COVER ME BOYS,
I'm Going In

TALES OF THE TUBE FROM A BROADCAST BRAT

I hope you enjoy the read

For information, or to order additional copies,
please contact:

Beacon Publishing Group
P.O. Box 41573 Charleston, S.C. 29423
800.817.8480| beaconpublishinggroup.com

Publisher's catalog available by request.

ISBN-13: 978-1-949472-94-3

ISBN-10: 1-949472-94-9

Library of Congress Control Number:
2013904936

Publishing in 2019. New York, NY 10001.
Printed in the USA.

DEDICATION

For Dad and Mom, who now frolic among the very stars for which they taught me to reach, and for Sarah, the most dazzling yet grounded person I have ever met and without whom one man's memories would still be just that.

"If you spend your whole life up there on the shelf, you got no one to blame but your own damn self."
Pat Green

COVER ME BOYS, I'M GOING IN

GETTING STARTED

I have been gainfully employed, with the exception of a few weeks here or a month or two there, for the better part of thirty-five years and am lucky enough to confess that it feels like I have never worked a day in my life. That's simply because I have been fortunate to have had a career in television.

My broadcast career began in 1975 as a wide-eyed nineteen-year-old with delusions of grandeur, but, thanks to my dad, my life in TV goes back much further.

My father was that rare combination of dreamer and doer. He was born March 23, 1925, in Reading, Pennsylvania, and was raised in Pennsylvania Dutch Country. He always loved sports; most kids in that part of Pennsylvania did. As was true for everyone in the mid '20s, life for the Hirshlands—my grandfather Harry, Grandmother Helen, Aunt Julie, and (father) Lee—was relatively simple. But nobody was surprised when it turned out my dad had a more adventurous one in mind.

He was not yet seventeen when historic and tragic events shocked our nation on December 7, 1941, as the Japanese bombed Pearl Harbor. The attack thrust our nation into World War II, but, being a resilient nation, as our military and its leaders prepared to exact our revenge, much of the country took care of business as usual (or as usual as anything can be in time of conflict). College football's Rose Bowl game, "The Granddaddy of Them All," was first played on January 1, 1902, as the "Tournament

East-West football game." Michigan, representing the East, beat Stanford, from the West, 49–0, beginning a tradition of New Year's Day football games that continues today. The games were played every year from 1902 until World War I interrupted that streak. On New Year's Day 1916, as a means to help fund a Pasadena parade, the game returned to stay, this time officially as the Rose Bowl. The actual Rose Bowl stadium was built in time for the 1923 version between the University of Southern California and Penn State and has been the venue for the New Year's Day extravaganza ever since...except for one year, 1942, and my dad was there.

As I mentioned, the game back then was an East versus West battle with a team from what was then the PCC (Pacific Coast Conference) against an opponent from somewhere east of the Mississippi. The Duke University Blue Devils, led by head coach Wallace Wade, played in the 1939 edition, coming in at 9 and 0, riding a defense that had not allowed as much as one single point during the entire season. That amazing streak continued until the final minutes of that game, when USC completed four straight passes, the last one finding the end zone, to beat Duke, 7–3. In 1942 Duke was again chosen to be the game's representative from the East, and this time the opponent was Oregon State College (later OSU). The invitation went out on December 1, 1941. Six days later, life in America was suddenly very different.

Fearful of another West Coast attack, the United States government ordered a prohibition on large public gatherings on the West Coast for the duration of the war. A football stadium with a seating capacity of close to one hundred thousand certainly constituted the potential for a "large public gathering." Lt. General John L. DeWitt recommended the game and the festivities surrounding it be cancelled and the Rose Bowl committee planned to do just that. But on December 16 Duke offered another idea. The university invited the committee, Oregon State, and the game to Durham.

My dad wasn't on that invitation list, but somehow he found himself in Duke Stadium (later named Wallace Wade Stadium after the legendary coach) for the only Rose Bowl ever played outside Pasadena. Being there was apparently not enough for Lee Hirshland. In fact, he ended up assisting Bill Stern, the play-by-play man for NBC radio that day. It was an introduction into the world of professional broadcasting that would inspire him long into the future. He eventually attended Duke for two years and then left to head west and enroll at the University of California, Berkeley. At Cal he served as the sports editor of the school newspaper, the *Daily Cal*, and in 1949 graduated with a degree in astrophysics. Space always fascinated him—and he taught my two brothers and me to shoot for the stars.

Dad was a natural leader his entire life. By all accounts he was well liked, but more importantly he was much respected. He was a navy man and served his country in the Korean War after graduating from college. I am told that, at the time, he was the second youngest commissioned officer in the navy and eventually the youngest commanding officer of a commissioned naval ship. He was in his midtwenties and leading sailors aboard the USS *Henrico*, patrolling the waters off Korea during the conflict. The son of a strict naval doctor and a brilliant and gregarious military nurse, my dad learned at an early age to be self-reliant and knew the value of integrity and hard work.

Dad left the navy in 1952, eleven years after the Japanese attack on Pearl Harbor, and chose Honolulu, Hawaii, to live, work, and start a family. The woman who would be his wife, business partner, and the mother of his three boys was Mary Virginia Davis Hirshland, his constant, loving companion until they died, less than a year apart, more than fifty-five years later.

My older brother, David, was born in 1953, and on December 19 two years later, I followed. I was born nearly a month premature. Mom and Dad said I couldn't wait to see the world. After doing what I've done, being where I've been, and seeing what I've seen, I guess they were right.

At the time, my dad worked at Honolulu radio station KGU—first as a salesman, calling on island retailers and automobile dealers, asking them to buy advertising on the station. In the five years he worked there he rose in the ranks to assistant manager and eventually national sales manager. But he wasn't just a behind-the-scenes guy. Dad's love of sports was evident during his work at KGU, and at one point he conceived, sold advertising for, and hosted *Sportslants* under the pseudonym of Lee Anders. The station promoted it as "a fifteen-minute sportscast from KGU with a special emphasis on predictions and discussions of Mainland football games."

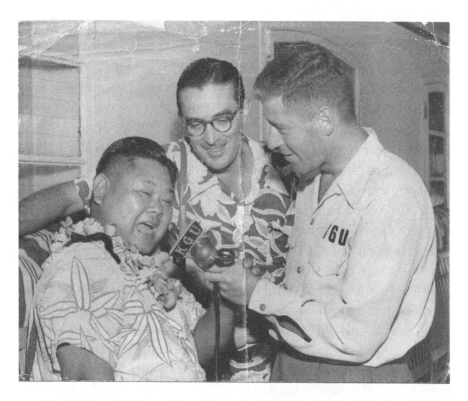

That chutzpah and hard work impressed the station manager and its owner, a gentleman by the name of Donald W. Reynolds, who owned not only KGU but a number of other broadcast properties around the country. Reynolds saw promise in my father and respected his work enough to offer him the position of sales manager of KOLO TV8—the station Reynolds owned in Reno, Nevada. Of course Dad accepted and, with my mom and two young boys in tow, the Hirshland family left paradise and moved to the Reno suburb of Sparks, Nevada. And this broadcast brat's life would never be the same.

In the late 1950s Reno was not in the top 150 of this country's top television markets. It may have been called "the Biggest Little City in the World," but it had only three TV stations: KOLO TV8, the CBS affiliate; KCRL Channel 4 (now known as KRNV), the affiliate of the National Broadcasting Corporation; and KNPB Channel 5, the public television station. The American Broadcasting Company (ABC) was America's third national network, and at the time my dad, mom, brother, and I moved to Sparks, it had no affiliate in Reno, so KOLO and KCRL shared ABC's programming. There was no FOX or CW, American television audiences were still years away from the glory of cable, ESPN, and 499 other channels, and nobody was even talking about DIRECTV or the Dish Network. If you watched the tube in Reno (and we had seven of them in our house), you watched either channel 8 or channel 4. When Dad took over the job of running the station in 1957, *Gunsmoke* was the country's most popular television show and was still in the top ten more than ten years later. CBS also had the *Andy Griffith* franchise, airing *Gomer Pyle, USMC* and *Mayberry RFD*, as well as the Brian Keith/Sebastian Cabot family comedy, *Family Affair*. In addition to those popular shows, Sunday night was reserved for CBS and the one and only Ed Sullivan. Needless to say, CBS was America's number one TV network and, much to the delight of those of us in the Hirshland household, everyone in Northern Nevada watched it on channel 8. Just as he had at KGU, my dad moved up the ladder in Reno. In the eight years he was there, he went from sales manager to vice president and general manager of the TV station, as well as manager of the radio station, and eventually supervisor of Nevada broadcast properties for Donrey Media Group.

Growing up in the Biggest Little City was pretty darn good. My younger brother, Mark, was born in 1960, and we enjoyed many of the perks afforded the family of a prominent local businessman. Reno was certainly not Las Vegas, but venues like Harrah's and John Ascuaga's Nugget lured the day's big-name entertainers like Frank Sinatra, Bill Cosby, Louis Armstrong, and Charlie Rich. We not only enjoyed the performances, but even got to go backstage on occasion. However, as kids, we looked forward most to the antics of Bertha and Tina—the famous performing pachyderms at Ascuaga's Nugget—a mother-and-daughter elephant team that did tricks on stage as an opening act.

We lived in a big house; Dad drove a Jaguar convertible with a telephone (again, long before cell phone towers sprung up all over America and everybody had a phone in their car); and Mom played golf every Thursday—Ladies Day at Washoe County Golf Course. But believe me, in almost every way, our life was normal for kids growing up in the '60s and '70s. We went to public school, attended church on Sundays, and Mom made dinner every night. We had a dog, friends, and played football, baseball, or golf until dark in the summertime and went skiing on the slopes of the Sierra Nevada and threw snowballs for fun in the winter. Then the dreamer in my dad decided to turn our lives upside down. There was always a poster in my dad's office that featured a quote from the poet Robert Browning that said, "A man's reach should exceed his grasp," and in 1965 my dad reached.

KTVN IS BORN

Lee Hirshland ran KOLO TV for close to eight years but knew that this growing city, just forty-five minutes from Lake Tahoe, was more than ready for a third local station that could carry the full complement of the brand new American Broadcasting Company's programming. In 1965 he put a plan together and, with the help of eleven other businessmen, he formed Washoe Empire—a corporation with the sole purpose of raising capital to start Reno's third local television station. My dad convinced Reno builder Robert Stoker, radio station owner Bob Stoddard, warehouse executive Frank Bender, and Link Piazzo, owner of the city's biggest and most popular sporting goods store (Link and his brother Chet would eventually host a weekly hunting and fishing themed show, called *Sportsman's Trails*, on KTVN. I just happened to direct that program on many occasions). Joining that group were four local pediatricians, John Palmer, William Pasutti (my pediatrician), John Scott, and Emanuel Berger. Rounding out the group were three businessmen from outside the Reno area: H. G. Wells and David McKay, who were former owners of KOLO Radio, and Bob Paisley. In all, the twelve men who formed Washoe Empire contributed close to $500,000; enough, at that time, to start a TV station in Reno. In the fall of 1964, my dad resigned his position with the Donrey Media Group and, with Washoe Empire, filed a petition with the

Federal Communications Commission to procure a television station license for Reno's third station.

A chunk of that half a million bucks raised by Washoe Empire came directly from the bank account and pockets of my parents. We went from living in a big house in one of Reno's nicer neighborhoods to spending nights in local hotels and, eventually, unpacking our bags in rental properties around town. Dad gave up his Jag and Mom ditched her Lincoln Continental, and we drove around in an Edsel station wagon that became our family's sole source of transportation (it even had plastic seat covers). But none of that mattered to my brothers and me. My parents made sure that the things that really mattered in our world changed little; that material things didn't define our life or family; and that we always had what we needed and wanted. And, in 1965, my dad got what he wanted more than anything in the world, his TV station. The FCC granted Washoe Empire a license to operate what would become KTVN.

Building a TV station in Reno was no easy task. The group rented ground-level space in a downtown building on Pine Street near the world famous Mapes Hotel. They also set about building the station's transmitter at more than seven thousand feet on Slide Mountain in the Sierra Nevada range. Staff was hired, including a University of Nevada School of Journalism graduate named Ed Pearce. He was a no-nonsense newsman in the tradition of Walter Cronkite who anchored the station's early newscasts and put together a team of reporters that turned TV news on its ear. Pearce did not suffer fools, but had the amazing ability to discipline and encourage. He wasn't a "rah rah" guy, but he got the absolute most out of his people. Ed Pearce had the respect of every single person in the building and, almost as important, the people in the community. Dad also hired a chief engineer, Al Richards, who would help build, maintain, and power a television station that became a model for local affiliates across the country. Al helped plan and construct a network of transmitter sights across Nevada that brought KTVN's signal to outposts in the most remote parts of the state. Richards also took Dad's vision of providing local programming, including sports and election coverage, and made it a reality by finding or building facilities with the latest and most cost-effective technology.

The station started with no more than twenty people and included creative minds like Will Chisum and Stuart Murtland, who were brought into the fold, as were a few enthusiastic, hard-working salespeople, led by a merry, gentle man named Jackson Fleming. In compiling his team, Dad chose people who not only shared his vision, but shared his passion, integrity, and hard-work ethic. But even with this talented team, everyone agreed that KTVN would never have become a reality if it weren't for my mother. Ginger Hirshland not only "bought in" to my dad's master plan; she leaped in with both feet. Mom served as the station's business manager/bookkeeper and head cheerleader, all while maintaining a household with three boys. She made sure we got to and from school and had clean clothes and a hot meal every night at the same time, whether Dad was able to join us or not (and most nights he was there). She shielded us from the hardships that they surely faced by making certain our daily lives were unaffected. I certainly remember the occasional hard times, but only as a very happy kid.

It took years of planning and preparation, months of beating back a lawsuit filed by dad's former employer, and the blood, sweat, and tears of the most passionate and dedicated group of people I would ever have the pleasure to know; and then on June 4, 1967, Dad, Mom and the team they had assembled flipped the switch and KTVN Channel 2 was on the air. I was eleven years old.

From the beginning, Channel 2 was different. Dad had experienced, from the inside, how to run a successful TV station with a corporate mentality. KOLO TV8 was one of many properties owned by the Donrey Media Group. Dad knew Channel 8 was the top station in the market by a large margin, but like Oz's Tin Man, it had no heart. The mom-and-pop operation that my mom and pop put together ran pretty much only on heart, especially in the beginning.

Team was the concept they fostered, and the station never would have made it if everyone hadn't believed in it. For example, at three o'clock every afternoon, always-smiling Sales Manager Jackson Fleming was asked nicely to vacate his office and make sure he turned out the lights on his way out. Jackson wasn't enjoying a short work day and people weren't concerned about the electric bill, Mr. Fleming was literally "shown the door" because his office was also KTVN's darkroom, where all the Super 8 film, on which each day's news and sports stories existed, was developed.

David, Mark, and I spent hours in front of the TV at home, not enjoying cartoons or our favorite shows, but instead watching soap operas, or, more accurately, the commercials inside the soap operas, and writing down the order and sponsor of each one so the station's official commercial log could be double checked. Production people also served multiple roles. Will Chisum, for instance, was not only the station's production manager, but he was also the creative director, built the station's sets, was the voice of station-produced promotional and commercial ads, and directed evening newscasts. Talent did in-field reporting as well as anchored newscasts and public service programs. Al Richards' engineering team not only maintained the station and its equipment, but spent hours, days, and sometimes weeks at remote sites making sure translators and transmitters on mountains all over northern Nevada worked properly.

Dad believed with all his heart that a local television station should be in business not just to make money, but to make a difference in the community, to serve its viewers. To that end KTVN was the first station in the area to provide hours of local, community-driven programming. Channel 2 was the first station to expand its local news broadcasts to sixty and then ninety minutes; the first station to air local community service programming like *Face the State*, a thirty-minute political forum; and the smallest local affiliate in America to become part of Westinghouse Broadcasting's Evening Magazine family by airing *PM Magazine* Monday through Friday.

KTVN was also the only station in Reno to air both the governor's inaugural address and his State of the Union message live, and, thanks to my dad, election night in Reno became a happening. With Dad leading the charge, election coverage was a labor of love for everyone at the station as the intelligent and creative minds figured out ways to get the results of local and statewide elections across Nevada in as-close-to-real-time as possible.

Those long nights are burned into my memory. Dozens of station employees manned phones, collecting information from hundreds of precincts. Armed with the information from each race, people would then take plastic, white numbers and press them into black sandwich boards for display on the screen as Pearce and his group of political experts discussed and dissected the results. Men like Dennis Myers, Larry Wisbeck, and Buddy Frank delivered well-written, concise analyses of the day's news and the impact each race would have on the various state communities. This was all done long before electronic character generators, the Internet, and laptop computers. Dad was pioneering election coverage in Nevada at a time when people had to wait (sometimes as much as a couple of days) for the newspaper to print the results of many political races. The look on his face as that engine hummed along during those hectic nights spoke volumes about his passion for what he was doing then and the vision he had for the station in the future.

In 1972, a historic television coup took place in northern Nevada. KOLO TV8 was still the CBS affiliate and KTVN flew the colors of ABC, but not for long. KOLO and its parent network weren't seeing eye to eye over the station manager's decision to preempt an inordinate amount of network programming. This dispute led Dad to petition CBS to drop KOLO as its affiliate and award that distinction to KTVN. CBS agreed, and Dad's station had a new network. KOLO became the ABC affiliate, and with it came what would become a Monday night phenomenon— *Monday Night Football*. The NFL "night" game of the week started in 1970; but when KTVN and KOLO swapped networks in 1972, the show had a new producer. Don Ohlmeyer was a brash, young talent with a healthy ego and an amazingly fertile, creative mind. He sat at the helm of the network's one- night-a-week football coverage for five years. I didn't know Mr. Ohlmeyer then, but that would change nearly twenty years later.

A FAMILY OF FANS

I have had a bird's-eye view of the earliest days of one local affiliate station and two television networks, ESPN2 and The Golf Channel, and some of those tales will be told in subsequent pages. As fate would have it, I was employed by each of those networks on days when events occurred that would change the way those networks would be perceived and forever alter the way they did business. I happened to be at the very heart of one of those incidents. But a whole lot happened before getting to either of those points in time.

During my broadcast career I have had the opportunity to meet, interview, and work alongside some of the world's greatest and most popular athletes, broadcasters, and entertainers. But none of that would have been possible were it not for the actions of two men: my father, who instilled in me my moral compass and my love of sports and gave me a role model to emulate; and Joe Bickett, a sportscaster in Reno, who, by being unknowingly selfish, gave me my start.

Neither my mom nor dad was an athlete. As far as I know there are no real athletes in the branches of our family tree. But that's not to say we weren't athletic. My aunt Julie played competitive tennis her whole life and still bats the ball around at nearly ninety. My folks' game was golf. They played with friends and together and encouraged us to do the same. Many weekends started with the five of us teeing it up as a family, and, thanks to encouragement, practice, and a certain amount of skill, we all got pretty good.

In addition to golf, like most kids who grew up in Reno at that time, we all played Pop Warner football, Little League, and Babe Ruth baseball, and swam and played hoops at the local YMCA. Reno was an hour or less away from world-class skiing, another activity we did with friends and family. It was also a great place to hunt, fish, and hike, but those were forms of recreation not on the Hirshland family agenda.

Mom and Dad supported us in every endeavor. At least one of them, if not both, came to every game, and when we weren't playing golf as a family, they knew we were with friends or in good hands thanks to Pete Marich and his staff at the Washoe County Golf Course. The "Shoe," as we affectionately called the county-run track in the middle of town, also served as our summer camp. Mom would drop us there in the mornings on her way to work, golf bag packed with a couple of peanut butter and jelly sandwiches and a dollar or two for a Coke and a bucket of balls, then pick us up on her way home in the evening. We'd spend hours riding bikes or skateboards and playing football, whiffle ball, or baseball with a tennis ball in the front yard, swinging at pitches or slinging passes until Mikey Mortensen's mom called him home or darkness and dinnertime broke up the game. There was no Nintendo or Xbox and nothing to watch on TV. Banks did not offer ATMs; moms and dads got money at the bank on Friday for the entire weekend or cashed personal checks at one of the many local casinos. We couldn't imagine a world filled with YouTube, texting, or twenty-four-hour news. We listened to our music on AM radio, played our favorite songs on vinyl or eight-track cassettes, composed our book reports on typewriters, and we got our kicks thanks to clubs, bats, and some kind of a ball.

The Hirshland family was a family of fans. Reno had a couple of minor league teams and has always been home to the

University of Nevada, but for professional sports we had to look a few hundred miles west to the San Francisco Bay Area. From the time we arrived in Reno, the baseball Giants and the football 49ers already had SF on their hats, and I became a lifelong fan of both. The Raiders and Athletics eventually arrived in the east bay city of Oakland, and my parents and brothers also became fans of those two franchises. As for me, I could watch and cheer for the A's and Raiders, but my loyalties lay with the original teams in the City by the Bay.

We watched and listened whenever we could. In the spring and summer Mom's transistor radio in the kitchen was permanently fixed on "the San Francisco Giants radio network" so she could listen to the play-by-play calls of, first, Russ "Bye-Bye Baby" Hodges and Lon Simmons, then, later, Al Michaels. Thanks to Mom and Dad, we even got in the car at least once a season and went to see our favorite teams in person. I remember watching John Brodie lead the 49ers in a losing effort against Fran Tarkenton and the Minnesota Vikings at Kezar Stadium.

While I don't remember getting to see a baseball game in Seal Stadium, I am fortunate enough to recall, as an impressionable kid, being awed in person by the Willies—Mays and McCovey—in sometimes sunny, usually frigid Candlestick Park. Even now I can close my eyes and find myself back in the car, Mark in the middle, David on his other side, the five of us filled with anticipation and excitement as Dad took the Paul Street exit off of the 101 freeway south; it was special every single time.

Our family was in the stadium or at the arena for some of sports most famous games and individual performances. I was only four years old, but on my Dad's shoulders I watched some of the world's most accomplished amateur athletes at the 1960 Winter Olympic Games at Squaw Valley (I have the Kodak slides to prove it). Two years later, I was driving my parents crazy needing to go to the bathroom or buy cotton candy and a souvenir at Candlestick as Willie "the Covey" hit a home run and Jack Sanford shut out the New York Yankees and Ralph Terry 2–0 in game two of the 1962 World Series. The Yankees would break our hearts (or so my pop said) a few days later when Bobby Richardson reached up and caught a McCovey line drive in the bottom of the ninth with the winning run in the form of Willie Mays on second and Matty Alou representing the tying run on third base in game seven.

We were among the 53,318 amazed fans that missed *Heidi* on TV because we were actually watching Daryle Lamonica lead the Oakland Raiders to a thrilling comeback to beat Joe Namath and the Jets on November 17, 1978. And we were back at Candlestick on January 11, 1982, in our seats in the opposite end zone when Joe Montana rolled right, avoided Ed "Too Tall" Jones, and hit a reaching Dwight Clark in the end zone for "The Catch." Then we held our collective breaths as Eric Wright tackled Drew Pearson, and moments later watched as Jim Stuckey fell on a Danny White fumble to send our 49ers to their first Super Bowl. Montana ran out the clock and we ran onto the field. I can still see my then-twenty-two-year-old brother Mark smiling like a kid at Christmas, looking for someone to slap on the back while stuffing a chunk of Candlestick Park turf in his pocket for a souvenir.

Nobody lived and died with the wins and losses more than my mom and my dad. Hers was an unconditional love, while he alternately loved and loathed his teams as they alternately exceeded his expectations then predictably broke his heart, many times in the same inning, possession, or game-winning drive or losing half inning. Dad and Mom were loyal and they taught us how to be fans. We were jubilant when the 49ers, Raiders, and A's won rings; but sadly the team we all loved most, the San Francisco Giants, never ascended to the sport's highest heights while Mom and Dad were able to listen on the radio or watch in the ballpark or on TV.

In 2010, a ragtag group of seasoned veterans and journey-men joined a future MVP rookie catcher and the best young pitching staff in baseball and celebrated a world championship for the first time as a team with San Francisco on the uniform. To get there they beat the favored Philadelphia Phillies for the National League pennant on the second anniversary of my mother's death. You can bet she and Dad watched every single minute. During the World Series victory parade in San Francisco, former Giants pitcher and current Giants broad-caster Mike Krukow addressed the crowd with a brief, but impassioned speech imploring the hundreds of thousands who were there to remember and honor the people in their lives who introduced them to Giants baseball. I sat in my living room watching and listening on my forty-six-inch HD televi-sion and thought of my mother and her transistor radio and my father, disappointed in the team one minute and delighted the next, and I cried like a baby.

But it wasn't just sports that ignited my parents' passions. My early childhood memories include, as a seven-year-old, see-ing both my mom and dad in tears, reacting to the assassination of President John F. Kennedy. I can't think of one other time when I saw my father cry. I also remember to this day the excitement in Dad's voice when, in the middle of the night on February 20, 1962, he woke David, Mark, and me because *Friendship 7* with astronaut John Glenn at the controls was about to be launched into space from someplace called Cape Canaveral in Florida. We sat on the couch, everyone but Dad rubbing sleep from our eyes, listening to the countdown and then watching with wide-eyed wonder as a human being rode a sixty-six-thousand-pound Redstone rocket into space. Like almost every kid, we loved to sleep, but we never squawked when we were awakened with a gentle shake on those monumental starlit nights.

I never wanted to be an astronaut, but like almost every kid growing up in America, at some point or another I dreamed of playing professionally in the major leagues, the NFL, or on the PGA TOUR. I loved sports—still do—but I learned early on that I had neither the physical talent nor the mental discipline to accomplish such lofty and impressive goals. But I grew up around and went to school with kids who did. Glenn Carano and I were friends as thirteen-, fourteen-, and fifteen-year-olds at B. D. Billinghurst Junior High School. Less than ten years later he took over the most famous position in team sports—quarterback of the Dallas Cowboys. As I was first contemplating a career in television, a fourteen-year-old kid named Greg LeMond was riding his bike around the Washoe Valley. It was only a decade hence that he won the first of three Tour de France titles. I went to school at the same time and played golf against an extremely talented young lady who broke ground by competing on the boys' golf teams in the school district; twenty-two years later Patty Sheehan had won two United States Women's Opens and was in the LPGA Hall of Fame. As for me, I did have some talent on the golf course, even played a little bit in college, but it was abundantly clear that shooting par wasn't going to get me very far. But both sports and television were in my blood, and deep down I knew what I wanted to be when I grew up long before I ever grew up.

Again, this is where Mr. Lee Hirshland and Mr. Joe Bickett became major players in shaping my career path.

SMALL MARKET, BIG DREAMS

Nobody who is really any good in this business started at the network level. Many of today's best broadcasters have come out of this country's top broadcast journalism schools; places like Syracuse University, the University of Missouri, and Northwestern University. Names like Albert, Costas, Vargas, and Greenberg started at those schools and are now among the top broadcasters in the business, but they really learned the business toiling in small-market America, perfecting their trade by doing whatever it took to be successful. They paid dues and worked their way up the ladder by doing local news and sports in places like Kalamazoo, Michigan, Hot Springs, Arkansas, and, yes, Reno, Nevada. The beauty of markets that size is that while working there you get actual "hands-on" experience with equipment. It's your sole responsibility on many occasions to complete a task from start to finish: come up with the idea for a story, make the phone calls, conduct the interviews (many times while also operating the camera), write the copy, and edit the piece for air; and then actually deliver the finished product during the evening newscast.

Chances are also good that you work for a news or sports director that has some time to invest in you, to work with you and, if you're smart enough to listen, make you better. Reno,

Nevada, market size 172 out of more than 250 in 1972, was that kind of place.

I graduated from Reno High School in 1973. I wasn't smart enough to follow in the footsteps of my brother, David, a straight-A student who went to Brown University and then on to UCLA Law School. I did, however, get decent grades, wrestled for two years under the watchful eye of Coach Ray Handley (the same Ray Handley that would later become head coach of the New York football Giants), and played three years on the Reno High Huskie varsity golf team. Near the end of my senior year I decided I would further my education and continue my golf career at Lewis and Clark College near Portland, Oregon. In subsequent years I have found Portland to be a beautiful, vibrant city bathed in copious amounts of sunshine. But when I attended school there in the fall and winter of 1973, it was the Portland that everyone who lives there would like outsiders to believe it always is: cold, rainy, and dreary. During one stretch while I was going to class and trying to play golf, the sun was obscured by rain clouds every day for more than a month, and for a kid who grew up in a place where the sun shines about 350 of the 365 days each year, it was too much to take. I went back to Reno and enrolled at the University of Nevada.

I found myself back home, not yet twenty, and sitting in the seats at Moana Stadium watching a Reno Silver Sox game with some buddies. The Silver Sox were the single-A minor league baseball affiliate of the San Diego Padres and were on their way to winning the first of two straight California League titles with future major leaguers Gene Richards, Butch Wynegar, and Juan Eichleberger. The Silver Sox were good, but whether they were good or not, they still merited coverage by local sportscasters for a highlight piece during the eleven o'clock news.

One of those local sportscasters on hand that night was Joe Bickett. Joe was a tall, blond, affable guy who always had a smile on his face and a good word for everyone. He was also the only sports guy KTVN had ever had. Ed Pearce hired Joe when the station went on the air in 1967. They were colleagues, drinking buddies, and fast friends. I had known Joe and seen him around the station since I was twelve. He knew me because I was the boss's kid. Regardless, it was no big deal for me, when I saw Joe holding his camera and getting ready to shoot baseball highlights, to get up out of my seat and walk up and say hello. Bickett returned the greeting and offhandedly remarked that he wished he didn't have to be there that night. Without a second thought, I offered to take the camera out of—and the responsibility off of—his hands and finish shooting the game. Much to my surprise, he smiled, handed me the Kodak Super 8 film camera, and walked away, telling me to drop off the camera and the film cartridge at the station after the game. I didn't realize it then, but I was nineteen and my career in television had begun.

In the mid-1970s, the University of Nevada's Journalism Department was like many around the country: it offered simply a bachelor's degree in journalism. At Nevada, there was no separate radio/TV department, no option of a broadcast journalism degree. So the classes and lectures I attended on the Reno campus concentrated almost exclusively on print journalism, with a special emphasis on newspapers. I worked for credits at the university radio station, played a very minor role on coach John Legarza's Wolf Pack golf team for a year or two (I even played well enough to accompany the team on a couple of road trips), and, with more and more frequency, continued to help Joe Bickett with various aspects as he prepared for his daily sportscast.

Armed with one of the station's Super 8 cameras and several cartridges of film, I attended and documented high school football and basketball games, Silver Sox baseball games, various sporting events at the University of Nevada, and the occasional exhibition game that professional leagues contested in Reno. Basically, I covered everything he asked me to cover, as well as the stories and games in which he had no interest, or without which, if I could convince him, the local sportscast would be incomplete.

I'll never forget getting the assignment to cover the arrival of the Los Angeles Lakers when they came to Reno to play an exhibition game against the San Francisco Warriors. I set up my camera in the corner of a waiting room and waited for the Lakers and their star center and reigning NBA Most Valuable Player, Kareem Abdul-Jabbar, to arrive. The Lakers' plane landed, and as it taxied the butterflies in my stomach kicked into full flaps.

The aircraft parked and I walked out on the tarmac toward the players as they were deplaning and heading inside. I saw Abdul-Jabbar immediately—at seven foot two, he was hard to miss—and waited for him to approach. As he got close, I reached out my hand to introduce myself and ask if I could trouble him for a few minutes to answer a couple of questions. My right hand was extended, but before I could utter a word, the man who many consider one of the five best basketball players to ever play the game looked unsmilingly at me and...handed me the small suitcase he was carrying. I managed to keep my composure, explain to Abdul-Jabbar that I was not a local porter, but a local *reporter*, and asked for the interview. He never smiled; he never offered anything close to an apology; but he did the interview, and, yes, I carried his bag into the building.

On another occasion I had convinced Bickett that KTVN sports needed to cover a high school wrestling match, and when an underdog upset the heavy favorite in the heavyweight division, I felt like my decision had been validated. I headed back to the station, wrote the copy for Joe to read on the air, and headed into the darkroom with the film. It developed, and I found the exact match I needed. I took the section of the film to the editing station, cut and taped the highlights together, and inserted it into the lineup along with the other stories that would make up the pictures to the stories Bickett would be telling in an hour or so. In those days, each reporter personally processed and then spliced the film clips together with tiny pieces of tape. You added a "stock" countdown at the beginning and made sure there was more footage of the story than you needed at the end so the director in the control room had time to change sources on the switcher and go from the film clip back to the camera shooting the anchor on the set. In addition to the copy I wrote for Bickett, I wrote a shot log and a TRT (total running time) for the director so he knew what pictures were coming next and, more importantly, when the last shot of the clip was on screen. I had done this hundreds of times and felt great as I sat in the newsroom, having done it again. On television, Ed Pearce handed the newscast over to Bickett to deliver that day's sports information. At that time, Joe had somewhere in the neighborhood of five to six minutes for his sports segment in each newscast. These days, sandwiched between several looks at "Doppler" weather and "Sky View" traffic, local sportscasters are lucky to get two.

That newscast, Bickett went through his rundown and, near the end, came to the wrestling story. To this day, I still get a rush when a story for which I am responsible hits the air, and it was certainly true that day. This wasn't my first story; probably not even my hundredth; I had even been called on during a news emergency to document a sheriff's department hostage situation. That was the first time I had ever heard a gun fired that wasn't pointed at a can, lizard, deer, or duck, and I still remember being scared and exhilarated at the same time. So there I sat, ready to watch the wrestling drama unfold. Joe read the introduction I had written; I knew upstairs that director Will Chisum was ready to push the button that would roll the projector and then push another button on the device that would actually put the images I had shot, developed, and spliced on television.

He did just that and on it came—in living color and *upside down!* I had inadvertently flipped the film while splicing it into the final clip reel; so on TVs all over northern Nevada, high school wrestlers were literally standing on their heads, thanks to me. Amidst the laughter, Chisum expertly warned Bickett that he would be coming back on camera early, and the sportscast ended with a verbal toss from Joe back to a chuckling Ed Pearce.

That was the first—and last—time I made that particular mistake. Believe me, in more than thirty years I have made hundreds of mistakes, but rarely the same one twice. Part of the reason I never made that mistake again was because I stopped getting the chance. In the late 1970s I got promoted, the station upgraded its equipment, and Jackson Fleming literally got his office back. My dad and Al Richards led KTVN out of the Super 8 film world and into the era of videotape.

In the early 1970s, the Sony Corporation was busy developing the three-quarter-inch, U-matic videotape format and had subsequently made it available to the broadcast industry. Videotape had long been a staple of both networks and local stations for use in recording and playing back programs. But the machines used before Sony's newer technology was developed were much too expensive, heavy, and bulky to use in the field; much like IBM's first behemoth computers compared to the devices we use today. That's why every station used some form of film to record stories locally. KTVN had a couple of Kodak 16mm and several Super 8mm cameras that reporters used to capture the footage that helped document the stories that made up daily newscasts. Sony helped spread the video revolution by making professional-quality videotape recording economical and accessible to a wide spectrum of users, including broadcasters who used it for electronic news gathering (ENG), local commercial- shooting and editing, and for recording complete programs.

As far as I was concerned, the Sony three-quarter-inch video-tape recorder was a mechanical marvel and a godsend. Before Stuart Murtland was finished taking ours out of its box, we knew it would immediately eliminate the hassles film exhibited, including the need for developing, splicing, and manually handling the film during editing. And the only way the subject matter being recorded could end up upside down was if you shot it that way on purpose.

The videotape process was simple. In fact, it worked pretty much the same way your old Betamax or VHS machine worked. Of course, if you're my son Jake's age, or younger, thanks to the advancement in technology responsible for Digital Video Recorders (DVRs) like TiVO, you have no idea what I'm talking about. Basically this machine used its technical genius to record pictures and sound on videotape instead of "burning" the images on a piece of film stock. So instead of waiting until you got back to the station to find out the picture was overexposed because you had the iris on the wrong setting, or what was supposed to be green turned out to be blue, or there was no sound to go along with the pictures, you simply pushed the play and record buttons simultaneously, pointed the camera at the action on the field, or the coach, or star of the game to be interviewed.

Upon completion of your task, you pushed another button to stop the recording, a fourth one to rewind the tape, and hit only play this time to view what you had just recorded. Right there on the spot! If it wasn't any good, you could hit play and record simultaneously again and start the process all over. It was so simple. What wasn't simple was getting it from place to place. The original versions came with several pieces: the camera and lens, which were about two and a half feet long and probably weighed fifteen pounds; a record/playback deck, approximately twenty inches tall by ten inches deep; and a battery that was the same length as the record deck but half as tall. It was all hooked together by a series of grey cables and fastened to a cart with wheels so it could be pulled or pushed wherever you needed to go. Add a tripod—or in some cases your shoulder, on which you mounted the camera—and a plastic-covered spool of videotape that resembled, in size, a three-hundred-page hardcover novel, and you had the greatest advancement in broadcast journalism history. KTVN was the first station in northern Nevada to have one.

FROM BEHIND TO IN FRONT OF THE CAMERA

Many other things happened in the late 1970s, including physically moving KTVN's production and studio facilities from a confined space in downtown Reno to a large, unoccupied warehouse on Energy Way, on the outskirts of town. I stopped playing competitive golf at Nevada and spent fewer and fewer hours in the classroom while working more and more hours at Channel 2. One day, Pearce and Bickett approached me in the newsroom and asked if I was interested in making the move from mostly behind the camera to in front of it. Of course I was interested, who didn't want to be on TV? As I look back, I see that Ed Pearce was rewarding both of us. I had shown promise as a writer and was doing a lot of the work anyway; but Joe was, after more than ten years, finally getting a chance to have a life, go home before midnight, and stop working weekends. I knew that Ed Pearce was taking a huge risk. I had done some on-camera standups for stories as a reporter, but never anything live; and never in a sport coat and tie with studio lights glaring in my eyes and thousands of people watching me sweat from the comfort of their living rooms and bedrooms all across Nevada. Maybe of greater consequence, Pearce was giving this gig to the boss's kid.

That was in no way lost on me. I knew I had been, and now with greater force would be, a target for criticism. "He's only on

TV because he's the station manager's son" would surely be spoken around town; and it would be potentially more damaging in the KTVN newsroom. Because I was Lee Hirshland's son, I had to work a hundred times harder and be noticeably better than the guy who wasn't. To my dad's credit, he never said a word. Did I work my butt off? Absolutely! Did I make my share of mistakes? No question. This was a time in television before the widespread use of the TelePrompTer.

That's a machine that takes the words printed on paper and "magically" puts them right on the lens of the camera so the person reading the news never has to look down. The TelePrompTer is omnipresent now. Every station has several, and even the president of the United States uses one, but back then it was a rarity. If a news or sportscaster wanted to say the words exactly as written, he or she had to either memorize the copy (impossible to memorize an entire newscast or sportscast), look down at the paper and read the script (not very effective when you are trying to make a connection with your audience), or perfect a combination of both (read a little, then look at the camera and recite those lines which you had memorized), and you had to do all of this while a director was occasionally talking in your ear. The best announcers made it look easy; it was anything but. And most of the time, I had a blast.

The fact that there was no TelePrompTer in our studio had nothing to do with my most memorable gaffes. During one sportscast, I referred to pitcher Mark "the Bird" Fydrich as "Detroit Tigers *pissing* ace" and described Jack Nicklaus as "*shitting* atop a two-stroke lead" during a golf tournament. Despite those and some less egregious faux pas, Pearce kept me around and I continued to learn on the job from him and others at the station, like Buddy Frank, Dennis Myers, Tom Lilley, Bickett, and many, many more. I never took myself too seriously (even did a number of sportscasts wearing a coat and tie and softball uniform pants because of a late recreation league game), but always took the work and the job responsibilities very seriously. I earned the respect of my colleagues and peers, and I learned something very important about myself. I absolutely loved working in television, and I, with equal passion, loathed being on television. So after a few years I made my way behind the camera and into the control room, producing and directing the men and women who wanted to be on TV.

IN TV TERMS, "TALENT" IS SUBJECTIVE

It takes a certain personality to be "on-air talent." It involves a weird combination of interest, insecurity, and ego. The best in the business, from my personal experience, have a ton of the first ingredient, a healthy dose of the one in the middle, and almost none of the last. The most difficult and, in my opinion, least talented ones have that order reversed. As a former on-air talent and current producer, I think to be really good on TV you have to be able to connect with your audience, and the most effective way to accomplish that is to actually care about your subject matter. That's easy to do for a play-by-play announcer in a particular sport, or a news anchor specializing in a specific area like politics or business. It's much more difficult for a station or network's news anchor that is charged with reading stories about a wide variety of subjects; add to that the extra variable of constantly having to read copy written by someone else.

It is rare in this business to have one person, during an entire newscast, write everything he or she reads on the air. Even in the 1970s in small market Reno, Ed Pearce and Joe Bickett wrote a lot, but not all, of what they read.

The best writers of sports copy know not only what to write, but how to write it for the person who ultimately reads it. For years I watched and listened to Joe Bickett deliver his sports-cast before I ever started to work and write for him. You hear and read about sportscasters and play-by-play announcers who spent endless hours as kids in front of the TV watching games with the sound off and pretending to be the announcer, calling the action. For me, turning the sound up and paying attention to other people's styles ended up being much more important than developing my own, and that distinction made all the difference throughout my career. When I wrote for Joe in the early days, and others later in my career, I wrote the words not in the way I would have read the story on the air, but in the way I knew that story would be read by them.

I have had the privilege of writing copy for some of America's best, and best known, sportscasters, including Brent Musburger, Brian Anderson, and the inimitable Vin Scully. In fact, one of my proudest career moments was the first time I wrote a tease for the legendary LA Dodger, NBC, and CBS announcer.

A tease is, many times, the very first thing a viewer sees at the start of a TV sports broadcast. The words, music, and pictures are designed to set the scene for the viewers, draw them in, give them a reason to watch, and, if you're lucky, create an emotional connection. Some of TV sports' top teases come from the fertile minds of the play- by-play announcer or anchor calling the game. CBS's Jim Nantz and the Golf Channel's Rich Lerner are two of the best. Most teases are conceptualized and first written by the producer or associate producer. Then that person spends hours combing through a dictionary and/or thesaurus to come up with just the right words. Of course, great teases can also be written in minutes, late at night, on a cocktail napkin.

Sometimes the tease script is nothing more than an outline, other times it is sixty seconds of verbiage written to specific pictures. But in every case, the ultimate decision on what is read or said falls on the shoulders of the announcer reading it. After all, it is his or her voice that will be forever associated with the beginning of the broadcast. Some are long remembered; others are forgotten thirty seconds after they are read. I have seen Jim Nantz at CBS take a look at the video and listen to the music one time and then, on the spot, write a poignant, memorable tease. I have also worked with Rich Lerner when he has developed an idea in his mind, turned that into words on paper, and then handed that script to a producer who was responsible for finding the right pictures and music to bring Lerner's vision to life. Both styles clearly work and have created some of sports television's most compelling and award-winning moments. Many of the announcers with whom I've worked, like Lerner, Grant Boone, and Musburger, have taken what I thought was a very good tease and, to my delight, made it so much better by changing a word or adding a phrase. But I have also seen far less talented, much more egotistical announcers try and do the same thing and end up taking perfectly well-written and moving pieces and make them much less so by changing words or inflection, just to say they added their personal touch to the work. Every announcer is different. Some are more fun to work with than others.

The Scully tease to which I referred earlier was written for golf's Skins Game in 1991, the first I had written for Vin. After editing the music and pictures with Tom Christine, a friend with whom I had worked years before at KTVN in Reno, I nervously delivered the copy to the booth where the legendary play-by-play announcer would deliver the day's action. He accepted the piece of paper, put on his headset, and turned his attention to the monitor so he could look and listen to the video and music that would accompany the copy. He gave me a little smile (what the heck did that mean?) and told the director in the production trailer he was ready. He cleared his throat, waited for his cue, and then read my copy word for word, with perfect timing and inflection, just like I knew Vin Scully would. I'll never forget the elation I felt that day, and again years later, when I would sit privately in front of a TV and, with a tremendous sense of pride, play the tape of the beginning of that broadcast.

Vin Scully was, and remains to this day, a great announcer; and whether you like their styles or not, so are Musburger, Nantz, Costas, and Jon Miller. I have worked with others equally as good, despite being not as well known. Brian Anderson is one. Brian worked in minor league baseball in the Texas League and as a sideline reporter for the San Antonio Spurs when I saw a tape of his work that was delivered by an agent to The Golf Channel. I knew immediately he was the perfect choice to be our new play-by-play announcer because he was polished, good looking, and had a great voice. When I picked him up at the Orlando airport, I learned right away that he had two qualities: one that almost always describes a great golf broadcaster—a large amount of golf knowledge—and the other that rarely described any kind of announcer—very little ego. I recommended we hire him ASAP. He was a dream to work with, setting up every situation beautifully and then doing what a great golf play-by-play guy does: hand the broadcast off to the experts. The players who have become announcers have forgotten more about the game than most of our viewers will ever know. Sadly, for me personally and The Golf Channel collectively, Brian left in 2006; but, happily for him, he is now living his dream working as the play-by-play announcer for the Milwaukee Brewers and doing playoff baseball for Turner.

I have also been a part of the maturation of at least one of America's most- watched newspersons. I was directing news in Reno back in the early 1980s when KTVN hired a female reporter who had gone to school, and was working, in Missouri. Elizabeth Vargas was definitely on her way up the television ladder. While at Channel 2, she quickly advanced from general reporter to being assigned the newscast's most important stories, to eventually becoming one of the station's anchors. Everyone, especially my Dad, knew she had the look, the smarts, and the drive to go places in the business, and she did: first to Phoenix, then Chicago, and eventually New York. Now you can see her almost every week on ABC News's 20/20. I am fortunate to say I knew her then, and I hope she would agree that I helped her career a little during her brief stay in Reno.

Another gem was Scott Van Pelt. Now a mainstay at ESPN and ESPN Radio, I first met Scott in the halls of The Golf Channel. He was confident, engaging, and smart. He was also one of the funniest guys I had ever met, and, like Brian Anderson, Scott knew there was plenty of hard work ahead and he was unafraid to put in the time. Scott gets better every day and, thanks to me, he got an unexpected addition to his bank account one day in 1996. He was on the winning end of the most embarrassing bet I have ever made.

We were sitting around the news room at The Golf Channel that summer as Tiger Woods was putting the wraps on his third straight US Amateur golf crown. In a fit of what I can only claim now was insanity, I bet Scott Van Pelt a hundred American dollars that the aforementioned Mr. Woods, who had just captured his record-setting sixth straight USGA title, would never, ever win on the PGA TOUR. Seventy-eight wins (and counting) later, how am I doing?

I think it's safe to say that if a team of the world's best psychiatric minds got a chance to examine, en masse, America's on-air talent, they would come to the universal conclusion that collectively this might be the most insecure group of people on the planet. If you ask me, there is a simple reason: it's because almost all of their self-worth depends on what other people think of them. In contrast, an athlete like Tiger Woods, Albert Pujols, or Michael Phelps knows when he has done a good job. The scorecard, scoreboard, or official time tells them loud and clear. But the only way any on-air broadcast talent can measure his or her worth is if another person tells him or her so. It could be a wife, or a friend, another announcer (though not likely), a producer, or a boss; but there is no scorecard, only opinion. You might disagree by pointing to the Nielsen ratings; after all, don't people keep their jobs or lose them because of ratings? But ratings are just opinions of the viewers. Good ratings mean the viewer says you're doing a good job, bad ones mean the opposite; but it's still a subjective measure. This is one of the most sought-after jobs in world. Millions want to do it, and millions more say they don't, but think, given the chance, that they could do a better job than the one on TV. There are hundreds of television networks and stations and thousands of on-air jobs available. Most people are hired after someone in charge sees a resume or watches an "only the good stuff" edited compilation reel of their work. It's what best-selling author Malcolm Gladwell would call a "blink" decision, made many times on a whim. This guy looks good, that girl sounds great. A station thinks it needs a male to do sports even though a dozen better, smarter women have applied for the job. Getting a job, more often than not, is pure luck; keeping it is purely subjective and, I believe, that subjectivity breeds insecurity.

BACK TO THE FUTURE

These days it seems every single college football or basketball game is on a TV somewhere in America. As an example, ESPN sent out an e-mail to production people working college basketball games in 2010 writing, "During championship week, presented by Dick's Sporting Goods, ESPN's family of networks will carry 177 college basketball games in 10 days." I'm no math wizard, but that's more than ten games a day, not counting the games covered and carried during the same time period by other sports-only networks like Fox Sports, the Big Ten Network, and others, and college basketball isn't the only sport available to fans. MLB Network now broadcasts Arizona Fall League and major league spring training baseball. Both the NHL and NBA have their own networks, and, thanks mostly to the Golf Channel, every round of every PGA TOUR golf tournament can be viewed at a fan's leisure. But nearly forty years ago in Reno, only one man was thinking about how to put games played by local sports teams on the TV in your living room, den, or bedroom. That man was my dad.

As it turned out, I made the transition from in front to behind the camera at the perfect time. KTVN was scratching and clawing for as many viewers as it could get. The shine of CBS's programming star had dimmed and suddenly both NBC and ABC seemed to have more popular prime time programs. This seemed to bolster my dad's resolve to increase local programming even more.

He went forward with his plan to provide viewers in northern Nevada programming that he was certain mattered personally to them, and he turned out to be right. He expanded the local newscasts to give people in Reno more information about the area in which they lived. He brought experts into the fold, such as Leon Mandel, who was one of America's foremost experts on the automobile industry, and Howard Rosenberg, who knew more about movies and why they were good or bad than almost anyone on the planet. This team of experts gave Reno fans pertinent and important information, and they were, in fact, the precursors to what many stations now call consumer reporters, and it made a difference. He also, with the help of Richards and his team of engineers, rolled out the KTVN Video Cruiser. This was simply a refurbished bread delivery truck that was transformed into one of the country's first, and Reno's only, mobile production studios. The back was cleared out and one end was filled with several small black and white TVs that served as a monitor wall for the producer/director. That person, doing double duty, sat in a folding chair facing the monitors and in front of a small switcher—the same type of equipment housed in the station's main production control room, allowing the director to change sources with the push of a button and put different pictures on the air. Behind the director, small shelves were added to hold two videotape machines, one to make a permanent recording of the broadcast and the other to either play the station's commercials or play back important plays during a game or moments of a news event—the video cruiser's version of instant replay. On top of the rolling production truck was a platform big enough for a couple of cameras and a desk for the announcers. In the first incarnation of the video cruiser, the cameras used came directly from the studio, so if there was a game that had to be covered, the crew would be in position for the evening newscast and then roll the cameras out into the garage and onto the cruiser for use at the sporting event. Later versions of the mobile production unit had smaller, more mobile cameras allowing for more complete coverage. Communication was set up from the command post inside the van to the announcers on top, and then the signal generated from the video cruiser was sent back to KTVN through telephone lines. Don't ask me how, because I couldn't tell you. I was just happy that someone knew how it all worked, and for KTVN that someone was Chief Engineer Al Richards and the talented team of Jack Antonio, who became the station's chief engineer, and Dave Briscoe.

So off we went to the ball park or high school football field. We headed to the University of Nevada campus, or Carson City and the governor's mansion, or the state capitol building. Stuart Murtland and Will Chisum produced and directed the news events and, thanks to their tutelage, I learned how to produce and direct the sports events. KTVN's ratings increased and we became more and more proficient at delivering events to northern Nevada's homes.

We did everything from a golf tournament (a Champions Tour event won by Peter Thomson) to the Basque Festival in Elko to the Annual Reno Air Races at Stead Air Force Base north of town. Eventually, we rode the wheels off the video cruiser and I was able to convince the station to buy and refurbish a cushy conversion van that Richards outfitted with better equipment. As we got bigger and better, the technology continued to advance and the equipment got smaller and more powerful. We were able to take Sony cameras, like the model we had used to revolutionize news gathering in Reno, and use them as sideline cameras (mounted on a plank in the back of a Toyota pickup) at Nevada football games, or on the shoulders of cameramen under the hoop at state high school basketball games. I would produce and direct with my colleagues and friends Tom Christine, Jim Irwin, Stuart Murtland, and Will Chisum running camera and

Joe Bickett on the other end of the headsets calling the action. We traveled with the teams all over the west. We followed the Wolf Pack basketball team to the campus of the University of San Francisco in 1977 where Nevada's future NBA player Edgar Jones outdueled the Dons' future NBA World Champion Bill Cartwright. When we arrived, USF, led by Cartwright, was 27 and 0 and number one in the land. When we left they were no longer unbeaten or top ranked. We hit the road to Moscow and Pocatello, Idaho, and parked our van outside the Walk-Up Sky Dome on the campus of Northern Arizona University in Flagstaff and watched future Oakland Raider Frank Hawkins and the Nevada football team play.

VITALE BEFORE "DICKIE V"

On one memorable trip we visited the Pacific Northwest for a college basketball tournament. Nevada was playing Seattle University in the first game, while the second game featured the University of Portland against a University of Detroit team coached by Dick Vitale. There was no such thing as a studio show at that time, so the road crew was responsible for providing all the content for the evening—including halftime. Commercial breaks were short and relatively few and far between, so we had to fill most of the time between the end of the first half and the start of the second. Earlier in the day, at the shoot-around, we learned that Coach Vitale was planning to watch most of game one with his team before preparing for their own contest, so Bickett and I arranged to have the coach stop by our announce position at courtside and join us between halves for a live interview.

These days every sports fan, as well as millions of nonsports fans, knows who Dick Vitale is. He is the volume set at ten, twenty-four/seven head cheerleader for college basketball on ESPN. He is also a major charitable contributor because of his admirable work with the "V" Foundation in its efforts to fight cancer. But this was years before Vitale would become the "Dickie V" we all know now. He had yet to build his reputation on energy and verbosity, but everyone watching the game on KTVN that night was about to get a glimpse of the future. Two separate commercial breaks were scheduled to air in the halftime portion of the show, and I knew how important they were. That's one thing that was no different than it is now. Commercial spots paid the bills, and I was most assuredly going to air the ones I had. We had about 12 minutes to fill, not counting the commercials, and the plan I had communicated to Bickett was a simple one: In the first halftime segment we would look at the first half statistics and then take a commercial break. When we came back live we would talk to Vitale in segment two and then take our last break; then come back, set up the second half, and be ready for the tip (they still started both the game and the second half with a jump ball in those days).

Joe did the first-half stats as planned, in about three minutes, and then tossed it to our first commercial break; so far so good. That left a little more than ten minutes to talk to Vitale, take another break, and get ready for the game's second half. In the break Vitale arrived, sat next to Joe, and put on a headset. I counted Bickett back from commercial and he introduced our special guest—the head coach of the University of Detroit, Dick Vitale. The coach started talking by saying he was honored to join us, and he *never* stopped. In fact, if the horn hadn't sounded to signal the start of the second half, he might be talking still. Vitale talked and talked and talked, and about five minutes passed. I knew it was time to take my next commercial break, so through the headsets I told Joe to "thank the coach for coming by"; that was my cue for him to wrap up the interview. To Joe's eternal credit, he tried—but Dick Vitale was having none of it. He was on a roll, talking about how much he preferred college ball and its athletes to the pros. Another minute went by, and I admit panic started to set in. I pleaded with Joe to end the interview and again he tried, but he couldn't even slow the runaway Vitale down. Finally, exasperated and well aware of the need to run the commercials, I simply rolled the machine on which the commercials were located, pressed the button on the switcher, and instead of Dick Vitale, northern Nevada saw several thirty-second spots featuring a local car dealer, a jewelry store, and a restaurant. Inside the arena and on the monitors inside the conversion van, Dick Vitale continued to talk—oblivious to the fact that he was no longer on the air. In fact he was still talking ninety seconds later. Eventually—and mercifully—the buzzer sounded to start the second half and, almost as if awakened from a trance, Vitale *finally stopped talking*. Joe thanked the coach, who removed his headset and returned to his team. Bickett, like a true professional, resumed the call of the game, without a hitch, after having just sat through the longest single statement in Reno television history—and he hadn't even asked a question!

A RUDE AWAKENING

We were on a roll in those days, having a blast and, by all accounts, doing a good job. So I admittedly got a little cocky and figured this was as good a time as any to take my talents to another level, like the top. So one day, in my dad's office, with his Robert Browning quote staring me in the face, I mentioned that I would like to work in sports production at the network level for CBS. Dad was well liked and respected in the industry, with contacts and friends at CBS headquarters in New York. He said if I really thought I was ready, he'd make a call or two. I said I was, he did what he said he'd do, and a few weeks later I had an audience with Terry O'Neill, who, at the time, made many of the decisions when it came to production at CBS Sports.

I went to the "City That Never Sleeps" armed with a tape that included what I considered the very best moments of my directing career, ready to wow the folks at CBS. I arrived at Black Rock—the nickname for the thirty-eight-story structure on West Fifty-Second Street, more than likely one of the very few who knew how to correctly pronounce Nevada and, without question, the only person in the building wearing rattlesnake-skin cowboy boots. With my three-quarter-inch resume reel in my sweaty palm, I sat in the waiting room outside Terry O'Neill's office with a handful of other hopefuls for more than an hour. Finally, I was summoned into the lion's den and met the very busy Mr. O'Neill, who immediately offered me a job as a broadcast associate. In CBS nomenclature, a BA was nothing more than a gopher, and by accepting the job I would be just that for NBA, NFL, and boxing announcer Tim Ryan. It would be a foot in the door, but my feet would be getting coffee and picking up dry-cleaning for Mr. Ryan. It would be my responsibility to make sure Tim didn't miss his flight and, if he did, to make sure he had a back-up plan; and I would be on the hook, thanks to all of this glamour, for about $15,000 a year. A little surprised, I thanked O'Neill for the offer, then countered by telling him I was overqualified for that particular job and was really hoping to get a shot at one of the director positions. All he had to do was look at my tape and, I was sure, he'd agree. Terry O'Neill looked across his desk at me, smiled, and said the following words I hope to never forget: "Kid," he started, "I appreciate your confidence; but I'm not hiring any director right off the street, especially one from Reno. If that's the job you really want—go to a bigger market, get some real experience, and come back and see me in ten years. But if you want the BA job, as a favor to your dad, it's yours. If not, I have a hundred other eager kids who will gladly accept it." I understood, then stood and thanked him. I shook his hand, then turned and left the office, having never let go of my resume tape. Someone else took the BA job that day—but to this day, I'll argue that I made a better decision than that person.

RENEWED RESOLVE IN RENO

A few years earlier, the FCC made a decision that would not only affect how Channel 2 and other local affiliates did business, but added another set of adventures to my life. Networks like CBS supplied local affiliates like ours with programming—basically, morning, noon, and night. Because of that, the networks controlled not only the airwaves, but the majority of advertising dollars available, except for about a minute an hour for a local station break. The more popular a network show, the more money a local station could charge an advertiser to run his commercial in that very exclusive window. Another way a station could make money was to actually produce and edit those commercials for the advertiser. In many cases, local automobile dealers were the top advertisers. Car dealers would send their pitchman (usually the owner of the dealership) with a couple of new car models to the station to record several versions of a commercial spot. At the station, the director would position the cars, light the set, and outfit the pitchman with a microphone.

The pitchman would deliver his thirty-second message and it was recorded on a piece of two-inch videotape on a machine about the size of a refrigerator. It was critical to record the commercial in one shot, start to finish, because editing on the behemoths was incredibly difficult. That was the case until the creation of the new and improved video cruiser. The remote capabilities of our newfound technology meant Fletcher Jones no longer had to leave Fletcher Jones Ford to make a commercial, because the commercial makers could come to him. The long walk along a line of cars on the lot had become a local commercial staple, and the prospective car buyer could now see the dealership where he or she would buy a car. Lots were decorated with banners, flags, and balloons, and the atmosphere seemed downright festive and much more conducive to sales than the sterile station studio. These commercials were produced on a daily, if not weekly basis and look today almost exactly the same as they looked in Reno thirty years ago.

Local casinos were also a mainstay for Channel 2 salespeople but you couldn't show drinking or gambling games on TV. You could, however, tell the world about the great restaurants and the world-class entertainers who visited our area on a nightly or weekly basis. Jackson Fleming and his team would sell the advertising and pass those orders on to Will Chisum, who would schedule the video cruiser. Out I would go and spend the day shooting, and then editing, the commercial spots. Between the sporting events, directing at least one of KTVN's nightly newscasts, and the commercial shoots, I was rarely bored.

CHARACTERS ABOUND

CBS ran soap operas until three o'clock in the afternoon, then Channel 2 would take over the airwaves, providing its viewers a number of choices, including the very first audience-participation talk show, hosted by a Chicago news and radio guy named Phil Donahue. More than a dozen years before Oprah made her way into our living rooms, Donahue was running through the aisles of his studio, allowing members of his live audience to ask questions of his guest. Donahue spawned Oprah, Ellen, Tyra, and all the rest, including a red-frame-spectacled New Jersey woman named Sally Jessy Raphael, with whom I would have personal experience years later.

For years, before Donahue, KTVN ran an afternoon movie hosted by longtime Reno socialite Betty Stoddard. She would interrupt the movie on several occasions each day and use the time to tell a story about one of the movie's stars, promote a local cause, or pitch a product. She was well liked, polished, and served as a spokesperson for a number of Reno area businesses, and Channel 2's production department shot all of those commercials, too.

The CBS Evening News with Walter Cronkite came on at 6:00 p.m. and was sandwiched between two half-hour local newscasts. Pearce, Bickett, and a meticulous, often gruff meteorologist named Tom Lilley comprised the main anchor team. Lilley was more than the station weatherman; he was an avid golfer, joining a group that included my dad, sometimes Mom, me, Richards, and several others for an early morning round every weekend. There were many instances when I'd had too good a time the night before and met the group after hopping the fence along Skyline Boulevard that bordered the second tee. Lilley was often grouchy, but always lovable, and would rarely if ever accept a compliment like "nice putt" from any of us without firing back, "It didn't go in, did it?" He was a decent golfer and an accomplished observer of the area's weather, having claimed the honor of becoming the state's first American Meteorological Society recognized meteorologist. He was uncommonly accurate in the days before "Accuweather" and "Doppler 5000" radar. Reno was far from San Diego when it came to changes in the weather, and forecasting what would come the next day, or the next week, was a complicated puzzle. At right around five thousand feet above sea level, and smack dab at the base of the eastern slope of the Sierra Nevada Mountains, Reno got its fair share of sunny, mild days, but it did snow every winter, and at least a handful of times while I was there, in the spring and summer. Often that snow was heavy—thanks to storm systems that would sweep in from the Pacific Northwest, hit the cold air above the Sierra Nevada, and dump copious amounts of snow. That snow pack still serves as the main water source for Lake Tahoe and its tributary, the Truckee River, which runs through downtown Reno. It is also the natural element that contributes to the recreational delight of millions every year. It was also a huge source of frustration for Tom Lilley. He recounted, on many occasions, the tales of aggravated viewers who would approach him, wondering how two and a half inches of "partly cloudy" ended up in their driveways.

Another Lilley story had him playing golf in Scotland with friends, including Richards. On the second hole, the caddie carrying Tom's clubs asked him what he did for a living in

America. Lilley answered that he was a TV weatherman. The caddie scoffed and said, "We don't need any of those over here, because, do you see that hill over there?" pointing to a bluff a few miles away.

"Yes, sure," said Lilley, "why?"

"Well," replied the caddie, "if you can't see it, it's raining, and if you can see it, it's going to rain."

Tom Lilley was a practitioner and worked in a time before appearance meant more than intelligence and weathermen became the stars of local news. He didn't care about being a star; he did his job and he did it well. The FCC ruling had little impact on Tom Lilley; but it would prove to be huge for my dad and me. My father and his news director, Ed Pearce, took some pride in the ability to find young talent from other markets and bring them into the KTVN fold. They did this with Vargas, and also with a young reporter from the neighboring state of California. Ray Murray was a tall, mustachioed, up-and-comer when Pearce hired him to report and anchor news broadcasts in 1976. Ray made friends easily and I was lucky enough to be one of them. That natural likeability would serve Ray well, because, as fate would have it, his days of covering Reno City Council meetings were coming to an end.

EVENING TV BECOMES
A MAGAZINE

After the 6:30 local newscast signed off at 7:00 p.m., the air-waves once again belonged to the networks, and opportunities to maximize local advertising were again reduced to about a minute an hour. The FCC changed all that in the early '70s with the Primetime Access Provision declaring that the hour between 7:00 and 8:00 p.m. would, in effect, belong to the local stations in each market. A federal government agency decision kick-started the engine that would fuel the industry of syndication. Stations were now looking for programming to fill that void, ideally in two half-hour chunks, and the easiest way to do that was to buy a show somebody else had produced. Television welcomed shows like *Jeopardy, Wheel of Fortune*, and later *Friends, Seinfeld*, and many others that would become both popular and lucrative for local affiliates. They also made men like Merv Griffin, who created both *Jeopardy* and *Wheel*, very, very rich.

Another program that may have never happened without the FCC ruling was *Evening Magazine*. The concept, conceived by the executives at Westinghouse Broadcasting, was simple and special. Westinghouse owned stations in five of the country's major TV markets: San Francisco, Philadelphia, Boston, Washington, DC, and Pittsburgh. The idea started at KPIX in San Francisco as a vehicle that would expose and highlight human interest stories in the Bay Area, and it was so popular, it quickly spread to Group W's other four stations. Each show would be hosted locally by a one-woman-and-one-man team. They would not only introduce the stories but, in most cases, would come up with the idea, do the research, conduct the interviews, write the copy, and help edit the story for air. The show also featured segments by "experts" in a variety of fields, from cooking (Chef Tell) to healthier living (Jazzercise and Captain Carrot) to medicine (Dr. James Wasco). The stories, produced and aired in each city, would then be offered to each of the other four stations, giving *Evening Magazine* a national feel. Then Westinghouse took it to the next level with the brilliant and, as it turned out, profitable idea to offer *Evening Magazine* to the first station in any city that wanted it and could pay for it, under the national name of *PM Magazine*. Among the stations that jumped on board early were Dallas, Denver, Charlotte, Detroit, Miami, Oklahoma City, Seattle, Portland, and Reno. My dad saw this as a terrific opportunity to add something new and different to KTVN's programming lineup and continue the mission to provide a community service.

This show accomplished that because it featured stories in Nevada, about Nevadans. Of course, my mom, still the station's business manager, wondered if it could pay for itself, let alone be profitable. After a brief discussion, they pulled the trigger, making KTVN the smallest station, in terms of national market size, to ever carry the show.

They tabbed Stu Murtland to be the executive producer, and he, in turn, hired a no-nonsense young woman named Nancy Lavin, from Pittsburgh, to handle much of the day-to-day duty of finding local stories and integrating the national ones from around the country to make a show each night, Monday through Friday. Murtland also robbed from Ed Pearce's newsroom by making the Californian Pearce had just hired, Ray Murray, the male host, and teamed him with a female TV neophyte with a million-dollar smile, Jan D'Atri, and they brought *PM Magazine* into homes all over northern Nevada. They were two hardworking, extremely friendly people who had a natural, welcoming way about them that translated beautifully to TV. They also approached the job without any hidden agenda or ego, and Reno welcomed them with open arms. Reno's version of *PM Magazine* was an instant hit, but it was not without its share of nagging headaches and minor disasters.

The technology in the electronics field specific to cameras, microphones, and recording devices in the electronic news-gathering field continued to explode. Other companies joined Sony in what would become a multibillion-dollar segment of the industry. One was RCA, which manufactured its version of the equipment Sony had sold to KTVN and which we were so excited about years before. RCA's camera didn't need a cable to connect to a bulky battery pack; instead, it had a smaller battery that would connect to and power the camera, right from the back of the unit. It also featured a pistol grip at the base of the housing, making it easier to use from the cameraman's shoulder and allowing the operator the ability to, with the push of a button on the grip, start and stop the recording device without ever having to take his eye away from the viewfinder. It made life easier, but also presented an occasional problem when the cameraman, now—thanks to *PM Magazine*—wanting to be known as a "videographer," would think he pushed the button to start or stop the tape, but instead did just the opposite. Many times a tape would come back to the station with several minutes of pictures of the ground instead of the shot of the subject everyone thought was being covered. RCA smartly marketed its unit as a "mini cam," and, despite weighing as much as forty pounds, it was all the rage in the industry, and Murtland had convinced KTVN to buy one for *PM Magazine*. It was blue and very cool and expensive, costing close to $50,000; but when it came to ease of production, especially for a show like *PM Magazine*, it was a godsend. It also wouldn't be the last one KTVN would have to purchase.

To shoot the introductions for the show each week, Ray, Jan, either Murtland or Lavin, and a cameraman—sorry, videographer—would throw their gear, a week's worth of changes of clothes, scripts, and themselves into a van brightly painted with the show's logo and hit the road. If there was a national story about an adopted dog who saved a child's life (and there were several), the crew would go to the Reno Humane Society. On other occasions, they would simply take advantage of the local scenery to shoot generic introductions, and Reno had plenty of local scenery. Lake Tahoe was less than an hour's drive from the station's front door, so it became a fairly regular backdrop for the openings on *PM Magazine*.

One time, Lavin got the idea to shoot the introductions, referred to as stand-ups, not at Lake Tahoe but actually *on* Lake Tahoe; so they talked a boat rental company into allowing the crew to take a boat out onto the lake for an hour or so to shoot. In turn, the company would get both a verbal thanks and a video credit at the end of that particular program; but it turned out to be quite a bit more expensive than that.

They found an appropriate spot and decided to shoot the stand-ups while the driver kept the boat at a steady, if not spectacular, speed. As Ray and Jan rehearsed their lines (again, everything had to be memorized, because while TelePrompTers had found their way to the studios in Reno, there still wasn't a device that could put words onto the lens of a remote camera), the cameraman, Lowry Stewart, took pains to set up his gear on a less stable platform than normal. Lake Tahoe is a large and very popular body of water, especially for boaters, fishermen, and water skiers. This particular afternoon was an average one on the lake in terms of activity. The driver motored on, Ray and

Jan continued to go over the script and Lowry continued setting up his gear; and then, in an instant, he leaned a little left; the skipper turned a little to the right; and the $50,000 mini cam toppled off Stewart's shoulder, splashed into the frigid blue water, and sank out of sight.

Insurance paid for a replacement and Lowry Stewart went on to shoot hundreds of show intros, but the boat rental company never got its credit, and it would be quite some time before Lavin got so adventurous in selecting a location. Ray and Jan became the most popular personalities in Reno television history by exhibiting that rare ability to connect with each other and their audience. They liked each other, loved what they were doing, and in turn Reno loved them back. So did a lot of other people. *PM Magazine* was exploding all across the country and there was someone doing Ray's and Jan's jobs in every city. Some were as good or better; most were not, and since Reno was the smallest TV market carrying the show, and Ray and Jan were effective and engaging, they became prime targets for *PM Magazine* "host poachers." It took less than two years for Philadelphia's producer to woo Ray away from Reno to become the host of *Evening Magazine* on KYW; and, at the same time, Jan headed south to host *PM Magazine* at the Phoenix, Arizona, affiliate airing the show. Dad was happy for, and proud of, both Ray and Jan; but their leaving was a huge gut punch to KTVN, Murtland, and, to a certain extent, my dad, but one for which they always had to be prepared.

That's how this business is built to work. Men and women get jobs across the spectrum at small markets; then an innate desire to want to improve, coupled with various amounts of hard work, talent, drive, and luck, provide the opportunity for advancement. You start in Reno or Corpus Christi or South Bend and then move to Omaha or Raleigh or Tampa/St. Pete; and from there, if the stars align; you're on to Chicago, San Francisco, LA, or

New York. That's what happened to Elizabeth Vargas, and it also happened to Ray Murray and Jan D'Atri. They made their mark in Reno and left for greener pastures. In Philly, Ray had the same effect on the viewers of *Evening Magazine* as those of *PM Magazine*; they loved him. He was hired as *Evening Magazine*'s second-ever host in the City of Brotherly Love, and, while there, worked with, among others, Nancy Glass.

Years later, when I was working in Connecticut, I took the train to visit Ray. He was as friendly and "normal" as ever, even though he was a big star in one of the country's top TV markets. He would eventually leave the show and the station and start Banyan Productions, an outfit responsible for well-known television fare like the Medicus golf club infomercial and the program *Trading Spaces* on the TLC network. Jan D'Atri went to Arizona and never left. She stayed in local TV, opened up several restaurants, authored and published cookbooks, and is still going strong.

Other well-known TV personalities who got their start or spent some time in the *Evening/PM* family were the *Today* show's Matt Lauer, *Dancing with the Stars*' Tom Bergeron, and long-time TV host and spokesperson Leeza Gibbons. Unbeknownst to me when Ray and Jan left Reno, I was soon to join the family. The departure of Reno's first *PM Magazine* team would leave a huge hole on TV screens in and around Reno, and it was up to Murtland to fill it. They quickly found a female host in a big-haired, outgoing blonde named Kim Shepherd, but finding Ray's replacement proved to be much more difficult. Despite the bad luck, they were prepared. Everyone knew Ray and Jan were leaving weeks before they actually taped their good-bye show, so Murtland had Lavin get the national story lineup as far out as they could and put several weeks' worth of episode lead- ins "in the can." Even with that, cushion time started to run out, and Murtland was starting to get in a bind. In hindsight,

he might say the solution he came up with was a panic decision. He filled the hole with a Band-Aid by asking me. They
thought I had a lot going for me, but, more critically they were
out of time. I was local, so I knew the area and the area knew
me. I could write, edit, and, if I had to, even shoot a story; and
I also had experience in front of the camera. Maybe even more
important to the station was the fact that I was already working
there, so they didn't have to pay for my relocation, and my salary was a known factor (although I did ask for a raise). Murtland
and Lavin called me into the *PM Magazine* office (a room big
enough to accommodate the producer, cameraman, and both
hosts) and made their pitch. Could I help them out and fill in for
Ray while they continued to look for a permanent replacement?
They were close, and it shouldn't take more than three months;
and during that time I could continue to do my "real" job at the
station—producing and directing. It was 1979, I had not yet celebrated my twenty-fourth birthday, and I said "yes." Then three
months turned into three years.

BACK IN FRONT OF THE LENS

In the beginning, ratings slipped, but only a little—a testament to the show's popularity, as opposed to the new host team—and despite the occasional "creative differences" with my co-host, I was having a ball. Serving as the host of *PM Magazine* was fun, and I still got to produce and direct sporting events and newscasts; what was not to like? The answer was simply—my co-host. From the very start, she made it a competition. Which one of us would open the show; who had the most interesting story of the night; who got to avoid doing the lead-ins to Chef Tell or Judy Missett's Jazzercise segment; could it be "*PM Magazine* with Kim and Keith," instead of "Keith and Kim," in promotional announcements; and, ultimately, who would get the most stories accepted by the national office? These were the feature stories that were made available on a weekly basis to the stations all across America. According to the national office, they had to be well done, compelling, and of national interest. Most of them came from the biggest markets, and especially the five Westinghouse stations, so even after Ray left, Reno got to see plenty of him. But smaller markets did occasionally get stories on the reel. "Tripod the Three-Legged Cat," "The World's Largest Ball of String," and "Dinosaur Tracks in the Desert" were examples of these. In the three years I was involved in the show, I was fortunate enough to have two of my stories accepted. Keep in mind, our mission was to have each host come up with, write, shoot, edit, and put to bed one local story a week, and while we didn't always accomplish that goal, we came close. Factoring in vacations, holidays, and preemptions, that added up to approximately forty-five weeks or forty-five stories a year, which means I was involved in, or responsible for, about 135 stories during my time on *PM Magazine*, and a grand total of two were deemed worthy to make the national reel and be seen by millions of people outside of Reno.

The subject matter and tenor of my two stories couldn't have been more different. The first to make the reel was an emotion-laced tribute to one of the world's great aviation pioneers and his "never-give-up-hope" wife. Bill Lear was an innovator who, among other things, came up with the world's first car radio in the 1920s. Bill Lear also made airplanes, and he made them near Reno. The Lear Jet was the standard for executive air travel, and it made Bill Lear a wealthy and well-known man. He made one fortune thanks to that plane and thought he could make a second fortune with an idea he had in the late '70s. The Lear Fan would be the next great achievement in private aviation. Designed to be made entirely of carbon composite material, it would be markedly lighter than anything in the air and, therefore, far less expensive to fly. It also had a peculiar and revolutionary "pusher" design in which two engines powered a single spinning propeller blade mounted not at the front, but instead the rear of the aircraft. It was a dream and a labor of love for Bill Lear and his wife, Moya, but it wasn't close to being a reality when Lear fell ill and died in 1978. On his deathbed, Lear turned to his wife and said two words, "Finish it," and Moya Olsen Lear did just that. Construction and design of the Lear Fan continued for more than two years, and on January 1, 1981, with our cameras rolling, it rumbled down a runway at an airfield north of Reno, took off, and flew.

From one of the Lear Fan's sister airplanes, a Lear Jet, the great aviation photographer Clay Lacy captured the moment, and the aviation history books actually recorded the date as December 32, 1980, because, for funding purposes, the plane had to fly before the end of the year. That little nugget, combined with the backstory of one of America's foremost inventors, made it national-reel-worthy. The emotional element of a tearful Moya Lear, first recounting the story, then crying tears of joy as the brand new bird finally left the nest, didn't hurt either.

The second story you may have seen, if you were living in Baton Rouge, Peoria, Toledo, or any number of other cities, was far less emotional, but a lot more fun. It was an up-close-and-personal look at the Virginia City Camel Races. In 1959, a man named Bob Richards was the editor of a Nevada newspaper called the *Territorial Enterprise*. If that paper sounds familiar, your high school English teacher would be proud, because it's the very same paper that had once employed a scribe named Samuel Clemens, better known as Mark Twain.

In true "Twainian" fashion, Bob Richards decided to perpetrate a hoax. He wrote, in one edition of the paper, the fictitious account of camel races held in the tourist town of Virginia City, Nevada, and went one step further by printing results. Virginia City is, of course, the home of the Comstock Lode: what many have called "the greatest single mineral find in history."

It was America, in the late 1850s, and thousands of prospectors were working the California hills hoping to find gold. Suddenly news came from over the Eastern Slope of the Sierra about a strike of a different color. Described by the earliest miners as "that blasted blue stuff," the silver found in the Comstock Lode was eventually responsible for the North defeating the South in the Civil War by pouring much-needed funding into the Union war effort. It also established Nevada as the nation's thirty-sixth state (nicknamed the Silver State) and brought nearly seventeen thousand fortune seekers to the Washoe Valley. Ramshackle buildings, tents, and tenements popped up all over the hills, creating villages and towns like Gold Hill, Silver City, and the biggest of them all, Virginia City. More than $400 million worth of silver and gold was pulled from the Nevada mines, and, at one time, Virginia City was second only to San Francisco as the most populated city in the West. Along with horses and mules, camels were introduced to the wild, wild West as pack animals. But prosperity brought progress, and all those people and all that silver meant the arrival of the railroads as the V and T laid tracks into, and through, town. The less-than-friendly, more-than-fragrant camels were soon abandoned and left to roam wild in the hills around Virginia City.

Richards knew of the camels and set about concocting his story featuring the not-so-fleet-footed, humped quadrupeds. His results featured both a winner, a champion rider from his very own newspaper, and a challenge to any other newspaper in the country to compete in the camel races the very next year. In what came as a surprise to Richards, the *San Francisco Chronicle* bit and showed up in 1960 with a camel of its own, borrowed from the San Francisco Zoo. Mr. Richards found a camel of his own, and the race was on. Academy Award-winning director John Huston was in the area filming the movie *The Misfits* and, legend has it, with Clark Gable and Marilyn Monroe in attendance, Huston rode the San Francisco camel to victory in the very first actual Virginia City camel race.

Some twenty years later I found myself receiving last-minute instructions before climbing aboard a saddled, stinking, spitting, braying, one-humped beast. The camera operator who dumped the station's first minicam into Lake Tahoe had departed for the same job (cameraman, not "anchor" man) in Boston, and our new guy behind the lens was an attention-to-detail, yet wildly creative young man named Jim Irwin. Through the viewfinder he watched, and simultaneously recorded, the camel expert asking for and getting my undivided attention by telling me to lie as flat on top of my mount as possible and stay alert. I will never forget his next words.

This was critical, he continued, "Because a camel can turn his head 180 degrees and spit in your eye or, even worse, easily bite you on the stomach, neck, or face."

I looked dubiously at Irwin and asked if we could do the story featuring one of the other fools who were climbing on camels all around me. He smiled, said no, and then added that it would be helpful to the story if I actually won the first race so we could get plenty of footage of me riding to support the story. Here I was, suddenly concerned about an angry wild animal ripping out my spleen or piercing my jugular vein with its teeth, and my cameraman and friend was worried about the b-roll (b-roll is a TV term to define the footage that covers the script, therefore illustrating the story). Priorities! The camels were saddled up and our group, consisting of various TV, radio, and newspaper personalities, climbed aboard. On my first attempt, I nearly went all the way from the ground on one side of the camel to the other; but I managed to get my hands on just enough saddle to keep me from making a complete fool of myself. Irwin captured my graceful mount on videotape; luckily for me, the camel continued to look straight ahead and didn't bat an eye.

The races were broken down into heats that qualified winners for subsequent races, culminating with the final race in which someone would be crowned National Camel Race Champion of the Year. As we were led to the start line, I looked around and noticed all I had to do was beat a handful of men and women who spent most of their time behind an anchor desk, typewriter, or microphone to advance to the next heat. Suddenly I felt confident...and then the gun went off.

As instructed, I kicked my camel, laid as flat as I felt was safe and held on for dear life. The camel on my left turned and ran the wrong way. On the other side, I remember hearing the camel bray, a woman scream, and then a distant thud as a reporter from KOLO TV hit the ground. The racetrack was no more than forty yards from start to finish, but it felt like it took forever to complete the race; but complete it I did. With my body parts rattled, but intact, I crossed the finish line first, claiming a beautiful blue ribbon and fulfilling Irwin's request for at least one more race worth of footage. The next heat for me was scheduled for an hour or so later, so we wandered, camera in Irwin's hand, microphone in mine, through the crowd gathering interviews and footage of onlookers, jockeys, and other races, compiling most of what we needed to finish the piece. Eventually, in time for my next and, you guessed it, last camel race, featuring the winners of four other heats, some of whom happened to be actual camel jockeys, I quickly summed up my chances as slim and none and, unfortunately, or if you asked me, fortunately, Slim was not my camel's name in this particular race. The best I can say is that I managed not to get bitten or fall off, but I did finish dead last and my camel racing career was, mercifully, at an end, left only to live on thanks to the *PM Magazine* national reel.

The Virginia City Camel Races celebrated their fiftieth anniversary in 2009, and the event is now an international phenomenon, featuring riders from all over the world, including jockeys Shorty Smith from Tasmania and reigning world champion Ian Rowan from Australia. It was a fun story then and remains an entertaining tale today.

Thanks to *PM Magazine* I was also fortunate to, among many things, ride with both the United States Navy Blue Angels and Royal Canadian Air Force Snowbirds flight demonstration teams. I witnessed the International Whistle Off (a mouthwatering music competition featuring thousands of "pucker uppers" from as far away as Germany, Russia, Argentina, and South Africa) held in Nevada's state capital of Carson City. I traveled both internationally and domestically, including a trip to the Hawaiian island of Molokai, where the crew and I spent two days and one night in Kalaupapa among the wonderful people suffering from the devastating disease of leprosy. I got to know and tell the story of Melvin Dummar, the man who claimed he found Howard Hughes in the Nevada desert and later became partial heir to his formidable fortune. There was an Academy Award-winning movie about Dummar called *Melvin and Howard*. *PM Magazine*'s Reno edition also went to the Bonneville Salt Flats to witness an attempt to break the land speed record; a New Mexico farm where tiny jojoba plants broke ground before anyone knew what that miracle bean could do; and on a helicopter ski trip in the Sierra Nevada Mountains. My friend Jim won a national *PM Magazine* award for his breathtaking photography for that story.

I met and interviewed '6os rock-and-roll icon Paul Revere and his Raiders; "Midnight Blue" singer Melissa Manchester; as well as Pong and Chuck E. Cheese mastermind Nolan Bushnell. I greatly enjoyed the company and the music of a raucous, extremely talented, iconic group of musicians from Montana called the Mission Mountain Wood Band; sat face to face with TV prognosticator Jimmy "the Greek" Snyder (who advised me to treat gambling as entertainment and "never play with more than you could afford to lose"); and doubled over in laughter at an up-and-coming, suspender-wearing, whirling dervish of a young comedian named Robin Williams (long before he was

"Mork" from Ork). I shared the stage, and a bit of the limelight, with some of the stars that, as a kid, I used to watch from my seat in the audience. I even hosted the Miss Nevada Pageant twice.

I also got married (for the first time) and fathered a son we named Jared—because we liked it—and Lee, in honor of his grandfather. Unfortunately, I was young and stupid and proved to be a less-than-spectacular husband and an inept father. The marriage didn't last long, but luckily for my son, my ex-wife was always a wonderful mother, and he is now a terrific young man, living in Los Angeles, working as a recording engineer for various bands. He also did a lion's share of the engineering work during the first two seasons of NBC's hit show *The Voice*.

Though my personal life was a bit of a disaster, my professional career was humming right along, and I almost ended up following the same path as my predecessor on *PM Magazine*, Ray Murray. Stations in both Denver and Dallas were looking to replace male hosts and inquired about my services. I went to the Mile High City first, met with management, and recorded some on-camera screen tests at various locations around town (if you haven't seen it, Denver has a magnificent capitol building). Around that same time, I also got my butt on a plane and flew to Dallas at the expense of WFAA TV 8, the *PM Magazine* station there. I went through the same screen test song and dance, this time with a female co-host named Leeza Gibbons. Michael, the producer, liked me and wanted me for the job; Leeza liked me, too, but not as much. Her complaint was that on camera I looked not like a contemporary, but like her little brother, even though she was only two years older. I went back to the airport knowing what Michael thought, but not what Leeza thought, so I thought I had done enough to land the job. Leeza knew I hadn't. Well, we all know what happened to Leeza Gibbons. She went on to host *Extra, Leeza* (her own talk show), and *Entertainment Tonight* on TV. She also hosted the Top 25 Countdown on radio, became the spokesperson for Sheer Cover makeup, wrote a book, appeared on *Dancing with the Stars*, and founded Leeza's Place, a non-profit organization aimed at finding caregivers for people with memory disorders. She even has a star on Hollywood's Walk of Fame. I went back to Reno, was surprised by the bad news delivered by Michael a couple of days later, and started considering the offer from the station in Denver.

That contemplation led to an epiphany. I realized then the same thing I came to realize years earlier. TV offered glamour and fun, but it was the nuts and bolts of the profession that I loved, and the recognition and randomness of it that I didn't—not even a little. A good story, good script, and good pictures never let you down. A producer or co-host, whether good or bad, often did. I phoned the folks in Denver and asked them to take my name off their list, and told Murtland and Lavin in person that the "three-month experiment" was finally at an end.

Among the candidates interested in becoming the third guy to host *PM Magazine* in Reno was the former lead singer of Paul Revere and the Raiders, Mark Lindsay. He had earned a modicum of fortune and fame by wearing tight-fitting pants and belting out hits, including "Kicks," "Arizona," and "Indian Reservation." He was now out of the band and living at Lake Tahoe. He had seen the show, heard KTVN was looking to replace me, and thought he would be a natural, so he came to the station for an interview and screen test.

He indeed might have been a natural; but before we even shot a second of video tape, Lindsay found out two things: how much work was actually involved and how little money all that work put in his "pocketless" pants. Mark Lindsay smiled, got up, and walked out the door without so much as a "nice to meet you." In the end, a really nice guy from Tennessee, named Andy Culpepper, took my place. I have no idea where he or Kim Shepherd is right now; I hope they are both happy and healthy.

MAJOR CHANNEL CHANGES

After my stint in front of the camera on *PM Magazine*, my colleague and good friend Jim Irwin and I decided the time was right to leave KTVN and start our own TV production company in Reno. We called the venture ViewFinders and, thanks to the time I had spent becoming somewhat of a known quantity in town, and with the help of a friendly banker and a couple of backers (Mom and Dad), we got a loan for enough money to buy a camera, microphones, and some editing equipment. We set it all up in an office building near downtown Reno and went to work. We made some money shooting and editing commercials in Reno, as well as working freelance, shooting vacation cruises for something called the News Travel Network. But our grand plan was to become program producers. The idea we had was to put together a *PM Magazine*-style, hour-long show, featuring music and interviews with the multitude of celebrities that worked in Reno and Lake Tahoe casino showrooms and lounges every week. We called the show *In the Spotlight,* and had a small amount of success selling it to a couple of stations (Channel 2 in Reno and Channel 11 in Sacramento). Thanks to the show, Jim and I were able to meet—and I was fortunate enough to interview—stars of the day, like the pop music duo America, superstar singer Diana Ross, legendary exotic dancer Tempest Storm, comic magicians Shields and Yarnell, and the '60s rock group Paul Revere and the Raiders (without Mark Lindsay). We also reconnected, both on stage and backstage, with the band of musicians from the Big Sky State of Montana who had since changed their name from the Mission Mountain Wood Band to The Montana Band.

They were about to release a new self-titled album, and the first single was a song called "In Without Knockin'." Coincidentally, a new television network called CMT had recently launched and was trying to make a name for itself by airing music videos produced by country music acts, like MTV did with rock and roll a couple of years earlier. I had forged a friendship with some members of The Montana Band, and so its leaders, Rob Quist and Terry Robinson, hired Jim and me to come up with a concept and shoot and edit the video for "In Without Knockin'." We took advantage of the terrain, the conditions, and some *PM Magazine* connections to make our music mini-movie.

Casino owner John Ascuaga also happened to be a big-time cattle rancher and agreed to let our cameras and our cowboy crooners saddle up and ride along as he and his real-life cowboys moved the herd from high ground to the lower acreage he owned for winter grazing. Jim was our director of photography as we had the guys mouth the words while moving the cattle; we built a roaring campfire and the members of the band sang the chorus and played their instruments around it. After a day at that location, we thanked Ascuaga's cowboys and relocated to a historic Virginia City saloon, complete with cards, cap guns, and corn whiskey, to shoot the rest of the video. The guys, still dressed as cowboys, were joined by their girlfriends and wives, resplendent in dance hall girl costumes, to finish the song. I can't remember having more fun at work. That day complete, it was finally up to me and Jim to take the two days' worth of footage, match it up with the professional studio recording of the song, and present the completed package to the program execs at

CMT for air. The editing process was painstaking. Working without modern-day computer technology, and on broadcast-quality three-quarter-inch videotape machines, the lip-synching process alone, at times, took days to match up one or two lines. In the meantime CMT had heard the song and was interested in airing the video. We worked late into many nights to get it right. I guess we did, because when we finished, the band was delighted, so we sent it off to CMT, where it aired on a number of occasions. I still proudly have the "master edit," three-quarter-inch copy of it. Sadly, tragedy struck The Montana Band and its thousands of fans on July 6, 1987, when six members, including the incredibly talented Terry Robinson, died in a plane crash after playing a Fourth of July party near their beloved Flathead Lake. Thinking about it breaks my heart to this day.

Jim and I (actually more Jim than me) made a go of ViewFinders for a year or so, but there just wasn't enough income to support us both. Channel 2 was still open to me coming back to direct newscasts and help produce commercials, and I was happy to do just that. Alone, Jim kept the business afloat for a while, thanks to his talent, dedication, and hard work, and eventually he left Reno for San Francisco, where he works to this day, having won an Emmy in 2007 for a documentary he produced, photographed, and edited.

So I went back to KTVN and back to work behind the scenes. My *PM Magazine* hosting duties and subsequent departure from the station left a huge production void. To fill it Chisum hired Tom Christine, a man who would become a great friend and colleague throughout my entire career. Tom took over the duties as production manager, responsible for most projects shot and edited within the walls of 4925 Energy Way.

I was still doing remote jobs, so the management at KTVN nicknamed us "Mr. Inside and Mr. Outside," and we worked hard and, as it turned out, very well together. Something else happened while I was off being a "TV star" and starting, then leaving, my first business: my dad and mom decided to sell KTVN.

I have witnessed firsthand media big fish devour little fish on several occasions. My personal experience showed me that mom-and-pop organizations build successful businesses through hard work and personal sacrifice. They find quality, passionate people and then give them the tools and inspiration to bring out the best in them so they can make that business the best it can be. In essence it's that "essence" that makes the small business attractive to a bigger, greedier one. My mom and pop built that kind of business at Channel 2; and so did a Birmingham, Alabama, businessman named Joe Gibbs, more than a decade later, at a start-up cable niche network called The Golf Channel.

In 1980, the group of investors who backed Dad in establishing KTVN decided it was the right time to "cash in," and they asked him to begin entertaining suitors. After wrestling briefly with the idea of buying those investors out and keeping KTVN all to himself, Dad decided maybe his business partners were right. So he let it be known that KTVN was on the market. The potential buyer that impressed my dad most was a multigenerational family-run corporation out of Indiana. Sarkes Tarzian made his fortune inventing and manufacturing radio and television equipment, tuners, and components. He sold off that concern in the '70s and started TV and radio stations in the Midwest. His son, Tom, was at the helm when the company decided to target a profitable, well-run station in Reno. On behalf of his company, Tom Tarzian made a good offer, not the highest offer received by the Washoe Empire group, but a solid one. What sold Dad on the deal was the "promise" that if Sarkes Tarzian was indeed the suitor chosen to be the new owner of KTVN, they "wouldn't change a thing" in terms of the way KTVN was run.

"We love what you're doing and have no plans to change a thing" appears to be a catchphrase among big corporations when they gobble up well-run, profitable smaller ones. They may even mean it when they say it; from what I've seen it doesn't take long before they don't mean it any longer. It happened twice to companies in which I had a personal stake, and in both cases it took approximately five years to either eliminate all the employees that made the original company great, or wring all the passion out of the ones who were left. I saw it happen before my eyes in Reno, and then again more than twenty years later in Orlando, Florida. When Comcast bought The Golf Channel in 2002, the niche network was millions of dollars in the black and worth every penny, and then some, that the Philadelphia cable giant paid. In a companywide Golf Channel meeting after the sale, a smiling Comcast CEO, Brian Roberts, addressed us all and said the magic words, "We are proud to be part of this team, we have every confidence in what you're doing, and we have no plans to change a thing." Of course, over the course of the next handful of years, they changed almost everything.

More on that transition later, because so many more adventures were in store for me in the meantime. Part of Sarkes Tarzian "not changing a thing" in Reno was a several-year phaseout of my father as the guy in charge. He knew it was coming, and at the time he may have even welcomed it, but in hindsight, the way it happened bothered both him and my mom for the rest of their lives. Sarkes Tarzian, Inc., had several stations in its stable and clearly saw people in management at those as worthy successors to the people running KTVN. "We love what you're doing" in 1980 would become "we can do it better ourselves and no longer need you" years later. But none of us felt it at the time—in the first part of the decade of the '80s—because we were living large in the "Biggest Little City in the World."

It was the wildest time of my life. I had stopped doing *PM Magazine*, stopped being married—and looking back, to my dismay, had stopped being much of a father to my firstborn son. My parents had already built a house on the North Shore overlooking Lake Tahoe and then, after considering Carmel, California, took the money from the sale of Channel 2 and bought a condominium at Kapalua on Maui, in Hawaii. Dad stayed on as GM of Channel 2 for a few years but left the station for good in 1985.

The master plan had them living six months of the year in Hawaii and the other six months in the Reno/Tahoe area, and they were masters at executing that plan. As for me, I had become very friendly with Ms. Vargas and we were starting to see each other more than professionally and very seriously. My friendship with Tom Christine and his wife, Vickie, also continued to grow. Tom and I were both big sports fans, and we spent more than a couple of college basketball seasons betting on games and actually making quite a bit of money. We were partial to what's known as a parlay bet, an option sports books in the casinos offered that combined games to give you a chance to multiply your winnings.

You could bet on three, five, or seven games, all tied together, and if you won every game, you won the parlay. Of course, it only took losing one of the games to "piss away" your entire bet. The odds were greater, commensurate to the number of games selected in the parlay. For whatever reason, college basketball in the mid-'80s seemed, for us at least, to be an easy bet (take Georgetown with Patrick Ewing minus the points) and we got on a roll, consistently picking parlay winners and collecting increasing amounts of cash. In what did we invest these new-found gains, you ask? Absolutely nothing—except more bets, booze, drugs, and good times. The drugs, especially cocaine, were becoming popular in certain social circles; and I didn't know it then, but I found out later that coke was popular in TV production circles, as well. Elizabeth Vargas had become a bigger and bigger part of my life, but wasn't in any way, shape, or form party to the partying in which we were engaged. She was all business and completely focused on her career—obviously for good reason. In 1986, she took a step onto the next rung of her career ladder and left Reno for a job at KTVK in Phoenix, Arizona. What that meant for me was that I would handle my duties at Channel 2, but as soon as the 6:30 newscast signed off on Friday, I would be out the door and off to the airport to catch the first available flight to Phoenix to spend the weekend with Vargas. This continued until one late summer day when I was summoned into the office of the general manager of KTVN, my dad's old office, and informed that my services were no longer needed at Channel 2. I guess being Lee Hirshland's son was perceived, for once, in the building as a negative. In the beginning of this missive, I mentioned that, save for a few months here or a few weeks there, I have been steadily and gainfully employed for more than thirty years. The summer of 1986 was one of those "few months." I was stunned for a day, angry for about thirty more, and bound and determined to prove they had made a huge mistake. Actually, it was no mistake at all, and it turned out to be the best thing that ever happened to me.

FATHER FIGURE

If you never had the pleasure of meeting and knowing my father, that's a shame. I knew him for more than fifty-one years and never once heard anyone make a disparaging remark about him or question his loyalty or integrity. I know I didn't appreciate that enough when I was growing up, but I sure as hell do now. He made an impression on, and helped influence, the lives of hundreds of people; many of them would go on to become influencers themselves. That, I guess, is what you would call a legacy—and one that I'm proud to say is his.

My dad died in a Honolulu, Hawaii, hospital on May 16, 2007. Doctors initially thought he had, and treated him for, pneumonia. He didn't; he had cancer. I feel blessed that he didn't suffer; but we did, and at times still do, because of our loss. When my dad died, people cried; and not just the ones you would expect—a wife, or sons, or grandsons and granddaughters—but the other people with whom my father and mother forged a life. KTVN was much more than just a TV station or a place to work. It was, in many ways, a living, breathing thing. It had a conscience, thanks to people like Ed Pearce; it had a brain because of men like Al Richards; and it had my mom and dad, so it most certainly had a heart.

A service at the mortuary in Kahului was attended by several people with whom my folks worked and socialized during their time on Maui—from Gary Planos and Nancy Cross, who ran the

PGA TOUR event at the Plantation Course, to the sushi chefs, Hadashi and his team, who served them at least once a week at the Ritz-Carlton Kapalua. We buried my dad in the Maui Veterans Cemetery at Makawao overlooking the Pacific Ocean. It was the second military ceremony I had attended (my grandfather's was the first) and its dignity will forever be burned in my memory. Naval officers from Pearl Harbor participated, played taps, and presented the American flag to my mother. That flag now has and will always have the place of honor it deserves in my home.

Weeks later, former employees, colleagues, and people who loved and respected him most gathered for a memorial service in Reno. Hundreds showed up to pay their respects to my mom, my brothers, and me; several spoke, many exchanged stories, and we all shared both laughter and tears. Later, we attended another informal ceremony as the building that had housed KTVN since 1978 at 4925 Energy Way was officially dedicated to my mom and dad.

What follows is a column written by Dennis Myers, the preeminent political reporter in the state of Nevada, just after my dad passed away:

> KTVN founder Lee Hirshland has died at the Queen's Medical Center in Hawaii.
>
> Hirshland, once general manager of KOLO, assembled a group of investors to start a third Reno television station at a time when it was uncertain whether the market would support it. KTVN went on the air on June 4, 1967, and was financially frail for many years. At one point he sold his car—a Mercedes roadster—to make payroll. "But, you know, he persevered and, boy, when we had good years, he shared the wealth with the people who worked for him," said Ed Pearce, who was the station's longest-serving news director.

Hirshland was known for innovations and experimentations. He brought the PM Magazine franchise—then a leading ratings winner—to Reno and launched an afternoon program called Live at Five. In the late 1970s after television news in Reno had been featuring the same two newscasts (6:30 and 11 p.m.) for 20 years, he added a 5:30 p.m., then a 5 o'clock, plus a Sunday news interview program, Face the State.

In the early years, before the days of lightweight live gear, the station's control room was in a huge van because Hirshland wanted to make it easier to do remote broadcasts.

He added a television station in Elko, KELK (which the Elko Daily Free Press denounced as the "perverse invaders from Reno").

Hirshland personally produced KTVN election night's coverage, setting up independent vote-total gathering systems around the state that ran ahead of the official counts.

By the late '70s, KTVN owned the local news market, with a firm grip on half the viewers, the remainder split between KOLO and KCRL (now KRNV). After Hirshland sold the station, he stayed on as general manager until he and Pearce were removed by the new owners in a dispute over programming. The news ratings collapsed, and the station never regained that kind of dominance.

Hirshland was a staunch supporter of the news department, providing it with a separate attorney and backing its decisions. On one occasion, on-air commentator Leon Mandel offended Reno car dealers, prompting them to stage one of their periodic snits, threatening cancellation of advertising. Hirshland gave a competing commentary but did not try to censor Mandel or take him off the air.

Hirshland was inducted into the Nevada Broadcasting Hall of Fame in 1997.

He meant so much to so many, but nobody more than my mother. She literally couldn't live without him and joined him at Makawao in July of 2008.

People to this day remember him, revere him, and realize what a great man he was. I'll never forget it. The other thing that won't be forgotten is the Mercedes mentioned in Myer's article. I remember how much my dad LOVED that car. Mom actually referred to it as "his mistress." It was an oyster white, 1964 230 SL with a blue soft top to go along with its factory-made hard top. The car only had a passenger side mirror, but Dad thought it would be safer with a driver's side one, too. Because Mercedes didn't make one, he bought a second passenger side mirror and flipped it, then installed it on his side. The car also had TLC touches, like a brand new cassette player and a solid gold plate on which Dad inscribed his signature. My brothers and I got to drive it, rarely, but when we did it was a thrill. It was my dad's pride and joy and one day it was gone...now I know why. Thankfully the story doesn't end there.

Mom and Dad made that payroll, and every single one after that, and in time he was able to buy his Mercedes back and drove it even more proudly through the streets of Reno. Then the car was stolen. Both the police and insurance company were notified, but the car was gone, and so was a little piece of Dad's heart. But my dad was good at everything—including moving on, and he did. Then one day, years later, he got a phone call. It seems the gentleman who expertly serviced the Mercedes while it belonged to Dad had made an incredible observation. Earlier that day a 1964 Mercedes 230 SL rolled into his garage. It was slightly different, but not different enough for the man whose hands had been all over it to know what he needed to know. "That car," he said to himself, "is Lee Hirshland's car."

Once again Reno's finest were called and the culprit was arrested. It turns out it was the tip of the iceberg of a huge stolen car ring in Reno. The thief who drove the car into the absolutely correct mechanic's garage was the son of a woman employed by the Nevada Department of Motor Vehicles, and the scam was simple. Steal cars, change the VIN numbers, and put them back on the streets. Fortunately for us, the car needed work, and the mechanic chosen by the car thieves was just one more person who knew, liked, and respected Lee Hirshland.

Unfortunately for my Dad, the car was now part of a major criminal investigation, meaning his vintage Mercedes sat unguarded in a Reno Police impound lot for months. He was finally able to convince the insurance company to sell him the car back, and then convince RPD to release it to him; but his beauty had been mistreated badly. By the time the car once again rightly belonged to Lee Hirshland, he and Mom were spending most of their days enjoying sunsets on Maui, and the islands were

no place for a classic Mercedes. So Dad called and asked if I wanted to buy it. I didn't hesitate for one second and quickly arranged for it to be transported to me in North Carolina (how I got there will be explained in future pages), and now, in the middle of a restoration project, it can be found in my wife, Sarah's, and my garage in New Jersey.

Some people who work in local TV markets can't wait to get out of jobs almost as soon as they get them. The goal, as I have mentioned, is to constantly move out and up to bigger markets and better-paying jobs. Others, and you have several in your town, get what they perceive is a good gig and never leave. It doesn't make them less talented, just more comfortable. That could have been my life, as I might have stayed in Reno forever, maybe even comfortably occupying the same office my dad had occupied once upon a time. But the truth is: I am absolutely fine with *not* being comfortable. I believe a little uncertainty makes you a lot stronger, and change creates opportunity. I also think having dreams is a huge part of everyone's life, and in 1986 it was time for me to chase a few of mine.

BRISTOL BECKONS

So there I was, unemployed, but with more than ten years of broad, local TV experience under my belt, ready to leave Reno and focus on the next phase of my career. My first hope was to join Vargas in Phoenix, and I readied myself for interviews with news directors and station managers in the Valley of the Sun. For the first time in my life, I heard the word "no." I know you're saying that I didn't get the job at CBS, but I was offered one, and in my mind I *chose* not to work at CBS Sports. Now I was being ushered out of offices all over Phoenix with kind words, but without a job offer.

Back in Reno, I found myself out of work, but not out of confidence or options. I still had many friends at KTVN and, thanks to them, I was able to use the facilities there to update my resume tape and began to set my sights on doing what I loved most— working in sports television. So, unaccustomed to any other approach, and with Robert Browning's words now part of my psyche, I aimed high and took a shot at "the worldwide leader in sports"—ESPN. As it so happened, by scouring the trade magazines I learned the Entertainment and Sports Programming Network was looking for a director. The advertisement asked prospective candidates to send a resume and compilation reel to a man named John Kosinski in Bristol, Connecticut. I did just that, and even went a step further by calling Mr. Kosinski to tell him that the twenty-four-hour sports network would be much better off with me than without me. Surprisingly, I actually spoke to Mr. Kosinski on the phone. He was quick to say that he liked my aggressive tactics but would have to wait to see my tape. So I sent it his way and waited. As it turned out, I didn't have to wait long. In fact, twelve days and a couple of phone calls to Bristol later, John Kosinski informed me that he liked my tape, saw potential in my work, and hoped I could come to Bristol very soon for a face-to-face meeting and a tour of the campus. I jumped at the chance and jumped on a plane headed to Hartford. A short drive later, I was in Kosinski's office listening to, and looking at, the energetic, fast-talking, long-haired man who now held my employment fate in his hands. We talked about what I had done and what I knew, and then about what I wanted to do and didn't know. After a little more than half an hour, he shook my hand and alluded to the fact that he thought there was a place for me in the ESPN family. Excited, I got back on a plane headed west, thinking pretty much the same thing I had been thinking leaving Dallas/Fort Worth a few years earlier. I was thinking I had a new job.

Two days later, Kosinski called and confirmed my hopes. ESPN would like me to join its group of studio directors responsible for putting shows like *SportsCenter* on the air several times a day. The offer had me starting in Bristol in a few weeks, and I gratefully accepted. I was living in a Reno apartment with a great friend named Jim Petersen. Jim was a pitcher in college for Cal State Fullerton and actually had a "cup of coffee" in the major leagues. He was, at the time, the sports director at KTVN in Reno. I told Jim I was leaving Reno for ESPN, but first would head down to Phoenix to spend some final "West Coast" time with Vargas. He congratulated me, said he was heading to Southern California to spend time with family, and we promised to connect again in the near future. What I didn't know at the time was that my good friend and roommate Jim Petersen had cancer and, sadly, would pass away before we could spend any more time together. What I did know was that it was late in the summer of 1986 and I had a new lease on life. I had a noticeable spring in my step, but what I didn't have was a mobile phone; in fact, no one would for several years, but looking back I wish I did.

After ten days in the Arizona sun, figuring out how Elizabeth and I would handle the increased number of miles between us, I headed back to Reno to pack all my worldly goods to go to Bristol, Connecticut. I called ESPN and asked for John Kosinski and, in a matter of seconds, my wonderful new world fell apart. On the other end of the phone, a very nice woman explained that John Kosinski "no longer worked at ESPN"; stunned, I told her both my name and my situation and asked if there was someone else with whom I could speak. With a sympathetic word or two, she transferred me to someone named Denis Sedory, who was, in the interim, taking over the recently departed Mr. Kosinski's duties. After a brief conversation, my new friend Denis dropped the hammer: he was going to start the process from scratch and, while he would be happy to consider my resume and tape, it would be one of many at which he would be looking. Deflated, I thanked him, hung up, and vowed to work as hard as I could to make sure I got that job for a second time.

A few days later, I called ESPN again and got Denis on the phone to ask him if he had seen my tape. He had good news and bad (at the time I had a great deal of trouble seeing the good), saying he liked the tape but had instead decided to hire someone else. As it soon became apparent, the problem with my employment, or lack thereof, at ESPN, he admitted, wasn't talent; it was geography,

"It would be much easier to hire you if you didn't live all the way across the country," he said.

While I couldn't, and still can't, understand what one subject had to do with the other, I asked him for advice on how I should proceed to one day end up employed by the "worldwide leader in sports." He said the man he decided to hire, a very talented director named Jeff Winn, was working at the local ABC affiliate in New Haven, Connecticut, and now that station was down a director. Denis said he would be happy to call the folks at WTNH and put in a good word for me. I thanked him, told him I would appreciate it, and put the phone back on its cradle with a renewed resolve to take advantage of this new opportunity on the East Coast.

Mr. Sedory, at ESPN, was true to his word and set the wheels in motion for me to become part of the production team at WTNH in New Haven, Connecticut. Stan Roman was the head of programming and production there, and Dennis Blader was its lead director. I met them both on my second trip to the Constitution State in a number of weeks; we reached an agreement and, once again, I had a job—this time in writing.

WTNH, THE "GREAT" 8

New Haven, Connecticut, is home to, among other landmarks, Sally's Apizza, Toad's Place, and Yale University. It is also where you'll find WTNH TV, the ABC affiliate serving Connecticut and parts of New York for more than fifty years. It started out as WHNC, but changed its call letters to WTNH in the early 1980s when the station was purchased by media giant Capital Cities Communications. New Haven's population, not including Yale students when in session, is in the neighborhood of 125,000 people, and in the fall of 1986 I found myself among them. I was thirty years old and, except for a brief stint in the Pacific Northwest, had lived my entire life in the shelter of the Washoe Valley and the Sierra Nevada Mountains. New England, and specifically New Haven, was, to put it mildly, a culture shock.

Immediately, I noticed a couple of things: First, it was cold; and not just temperature cold but bitter, bone-biting, face-freezing cold. A port city, New Haven is on the Long Island Sound, and when the winter winds blow off that body of water, it can sting right through most outerwear, especially a San Francisco 49ers team jacket (which, by the way, was the warmest thing I brought with me). The second thing I realized in a hurry was that a football-crazy New England sports town was no place to wear a San Francisco 49ers team jacket. This was an NFL-savvy spot almost equally divided between New York Jets and New York

Giants fans, and at that time the Niners and the Giants were the most bitter of enemies. San Francisco had won the Super Bowl in 1984, but the following year, despite the presence of rookie wide receiver Jerry Rice, my beloved Niners were sent packing in the first round of the playoffs by Lawrence Taylor, Phil Simms, and the rest of the New York football Giants. The exact same fate would befall the Forty Niners in 1986; but I would extract a measure of revenge a few years later when Joe Montana, and then Steve Young, led San Francisco to back-to-back Super Bowl wins in 1988 and 1989. But, despite records and which team won what championships, Giants fans, with whom I became acquainted and worked, were quick to point out how superior their team was to mine when I arrived in Connecticut in 1986.

One of those fans at the time was the sports director at WTNH, Bob Picozzi. These days you can hear Bob on the radio delivering the sports news in quick, informative bursts during ESPN Radio's *SportsCenter* or calling Seton Hall Pirate basketball games. In those days, Bob was a no-nonsense, hardworking proponent of the importance of local and national sports' place in an evening newscast. He loved sports, loathed mistakes and laziness, and settled for nothing. He was always at his best when he went on the air and he expected the same of everyone around him, including his director, me. More on Bob a bit later, but first let me set the scene at WTNH in 1986.

Experts call cities, or areas that local television stations reach, "markets," and each year they measure or rank 210 of them. At the top of the heap is New York City. The perennial number one reaches close to seven and a half million households; nearly 6.5 percent of the nation. Sitting in second, every year, is Los Angeles, followed now by Chicago, Philadelphia, and Dallas. All the way down at the bottom, and wearing the crown as the smallest measured market in American television, for as long as I can remember, is Glendive, Montana, with just under four thousand households. As I mentioned earlier, there are hardworking men and women at every single one of them, delivering news, sports, and weather to folks sitting around the dinner table, readying themselves for bed every night, or preparing for another day bright and early in the morning. Others are producing local public service programming or helping local businesses sell goods, thanks to the commercials they put together; and still more are sitting at desks in accounting department cubicles; hitting the streets as part of a sales staff; or working from corner offices, programming, managing, and running the operation.

At the turn of the century, the United States government estimated that the broadcasting industry was responsible for more than 327,000 jobs (including radio and television); and I can guarantee you that many of the ones working as on-air talent in most markets spend at least part of their day thinking about, or working on, a way to move up to a bigger market, city, opportunity. Thanks to geography, WTNH was, and is, one of the stations in Connecticut that benefits from being able to reach households all across the state (the station's main competition comes from Hartford-based stations) and into Westchester County in New York. That reach puts New Haven squarely at number thirty on the above-mentioned market size rankings, and, thanks to its proximity to New York, a prime target for the ladder climbers. Now, it only stands to reason that the higher the market on the list, the harder it becomes not only to move in—but to move up and out. There were people working at WTNH long before I got there in 1986; they were still working there when I left in 1989; and many still punch the time clock on State Street in New Haven today. Most are consummate professionals—among the best in the business at what they do—and they still do it right there in New Haven because they want to be there. I am proud to say I worked alongside them for three years, although at first many would say, to this day, that they would have been surprised if I lasted three weeks.

In 1986, WTNH was a busy, bustling place, especially in the newsroom run by News Director Wendie Feinberg. Ms. Feinberg was fairly new at the job but managed the process professionally. She went on to run the newsroom at WSVN in Miami, Florida, and is now the Emmy Award-winning managing editor of the *Nightly Business Report* on PBS. But a quarter of a century ago, she had her hands full running the operation of a very busy New Haven newsroom. The city's crime rate has long been at least double the US average, which made for almost constant chatter on the newsroom police scanner and frequent dispatches of news teams (reporters, camera operators, and live vans) throughout the day; and the day started early.

Like many medium to large-market TV stations, WTNH started informing its viewers of the day's events at or before the crack of dawn. As an ABC affiliate (the station is obligated to air American Broadcasting Corporation programming throughout the day and night), it entertains its viewers with the live nationwide broadcast of *Good Morning America*, starting at 7 a.m., and at various points during that program (usually the top and bottom of each hour), the local station interrupts the national broadcast with local news, traffic, and weather. Staff has to be in place to provide this service; but that staff is responsible for more than just those few minutes every half hour. At WTNH, now and in 1986, *Good Morning America* was preceded by at least thirty minutes of local news. That meant producers, reporters, and assignment editors would sleepily arrive at work, sometimes as early as 4 a.m., and start preparing to deliver the morning's news and information. While those folks entered the building from the newsroom side, a different set of folks were, most times just as sleepily, walking in the production doors. A director, an audio technician, a graphics operator, a videotape operator, and a technical supervisor all joined a master control operator who made sure the station stayed on the air during the overnight hours.

In the newsroom, the producer spent most of his or her time completing several tasks. One was what they called "poring over the wires," or looking at overnight reports from either the Associated Press (AP) or United Press International (UPI) for important and relevant stories, both locally and from around the world. Another job was to review the rundown, or list of stories, from the newscast that aired at 11 p.m. the night before to see if there was anything that needed a follow up, or new information that had come to anyone's attention in the hours since the story aired last. After compiling what the producer felt were the relevant stories for that morning's news broadcast, he or she would then go about the task of putting together his or her own rundown: deciding how much time each story would be allocated and in what order the particular stories would be delivered; the videotape or graphic support for each story; and in what segments the viewer would be treated to things other than news, like sports or weather. The weather was delivered live, and the weatherman, a delightful gentleman named Dr. Mel Goldstein, joined the producer, the anchor, and the rest of us bleary-eyed employees at that ungodly hour of the morning. Sports, on the other hand, was delivered via a piece of videotape, recorded the night before and left on the morning producer's desk by the sports anchor, now sleeping soundly in his comfortable bed.

The good and bad thing about time, when it comes to broadcast television, is that it is both a constant and finite thing. There are exactly thirty minutes in a thirty-minute newscast; and a producer has to manage each one of them down to the second. But a thirty-minute newscast does not mean there are thirty minutes of news. First, the producer has to account for commercials (someone or something has to pay the bills), so if there are six minutes of commercials, the time allotted for news now becomes twenty-four minutes. If the sports anchor from the night before left a two-minute wrap-up on the producer's desk, the time for news now gets shaved to twenty-two minutes. Some parts are set in stone; others, like the weather, are more fluid. On many occasions, I witnessed Dr. Mel react with the same smile when he was asked to either extend his on-air time to fill a hole in the rundown, or contract the time he would be on the air because the producer had stuffed too much into the rundown on a particular day.

If you boil it down to nuts and bolts, producing news, or any studio show, for that matter, is basically a combination of decision making (choosing which stories deserve to be told and for how long), babysitting (making sure the talent is in the right frame of mind), and a simple math exercise (when it's time to start, you better be ready, and when the time is up, you better be finished). So it's the producer's job to put it all together; but it's the director's job to put it on the air. For most morning newscasts in the late '80s in New Haven, an intense Ohioan named Mary Beth Laskey was the producer and I was her director. Before we both left WTNH, around the same time, years later, Mary Beth and I had become friends and developed a great professional respect for each other. But it took a while, mainly because I was a disaster.

My first days at WTNH were spent introducing myself to the many dedicated employees with whom I would now be working. My experience in Reno taught me that broadcast television worked much like a sports team in that a successful product depends on everyone involved working together and doing their job. Having actual hands-on experience at many of those jobs, I had an appreciation for each and knew that none was more important than another. But I was a stranger—the "new kid," an unknown quantity—and I had to prove myself worthy before being accepted into the "club." Luckily for me, I made friends easily, always had, so my coworkers liked me, or acted like they did, early on. It took some time for them to respect and trust me in the director's chair. After finding an apartment (a couple of rooms in a beautiful Victorian house) walking distance from the station, I began my daily routine of getting up before the sun and learning how the pros at WTNH put newscasts on the air every day. In the beginning, I would watch the interaction between the producer and my boss, Dennis Blader. Dennis had been directing the morning shift for a while, thanks to the departure of Jeff Winn and the hole in his staff created by that departure, but he was a family man and, through his own experience, had earned a much higher place in the WTNH production pecking order. In short, he was tired of this early-morning, entry-level shift, and he wanted me up to speed as quickly as possible.

The basics of directing a newscast at the local level are fairly universal. You have cameras, videotape machines, microphones, graphics (both words and pictures that accompany each story on the screen), people to operate all of that equipment, a producer, and talent. In many large markets, there is also a technical director, or "switcher." That nickname came about because the piece of equipment the technical director is responsible for operating is called, oddly enough, a switcher. An easy explanation of this particular piece of gear is that, by virtue of a push of a button, it switches the source that goes on the air; or, in layman's terms, the picture you actually see on TV. If you can visualize the switcher as a piano hooked up to your television set, then imagine yourself pressing different keys. Now wrap your brain around the idea that each time you press a different key, the picture on your TV set changes. Middle C might be a camera pointed at the talent, A sharp might be a videotape machine that contains a story about a bank robbery, F might be a picture of Tiger Woods—because the sports anchor is, at some point, going to read a story about the golfer, and the G key is black (which is exactly like it sounds: push this key and the screen goes dark). The timing and order of when the technical director pushes each key, or button, on the switcher is crucial to the success of a newscast. Get them all in the right order and at the right time, and it does, in some ways, resemble a symphony. Get one thing wrong, or slip on the timing, and it might as well be junk. The problem is that in live TV, if it's junk, you can't just rewind the recording device and start again; your mistakes are there for everyone watching to see. In the various markets that employ both a director and a technical director, it's the director's job to call out each order that the technical director eventually executes. The director will use terminology like "ready camera one"; this tells the technical director that the button that represents camera one is the next source that everyone expects to be on the air. The director, when the time is right, will then call out, "take camera one" or "take one." On the "take" command, the technical director, or TD, pushes that button or "takes" that source. There are a million TV stories about nervous, or under qualified, directors issuing counterintuitive commands like, "Ready one, take three," and, at that point, all bets are off as to what the director wanted and what actually ends up on TV. At WTNH in 1986, and maybe still today, there was no technical director, so the person responsible for not only giving the commands, but executing them, was the director, yours truly.

The situation was the same in Reno, but at a market size in the hundreds, compared to WTNH's thirty, there was much less equipment and far fewer sources on the switcher from which to choose. Adding to the angst was the attitude that what they were doing at WTNH was far more important than what my colleagues and I happened to be doing at KTVN, and they were probably right. More people were watching, and sometimes that bigger audience included important people: movers and shakers in the industry, executives at New York stations and network headquarters, who just might be getting ready for work and watching WTNH from their Westchester County homes. In addition, the talent employed by WTNH included Emmy Award winners and broadcast veterans with hundreds of years combined in the business. This was not a training facility; you were expected to bring your best and be your best, every show, every day. It was nerve wracking, and I was nervous.

I knew it at the time, but looking back it seems even more important to recognize and thank those that supported and befriended me as I made my way at WTNH: Dennis Blader and his boss Stan "the Man" Roman; lead director Joe Cook (who left WTNH to head up production at *Live with Regis and Kathie Lee* for a while); Phil Skender; technical supervisors and technicians like Francine DuVerger and Tom Sgro; Gary Banderas; Curtiss Anderson and Tim Wright; other friends, like Mark Nelson, Tony D'Angelo, Bob Bentz, and Sheila Crowley; and the hundreds of others who I have failed to mention, but will never forget because they made going to work a joy every day. I learned something from every one of them, and they made me both a better broadcaster and a better person. I'm sure they'll all admit that my early days at WTNH were an adventure. Such an adventure that one anchor compared working with me to an amusement park ride.

I had been at WTNH for a few months and, after a few early rough spots, had been doing a good job directing the morning newscasts and cut-ins that accompanied *Good Morning America*. The lead director at the time, Joe Cook, decided I was ready to tackle the next rung on the WTNH director's ladder, the *Noon News*. Joe was a smart guy and one of the best local news directors that I had ever seen. His command of the control room and work with the switcher was flawless, and every single producer working at the station breathed a sigh of relief when they saw on the schedule that Joe Cook was directing their show.

So if he thought I was ready, who was I to argue? I had been observing Joe direct the *Noon News* for a few weeks, and had even sat in for a segment or two on several occasions. Adding to my comfort level was the fact that the *Noon News* producer was Mary Beth Laskey, alongside whom I had worked during many morning newscasts. She was okay with it; Joe was okay with it; Dennis and Stan were okay with it; and so the day came for me to direct my first noon newscast for WTNH.

The worst thing a director can do to an anchor on the news set is to surprise him or her. Going off script for immediate or breaking news is one thing; the best anchors in the world can react to the immediacy of a plane crash or an impromptu presidential news conference without missing a beat. But plain old-fashioned screwups, like being on camera when the other anchor is reading the news, or seeing pictures of a quilting convention when the words you are reading describe a downtown apartment fire, can be hard to overcome.

The talent for that very first show was a team of WTNH's longtime and best anchors, Diane Smith and Mark Davis. Bob Picozzi was the sports director at the time, but the person who handled sports at noon was a funny, friendly guy named Skip Church, and the weather was handled not by Dr. Mel, but by a young, energetic, slightly arrogant weather junkie named Geoff Fox (he's still working in the market, by the way). The rundown was in; the scripts loaded into the TelePrompTer (the machine that didn't exist when I was on air in Reno); the videotapes stacked in the right order, ready to be loaded into, and played by, a bank of machines; the microphones were placed on Mark and Diane and checked; and the entire crew was in place and ready to go. I won't go into a lot of detail, but remember the piano story I told a few pages ago?

The clock struck high noon; I gave the commands to "roll" (the videotape technician would push the button to play the tape); track (the audio supervisor would open the fader to make sure the sound would be heard); and "take" (that command was to me, so I would push the button on the switcher—the piece of videotape on which lived the opening to the *Noon News*), and that was the last thing I did right for half an hour. Everything that could go wrong went wrong, almost exclusively by my hand. If Mark was supposed to introduce the story, I pushed the button for the camera that was pointing at Diane. I missed roll cues on tape machines, put the wrong names on people featured in stories, called for the audio supervisor to open the wrong person's microphone—and that was just in the first segment. Thirty minutes felt like thirty hours, but, mercifully (thank you, Father Time), those thirty minutes came to an end and silence hung over the control room. Mary Beth just got up and left, as did the camera operators in the studio, the videotape techs, and the audio supervisor. Stunned, I sat there trying to figure out what had gone wrong when the control room door opened and in walked anchor Mark Davis. Without so much as a glance my way, he put a piece of paper on top of the switcher in front of me and walked out. It was the last page of his scripts for the *Noon News*, and at the bottom, in black marker, he had written four simple words: "thanks for the ride."

With that debacle clearly etched in my memory, I got better, earning the respect and friendship of my colleagues. Working at WTNH was fun and afforded me a diverse selection of opportunities. I was fortunate enough to direct a Yale basketball game, a live performance of the New Haven Symphony, and a studio show hosted by Picozzi that featured the 1988 NIT Champion University of Connecticut Huskie basketball team and their third-year coach, Jim Calhoun. New Haven was also home to the Walter Camp Foundation, a proud organization that has, among other things, selected an All America college football team since 1889. Camp played football at Yale and is widely regarded as the father of American football. Derived from rugby, the game changed thanks to Camp, who dreamed up things like the play from scrimmage, assigning a certain number of points for goals scored, and the long-standard offensive arrangement that features seven men on the line as well as a quarterback, two halfbacks, and a fullback. Every year, the best and the brightest in college football arrived in New Haven, Connecticut, for a gala weekend, and I thought it would be fun to put together a half-hour program that chronicled their time spent in "the Elm City." Stan Roman gave me the thumbs up, and cameraman Tim Wright and I followed future NFL players Vinnie Testaverde, Keith Byars, Deion Sanders, Cris Carter, Tim Brown, and Keith Jackson as they partied, prepared, and pronounced themselves the best of the best. The show was fine and fun, and we did it a couple of times before the novelty wore off and other exciting programming came knocking on WTNH's door.

In 1987, the knock on the station's door came from the knuckles of Sally Jessy Raphael. She brought her trademark red spectacles and her entire crew to the studios of WTNH to tape her daily talk show. She also brought some of the world's most interesting and psyche-riddled guests into our lives, all in front of a studio audience that had just about everyone at the station in awe, in stitches, or in shock, depending on the day. People would line up around the block for the chance to be part of the studio audience on taping days, and because they put together multiple shows per day, everybody who waited in line got a chance to see at least one broadcast. Sally Jessy was a phenomenon; she was Jerry Springer before Jerry Springer, bringing to light stories of people with multiple personalities, troubled homes, and confrontational in-laws, but also welcoming and interviewing the occasional celebrity. The show was produced by a longtime Raphael staffer, but directed by the guys and girls with whom I went to work every day. Joe Cook got most of the assignments, but once in a while others like Dennis Blader, Phil Skender, and Deb Troutman got the nod. I even directed one or two, but at the time I had pretty much moved off the day shift and found myself directing the 5 p.m. news and the nightly news show that aired at 11 p.m., after primetime programming and before ABC's *Nightline*.

Around town, WTNH had earned the nickname "The Late 8" because, in some people's minds, the station's news department had a tendency to be the last to arrive at a breaking story or crime scene. Wendie Feinberg was working hard to fix that and hired some younger, harder-working reporters to rebuild the station's reputation. So into the newsroom, and subsequently my life, came people like Ann Nyberg, Charmaigne Wilkerson, Keith Kountz and Carla Wohl, who teamed up with Davis, Smith, Picozzi, and others already there, like Al Terzi, Mike Boguslawski (he was "on your side"), and Peter D'Oench to comprise a formidable news operation that battled WFSB in Hartford for the ratings top slot. Style seemed to be as important as substance at the time, because management adopted the "Action News" philosophy successfully employed at stations in Philadelphia and other markets. It was a fast-paced, high-energy newscast filled with shorter-length reports, stylized graphics, and a method of delivering sports news, scores, and highlights called "Big Board Sports." Instead of sitting behind a desk, Picozzi, Church, or anyone tasked with giving viewers the sports scores would stand next to a wall painted green that, through technology, would transform into a veritable smorgasbord of sports information. The computer-generated screen would magically "open up" to reveal a team logo; highlights—thanks to a piece of videotape;

a picture, transmitted live via a camera hookup somewhere in the city; or a graphically generated list of scores from any sport or league. It was exactly the same as the technology employed then and now by many weather operations for segments during local evening newscasts across America or behind home plate in baseball stadiums these days. In person, the fan sees a lime green square, circle, or rectangle; but on TV, the viewer sees whatever electronic image a director or technical director selects. It could be a weather map showing both high and low pressure ridges, an advertisement, a promotion for an upcoming show, or, in the case of "Big Board Sports," any of the previously mentioned sources available on the house of horrors that is the switcher. On several occasions, and regardless of who was directing, the Big Board would open up to show baseball highlights when Picozzi was talking hoops or American League scores when Skip Church called for the National League. The viewer at home might have also seen black, color bars, a shot of Yale University, or even Ann Nyberg in that big board, much to the dismay and, if I'm being honest, at times the profound amusement of me, my colleagues, and Bob and Skip. We directors hated "Big Board Sports" and were thrilled to finally see it go.

In New Haven, I learned to order my morning coffee "light and sweet," that the white clam pizza at Sally's was a delicacy respected around the world, and that the concerts were raucous at Toad's Place (I saw Springsteen and many others there). I also learned that you didn't really want to wander the streets of New Haven alone at night. The fact that New Haven had a fairly high crime rate did make my shift directing news interesting. I came into work most days around 2 p.m. and stayed until everything had been cleaned up after the 11 p.m. news. But just because my shift ended close to midnight, my "day" was far from over. On most occasions a group would leave the station just before midnight and head over to our favorite watering hole, a New Haven tradition called Archie Moore's. At Archie's we'd talk about that night's newscast over a few drinks (have you ever had something called Alligator Piss?) and on more nights than not we would close the place and then stay and continue to imbibe. The owners and service staff knew us, knew we tipped well, and, within reason, let us stay after hours for another drink or two. We'd say goodnight, find our way home, and then sleep the morning away before getting ready for another 3 to midnight shift. It was not a very healthy lifestyle and, quite frankly, it got boring.

AS BOWIE ONCE SAID...
CH-CH-CH-CHANGES

Something else happened during my tenure at WTNH. The distance between Phoenix and New Haven proved to be too big an obstacle for my relationship with Elizabeth Vargas. We broke it off after one too many cancelled trips or missed opportunities to be together. Subsequently, I watched with pride as her career continued to skyrocket, taking her from Phoenix to Chicago and then, eventually, New York and ABC. She anchored ABC's national evening newscast, hosted *Good Morning America*, was a correspondent on *20/20*, married and had children with "Walking in Memphis" writer and singer Marc Cohn, and has become one of American television's most recognizable personalities. While not as impressive, my career ended up being a better than average one, too (if I do say so myself), but it took a little longer for me to get there.

After Vargas and I called it quits, I spent more time with the folks who had befriended me at WTNH, both at work and around town after work. I lived, on separate occasions, both alone and with roommates in apartments that lacked washing machines and dryers. Like most bachelors, my MO was to wait as long as possible before I had no choice but to go the Laundromat and clean my clothes. One Sunday, I was down to the last pair of everything, so I crammed the dirty clothes into a pillowcase, grabbed the Tide, and headed for the Laundromat on the corner.

I washed my clothes like a guy, basically still do. What I mean by that is, there is no separation of whites, darks, and colors, and there is no change in water temperature. There is simply the exercise of cramming as many clothes as possible into the machine, dumping in a cupful of detergent along with it, and pushing start. When "clean," the entire bushel of clothing is then transferred into the same dryer for that part of the process. It's simple, and it happened the same way every time I went to the Laundromat, except on this day. As the drying cycle was winding to an end, a very pretty brunette walked into the shop with her own basket full of clothes to be washed and dried. I liked her looks and instantly wanted to figure out a way to start up a conversation, but my time in the room was at an end and hers was only just beginning. So I did what any red-blooded American male bachelor would do in the same situation...I retrieved my clothes from the dryer and washed them again. That "smooth" move allowed me to meet Kathryn Freeman, the woman who would become my second wife and the mother of two more wonderful children. But initially, she wasn't buying my shtick. In fact, my elaborate if impromptu scheme nearly got me a slap in the face. While I watched my already-once-cleaned clothes go around and around, I tried to work up the courage to approach this person who had just strolled into my life. When her clothes were ready for the dryer, I saw my opportunity and approached as she was scouring her purse for dryer change. "Do you need some quarters?" I offered with a smile. With nothing even remotely resembling a smile she shot back, "I have my own money." Appropriately chastened, I turned tail and headed back to my now twice-cleaned clothing. I assumed that encounter was the end, but instead it turned out to be just the beginning of marriage number two for me.

Ms. Freeman, I soon learned, had just returned from a trip Down Under in what was an effort to mend her broken heart.

Kathy had just lost her mother, killed by a drunk driver. Doubly sad was the fact that she had lost her father to cancer when she was a child. Despite the fact that she had lost both of her parents, it wouldn't take long for me to learn she had an amazing support system of friends and family, led by two older sisters and their loving husbands.

That day in the Laundromat, we ended up striking up a conversation that turned into an exchange of phone numbers and a promise to spend time together soon. I walked back to the apartment I shared with Mark Nelson from WTNH and another friend, my mind full of scenarios and thoughts about how long I should wait to call on Kathryn Freeman again. As it turned out I didn't have to wait long; she beat me to it. When my phone rang later that day, I was both surprised and delighted to hear her voice on the other end. She had friends who were in the middle of making preparations for their wedding and the plan for that evening was to head out to the local VFW hall and listen to a band they were considering. They were dragging her along and now she was, in turn, trying to drag me. For my part I was all too happy to be dragged. We agreed on a time and hung up. Minutes later, the plan changed. She called back to say she was meeting her sisters and some friends for dinner at Pepe's Pizza, one of the two (Sally's is the other) famous New Haven, Connecticut, pizza joints, and how did I feel about joining her? Part of me wanted to go, and it was clear she wanted me to, but for goodness sake's I had just met her and now I was being asked to meet her entire family and whichever family friends had decided they wanted to meet this latest interloper. But what the heck—a guy has to eat, right? And Pepe's pizza was amazing, so I said yes.

I don't remember how the band was, but I do remember shaking a bunch of hands and being both overtly and covertly the focus of attention for most of the night. I must have passed enough tests to warrant subsequent audiences with Kathy, her family, and her friends. We started spending a lot time together, a framed photo on my desk became one of her, not Vargas, and more and more of my belongings started ending up in her State Street apartment. I was still working the late news shift at WTNH, but as I was starting to enjoy Kathy's company more and more, I enjoyed my time at the station less and less. Maybe it's human nature to examine many things in your life when one thing in your life changes; or maybe I stopped liking the night shift when suddenly I actually had someone to spend my nights with. Whatever the reason, as I realized thirty-five was right around the corner, I started thinking about what I wanted to do with my life. I knew it wasn't a professional change that I was after. I had worked in television for more than a dozen years, really had never done anything else (well, there was one stint as a shoe salesman), and I knew, in my heart and my head, that I never wanted to do anything but work in television. But my whole professional life had been at the local TV station level, and a lot of the work was in and around control rooms and local newsrooms. I was a sports fan, as well as a competitor briefly, at a reasonably high level; and as much as I appreciated the contributions of men like Dennis Blader, who hired me at WTNH, I didn't want to end up being him. Now, all of a sudden, I knew where I wanted my career to go next, but I had no idea how to get there. So I picked up the phone and called the guy who would—my dad.

Not really the retiring kind, my parents were working and living both in Reno and on Maui after the sale of the station. Part of the terms my dad signed in 1980, before saying good-bye for good to Channel 2, was a noncompete agreement, which meant he couldn't work for another television station or broadcast entity for several years. He couldn't, but my mom could. The television universe had expanded to the extent that, at the beginning of the decade, Reno seemed ready for a fourth affiliate, and nobody knew more about putting together a group of folks interested in investing in a startup TV station than my folks. So, with my dad behind the scenes and my mom out front, work began on getting the Hirshlands another station in Reno. After a minor financial investment, and a fairly major intellectual one, the quest for station number two ended, but the desire to contribute to whichever community they belonged never did. Simultaneously, Dad also kept himself busy by starting and running a small public relations firm and invited some old friends like Ed Pearce to join him. They were also enjoying more than just going to the beach while in the islands. Being TV people and avid golfers, they were naturally drawn to the broadcast teams that came to Hawaii each year to televise the various professional golf tournaments. In the early '80s, that group of professionals worked under the watchful eye of Don Ohlmeyer, who had gone from ABC to NBC to forming his own production company in 1982. His production teams were responsible for bringing Indy Car Racing and golf into American homes on the cable sports network ESPN. Those assignments included golf telecasts in Hawaii.

When in Hawaii, my parents played golf almost every day, and mostly on the Arnold Palmer-designed Kapalua Bay Course (the par three 8th green is located right outside their condominium's front door). Golfers, certainly ever since I can remember, they knew the game, and obviously knew TV, so volunteering to work alongside producers, announcers, and technicians seemed a natural continuation of both professional and leisure activities. So they met and worked for the likes of Ohlmeyer; his producers:, Paul Spengler and Andy Young; and directors like Steve Beim and Bob Goodrich. They earned and returned the respect of, and became, at least on the edges, members of a most accomplished television sports brotherhood. Dad and Mom knew the guys on the crew and all the announcers including Vinny and Jim, Rolf, Gomer, Dawg, Swanny, and Hoagie, too, and they all knew Lee and Ginger. My parents showed up on time, kept score, carried tripods, drove golf carts, answered phones, or anything else anyone asked them to do, then went home, had dinner and a glass of wine, and did it all again the next day. They loved it, and the people who put the sport on television loved them back. Those cameramen and announcers (with whom I now have the pleasure of working these days) still remember those days with Mom and Dad fondly.

Nights at WTNH could be both eerily quiet and maniacally busy. I could sit at my desk in complete silence, left to my own devices, or occupy a desk in the newsroom surrounded by devices. Rattling keyboards, ringing telephones, crackling police scanners, and cackling reporters, assignment editors, and producers were all part of the soundtrack of a busy news operation at night. That was when, especially in a city like New Haven, the action seemed to ratchet up a notch. The people who manned the news assignment desk and the reporters who carried out their orders were usually doing double duty, working on a pre-assigned story while waiting for the scanner to announce a more immediate story that required everyone's undivided attention. A rolled-over big rig on I-95, a robbery on Crown Street, or a shooting in the projects meant a release of adrenaline in the newsroom as coats were grabbed, gear was assembled, and live trucks hit the streets. One night, I opted for the relative anonymity of my upstairs desk and picked up the phone to call my father.

Those who know me best know that my relationship with the telephone can be described as reluctant. The 1992 Masters champion, Fred Couples, once famously said about answering the phone, "I don't answer the phone. I get the feeling, whenever I do, that there will be someone on the other end." I know what you mean, Freddie. It's not that I am anti-social; I guess I just don't like talking on the phone. I loved my parents and they loved me, but there were times when we wouldn't speak on the phone for weeks at a time. I didn't think anything of it; but clearly others did. Years after I left Connecticut and wandered down the career path I now occupy, I would be standing in the catering line waiting to grab a bite to eat before a golf telecast when a cameraman who had just worked a show in Hawaii before joining our crew would approach with a smile and simply say, "Call your mother," then walk away. I admit now, sadly, that I didn't call them enough; but I did call on that Connecticut night.

Because I didn't call often, my parents knew something was up. We briefly caught up on how everyone was doing, my older brother, David, in LA and younger brother, Mark, either in Reno or on Maui with them. I mentioned I met someone new and, personally, things were good. Those trains of thought weren't very meaty and, therefore, only lasted a few minutes; so it wasn't long before I got to the real reason for the call. I was unfulfilled at work; tired of punching buttons on a switcher and putting stories about criminals, politicians, and athletes on the air. I was okay with the climate in Connecticut, but bored with being partly responsible for bringing the nightly weather forecast into Connecticut's homes. I didn't want to continue working around the day-in, day-out drama of the local news in whichever locality I happened to be living. I loved live sports and wanted to find a way back into that world. My dad understood and wondered, out loud, if the contacts he had made through the golf tournaments at which they volunteered might be of help. He had this person's business card and that person's office phone number, and he would make some calls. The timing around what happened next is a little fuzzy; but that conversation resulted in another one in which my father had gotten in touch with Paul Spengler, Don Ohlmeyer's golf producer, who told Dad that I should give him a call at my convenience. The next available moment became my most convenient.

Kathy knew that while she and I were getting more and more comfortable with each other, I was becoming less and less happy at work. I mentioned my conversations with my dad and told her about the phone call that I was certainly going to make. She had family (a sister, brother-in-law, and a very close cousin) in Connecticut, but her oldest sister had already moved to Wisconsin and more moves seemed to be imminent; so, she reasoned, there was nothing really keeping her in New Haven. I was able to reach Mr. Spengler on the phone, and he informed me that if I could get myself to LA, the fine folks at Ohlmeyer Communications Company (OCC) would find something for me to do, and I should give him a call as soon as I got to the West Coast and settled. I didn't need further prodding. Always ready for an adventure, I thanked everybody that meant anything to me at WTNH and gave my two weeks' notice. Then Kathy also gave notice on her apartment lease. We sold her car, loaded up everything we could fit into mine, and hit the road— headed from one coast to the other. It was springtime in 1989.

ACROSS THE COUNTRY, THANKS TO AN ASSURANCE

If you have never had the experience of driving across this great country, I highly recommend it. The American interstate highway system is a magnificent, meandering thing. Authorized by Congress in 1956, it is named for president Dwight D. Eisenhower, who championed its formation. The Interstate Highway System is made up of hundreds of roadways, with pavement touching some part of each of the forty-eight contiguous United States, Alaska, and Hawaii. In 1992, a stretch of road through Glenwood Canyon in Colorado was finished, signaling the completion of the original project. The initial cost estimate for that was $25 billion, and experts expertly figured it would take twelve years from start to finish. Instead it required thirty-five years to complete at a cost, in today's dollars, of more than $425 billion. But I would argue it has been worth every penny.

Even-numbered highways traverse the nation from east to west, and odd-numbered interstates travel north and south. The longest stretch is I-90, which winds from Seattle, Washington, to Boston, Massachusetts, running slightly longer than 3,020 miles, through thirteen states. Interstate 80 is a slightly shorter stretch, logging 2,902 miles from San Francisco, California, to Teaneck,

New Jersey, and I have motored along most of that stretch, on a single journey—once. In case you're curious, the longest north/south stretch of interstate highway is I-95, running from the Canadian border to Miami, Florida. New Haven sits happily along a very busy I-95. There isn't one continuous interstate roadway that goes from New Haven, Connecticut, to Los Angeles, California, but there are several ways that can get you from point A to point B. The route we chose was a combination of five interstates, crisscrossing just a little more than three thousand US miles. The plan was to drive around ten hours a day at an average speed of sixty-five miles an hour. If we could adhere to that pace we could get from New Haven to the Hollywood sign in five days, so off we went. Heading south on I-95, you have the pleasure of driving through the great American cities of New York, Philadelphia, Baltimore, and Washington, DC, and, while we weren't in that much of a hurry, we also were not on a sightseeing trip, so we drove by looking out the window and marveling at our country's most famous landmarks. Interstate 95 took us south to North Carolina, where we made our right turn onto Interstate 40 at the capital city of Raleigh. I-40 is the nation's third longest interstate, and it runs through eight US states. In fact, we could have taken it all the way from where we picked it up in Raleigh to where we wanted to be let off in LA; but we didn't do that. Most nights, we planned to sleep in the first Comfort Inn or Red Roof Inn along the road when we got too road weary to continue; but we planned the trip to take us through Dallas, where my great friend Tom Christine and his wife, Vickie, were living. I guess we figured catching up with friends and spending one night not in a hotel bed was worth the slight detour. We hadn't figured on the seemingly endless, certainly straight-as-an-arrow miles of Texas asphalt.

Before we got to the Lone Star State, we spent several enjoyable hours winding our way through the Smokey Mountains and stopping for a meal in America's "Music City," Nashville, Tennessee. We also looked forward to what awaited us in the Volunteer State's easternmost city of Memphis. I had seen Elvis Presley once in concert, and it was near the end of his amazing life during what many people call the "fat Elvis days." He was indeed filling out his sequined jumpsuit, but he also put on a great show, thrilling a sold-out crowd at Harvey's Hotel Casino in South Lake Tahoe. This trip through Tennessee would take us right into Memphis and right by Graceland—the iconic estate of "The King"—and both Kathy and I were excited to see it. I mentioned before, these were the days before everyone had a cell phone; they were also the days before drivers were accompanied by a disembodied voice recalculating which way to turn or how far to go. We relied instead on incomplete road signage and inadequate map reading. As we were looking for signs along the interstate pointing us to the proper exit for Graceland, we approached then found ourselves on a bridge crossing what turned out to be the awe-inspiring Mississippi River. Grade-school geography students know that the Mississippi is a historic source of interstate commerce, a free-flowing inspiration for thousands of adventures, accounts, and articles about the American way of life, and the unofficial border between a number of states, including Tennessee and Arkansas. By the time we realized where we were, we were getting closer to the residence of the current governor of Arkansas and future president of the United States, and further away from the jungle room in the basement of Graceland. Unwilling to return to Tennessee, we agreed that we would get back to Graceland at some point later in life. That point in time would never come for "us," and I still haven't found the time to see it. We made it through Arkansas and into Texas, spent the night at the Christine household, and headed out bright and early the next morning to once again follow the setting sun.

Texas is a great state, full of wonderful cities, communities, and people. It is also incredibly boring to drive through. El Paso is the biggest city on Texas's westernmost border, and it is 570 miles from Dallas. You can drive seventy miles an hour across the state, but after having done so, I can count myself among those who wish they could've driven seven hundred miles an hour. While Texas may have a lot to offer, believe me, there is a whole lot of nothing east of DFW; but we made it and found a place to rest our weary heads on the outskirts of El Paso, knowing if we hit the road as the sun was coming up, we would be in LA before it set the following day. The plan was to stay with my older brother and sister-in-law until we found a place of our own in Los Angeles. As we got closer to California, I had also made a phone call to Paul Spengler at OCC to update him on our progress. While I never spoke with Paul, his assistant assured me Paul knew I was coming, and to call and make an appointment when we had officially arrived. In addition to my brother, I also reconnected with a friend who had been a reporter at KTVN in Reno: Les Kumagai was a terrific guy and a good reporter. The fact that he was handsome didn't hurt his upward mobility in the TV business. After spending a little more than a year at Channel 2, Kumagai made the leap to the number two television market in the country as a reporter for one of the independent stations in Los Angeles. Once he knew I was in town, he was quick to help us find a place to live.

Les' sister Denise was what hundreds, if not hundreds of thousands of men and women want to be: a successful working actor. You might remember her as Aunt June on the television series *The Gilmore Girls*; or Judge Leslie Yang on *Family Law*; but when we met her, she was portraying Quon Le Robinson on the extremely successful NBC network comedy series *Night Court*. She was living, at the time, in an eight-unit apartment complex, just over the hill from Hollywood. A couple had just moved out, so an upstairs apartment was available. Thanks in part to Denise's recommendation, we got the apartment and moved in. The first order of business was to set up accounts with the various Southern California utilities, including the phone company, so I could let Paul Spengler know I had an LA address. I was ready to meet with Paul; but Paul apparently was not ready to return the favor.

I LOVE LA (PART ONE)

Los Angeles, California, is a great place to live: sunny, warm, active, almost every day of the year. Sure, there's traffic; but, quite frankly, there's traffic everywhere, and LA is not just everywhere—it's somewhere. The City of Angels is an especially nice place to live if you can afford it. Kathy and I had some money saved and we also had the safety net of my parents, in case of an emergency, but I wasn't really worried about money (actually then or ever) because I knew for sure that I would be gainfully employed by OCC in a matter of days. I just had to get Paul Spengler on the phone. While I waited for my date with destiny, Kathy, to her credit, realized that, while we were eating into our savings, we had to continue to eat, so she went out and got a job.

The daily routine went something like this: Alarm clock rings, Kathy awakens, showers, dresses, and heads off to a Century City high rise for an eight-hour workday. Shortly thereafter, Keith rolls out of bed, showers, dresses for a meeting, and picks up the phone to call Ohlmeyer Communications Company. In 1989, I wasn't all that familiar with the phrase "He's in a meeting," and the first dozen times I heard it uttered, I believed it. Then I kind of believed it; then I got realistic. I was told Paul Spengler was in a lot of meetings in 1989 and, unfortunately, none of them were with me. The lack of any quality time with the man I hoped would be my future employer left me with a ton of just plain old time on my hands. So I did what any responsible, self-respecting, thirty-three-year-old man would do: I changed my clothes and headed to one of the many public golf courses in the LA area. On an almost-daily basis, I parked myself at either Rancho Park or Griffith Park or DeBell or the Rose Bowl Golf Course or Wilson Golf Course or Hansen Dam or any of the many other places to play in town, signed up as a single, and waited my turn to engage in the more than five-hour tango that is public golf in Los Angeles. The whole time, I knew that the next day would be the day I finally got a face-to-face meeting at OCC.

I wasn't able to establish a relationship with Spengler; but his assistant, a nice young lady named Tracey Adelstein, and I became fast phone friends, and while she couldn't, with any certainty, tell me when I might actually see her boss, she must have felt some sympathy for me. She gave me the names and numbers of several people whose job it was to hire the crews for the various televised sporting events going on in Southern California. Thanks to those contacts, I applied for, and was hired to be a part of, several TV crews broadcasting swim meets at USC, motocross events at the LA Coliseum, and baseball games in Anaheim. I offered my services for any task and ran camera, served as the technical director (the one that pushes the buttons on the switcher), and pulled cable. For some jobs, I received as much $300 a day, while others paid as little as $75. I could work two events in one week; but I also found myself not working for weeks at a time. It was invigorating and exciting and demoralizing and discouraging; but it wasn't steady. Steady or not, I never gave up hope, and I always knew I had made the right decision.

I WATCHED, THEREFORE I AM

American ingenuity is an amazing thing. My children grew up in a world much different from the one in which I spent my childhood. As I already mentioned, we didn't have cell phones, portable video games, or e-readers. I spent my preteen and teenage years in a world without ATMs, hybrid cars, and espresso makers. Amana didn't introduce the very first personal microwave oven until I was twelve years old. We amused ourselves until the sun went down, went into the house for dinner, did our homework, and watched TV. What we watched would be foreign to my kids, too. Watching television in Lee and Ginger Hirshland's house was a family affair, especially in 1966 when *Family Affair* debuted. Together, we also watched *I Love Lucy, Lassie, Bonanza, The Man From U.N.C.L.E.,* and *Mission: Impossible* ("Your mission, Jim, should you decide to accept it..."). The pop group the Monkees even had a TV show for a couple of years. The reality was—there was no reality TV. It was comedies, westerns, dramas, variety shows, and cartoons. Sunday nights belonged to Hanna-Barbera and we loved it. The first animated prime-time American television sitcom series was *The Flintstones,* premiering on my brother David's seventh birthday, September 30, 1960. It was on Sunday night and it proved to be so popular that *Top Cat, The Jetsons,* and *Johnny Quest* followed. Cartoons weren't the only daytime shows that crossed over to the evening hours. Game shows also were a part of every network's prime-time lineup, as *What's My Line, To Tell the Truth, Match Game, Hollywood Squares,* and others made Gene Rayburn, Peter Marshall, Soupy Sales, Gary Moore, and others household names. My mom loved the game shows best and watched everything from *Truth or Consequences* to *Password* to *Queen for a Day.* She also watched a show called *Concentration,* and at times I'd watch with her.

Concentration first aired in 1958 and was hosted by Hugh Downs. The game was relatively simple. Pairs of prizes were hidden behind numbered squares, and if the contestant matched the prizes, those squares revealed segments of a rebus puzzle. If the contestant solved the rebus puzzle, all the prizes he had claimed were his or hers to keep. A rebus is a type of word puzzle that uses pictures to represent words or parts of words; for example, the word "may" plus the picture of an eye, plus the letter *C,* followed by the letter *U,* plus the picture of a house would translate to the question, "may I see you home?" You had to be good at clichés and willing to take a chance. Apparently, I would turn out to be both.

By the time I arrived, unemployed, in Los Angeles, *Concentration* had become *Classic Concentration.* Hugh Downs had given up his hosting duties to a mustachioed Canadian, Alex Trebek, who was double dipping as host of this game show while being the front person of another, more popular one—*Jeopardy.* As spring started to turn to summer in Southern California, it dawned on me that waiting for a face-to-face meeting with Paul Spengler was just as difficult as it had been on the day we crossed the Arizona/California state line, so I began to add an element or two to my daily routine. I'd grab the *Los Angeles Times* and look through the help-wanted pages.

The other thing I did, somewhere along the way, was ask Kathy Freeman to be my wife. I have been married three times, and I hope these pages are testament to the fact that I remember a lot about my life both with the people in it and without them, including each wife. But I couldn't, for all the tea in China, tell you the first thing, or anything for that matter, about how I proposed to Donna Fortin or Kathryn Freeman. Oddly (or maybe not so oddly) enough, I will never forget how, where, and when I asked Sarah Caitlin MacDougall to marry me.

Obviously, Kathy said yes, but you wouldn't find it in the paper. What you could find in the *Times* were the usual requests for help and pleas for work that you find in every single newspaper in the country. There was something else as well; something quite possibly unique to a paper that was printed in the entertainment capital of the world: one-and two-column-inch advertisements for game show contestants. The folks at Goodson-Todman Productions were looking for people who wanted to play old standbys like *High Rollers* and *The Price Is Right*, as well as newcomers to the scene, like *Pictionary* and *Now You See It*. One of the shows looking for contestants was *Classic Concentration*. I watched that show, liked it, and, if I do say so myself, sitting on the couch in my living room, I was pretty good at it. I didn't have anything else on my calendar at the time, so I figured why not? As someone who had watched a game show on television but hadn't the foggiest idea how one was put on television, I figured it would be a breeze. I had all my hair, all my teeth, and all the time in the world. I was well educated and reasonably good looking; how hard could it be? Like I just said, I had no idea.

MORE TROUBLE THAN IT'S WORTH?

So one sunny, Southern California day, I decided, instead of concentrating on drivers and wedges at the local municipal golf course, I would concentrate on the personal ad for *Classic Concentration* contestants. I had already made my again-less-than-fulfilling phone call to Paul Spengler, so my day was free and, as it turned out, I needed it to be. Here's what I thought would happen as I headed toward Beverly Hills and the Wilshire Boulevard address listed in the ad: I'd enter the building, be greeted by a receptionist, who would take one look at me, call a producer or associate producer, and sign me up to appear on the game show that day or, if they already had that day's show booked, the next. I have no idea why I thought it would be that easy; after all, it hadn't been that long since I watched how the TV talk show *The Sally Jessy Raphael Show* was put together. I witnessed multiple show tapings during singularly very long days. I said hello to a multitude of guests sitting in a green room waiting, sometimes for hours, for their turn at what Andy Warhol called their "fifteen minutes of fame." I should have known better, and my vision for what was about to happen was much more simplistic than the reality that would follow.

I found the building, pulled into the underground parking garage, and parked the car. The expansive and expensive-looking lobby offered a building directory next to a bank of elevators.

After pinpointing the precise office, on the exact floor, I entered the elevator to take the ride to what I was sure would be a moments-long interview that would lead to a spot on national syndicated television. The office door opened to a small area which served as home to two chairs and a desk, behind which sat a phone-holding, pen-toting, twenty-something receptionist.

Without a smile, she looked my way, put her hand over the phone's mouthpiece, and perfunctorily asked, "Which show?" I attempted my most winning smile and replied, "*Classic Concentration.*"

She pointed to one of three wooden doors and immediately returned to her phone call. There was no rush to call a producer, no fast track to cash and prizes, just a finger pointing to door number two. Undaunted, I took the requisite steps, turned the knob, and entered a room filled with dozens of other people with all their teeth, all their hair, and all the time in the world. They were young and old, short and tall, male and female, seated and standing, and holding clipboards and yellow number two pencils. In the middle of the room was a plastic card table and a folding chair, occupied by what I'm sure was another twenty-something, minimum-wage employee.

"I'm…," I started.

"Fill this out," she interrupted, handing me a clipboard and a number two pencil of my very own.

Attached to the clipboard was a single sheet of paper that resembled the questionnaire you fill out when you visit the doctor for the first time. Name, address, phone number, age, gender, and level of education were all questions that needed answers; but so were days of the week you are available, and last game show you were a contestant on. I mimicked everyone else in the room and jotted down my answers, penciling in "All" and "None" for the last two. I completed the questionnaire and set my clipboard on top of what appeared to be fifty others and then found an unoccupied portion of the wall on which to lean and wait…and wait…and wait.

I arrived at the Wilshire Boulevard building at the appointed time, 10 a.m., and two and a half hours later, my day consisted of riding one elevator, walking through two wooden doors, and uttering three words. Utterly and completely unprepared, I watched as people pulled sandwiches and pieces of fruit out of paper sacks, tore open bags of potato chips and salted peanuts, and twisted caps off bottles of soda and water; and I listened as they told each other tales of trying to get on this show last month and that show last week. I underestimated my competition so completely that I hadn't even considered there would be any, and as each minute ticked by, I realized they were not only there, but they were better fed, better watered, and far better prepared than I for the long, arduous task of landing a spot alongside Alex Trebek. Eventually, two women and a fellow, who appeared to be a few years younger than me, entered the room, grabbed their share of the clipboards, and began to call out names.

I was lumped into a group of about twenty, under the watchful eye of one of the women, who thanked us all for coming and then led us out the wooden door, down a corridor, and into my third room of the day. Instead of one table, this room had rows of desks and resembled a fourth-grade classroom at Jessie Beck Elementary in Reno. We each took a seat and faced our leader, who had assumed a position at the front of the room. She reminded us that we were there to try out for the Goodson-Todman game show *Classic Concentration* and asked again if anyone in the room had appeared on any game show in the last sixty days and a Goodson-Todman game show in the last six months. I didn't know why, but clearly this was a sensitive subject, and, while I sat in my grade-school desk with a crystal-clear conscience, one person in our group wasn't willing to risk public shame, personal humiliation, or, for all I knew, a prison stint, and got up, averted eye contact, and slunk out of the room.

"Anybody else?" our *Concentration* captor asked, looking around the room. "We check, you know."

Confidently clean, we all kept our seats and waited for the next step in the process. That next step turned out to be another clipboard and another yellow number two pencil, but instead of another questionnaire, we all got our chance to solve as many rebus puzzles as we could in ten minutes. Our Goodson-Todman team member thanked us for coming, told us accuracy and quantity were equally important, started the clock, and walked out of the room. I already mentioned that I was pretty good at solving these types of puzzles, and I got started immediately. I don't know if I was focused, hungry and in a hurry to leave, or actually having fun for the first time during that day, but I was solving the puzzles with relative ease and had amassed a fairly impressive pile by the time our ring leader reentered the room and told us all time had expired. I sat proudly as she marched up and down the aisles, gathering up each person's rick of rebuses, trying to get a glimpse of a stack more impressive than mine. Quite sure I hadn't seen any, I waited for what surely would be an invitation to the nearest television studio for a seat in front of a makeup mirror and a congratulatory handshake from Alex. Instead, I got what everybody else in the room got from the woman who held our game show fates in her hands: a slight smile, a "nice job," and her back as she left the room. No one else seemed worried, frustrated, or angry, so I decided not to be either, and sat there patiently waiting, trying to enjoy experiencing something of which I never thought I'd be a part. Then she returned. "Here we go," I thought to myself; but it quickly became apparent I wasn't going anywhere but home.

"Goodson-Todman wants to thank you all for coming in today," she started. "We really appreciate your time and effort and will let you know within the next thirty days if you've advanced to the next stage," she finished, and left the room again, this time for good.

PLAYING GAMES

The weeks immediately following that experience greatly resembled the ones that preceded it: working an occasional event, cementing the relationship with my Reno friend Les Kumagai, and hoping to land a permanent job in sports television. Now, in addition to calling Paul Spengler, I was anticipating a call from the powers that be at *Classic Concentration* but, unlike the stonewalling Spengler, the folks at Goodson-Todman said they'd call within thirty days, and they were true to their word. I picked up the phone to hear an invitation to return to the office building on Wilshire Boulevard to participate in what the voice on the other end referred to simply as round two. I accepted the terms and kept the appointment, much better prepared this time for the possibility of anything—or, for that matter, nothing at all—happening.

This time, I was met in the reception area, offered and declined something to drink, then led into the same room where I had successfully completed enough rebus puzzles to earn a return trip. This time, the rows of desks were gone, but the classroom vibe remained, thanks to a six-foot-tall easel with what appeared to be a full sheath of paper. Next to the easel was a tripod, and on top of the tripod, a videocamera with its lens trained on two of the desks leftover from the previous visit: one occupied by a woman who appeared to be close to the same age as I; the other occupied by no one, and clearly reserved for my behind. I smiled, said hello, assumed I was supposed to sit at the empty desk, and did. Seconds later, the door opened and in walked a determined-looking lady, clutching a yellow legal pad, who introduced herself as an associate producer. Unsmilingly, she verified our identities, then turned our attention to the easel and said we were about to be shown another set of rebuses and we should shout out the answers as soon as we deciphered the puzzles. She stood next to the camera, turned it on, and began flipping the pages.

Back and forth we went, barking out "better late than never," shouting "save it for a rainy day," and hollering "hope springs eternal." This lasted about ten minutes, and then we were done. The associate producer made a few notes on her pad, switched off the camera, and left the room, saying one of the show's producers would be right in; and he was. While the woman who left was phlegmatic, the young man who took her place was animated and enthusiastic. I remember, he congratulated both of us on exhibiting excellent rebus puzzle solving skills, but proudly announced that *Classic Concentration* was about more than skill; it was also about pizzazz and personality. I wanted to laugh out loud, but thought it might undermine my chances to advance to whatever came next, so I simply nodded knowingly and continued to listen. Taping was scheduled to begin within the next four to six weeks, and he wondered if we would be available in that time frame. Since I had no idea whether I would be available or not, I said yes, and so did my *Classic Concentration* co-conspirator. That was apparently the correct answer, because he shook hands with us both and bade us farewell, saying someone from the show would be in touch. So a process that, upon its undertaking, I was sure would be over in a day or two, now threatened to follow summer into fall. Sadly, I didn't have one single thing better to do.

The fine folks at Goodson-Todman were nothing if not true to their word again, because a little more than a month later, they were on the other end of the line when the apartment phone rang. Congratulations were in order because I had been selected to be in the contestant pool for the current series of show tapings for *Classic Concentration*. I guess I heard "selected," "contestant," and "tapings" loud and clear; the part about the pool, in hindsight, was a little vague. For the remainder of the call, the "very happy for me" person barked out orders…I was to get myself to NBC Studios in Burbank by 9 a.m. the following Tuesday and, if I had a car, I must park it in a very specific section of a certain lot. It was critical that I bring "at least" four changes of clothes, because my appearance might last as long as a week's worth of shows, and I needed to be sure to clear my schedule for a minimum of three days. Every command was easily accomplished, especially the last one. I told Kathy, called my parents and my brother, and let Les know that I was going to be a contestant on *Classic Concentration* on Tuesday, or so I thought.

The big day arrived and, with my requisite changes of clothes, I found my way to the predetermined lot at NBC Studios in Burbank. Driving around the building, I was reminded of the many iconic personalities that had worked there on many of network television's most famous programs. *Rowan & Martin's Laugh-In*, *The Tonight Show* with Johnny Carson, and *Sanford and Son* were just three of the more than ninety programs that had originated, at one time or another, inside those walls since NBC's Burbank Studios were officially dedicated on March 27, 1955, nine months before I was born. Now I was headed inside to be on a TV show taped there in 1989; or was I? The phrase "contestant pool" didn't sink in when I heard it on the phone, but it smacked me squarely in the face upon entering the waiting room for *Classic Concentration*. I wasn't the last to arrive with my four days' worth of shirts and slacks, but I was a long way from the first. By the time the clock struck nine, I found myself part of what suddenly seemed like a very large group. That's because it was—thirty of us in all, fifteen women and fifteen men—and I figured there had to be another elimination coming on the horizon. Each of us was given a locker in which to hang our clothes, and then the entire group was led down the hallway and into Studio 3, where we were greeted by two more *Classic Concentration* producers (neither of which was the exuberant young man who had congratulated me weeks earlier). They filed us into a group of men and a group of women and filled us in on what was about to happen next. Our handler explained that one of us would be randomly selected to play the game against one of them in a best-two-out-of-three competition. Then they reminded us to be enthusiastic, have fun, and make the audience believe that we had the perfect use for every single prize and had secretly hoped to own each one for as long as we could imagine. Finally, they said that they could tape as many as a dozen shows today and the same amount the next day, and the next, but the game had to be played with one guy against one girl, so if one of us guys kept winning the rest of us guys wouldn't get in the game, and some of us guys may not ever get the chance to play.

"Okay, everybody ready to have some fun and win *lots* of prizes?" they exhorted loudly.

"Wait. What?" I said under my breath.

We walked by the set, around the cameras, parked ourselves in the bleachers that would face the contestants, and waited for our names to be randomly called. Mine wasn't; not immediately, nor for the rest of the first day of taping.

FINALLY I MEET
MR. TREBEK

Alex Trebek was a broadcast veteran and had been a professional game show host since 1963, when, in his native Canada, he was the master of ceremonies of a Canadian music program called *Music Hop*. He moved to the United States a decade later and subsequently gained employment with game show producers Merrill Heater and Bob Quigley, who assigned him to host their show *High Rollers*, which was airing on NBC. It fell out of popularity two years later, and Trebek joined forces with Goodson-Todman on a short-lived something called *Double Dare*, as well as the much more popular syndicated series *The $128,000 Question*. He found himself on both American and Canadian television, hosting various shows for the next several years while continuing to shoot pilot programs for game show producers like Heater and talk show host turned television program producer Merv Griffin. One of Griffin's projects in the early '80s was the revival of a "made for brainiacs" game show called *Jeopardy*, which would become Alex Trebek's calling card from the first syndicated evening it aired in 1984. Three years later Goodson-Todman called on Trebek again, this time asking him to return to daytime television to host *Classic Concentration*, making him the host of two TV games shows simultaneously, and that was when I finally got the chance to shake his hand.

I had returned to NBC Studios in Burbank for day two, more annoyed than excited, and determined to either become a contestant or a casualty of the process. Months prior, Kathy and I had set both the wedding venue (back in Connecticut) and the date (in a couple of weeks), and we were set to travel from west to east in a matter of mere days. I had decided to participate in the game show on a whim, thinking the whole process would be fast and fun. Over time, it had become neither. Changes of clothes hung in lockers for the second straight day. The slowly dwindling group of us marched back through the studio and onto the cold, hard steel bleachers. As I said, one way to get on the show was to replace a vanquished same-sex member who had failed to win the best-of-three puzzle-solving contests; but I failed to mention it wasn't the only way.

The ultimate prize in *Classic Concentration* was a shiny new automobile, and, in the 1989 incarnation of the daytime prize grab, once a contestant accomplished that goal, he or she went happily from the ranks of contestants to those of former contestants and past champions. If that was the result, both a new female and a new male were selected to compete in the next round. Such were the circumstances under which I came to hear my name announced, met one of the world's most recognizable game show hosts, and faced Sheila in the first of what would end up being many nationally televised rebus puzzle-solving contests. I remember how bright the lights were, how nice Trebek was, and how dry my mouth was when it came time for me to open it and actually speak. This wasn't playing the game from the comfort of my living room couch, or even in a windowless room in front of a fresh-faced college kid with a clipboard; it was for real and on TV, and even though I had some experience in that regard, I was a little unsure and relatively certain I was about to make a fool of myself. Off-camera introductions and pleasantries were exchanged, and then it was time for "Lights, camera, and action," and away we went.

Sheila and I matched numbers, collected prizes, and were allowed glimpses of the puzzle behind the yellow and black squares. The clichéd sayings and familiar symbols came flooding back, both calming me and giving me confidence. I won a couple of prizes, including a Caribbean cruise, but couldn't solve the puzzle and lost control of the board. Sheila then rattled off three straight matches, opening up the board enough for me to figure out the underlying answer, but I couldn't reveal my knowledge because Sheila was in command. Two more prizes matched, revealing another chunk of rebus and giving Sheila the allotted five seconds to come up with the solution, but she couldn't, and the buzzer sounded. This time around, Sheila missed her match, and it was my turn again. I quickly called out the numbers I knew would reveal matching prizes, giving me the opportunity to solve the puzzle and win game one. There was a piece of an *F*, an awl, an arrow pointing to a singular link in a chain, and two chickens ("hens" in rebus parlance), the last one having laid an egg, bookending the word "love" above a picture of two people kissing on a tennis court. Easy.

"Is it 'falling in love again'?" I asked, knowing it was.

"Is it 'falling in love again'?" Trebek repeated, knowing I was right.

Ding, ding, ding went the chimes, and I was summoned to Trebek's side to show all the folks at home, by pointing to the game board like a local station weatherman, how I had solved the puzzle. Staff announcer Gene Gilbert described my prizes (the cruise, a brass bed, and a brass telescope), Alex tossed to commercial, and I walked back to my seat, emboldened and ready to dispatch Sheila in game number two. But Sheila had other ideas, and the second game was hers to win again; and this time she did. Instead of playing a third game, like the first two, the rules of *Classic Concentration* allowed for a tiebreaker; that simply meant that backstage a deciding puzzle would be configured, then covered up with numbered squares: five rows of five squares each. At Trebek's command, the placards that concealed the rebus would quickly reveal what rested behind them, giving the contestants, in this case Sheila and me, the chance to buzz in and be the first to solve the riddle. I knew from practice it was critical to go with your gut, and the first row of five squares disappeared, revealing what looked, to me, like the top of a box, followed by a representation of the two of diamonds playing card. The next row of numbers flipped open one by one, showing that it was indeed a box with an arrow pointing in the "up" direction on its side. I knew immediately the first two words of the saying had to be "up to," and subconsciously my mind flipped through its rolodex of clichés that began with those two words. I knew Sheila hadn't figured it out yet, because the first two squares of row three began to flip aside without her pressing the button in front of her, setting off the buzzer. Not hearing the sound that could very well end my concentration, and my *Classic Concentration* career, I continued to stare at the puzzle and saw the curve of what had to be the small-case version of the letter *n*, followed by the cap-laden head of a boy; and I hit my button, sounding the buzzer.

"Is it 'up to no good'?" I said, this time not nearly as confident as I had been minutes earlier. If I was wrong, the entire puzzle would be revealed, giving Sheila a complete look and the chance at an almost certain win. Alex looked at me with a slight smile and said, "That would be a great anticipation on your part. Is it 'up to no good'?" The dinging was the only answer I needed. My guess had been correct, and I knew there was a bunch of bleacher-bound boys beyond my field of vision, sitting disappointed as we bade farewell to Sheila. I didn't care and got ready for my first, and maybe only, chance to win a freaking car.

AGAINST THE CLOCK FOR A CAR

The odds were against winning an automobile on *Classic Concentration*, especially on your first try. You had the minimum amount of time, thirty-five seconds, to match, one by one, the names of eight different cars. Up for grabs were brand new versions of the Volkswagen Cabriolet, Ford Escort, Pontiac LeMans, and Jeep Wrangler, among others; but I wasn't thinking about which one I wanted. I didn't have the luxury of time to pick the most desirable model. I stood next to Alex; I think I remember feeling his hand on my shoulder, offering encouragement, and staring at a board featuring fifteen numbered squares. I knew that meant seven cars were named twice and the eighth was only on the board once. If the contestant matched a certain model—for instance, the Jeep—the picture of that car took the place of the name and the numbers disappeared. What also disappeared was the chance to win that particular car, because the last car matched would be the one that ended up in your garage. If the names of the car didn't match when you called out the numbers, then the numbered squares would simply reappear over the car name and it was incumbent upon you to remember behind which number rested the Escort or the LeMans, and the whole time the clock kept ticking. As if it had slipped my mind, Alex reminded me and the audience that people rarely won a car on their first try, and he gave the order to start the clock.

"One, two," I said robotically. No match.

"Four, five," were the next words out of my mouth, adopting the strategy I had seen others employ, going vertically down the board as two more car model names appeared where numbers had been seconds before. Again, no match, and the thirty-five-second clock now showed thirty-one.

"Seven, eight," I continued; still nothing but numbers on the board. I finally connected, matching the Honda Accord, but with only twenty-four seconds left on the continually ticking clock, I had no chance to collect keys that time. When the buzzer mercifully sounded, signaling the end of the round, I had successfully matched four of the eight cars; not enough to win, but not bad, according to Alex, who reminded me that I had won $6,319 in prizes by beating Sheila, and that I could add to that total if I could outwit and outplay my next challenger tomorrow. Because it was just past 9 a.m. in a television studio somewhere in the LA suburb of Burbank, tomorrow meant right now, as I was instructed to quickly change clothes and return to meet and play against a different female opponent. She turned out to be a very nice housewife from Claremont, California, named Dottie Breiner, and she didn't stand a chance.

I COULDN'T LOSE BUT I COULDN'T WIN EITHER

Dottie turned out to be a good-natured, soft-spoken woman who had an impressive memory, matching prizes time and time again. But matching prizes and revealing puzzle pieces was only part of the game; once the pieces and parts of the rebus were revealed, you had to solve the problem, and this is where the downright neighborly Dottie fell woefully short. Her proclivity for remembering which numbers concealed what prizes was admirable. It was also advantageous for me. She missed; I matched and then solved the puzzle, adding a washer, dryer, and a set of luggage for coming up with "clean slate" and cashing in on a refrigerator, a sewing machine, a motorcycle (actually a mini-bike), and a trip to Singapore when I solved "hot chocolate." So Dottie and her remarkable ability of recall were a memory, and I was back at Alex Trebek's side, trying to win a car.

The same eight cars were up for grabs, but five extra seconds were on the clock—my reward for returning to the lightning round. Alex again wished me luck as he started the clock. I utilized a different strategy in my second attempt to leave the show in the driver's seat. This time, I chose the numbers at random, hoping that good fortune would deliver me a quick match or two. No such luck. A different approach actually resulted in a less successful outcome, as I matched a mere three cars, meaning I would have to defeat yet another contestant if I wanted a third shot at glory. I returned to face Jan Scheurmann with an additional $8,200 worth of booty.

Jan wasn't as nice as Dottie, or as good at playing the game, and I collected another parcel of prizes, including a second cruise (this one sponsored by Disney), a diamond sapphire necklace, and a vacuum cleaner, by beating her, which meant a third trip to Trebek and another five seconds on the "car" clock. This time, Alex was certain I would collect the grand prize, calling the time I had in which to do it "an eternity," and I was confident, too. I went back to the tried and true call-the-numbers-vertically system as the clock ticked down from forty-five seconds.

"One, two" resulted in two different cars.

"Four, five," again no match, so I continued to call out numbers, still confident but less so. The seconds ticked away, but my luck didn't change, and it was a full nineteen seconds before I was able to come up with my first match. In the next ten seconds, I managed two more matches, leaving ten seconds on the ticking clock and nine numbers and four cars on the board. I got three.

The additional $4,863 in prizes was little consolation at that very moment. I wanted to win the car more than ever, and my failure just a few seconds before meant I was going to have to win another two games to have the chance to do it. Before I learned the name of my next opponent, the show producer announced that this would be the final game of the final set of that week's show recordings. They thanked us all for our time and then revealed that the next set of tapings would be three weeks from Tuesday. That turned out to be a problem for a number of people in the group, including the three-time defending champion, me. I happened to have a scheduling conflict—namely a wedding ceremony that was slated to take place during that time frame. I explained my dilemma to the producer, and clearly Alex Trebek overheard, because he slapped me on the back and said:

"I guess you better win the car today then, my friend."

"I guess I better," was my four-word response.

CASHING IN

The show's schedule was also problematic for several of the women who had been waiting to take me on. In fact, it was a problem for all of the remaining female contestants. Because none could commit to coming back in three weeks if they happened to defeat me in the last game of the day, my fourth opponent would come from the male pool. The cameras were set, the tape machines put into record, and Tom Hogan was introduced to the daytime-game-show-watching world. Tom described himself as being "in a transitional period of his life," having driven across the country to come back to Los Angeles and be on the show. Alex, probably having been in a few transitional periods himself, looked at Tom, then the camera, and said with a smile:

"A transitional period means you don't have a job."

Me neither, I thought, but didn't say. At that moment, my job was to win two games and then a car. I won the first game, a mantle clock, and a wok set by solving "wishful thinking," but Tom won game number two when I couldn't come up with "magnificent seven" because the rebus began with the picture of a coffee cup and I couldn't turn that into the required "mug." So, all knotted up at one a piece, Tom Hogan and I prepared for the tie breaker that would either send me home or back to try and win a car, with fifty seconds in which to do it.

Trebek implored us both to concentrate as the numbers flipped away, revealing the final puzzle of the day. Two rows of numbers disappeared revealing the letter *H* and a man's head with arrows pointing to his right eye. It was "high something," I knew as the board continued to come into focus. The third row was now gone, leaving behind two more heads: a man's across from a woman's, and the very top of another letter. Numbers sixteen through nineteen went away, revealing the woman pulling on a necktie worn by the man and a little more of the final letter, but I had all I needed. Pushing my button before Tom pushed his, the game was now mine to win or lose.

"Is it 'high tide'?" I asked Trebek.

"Yes, it is," answered Alex, as the familiar bells began to ring. It meant Tom Hogan was gone and I was going back to try and win that damn car. After a commercial break that ended with a promotional spot for an NBC soap opera called *Generations*, Alex and I were back on TV.

"Here are the fifteen numbered squares, and here is the clock," Trebek began. "I think you can do it. Concentrate, and good luck," he ended, and off I went.

"One, two," I started, and for the fourth straight time produced no match, so I kept going.

"Three, four" wasn't a match either, but one and three were, and I knew it.

"One, three," I said, and five seconds into the process, I had my first match. It took twenty more seconds to get the next one and the Jeep Wrangler was gone. Three more quick matches meant I had two cars left on the board and fourteen seconds to find and pair them up. It was plenty of time and, as it turned out, I needed every second. After several misses revealed the location of every car on the board, I used the final five seconds on the clock to match the Ciera and then win a Pontiac LeMans with one tick remaining. I had invited Kathy and my older brother David down to the studio to watch and, as I pumped my fist in jubilation, they both ran on the stage to help me celebrate.

As confetti fell and the music played, we all could hear Gene Gilbert say:

"Keith, you finally did it," as he started to describe the various attributes of my new $9,000 car.

If you watched those particular episodes of Classic Concentration, you might recall: I won exactly $29,152 in prizes, which included the car, three vacations, a brass bed, a washer and dryer, and dozens of other toys, trinkets, and gadgets. We kept, used, and enjoyed much of what I won, and what we didn't want we gave to friends or sold back to the various dealerships; but whether we wanted the stuff or not, we were responsible for paying taxes on all of it. The valuation of each prize was negotiable and, from what I was able to figure out, the game show received the items from the manufacturer and claimed the maximum amount of worth when it distributed the prize to the "lucky" winner. The negotiation part of the equation occurred when the "lucky" winner—me, in this case—didn't want to keep something he or she had won. Take, for instance, the motorbike I had won while playing against Dottie. I didn't want it, so my option was to sell it, either through the want ads or back to the dealer from whence it came. The bad news was the dealer didn't think the bike was worth as much as the game show thought it was; the good news was that I could claim the "fair market value" of the prize, and not the actual number attributed to it by the folks at Goodson-Todman. But there was even better news for me.

During the entire process I had been in what counts for me as fairly constant contact with my mom and dad, who were at home on Maui. Disappointed that I had been unable to connect with Mr. Spengler, they were nonetheless delighted that I had managed to qualify for potential game show fame and fortune, especially Mom. Needing a new car, and knowing I just might win one, my dad and I struck a deal. They would pay all the taxes associated with my appearance in exchange for whichever car I happened to claim the keys. Early on, it seemed like a win-win situation; but as my prize total added up, while my capacity to win a car stayed stagnant, I felt I was getting the better of the bargain. They gladly accepted the two-door, four-cylinder LeMans, took it immediately to a Pontiac dealer, traded it in on a four-door LeSabre, and wrote a check for me to give to the Internal Revenue Service. How cool was that? Shortly after accepting delivery, and for several years after, Dad never missed the opportunity to chide me by asking, "Why didn't you win the Jeep?"

Like I had a choice.

BIDING MY TIME

We sold back some of the spoils, gave away some other things, and packed the rest of the prizes into the empty second bedroom of our Glendale apartment before flying across the country to get married. The ceremony took place in a small white church on a rainy September, New Haven, Connecticut, day. My dad and mom were there (Dad was my best man) as were friends from both the East Coast and the West. One couple that made the trek all the way from LA was my reporter friend Les Kumagai and his wonderful wife, Linda.

The reception was a celebration, filled with plenty of food, drink, and music for dancing. Kathy and I smiled, shook hands, and accepted congratulations, trying to make sure we thanked everyone for making the effort to come. On one rare occasion, when there was some down time, I sought out my dad, who was sitting at a table with Mom and the Kumagais. Les had worked for a brief time as a reporter at KTVN, and he and my folks were catching up when I plopped down, interrupting the conversation. We laughed about my game show appearance, exchanged pleasantries about the ceremony, and then, I remember, Dad got down to business,

"How's the job hunt going?" he asked, knowing I would have to tell him things in person that I hadn't over long distance on the telephone.

"Could be better," I admitted. "I can't seem to figure out how to actually get a face to face meeting with Spengler."

"He still hasn't met with you?" Dad said, surprised. "I didn't figure him for that kind of a guy."

"He's probably not," I replied, wanting to assure him that he was still a very good judge of character. "My guess is he never considered that I would actually pull up stakes and come to California." We both laughed, and then Les spoke up.

"I know they're looking for a few tech guys at my station," referring to Channel 9 in Los Angeles. "It's not exactly what you're looking for, but it's a job."

"And it keeps your hand in the industry," added Dad, "and that's never a bad thing."

Buoyed by the conversation, I asked Les if he wouldn't mind digging a little deeper; and then I asked my mom to dance.

MICKEY AND ME
(TAKE ONE)

We slept in the brass bed, took the trip to Singapore (an amazing place, with the cleanest streets of any major city in which I've walked), and discovered, thanks to an ocean liner that doubled as a floating hotel casino, the islands of the Caribbean. While exploring St. Barts, St. Kitts, and St. Thomas, I learned there are two types of people in this world: those who love "cruising" and do it vacation after vacation, and those who go on one cruise, out of curiosity, and are unable to adapt to the confines of both the ship and the schedule and never do it again. I am the latter, and, agreeing with me, Kathy happily gave the second cruise—the one sponsored by Disney—to friends who would and did enjoy it more.

So, I was back in LA and energized to start collecting a steady paycheck. I promised myself I wouldn't stop trying to crack the OCC barrier; but, thanks to my dad's suggestion and Les Kumagai's recommendation, I started working at KCAL TV. The station went on the air in the summer of 1948 as KFI TV and was, for a brief period of time, Los Angeles's first NBC affiliate. In subsequent decades, it became an independent station, changed its call letters to KHJ, and switched owners on several occasions. Original owner Earle Anthony sold the station in 1951 to the General Tire and Rubber Company, which purchased and then merged with RKO Pictures four years later. The newly formed

RKO General ran the property for thirty-four turbulent years before selling it to Fidelity Television, who owned it for a blink of an eye before the Walt Disney Company took control in 1989. Disney wanted a clean slate, so they gave pink slips to most of the employees and changed the call letters to KCAL.

Les was right: the job wasn't exactly what I was looking for; but it was one for which I was certainly qualified. It's best to describe it as a "jack of all trades" technician's position. One day I would find myself sitting at the switcher, serving as the technical director for the midday news, then the next the schedule would have me in the station's bowels staring at a giant videotape machine, recording and watching the East Coast feed of *Regis and Kathie Lee*, making sure there were no breaks in the broadcast, because it would air on our station a few hours hence. I also might receive the "plum" assignment of floor director for one of the many programs broadcast or recorded in the spacious KCAL studios. A floor director may sound important, but the job was really nothing more than counting backward from ten and pointing to the correct camera, so when the show came back from commercial, the host, announcer, or reporter was looking into the lens with the red light glowing atop it. It wasn't challenging work, but it was five days a week, and it was for more money than I had ever made in my life.

To work in the production department at KCAL, and around its millions of dollars' worth of equipment, you had to join a union; so, shortly after accepting my new position, I was welcomed into the International Brotherhood of Electrical Workers (IBEW) and began reaping the rewards of what that meant: primarily, double hourly wages for working overtime, which helped my bi-weekly paycheck balloon considerably. There were non-union-related perks as well. The Walt Disney Company owned the station, so each person working within its walls was considered employed by the entertainment giant. That meant we all had to endure a half-day indoctrination at Disney's Burbank studio, at which we were made privy to the secrets that made the so-called House of Mouse so successful. It wasn't exactly equivalent to learning the formula for Coca-Cola, but it was important enough for our training leaders to demand our undivided attention for several hours. I learned, among other things, that I had to wear my Mickey Mouse engraved, oval-shaped name tag at all times while I was on duty, and I couldn't have facial hair unless my character compelled it of me. Since my job description didn't include wearing a Captain Hook costume, my lifelong goal of growing a beard or moustache was put on hold. We also learned that Disney employees respected one another (that was nice to hear), didn't smoke on the job (another plus), and were entitled to free admission to any Disney theme park and every Disney movie premiere (*jackpot!*). So, we now had that going for us.

For months, I shaved every day (even though I didn't need to), went to work, wore my name tag, respected my coworkers, and didn't smoke. I also rode the Disney "mountains"—Space, Big Thunder, and the Matterhorn—and was one of the first people on the planet to see *The Little Mermaid* and *The Rescuers Down Under*. But, despite the benefits, I was more than a little bored, and I still wanted to work for Don Ohlmeyer. I continued to call his company and speak not with my presumed contact, Paul Spengler, but with my friend Miss Adelstein, and still hoped one day she would surprise me by saying, "Paul is available to speak with you." So far, she hadn't said those words, but she also didn't tell me to stop trying, so I didn't. I had, on a previous call, left the number of the station (remember, only a few people owned mobile phones at the time, and one of them wasn't me); but, frankly, I never expected to hear her voice on the other end of the line. But one day I was paged while sweeping the studio, and I did.

"Hi, this is Keith," I said, expecting to hear Kathy on the other end.

"Hi, Keith, it's Tracey Adelstein from Ohlmeyer Communications. Surprise."

Yes, it was.

"Hi, Tracey," I managed to blurt out, hoping my excitement wouldn't soon turn to disappointment. My muddled brain determined she was calling to either tell me my chance had finally come, or that the OCC switchboard had detected a criminally abnormal number of calls from me and this was a "cease and desist" message. It was the former.

"How would you like to come in for an interview?" she said, knowing full well how much I would like that.

"When?" Was my answer, before the dot completed the question mark.

"Tomorrow afternoon at 3; does that work for you?" She knew it would.

"I'll be there." I practically screamed with excitement.

"Okay, see you then," she concluded, but before she hung up, I made sure to say six more words:

"Thank you, thank you very much."

The end of that day couldn't come quickly enough. I didn't care what news Jerry Dunphy had to deliver, or what guest Regis and Kathie Lee were bothering with bad questions. I had an interview to prepare for; one for which I had packed up my life and travelled across the country; one for which I had waited almost a year; one that just might represent the only shot I had at landing my perfect job; everything had to be perfect. Kathy shared my excitement and nervousness over dinner, and I remember a restless night in bed. Then the next day dawned and I tried to busy myself before leaving for West Hollywood in plenty of time for the interview. I readied my clothes, read and re-read my resume, showered, dressed, and headed off for my date with destiny.

I arrived at 962 La Cienega Boulevard fashionably early. The building was a two-story, Mediterranean-style structure, up the street from the fancy designer shops in the Beverly Center and down the block from the famed Sunset Strip. It looked like a wizard's castle to me, and I was Dorothy. I entered the massive wooden double doors and turned toward the receptionist for help when I realized Tracey Adelstein was the only person from the company with whom I had spoken. So I asked for her.

"Have a seat," the young lady said, without so much as a smile, and then she picked up the phone and I heard her tell Tracey someone was out front to see her; but her tone intimated I probably wouldn't be around long. I sat, clutching my resume, on a leather sofa. I had settled in for no more than ten seconds when a door to my left opened and a smallish young woman walked out. She had the biggest smile I had ever seen, and she extended her hand as I stood.

"I'm Tracey," she took my hand and shook it. "Come on back." Saying nothing, I followed.

I remember a hallway with a handful of cubicles fronting offices on either side. Most of the doors were closed, but Tracey's was wide open, and I followed her in. We made small talk for a few minutes; after all, she knew pretty much everything about me from our previous conversations, and then she said something I wasn't sure I wanted to hear,

"Paul's not here," she started, and I slumped in my seat. "But he's not the guy you need to talk to anyway. I mean, he's a great guy and all, but the person making the hiring decision is someone else." She stopped and looked over my shoulder and across the hall.

"His name is Steve Beim," she said, looking back at me. "He's one of our directors, and he's ready for you." I gulped and slowly got up.

146

"Good luck." She sounded like she really meant it. I smiled and turned and left her office.

It was less than ten steps from Tracey's office to Mr. Beim's, but a million thoughts rattled through my head as I took each one. I had spoken to my dad the previous night and he gave me several pieces of advice.

"Listen first, talk second," he counseled, over the phone, as I made mental and physical notes. "Sell yourself, but don't sound desperate," he continued. "You are perfect for this job and you've been preparing your entire career for it."

"But Pop," my turn, "I am kind of desperate. I really want this job."

"I know you do, son," my father said, sounding fatherly, "and so do *they*," he said, sounding even more fatherly.

"Got it," I replied, and I did. I was recalling our conversation when I reached the office door and knocked.

"Come on in," said the voice inside, so I did. My first thought, upon laying eyes on the man who would hold my professional fate in his hands, was, "Man, he looks so young." I said hello and extended my hand.

"Wow, you're older than I imagined," Steve Beim said, taking my outstretched hand. "Have a seat."

Uh oh.

"How old are you?" he asked, and apparently the interview had started.

"Thirty-four," I said with a smile as I handed him my resume. He took it and began to look it over. I took the time to steal a quick glance around his office. On the wall hung a couple of signed Skins Game posters, along with a framed diploma from the University of Southern California. On his desk, among other knickknacks, was a framed photo of young Mr. Beim and golf legend Arnold Palmer. Both were smiling like they were old friends; Palmer had signed the photo.

"You certainly have a lot of experience," Steve said, looking up at me. "What brought you to LA?" he asked.

Are you fucking kidding me? I thought, but I smiled and said, "I came out here to work for you. My mom and dad volunteer for your crew when you're in Hawaii." I stopped, remembering Dad's advice.

"Who are your mom and dad?" he wondered aloud.

"Lee and Ginger Hirshland," I answered, and a big smile spread across his face.

"You're kidding me," he laughed, "they are the greatest."

"I think so." I said, but I thought, "what about me?" He considered my resume a second time.

"Here's the deal," he started. "The job is associate producer for golf, and it entails a number of responsibilities." This was all positive, I thought, as he continued, "and you are clearly qualified for the position."

"Thanks," I interjected.

"In fact," he continued, "you might be a little too qualified." What the heck did that mean? I thought to myself.

"It's really an entry level position and it doesn't pay very much," he finished. Oh, that's what that meant. Then I disregarded Dad's advice.

"The money isn't really that important," I admitted. "I realize I'd have to start at the bottom rung of the ladder and work my way up. I think I can be a valuable addition."

"The problem is, Don really wants to hire a kid right out of college"—Don being the head honcho himself—"and I'm not sure I can talk him out of it," said the guy who looked like he had just graduated himself.

"I realize I'm nowhere near just getting out of school, but I'm as enthusiastic as a recent college grad and I'm willing to work for entry-level pay." Was that begging? "I really want to do this." The defense rested.

"I'll talk to Don and Andy (producer Andy Young) about it, but my gut tells me Don is going to want to go with this college kid, Eric," he said a little sadly, and pushed back from the desk to stand. I stood too, feeling like I was falling. There had to be something I could do or say, but before I thought of what it might be, Steve said:

"Here's what you should do. Check in with me every couple of weeks, because while Don may have a feeling that he wants a kid right out of college for this job, I have a feeling it's not going to work out. We have your number, right?"

"Yeah, Tracey does," I said. Then I shook his hand, thanked him for his time, and walked to my car, still with no idea what Paul Spengler looked like.

CALLED AWAY FROM KCAL

My job at the LA TV station could be boring, but my days rarely were. KCAL was located on Melrose Avenue, just west of the Hollywood Freeway (known in LA as the 101), right next door to the famous studios of Paramount Pictures; in fact, we shared the same cafeteria. If you walked out the back door of the station's studio, you could walk right onto a courtyard fronted by sets being used for movies and television shows, including *Wings*, *MacGyver*, and *Ghost*. There were countless times I stood in the cafeteria lunch line, waiting as Richard Dean Anderson and Crystal Bernard paid for their soup, salad, or sandwich, or waited as Tim Daly or Tony Goldwyn refilled his favorite fountain drink. I never saw Patrick Swayze, Demi Moore, or Whoopi Goldberg, but they were around somewhere. The food was pretty good and it was surprisingly cheap. Thanks to my IBEW brothers, I was guaranteed an hour for lunch every day, but rarely took the entire sixty minutes, and it was always during that time that I made my occasional calls to OCC. One time, near the end of April, I actually got the answer I was hoping for. I called Tracey, just to check in, and immediately recognized that something was different—mostly because, instead of just asking how I was doing or making equally meaningless small talk, she said, "Hang on a minute. Steve needs to speak with you," and put me on hold.

"Really? Right now?" I said to the music, which soon stopped, replaced by an actual human being.

"Hey, Keith, how are you?" It was Beim.

"You tell me," was my snappy reply.

"Here's the deal," he got right to it. "We're not sure the thing with Eric is working out."

Way to go, Eric! I thought, but didn't say.

"Uh huh," I did say.

"Are you still interested?" he asked.

Nah, I'm getting to love recording *Regis and Kathie Lee* and am hoping to make it a career, I thought, but didn't say.

"Absolutely," I did say, trying not to sound too excited.

"Okay, good," he continued. "There's a tournament in Las Vegas the first week in May. Can you work it for us?"

"Sure," I blurted, not knowing, or caring, about my schedule at, or commitment to, KCAL.

"We can't pay you," he said, knowing I wouldn't care, "but we can take care of your travel and get you a hotel room."

"That works for me," I said, and it did.

"Good. Call Tracey and she'll help with the travel arrangements."

"Thanks for the opportunity," I started to say, but he was long gone. I stood there smiling, listening to a dial tone and wondering, now what?

I got the time off from work, and a few days later received a packet of information in the mail that included an airline ticket and directions from the McCarran International Airport to the famed Desert Inn on the Las Vegas strip. Standing in the middle of the apartment's living room, holding on to the manila envelope suddenly made it all feel very real. I understood I had been given a chance, and I knew I needed to make the most of it.

VEGAS, BABY

I had been to Las Vegas dozens of times in my life, mostly to play golf in various Nevada state amateur competitions, but never for work. It was then, and is now, an amazing place; and, while Las Vegas Boulevard was not quite as glitzy in 1990, it was still luminescent and illuminating. More than a dozen hotel casino buildings towered above the strip, including the brand new Mirage, opened in November of the year before by mega-mogul, Steve Wynn. There was no Excalibur, New York New York, Mandalay Bay, Luxor, Bellagio, MGM Grand, Paris, Planet Hollywood, or Stratosphere; but there was the Desert Inn. Nicknamed "the DI" by locals, it was the fifth hotel on the strip, started by a man named Wilbur Clark and finished in April of 1950, thanks to new owners and an influx of mob money. Almost every major star of the day appeared in the hotel's famous "Crystal Showroom"— from Paul Anka and Tony Bennett to Frank Sinatra and Dionne Warwick—but its most famous guest was the mysterious Howard Hughes. The Vegas businessman first showed up on Thanksgiving Day 1966 and reserved the hotel's entire top two floors for a ten-day visit. Hughes wanted to stay longer, but the hotel had high rollers to accommodate, so the reclusive billionaire was asked to leave. Instead, he plopped down $13 million and bought the place. Almost twenty years later, Hughes was gone, having died in 1976, but the PGA TOUR's over-fifty set arrived to play, for the first time, on the hotel-owned golf course. The tournament's four-year list of champions was unimpressive when I showed up, as part of the OCC production team, to broadcast the fifth edition for ESPN in 1990.

Technically, I didn't have a job title because I didn't have a job, since the person I hoped to replace as associate producer was still on the staff. His name was Eric Sweringen, and he was exactly what Don Ohlmeyer wanted: a fresh-faced college graduate who would work hard, work cheap, and metamorphose from inexperienced TV caterpillar to veteran production butterfly under the tutelage of the great man himself and his underlings. It may have been what Don wanted, but it wasn't what producer Andy Young wanted or was willing to put up with for long. Andy had a job to do, a difficult one at that, and needed people on his team to contribute more quickly than young Eric seemed to be able to manage. Enter the old guy, who, uncomfortably, showed up before the youngster had exited. I knew golf and I could recognize Al Geiberger, Charles Coody, Miller Barber, and other players on sight, which was helpful. On the other hand, I didn't know any of the people involved with the production except Mr. Beim, who was nowhere to be found when I located the area set aside for the TV truck and mobile office trailers (I would later learn that this was referred to as "the compound"). I introduced myself and asked where I might find the one person with whom I was familiar. They pointed me toward a silver eighteen-wheel tractor-trailer with the twenty-four-hour sports network's logo painted on the side, and, after thanking them, off I went. I also knew TV, or thought I did. I climbed the steps of the mobile unit and knocked on a door labeled "production." No one answered, so I knocked again and again. No one came to the door.

"Just open it and go on in," said a burly fellow who had looked up from making some repairs to what appeared to be a great big microphone.

I followed his advice, pulled on the door, and entered a magical world of flashing lights, television screens, and several very busy people. It turned out, the kind of television production about which I actually knew had very little in common with this kind of television production, and what I did know wasn't going to be very helpful. So, right on the spot, I made what would become an astute and important decision—keep my mouth closed and my ears open.

A television production truck is a technological tour-de-force. On the outside, it's a typical-looking tractor-trailer, seen on American highways by the hundreds every day; but inside, it's anything but commonplace. It's not crammed full of freight or piled high with personal belongings, but instead is outfitted from top to bottom, stem to stern, with the latest and greatest high-tech electronic components. It looked a lot like television station control rooms I had seen throughout my career, but this one was fully functional and perfectly portable. It was, without question, where I wanted to work.

Most of the week was an absolute blur, meeting the production staff, announcers, and technicians. They all knew I was there, but wondered why; especially young Eric. I realized very quickly that camera operators are very intuitive, and most put two and two together before my first day was done. They figured change was most likely on the horizon and wasted no time trying to find out more about me.

"Why are you here?" was one question. "Are you Eric's replacement?" was another, more direct inquiry, and "What's your background?" was a third, easier question to answer. In fact, I was with a cameraman named Bob Swanson during the afternoon, getting several minutes of footage of the tournament trophy, when the conversation turned to me.

"How did Steve and Andy find you?" Swanny (I learned that was what everyone called him) wondered.

"Actually, I found them," I answered, wondering how much I should reveal. "More truthfully, my mom and dad found them," I completed my thought.

"How did your mom and dad know them?" Swanny pressed on.

"Golf tournaments in Hawaii," was my response. "They volunteer."

"What is your name again?" he asked, trying to make some kind of connection in his mind.

"Keith Hirshland," I said, expecting what came next.

"Are Lee and Ginger your parents?" he smiled as he asked.

"They are," I said, knowing it was a good thing.

"My God!" he exclaimed. "They're the best."

"So I've been told," I smiled, inside and out.

"If you have half as much on the ball as the two of them, you'll be just fine," he said, turning back to his trophy. Didn't I know it?

Bob Swanson and I would become fast friends, teaming up for countless adventures, some of which will be detailed here a bit later; but first, I had to impress Steve Beim and Andy Young during this trial week, and, as we headed back to the compound in his golf cart, he gave me one last piece of advice.

"Work hard and work smart," he said, "but if you don't know what you're doing, don't pretend you do. These guys can spot a phony from a mile away." He parked the cart and gathered up his gear. "I look forward to working with you," he said, and walked away.

Me too.

I finally connected with Andy Young, who was OCC's main live tournament producer. Andy came to Ohlmeyer's team after an extended stint at ABC Sports, working under that network's top dog, Terry Jastrow. Andy, I would later find out, butted heads on numerous occasions with Jastrow over coverage philosophy and came away with the headache most of the time. When Ohlmeyer offered him the reins to the golf wagon at OCC, he gladly jumped off the ABC ship. He was smart and he was cynical and, over time, I found him to have the driest sense of humor of anyone I had ever met. He would also prove to be the best live golf producer I've ever known. Upon meeting Andy Young for the first time, he informed me that my job that week was simple,

"Impress me," was all he said, as he turned his attention toward more important things. I did my best to do just that.

One of the elements Young brought with him from ABC was something called "bumpers." These were simply short, succinct features about everything from past champions of the event to interesting characteristics or attractions about the city in which the tournament was being contested. I heard from several people that this was a particular area of interest for Andy and a prevalent shortcoming of Eric's, so that's where I turned my attention. Armed with guidebooks, travel magazines, and my own personal knowledge of the area, I spent hours in my hotel room crafting my thirty-second stories on the pages of a legal pad. At the compound, I commandeered the company's black Royal typewriter and transferred what I had written to the five-by-eight-inch index cards preferred by announcer Jim Kelly. Since laptops didn't exist, I hunted and pecked my way over the keys, manually correcting every spelling mistake using my trusty bottle of Wite-Out; when the mistakes became too plentiful, I started all over again, from scratch. With the help of the guys in the tape room, I edited the video for each bumper and read with pride as my script matched the pictures on the nine-inch color television screen. When the time was right, I handed the cards to Kelly, who read each one, marrying words and video together for the broadcast. Apparently, I made an impression on Jim Kelly, but more importantly, I had done the same with Andy Young, because three weeks later Eric was gone and I had his job.

My job and I have been sleeping out of a suitcase, eating off paper plates, and going to the bathroom in a plastic box ever since.

IT'S A PLEASURE TO FINALLY MEET YOU, MR. SPENGLER

Days after returning from Las Vegas, I was once again called into Ohlmeyer Communications Company; this time not to make an offer, but to listen to one. I sat in Steve Beim's office, along with Andy Young, as they outlined what they had in mind for me. The associate producer's job was mine if I wanted it, effective immediately, but with a caveat or two. It seemed my predecessor was still on the payroll, so the offer to me was on a per-event, independent-contractor basis and would not, at this particular time, include benefits like health insurance. It would include a per-tournament fee, travel to and from each tournament, a hotel room on site, and $40 a day per diem. I could barely contain myself and accepted on the spot. As we shook hands, Steve left me with an interesting bit of irony. My first official event as a paycheck-collecting member of the OCC production team would be Paul Spengler's last—the very first LPGA Skins Game. It had been more than a year since I packed up everything I owned and moved across the country because of an assurance made by a man I had never met. I still hadn't made his acquaintance when I was advised that I was about to take orders from him.

The Skins franchise had been one of TV sports' most successful, spawning an over-fifty edition in 1988 and an all-ladies version two years later. Don convinced department store giant J. C. Penney to sponsor it, after agreeing to hold the event in the company's corporate backyard, Frisco, Texas. The CEO's sprawling Lone Star State mansion was one of many that dotted the fairways of the Stonebriar Country Club. The Dallas suburb couldn't compare with the beauty of the Senior Skins Game's home in Hawaii, or the allure of the original's Thanksgiving weekend spot in Palm Springs, but it did have eighteen holes and was the only reason J. C. Penney was willing to put up a nickel in prize money. Ohlmeyer chose the Memorial Day weekend and worked with the Ladies Professional Golf Association to invite four of the most famous female golfers of all time: Nancy Lopez, JoAnne Carner, Jan Stephenson, and Betsy King.

I don't remember much about working for Paul Spengler because Andy Young ended up doing most of the producing. Paul had essentially checked out, having accepted a job with the Pebble Beach Company running that famed golf resort. He was an extremely supportive, remarkably nice man who was happy things had worked out and wished me the best. He hoped I would send his regards to my parents, which reminded me that I hadn't called them since I had officially been offered the job at Ohlmeyer (I told you I wasn't very good at that).

Because the Skins Game features just four players, the television show relies on pre-produced pieces and interviews with the participants. Putting these together was my main responsibility before we went on the air the last weekend in May. My old friend and colleague Tom Christine had moved to Dallas with his wife, Vickie, and he was working as an editor in the very lucrative, flourishing, postproduction industry, putting together everything from television commercials to video versions of annual reports for corporations to two-minute tales about well-known women golfers. I was the reason he was doing those. The ladies couldn't have been nicer, and all had incredible stories, ranging from major championship victories to overcoming injury and breaking down barriers. I wrote the words, matched them up with pictures, and pounded out scripts on the trusty Royal typewriter, presenting a finished product that aired on NBC with the voice of announcer Charlie Jones.

Of the four players, Australian Jan Stephenson was the least accomplished. She had won three majors, but the last had come seven years earlier, and in 1990 she was more famous for promoting her image than producing victories. Stephenson claimed that women golfers needed to embrace a sex-sells attitude and apply it to the way their sport was marketed. She posed for pin-up calendars and prodded her fellow professionals to play along. Her attitude didn't make her many friends on tour, but it did get her invited to the first made-for-TV tournament featuring females. Then she collected $200,000 worth of "skins" for playing eighteen holes and walked away the champion.

My work had continued to impress the higher-ups at OCC, and by the end of June I had been offered a full-time position, along with health benefits, which turned out to be beneficial indeed, because that summer Kathy and I happily learned we were going to be parents.

PALMER PAVES
THE WAY

It's been said that golf is a game for a lifetime, but there was a time that wasn't true if you wanted to make a living at it. Arnold Palmer is credited with bringing the gentleman's game to the masses and, from the time he won the US Amateur golf championship in 1954 until long after he's gone, he'll be remembered as the most popular player of all time. He will never be considered the best or lay claim to the most trophies, but he will always be the most beloved. He won the Masters Tournament every other year from 1958 to 1964; came from seven shots off the lead on the final day to win the United States Open in 1960; and won back-to-back British Open claret jugs in 1961 and 1962. In fact, Palmer is given most of the credit for making the British Open popular among American players when he travelled overseas to compete. American golf legends Bobby Jones, Sam Snead, and Ben Hogan had all played and won in Europe; but after Hogan's victory in 1953, the luster of the Open Championship faded among American players because of the grueling travel schedule, inclement weather, unimpressive prize money, and links-style golf courses. Then, Palmer won the Masters and US Open in 1960, and business partner Mark McCormack convinced him that adding the British Open crown—like Jones, Hogan, and Snead had done before him—would make him a true global star. Palmer lost that tournament by a single stroke to Kel Nagle, but his go-for-broke style and swagger helped him win the hearts of European golf fans and made McCormack an oracle and a multimillionaire.

Between 1955 and 1973, Arnold Palmer won sixty-two professional golf tournaments and is considered the player of the decade for the 1960s; and in 1963, he became the first professional golfer in history to earn $100,000 in prize money in a single season; but ten years later, when he won for the sixty-second and last time on the PGA TOUR, at the Bob Hope Classic, it was evident that Palmer no longer had the game to compete every week with younger, stronger players like Jack Nicklaus, Tom Watson, Hale Irwin, and Lee Trevino. By 1980, a fifty-year-old Arnold Palmer had fallen to 136th on the official PGA TOUR money list, making slightly more than $1,000 per event, but was still charismatic enough to draw the biggest galleries at every event. The brass at headquarters knew it was time to give Arnold Palmer another vehicle.

Two years earlier, an Austin, Texas, entrepreneur named Fred Raphael had decided to create his own golf tournament with two-man teams of players fifty years of age or older. He solicited the insurance company Liberty Mutual to be the tournament's title sponsor and created the Liberty Mutual Legends of Golf. Sam Snead and Tommy Bolt beat a handful of other teams and won the first one, then Julius Boros and Roberto DeVincenzo partnered to win against a significantly bigger field in 1979, and the PGA TOUR took notice. With Raphael's tournament as impetus, the Senior Tour was born in 1980, boasting a four-tournament schedule with a fifty-year-old Arnold Palmer as its headliner; and he didn't disappoint, winning the only event in which he played, the PGA Seniors Championship. Three tournaments were added to the schedule the next year, and Palmer played in four, winning one. By 1984, the tour had begun visiting twenty-two cities and playing for more than $5 million in prize money. Don January, Peter Thomson, Miller Barber, and Lee Elder were all winning golf tournaments again, but people were coming to the course to see Arnold Palmer. The bigwigs in Ponte Vedra created the Senior Tour in 1980, but Palmer popularized it. He made it viable, allowing those that followed in his footsteps decades earlier to find and follow in those footsteps again.

Playing golf can be a great way to make a living, especially today, but forty years ago it was completely apathetic to aging. Once past his prime, a player had few options in regard to remaining in the game. Some were able to transition to television, but there were precious few jobs. Others found head professional jobs, teaching at country clubs across the land, but many found that unfulfilling. Then the PGA TOUR lobbed a lifeline. The Senior Tour was tournament golf, in some respects, but pure theater in many others. They played for a paycheck, but nobody who came to the course to watch cared who won. It was a parade of personalities, a chance for people to pay their respects to the game's greats, and a time to turn back the clock and celebrate a memory. They played fifty-four holes instead of seventy-two; no player was sent packing for poor play; and they stayed for hours after the last putt dropped to sign hats, flags, and programs for each and every fan. No one stayed longer, or used more ink, than Arnold Palmer. For many, it was reason to live; but for others it was a revenue stream, a new way to get rich, and that's precisely what Lee Trevino was doing when I joined him on the Senior Tour scene in 1990.

My first Senior Tour event was the nineteenth one on the schedule that year, something called the Northville Long Island Classic, which had been played since 1988 and boasted such luminous past champions as Don Bies and Butch Baird. Twenty-nine-time PGA TOUR winner Lee Trevino had turned fifty on December first of the year before, making him eligible to play on the Senior Tour in 1990, starting with the Royal Caribbean Classic in February. He won it. Then he won two weeks later, and again two weeks after that. By the time the tour had made it to Long Island, Trevino had won six tournaments, including the United States Senior Open the week before our cameras showed up. He was the undisputed king of the hill and didn't miss any opportunity to let folks know it. Relentlessly jocular, Trevino was just what the Senior Tour doctor ordered. He constantly and consistently kidded around with the crowd, joking, making merry, and cracking wise, especially when the cameras were rolling.

"Pressure is playing for five bucks a hole when you only have two in your pocket," he would famously tell a gathered crowd.

"There are two things that won't last long in this world, and they are dogs that chase cars and pros that putt for pars," I heard him say a hundred times.

"You can make a lot of money in this game," he began, getting everyone's attention. "Just ask my ex-wives," he'd finish, as the gallery exploded in laughter.

"I'm going to make so much money this year, my caddie will make the top twenty winners' money list," I heard him utter in 1990, and he meant it.

People couldn't get enough of Trevino, and in every piece of videotape I've ever seen, the feeling is mutual—but I have seen Trevino when the cameras stopped rolling, and on several of those occasions he was far less gracious. He was a great player— in 1990, a record-setting one in senior golf—and a shot in the arm to a tour that had seen the great Arnold Palmer play less and less and the greatest of all time, Jack Nicklaus, rarely play at all. People came to the golf course by the thousands to listen to Trevino talk and watch him work his magic. He was the star of the show, so he was in constant demand, and it was my job to find him during pro-ams and practice rounds and make sure we captured every ounce of wisdom that he was prepared to promote each week. He was always easy with a word, but when our cameras arrived, he made sure to let everyone know getting an interview was going to be difficult.

"Here comes ESPN," he would say loud enough for everyone, including us, to hear, "always wanting something for free."

"Hello, Mr. Trevino," I would say respectfully, asking, "Can we trouble you for a few minutes of your time?" as the camera set up behind me.

"How much are you going to pay me?" he'd ask, only somewhat facetiously. "I'm the top dog out here and you want me to bark for free?" I did.

At first, I was intimidated, and he knew it, and then took advantage of it; but once he realized that I realized it was all part of his act, we forged a much more respectful relationship. Trevino was many things, but dumb wasn't one of them. He knew we needed him, but the reverse was equally true: he needed us, more specifically the forum we offered; and, while he always tried to make the asking uncomfortable, he never refused. We got away unscathed and with the sound we wanted. Trevino won seven tournaments in 1990, four of them on ESPN, and ended up being the tour's leading money winner, with a record $1,190,518, scoring leader, Rookie of the Year, and Player of the Year, as well as its consummate pain in the neck. That command performance also got him invited back to a Skins Game—this time the senior variety, joining Nicklaus, Gary Player, and defending champion Arnold Palmer.

FRIENDSHIPS ARE FORGED

While 1990 found me busy in Los Angeles getting, first, a meeting, then a job, and ultimately making friends with professional golfers, America's most iconic golf pro was making a new friend of his own. That year, the PGA Championship was being played at the Shoal Creek Golf and Country Club in Birmingham, Alabama. The PGA Championship is the last of four major championships played each year. Like the US Open and the British Open, but unlike the Masters, the PGA of America moves its championship around and plays at various venues around the country. The Masters is always held at Augusta National Golf Club in Augusta, Georgia, and, while the other majors move, they often return to golf courses where championships have been held in the past. Shoal Creek, in Birmingham, also hosted the PGA Championship in 1984. Arnold Palmer played in that one; he played in the 1990 edition as well. The fact that Palmer was playing was not noteworthy; there were no shades of gray when it came to Palmer and the PGA. He had played in thirty-two in a row—every one since 1958, never winning, but finishing second on three separate occasions. In fact, the PGA Championship would be Palmer's major championship Achilles' heel; the only major trophy he would never collect.

Network news vans found their way to the Birmingham suburb of Shelby for another reason, and it was black and white as well. Shoal Creek was one of many private golf clubs in America that had yet to offer membership to a person of color. Club founder Hal Thompson said the club would not be pressured into accepting an African American member, telling anyone who would listen:

"This is our home and we will pick and choose who we want."

That public comment was all civil rights groups needed to protest the upcoming golf tournament, force sponsors to start to pull their advertising from the CBS broadcast, and make the PGA of America consider pulling up stakes and staging its premiere event somewhere else. In the end, a compromise was reached as Shoal Creek agreed to offer an honorary membership to local insurance executive Louis Willie, with the promise of full membership after completion of all club requirements. The episode forced golf's governing bodies to change the way they did business, focusing more on minority involvement in the sport and vowing never again to hold a major championship at an all-white club. Mr. Willie would now be one of hundreds of people who belonged to Shoal Creek; another was Birmingham businessman Joseph E. Gibbs.

Gibbs was an Alabaman through and through. He was born in Oneonta in 1949, grew up on its streets, and was educated in its schools, graduating cum laude from the University of Alabama in 1975 with an accounting degree. He spent four years in the navy before starting his professional career with Price Waterhouse as an accountant, but he had bigger dreams. The entrepreneurial Gibbs saw a bright and lucrative future in cable TV and cellular telephone technology and served as a principal in two different cable system companies in Birmingham between 1982 and 1986. He then founded Crowley Cellular Communications and grew it to be the largest private cellular operation in the country, until it was sold in 1994. Somewhere along the way, Gibbs took up and, like so many of us, fell in love with the game of golf.

He was living along the fairways of Shoal Creek when the PGA of America came calling with its annual major championship. It is customary for local residents and club members to open up their homes to the professionals competing in tournaments, and that's exactly what Joe Gibbs did, telling the tournament officials that he would be happy to host one of the players in his guest house. The club thanked him and then told him that two-time Masters champion Ben Crenshaw would be delighted to accept. Gibbs was delighted as well, but then disappointed when he learned that Crenshaw's plans had changed and he would no longer need Gibbs' generosity. The disappointment once again turned to delight when Joe Gibbs found out that the most famous golfer of all time, Arnold Palmer, would be taking Crenshaw's place. The two men liked each other immediately and shared an easy conversation over dinner and drinks when Palmer returned from the golf course. They talked about business, they talked about life, and, of course, they talked about golf and, somewhere along the way, the seed of an idea for a twenty-four-hour television network devoted to the game was planted in Gibbs's mind, a seed that over the next three years would blossom into a reality. But I didn't know anything about any of that, yet.

BIG ISLAND, BIGGER STARS

We ended the 1990 season on a high note, thanks to Trevino's sensational season and the barefoot Skins Game heroics of Curtis Strange. Kathy was healthy and happy and seven months pregnant when we spent the holidays in Hawaii with my mom and dad. They were thrilled about the prospect of being grandparents again and the positive turn of events that had me doing what I wanted to do. Life was good when I informed them that I would be back in less than a month to work on my first Senior Skins Game at the Mauna Lani Resort on "the big island" of Hawaii. I would be coming by myself because our ob-gyn felt Kathy would be too pregnant to travel, especially having just made this trip, but as it turned out I wasn't alone. Mom and Dad had served as volunteers at the first Senior Skins Game, two years earlier at the Turtle Bay Resort on Oahu, and had put in their request to work when the tournament returned to the fiftieth state.

I took every tournament seriously—still do—but Skins was different. It was a big deal for several reasons. It was always on network TV and, back in the '80s and '90s that still meant something. These days, many of the big sporting events are carried on cable television networks like ESPN and Golf Channel, because those networks can boast a hundred million subscribers or more, but more than thirty years ago, the Golf Channel didn't exist and ESPN didn't count when it came to top-notch events. Skins was one of the few opportunities the hardworking OCC production and technical folks got to show their wares on TV's biggest stages, and they took that seriously.

It was also a showcase for just four players, and they were the most recognizable players of their time, or all time. At the Senior Skins Game, it was the "of all time" that made the contestants so impressive. When Jack Nicklaus, Arnold Palmer, Gary Player, and Lee Trevino stood on the tee together in January of 1991, they carried with them the combined weight of 188 PGA TOUR wins, forty major championships, millions of dollars, and hundreds of millions of fans. They commanded respect and got it.

The third reason (or maybe the second, or even the first) you knew Skins was a big deal was because Don Ohlmeyer showed up to produce it. I've already mentioned that Don was a larger-than-life figure, but his stature increased even more at an event like the Skins Game. I had learned by observation, during my first few months, that Don had hired Steve Beim right out of USC and taken him under his wing. Steve started at OCC as a "gopher," running errands for Ohlmeyer and others in the company while inserting himself into the process and soaking up all the knowledge and experience he could. You could tell he idolized his mentor, and when it became time for Steve to direct at Don's side, it was like looking at a mirror image, at least in the way both men behaved. Don ran the show and ruled with an iron fist, and when he wasn't around Steve tried to do the same thing. Because of Don, Steve became a good, then great director; but his bedside manner left something to be desired, and that behavior, in an industry that, over time, became more and more conscious of political correctness, eventually led to difficult and uncomfortable situations. But in 1991, those worries were years away and the awful words and absences of decorum were considered confirmation of competence. Everybody got yelled at (as I will attest), but nobody wanted to be on the receiving end. Even after Steve rose through the ranks to sit at Don's side as his director, he still showed his superiors, especially Don, the same respect he did at the beginning of his career. He and I flew together (Steve in first class, me in coach) from Los Angeles to Kona and shared a car from the airport to the magnificent Mauna Lani Resort on Hawaii.

The Mauna Lani Hotel and Bungalows Resort was built in 1983 as a big island luxury alternative to the massive Waikoloa and the aging Mauna Kea resorts. Looking for exposure, the ownership decided to partner with Ohlmeyer and agreed to host the Senior Skins Game, starting in 1990. That first year was a success, thanks to its prestigious champion (Palmer) and the stunning scenery, so everyone was excited about year two. We arrived, checked in, and were about to be shown to our respective rooms when Steve addressed the attractive Hawaiian woman behind the desk,

"Can someone show me Mr. Ohlmeyer's accommodations?" he asked.

"I beg your pardon?" she replied, obviously curious.

"Mr. Ohlmeyer will be checking in later and I want to make sure his room is in order," Steve said, looking her in the eye.

"Excuse me for just one moment," was her reply, and she turned and walked away.

"If Don's room isn't perfect, we'll all pay," he said to me, shaking his head.

"Holy crap" was all I could think.

The woman who was handling our check-in returned with a smile,

"Mr. Ohlmeyer is in bungalow number one and we'll be happy to show you," she smiled at Steve as she called a bellman over.

I was not in bungalow number one, but I was in one of the nicest hotel rooms I'd ever seen, and on the bed was a package. I set my bag and briefcase down and went over to the bed to examine my gift. A card welcomed me, by name, to the resort and offered wishes for a successful week. I carefully peeled away the Mauna Lani wrapping and opened a box in which I found a golf shirt embroidered with the resort's logo.

"Very cool," I said softly to myself, setting the shirt aside and starting to unpack.

That wasn't the only gift I would receive that week. In fact, there was a different surprise in my room each day, and it was far from my only surprise. Because Senior Skins was played in Hawaii, the crew had to go to work before the sun rose in the western sky. Portable lights were set up in the compound and each member of the crew had, or was given, a flashlight to help him or her find his or her way around. I wasn't the first to arrive at work each day, nor was I the last, but there was always someone already there when I showed up for work. One morning, there appeared to be more folks than usual in the catering tent as I approached to get a plate of bacon and eggs. That was strange, but what was even more bizarre was that everyone under the tent was wearing the bathrobe clearly appropriated from the hotel room closet. Before I could ask what prompted this display, I heard a roar and then applause, which prompted me to turn, just in time to see a bathrobe-clad Don Ohlmeyer, with a Coca-Cola in one hand and a hot dog in the other, clamber out of a golf cart and head, smiling, right for the tent. I realized, despite the hazards, this was perhaps the main reason everyone on the crew would run through a wall for Don; he was one of them.

Another surprise came as I was hunkered down in the tape room during the first day of competition, making sure I didn't make the same mistake I had made at the Skins Game a few months before—or any mistake, for that matter—when I heard, but didn't turn around to see, the production truck door open behind me. Then I felt a hand on my shoulder,

"Is Don Ohlmeyer here?" came the question, as the hand was removed.

"We're a little busy in here," was my abrupt reply.

"I'm looking for Don Ohlmeyer. He told me I could find him here."

Persistent devil, I thought,

"I'd give you a tour if I had time," is what I said, snarkier than I needed to say it. "You'll find him in there, but we are on the air." I pointed to the sliding glass door, without ever turning around.

At that time, Kevin Costner was a bona fide movie star, having appeared in *The Big Chill, Silverado, The Untouchables,* and *No Way Out,* and responsible for the success of *Field of Dreams* and *Bull Durham.* But what made him really famous was the Academy Award he had won months earlier as best director for the 1990 release *Dances with Wolves,* a movie for which he also won an Oscar for best picture. Apparently he was also a golf fan.

"Do you know who that was?" said an incredulous Eddie Beddingfield, currently operating tape machines red and white.

"Know who *who* was?" I asked, still concentrating on Nicklaus's golf shot.

"The guy that was just here asking for Don," he answered, smiling.

"How would I know? I never looked at him."

"Maybe you should have," he smirked. "That was Kevin Costner."

"No shit?" I said.

"No shit," said he.

One last surprise came after Jack Nicklaus had won ten skins and $285,000, thanks mostly to a thirty-five-foot eagle putt on the third playoff hole. Ohlmeyer's helicopter had left for the airport, the crew was busy breaking down all the equipment and stowing it away in cases, and my parents were at the bar enjoying a cocktail after completing their volunteer services (Mom kept score for the announcers in the booth, while Dad was the golf cart driver for hand-held camera operator Mark Bowden). I was also getting ready to call it a week, having cleaned out the office, packed away the Royal typewriter, and made sure every videotape was returned to its proper case, but I had one last thing to do: return to the pro shop to exchange the shirt I had received as a gift for the proper size.

The Skins Game was Don Ohlmeyer's brainchild, but it couldn't have made it to living rooms all across the world without help, and the lion's share of that help came from media and marketing giant IMG. International Management Group was the name superagent Mark McCormack had given his company after he signed its most high-profile athlete, Arnold Palmer. With Palmer front and center, McCormack had built the company into a billion-dollar behemoth. It was the biggest athlete representation company in the world, and its tentacles reached into TV production, rights fee negotiations, and global acquisitions. When Ohlmeyer was pitching Skins as a concept, he knew he needed help securing the athletes, and IMG had them, so a partnership was born. I had the chance to meet Mr. McCormack once, but only in passing, and never at a Skins Game. I did have the opportunity, more than once, to work alongside one of his more valued lieutenants, Barry Frank. Frank was a small man with a huge reputation in the sports industry. He joined IMG in 1970 after serving as vice president of sports programming at ABC for six years, and left IMG briefly in 1976, returning to network television as president of CBS Sports. That stint lasted two years, and he returned to the marketing and management company, where he has been ever since. Extremely successful,

Frank's most high-profile deal took place when he took a seat at the Olympics rights negotiations table to help broker a deal for the broadcast rights to the 1988 Winter Games. Prior to that year, the highest price paid for the broadcast rights to any Winter Olympics was the previous one in 1984. The Sarajevo games went to ABC TV for an impressive $91.5 million, but four years later all three networks were back at the trough hoping to get the rights for the Calgary games. Accounts of the negotiations all say Frank was in charge from the beginning and started the bidding by having all three American networks sign identical broadcast contracts with only the price tag left blank. That way, Frank contended, there could be no negotiating after the deal was signed, and after each signature hit the paper, the bidding began.

Frank conducted the negotiations on a round-by-round basis, and as long as two networks' high bids were within 10 percent of each other, the bidding would continue. After several rounds, the number had reached $300 million and CBS was long gone, and straws were drawn to see whether ABC or NBC would submit the first bid. ABC won and wrote down $309 million. NBC didn't offer a counter and left the table, leaving the broadcast rights to ABC at a fee increase of more than 300 percent.

Barry Frank also rightfully claims to be a major influence in nurturing the broadcasting careers of notable announcers Jim Nantz, Greg Gumbel, Bob Costas, and Mike Tirico, and he was standing in line in front of me Sunday afternoon in the pro shop at Mauna Lani exchanging a number of gifts.

"How can I help you?" asked the clerk

"I'd like to exchange these gifts," said Barry Frank, pushing a pile across the counter.

"Everything?" asked a surprised young man.

"Yes, everything," said Frank, matter-of-factly.

In addition to two golf shirts, the resort had, for no other reason than to simply say "thank you for being here," given us a set of rocks glasses, a jacket, a golf towel, and a cashmere sweater.

"What size do you need?' asked the clerk placing each item into a separate pile behind him.

"I'd like cash," said Barry Frank.

"I'm sorry," said the assistant pro, knowing the items were offered as gifts.

Standing behind Frank, I was sorry, too, and embarrassed.

"I'd like cash, please," Frank repeated.

I have no idea how the exchange ended, because I turned on my heel and walked out of the pro shop, keeping my too-small shirt because I didn't have the stomach any longer to return it.

DIFFERENT SPORTS, DIFFERENT DUTIES

A cynically simplistic vision of a TV sports producer's job would include the completion of three simple tasks: get on the air on time, get off the air on time, and get in all the commercials. A slightly more accurate and detailed description, given by someone who's actually done the job, would have to include these six words: tell the story of the event. In my experience, the easiest sports to produce, in alphabetical order, are: auto racing, baseball, basketball, bowling, hockey, soccer, volleyball, and water polo—and that's only if you're willing to suspend your disbelief enough to consider bowling a sport. All of these sports are uncomplicated to produce because of the number of actual decisions the person sitting in the producer's chair has to make. But producing the three *B* sports, hockey, and others means never having to decide when to take your commercial breaks, because they are already woven into the fabric of the game. Baseball naturally stops after every three outs or when a manager makes a pitching change. In a college basketball game, TV timeouts are built in after the first whistle at various time intervals, hockey gives you ten minutes to run all your commercials during the intermissions between periods, and volleyball takes a TV break when the first team reaches fifteen points in a set. In fact, on many occasions, especially at the local and regional level, one person serves as both producer and director for baseball, basketball, and hockey. Only auto racing diverts from this paint-by-number method of going to commercial, because someone sitting in a producer's chair actually has to decide when to go to commercial, especially under green flag racing conditions. They take a break with fingers crossed, hoping Dale Earnhardt Jr. doesn't wreck his car while folks at home are watching a Nationwide auto insurance company commercial featuring Dale Earnhardt Jr.

That's not to say hundreds of decisions aren't being made every minute during the broadcast of these sporting events; they just aren't being made by a producer—those decisions are made by directors. That's why these, and most other "stick and ball" sports, are director's sports. If one of the main tenets of producing a sport for television is "telling the story" of the event, and that story can be told by just pointing the camera at and focusing on who has the ball, then that job, in most sports, is being done by the director. Most sports have one or all of the following ingredients: one ball (or puck), one offense, one defense, and one field of play, so, if the director is smart enough to have the cameraman find the athlete with the ball, he's done the lion's share of informing the viewer what is most important in the game. These sports have many challenges, for sure, but producing isn't one of them. Not golf, not by a long shot.

On a Thursday afternoon telecast, golf features not one, but as many as seventy-eight balls; not one, but up to eighteen fields of play; not one offense, but *everybody* playing offense (many at the same time); and no TV timeouts, so a producer has to decide, among other things, which player to show on what hole, whether to show that shot live or recorded earlier, and when to break away from the constant action to take a commercial break. Then, even during the commercials, the decisions don't stop because one has to decide which player's shots to record and in what order they will be played back, and exactly which shot to show when the commercial break is over—all the while giving the information to the director and the announcers so everyone knows what's going on in the broadcast. The producer and director sit in the production mobile unit in front of a monitor wall that includes as many as seventy screens showing cameras pointing at all the golf holes, as well as the recording devices, graphics generators, and what his own, and probably what other networks, are showing at the time. The announcers, to whom the producer gives instructions, sit in a tower or booth and see screens that show only the holes for which they are responsible, or one larger screen that shows what's actually on the air. They fly blind, not knowing what they're going to have to talk about until the producer tells them, and/or they see it for themselves, and by then it's too late because it's already on TV. There has to be a tremendous amount of trust between producer and announcer in TV golf because the announcer can't simply look out a window at the stadium below and inform the fan what's going on in the game. Many try to produce a golf telecast. Few do it well, and Andy Young did it, and still does it, better than most.

ROAD WORK

It takes in the neighborhood of a hundred people to put an average golf tournament on television, many more for a high profile event, and more still for a major championship. Fifteen to twenty work on the production side, and a handful of those find themselves in the producer's "inner circle." In the OCC golf production world, the replay producer was one of those jobs, and I was one of those guys. I can say, with certainty, the replay producer job was, and still is, the toughest job on a golf crew, and the reason is simple. The producer decides which character is the most important and then builds his story around that character, showing his or her shots live, going to commercial when he or she finishes a shot or completes a hole. But every story has more than one character, and while the producer focuses in on the one he perceives to be the main one, the replay producer then has to keep an eye on every other character on the golf course. Sometimes that's two, sometimes its twenty-two, and you never know when, or if, the shot you are recording might become the most important golf shot of the tournament. That was the pressure cooker in which I spent a hectic two or three hours each Thursday through Sunday, but on Tuesday and Wednesday my job was interesting for other reasons. Those were the days when interviews were conducted and features were shot and produced. Since those first unpaid days in Las Vegas, I had developed a special affinity for the videotape pieces that featured sights and attractions unique to the areas at which tournaments were played, and I sought them out each week.

Cameraman Bob Swanson and I would take Tuesday road trips, and my curiosity and our travels took us to some interesting spots. Have you ever visited the original Floyd's Barber Shop (where Sheriff Andy Taylor got the latest Mayberry gossip), Jesse James's homestead, or the William Taft presidential museum? Have you seen the world's largest chest of drawers or the world's smallest church? How about America's first traffic light, ATM, or urinal? I have. I found a book called *Roadside America* and went to town, literally.

We travelled from Los Angeles to Miami one week for the Senior PGA Tour's Royal Caribbean Classic, and I was intrigued by an entry in my book of interesting places that was just a few miles away, in the Miami suburb of Homestead: the Coral Castle. Ed Leedskalnin was a five-foot-two-inch, one-hundred pound Latvian immigrant who loved, and asked to marry, Agnes Scuffs. But instead of a lifetime of bliss, Leedkalnin's heart was broken when his bride-to-be left him at the altar, for reasons known only to her. Maybe she decided Ed was too poor, too uneducated, too old (Agnes was only sixteen), or maybe it was because she came to realize Ed was just plain crazy. After all, he had spent twenty years building a coral compound, complete with rock tables, chairs, and beds, hoping, someday, someone like Agnes would occupy it with him. The tiny immigrant carved walls, gates, and crescents (some weighing as much as thirty tons) and moved them into place, creating his castle, mostly at night and always by himself. Ed died in 1951 and the Coral Castle opened as a tourist attraction two years later. We visited in 1992, each paying the requested ten cents to enter, and documented this amazing attraction. I'm sure the structure, just north of the corner of 157th Avenue and the Dixie Highway, is exactly the same more than a quarter century later.

Swanny and I looked forward to our Tuesday afternoon adventures, with me diligently researching the sideshows that surrounded the tournaments, while he focused on the most attractive angles, best backgrounds, and appropriate approach to showcasing many of America's off-the-wall places. He was happy when we loaded up the gear and hit the road, stopping at, and capturing on videotape, the cell at Alcatraz that Al Capone called home or the final resting place of author, humorist, and American icon Mark Twain. During our travels, I discovered my cameraman companion and I had a lot in common, including the fact that our first love, when it came to sports, was baseball. Swanny's a lifelong, long-suffering Chicago Cubs fan, and his love of America's pastime made one road trip especially enjoyable.

In 1989 Kevin Costner starred in a drama/fantasy/baseball movie titled *Field of Dreams* about an Iowa farmer who turns his cornfield into a baseball diamond because of the nocturnal whisper, "If you build it, he will come." The movie earned three Academy Award nominations and helped establish a tourist attraction. A few years after the film hit the nation's movie screens, Swanny and I took the camera to see it for ourselves (the ball field, not the movie). If you've seen the movie, you know the house, the porch, and the regulation baseball diamond just a few feet away. The same bleachers from which Costner's movie daughter fell, precipitating the movie's climactic scene, sat in the sun, waiting for our rear ends. There was no admission, and we were joined by several others who had made the trek along one of Iowa's rural highways to get to the renovated cornfield. I wandered around the bases and out into the rows of corn in the outfield, from which Shoeless Joe Jackson (played by Ray Liotta) and the rest of the imaginary characters appeared in the film, and, before leaving, I picked an ear of corn and plopped a $20 bill into the Mason jar attached to a fence. I have no idea what happened to the corn, but I'll never forget the visit to the field of dreams.

We also dropped in on the Venthaven Ventriloquist Dummy Museum outside Cincinnati (that was creepy), the site of the Salem witch trials, and Daniel Boone's gravesite, and we did it all under the assumption that these places would be interesting to golf viewers on ESPN. I don't know if they were or not, but they were interesting to me. Putting a golf tournament on television was also interesting to me, and, as I continued my progression, my friend Steve Beim was constantly trying to get me to move into the main production truck and direct a few segments. Beim had worked his way up the Ohlmeyer career ladder from errand boy to director and had made a stop at replay producer along the way. Naturally, he thought my best course of action would be to follow in his footsteps, but I knew all along that I wanted to do what Andy was doing, but I didn't want the job at his expense. I would have been perfectly happy to work with Andy and Steve for as long as possible, but plans change when life gets in the way.

THE GOOD, THE BAD, AND THE UGLY

I have met thousands of golfers, been friendly with hundreds, and call dozens my friends and can say, with utter certainty, that as a whole they are the most accommodating professional athletes when it comes to dealing with the media. There are probably a bunch of reasons for this, but the one that comes to my mind is that, first and foremost, they are nice guys playing a "nice" sport. You can also make the generalization that they are privileged, well-spoken, and comfortable in social settings, but there is also a monetary explanation. Save for a modest amount of product endorsements, the world of professional golf does not include guaranteed contracts. If they don't play, they don't get paid; in fact, even if they do play, if they don't make the cut they go home, not only empty-handed, but out of pocket for expenses like travel, accommodations, and whatever sum they've agreed to pay their caddie. They are well aware that any exposure is good for their brand and the business of the brand that is on their cap, chest, sleeve, or golf bag; so, if a camera comes around with a network logo plastered on the side, chances are good that a request for a sound bite or interview will be met with a positive response.

Dan Forsman, Jason Gore, Rocco Mediate, and Jay Haas are just a few of the guys who will talk to you anytime, anywhere. Curtis Strange, who I happen to like, will almost always, not very politely, decline, especially if the interview was your idea and not his. Craig Stadler and Lee Trevino will do it, but they'll let you know the whole time they're not happy about it. Jack Nicklaus will do it, too, but he'll make you wait (sometimes for hours). Phil Mickelson will only do it once in a great while and hardly ever one on one, and you can forget about Tiger. Nice or not, they are all creatures of habit, and the best time to get to them is on the professional tee box during a pro-am, or at the practice tee *before* they start their warm-up routine. As soon as the player you hope to talk to reaches for that first wedge, your window for an interview is pretty much over until he's hit his last practice driver, an hour or so later. In between the easily gettable and the impossible-to-talk-to guys are hundreds of hardworking, best golfers in the world who, under the right circumstances, are happy to give you what you need, especially if they know you, your cameraman, or your network. If a tournament comes to a town in which you happen to be the local sports anchor or one of a handful of sports reporters, your chances of just walking onto the practice tee and grabbing just anybody go down exponentially, and the task gets even more difficult at a big event like the United States Open.

In addition to producing live tournament golf, the OCC production team was also responsible for a number of major championship preview shows on ESPN. These programs would include a detailed description of the golf course, a look back at past championship winners, and predictions from the announce team and a panel of ESPN experts on which player might win the next one. The show would feature dozens of player interviews, and at the US Open at famed Baltusrol Golf Club in 1993, I was in charge of collecting many of those interviews. The club has a rich history and, at the time, it was about to host our national championship and "golf's toughest test" for the seventh time. Nicklaus had won there twice, but he was well past his prime, giving way for the likes of Payne Stewart, Nick Price, Paul Azinger, Greg Norman, and the other heavy hitters of the early 1990s. As I was staking out my spot on the practice tee, waiting for the right opportunity to speak with Lee Janzen or Fred Couples, I noticed an unfamiliar reporter pacing up and down the range. He would approach a player, only to be stopped dead in his tracks by a protective caddie who knew his man wasn't available,

"Poor guy," I said to my camera operator. "He's got no shot."

"Why don't you help him out?" he asked, more than half joking.

"Yeah, why don't I?" I said, making a step toward the stymied sports reporter who was coming my way.

"Having a hard time?" I asked as he got close enough to hear.

"I'm good," he said, walking past.

"I can tell," I replied as he approached and was rebuked by another player.

The player that denied my confident friend's request happened to be Tom Kite, the defending US Open Champion, who had been kind to me whenever I had asked for interviews since meeting him for the first time in 1991.

"Hi, Mr. Kite," I said loud enough for Mr. "I'm good" to hear. "Keith Hirshland with ESPN."

"Yeah, Keith, how are you," said the talented Texan, "and for the last time, it's Tom. What can I do for you?"

"Just one quick question and I'll let you be on your way," I said, as my cameraman moved into position and handed me the microphone.

"Fire away," said Tom, and I did.

After the interview I moved back into position near the end of the practice tee when the reporter, who to the best of my knowledge still hadn't gotten one single player to speak to him, walked over,

"How come they'll talk to you and not to me?" he asked, in a more than slightly condescending tone. "I'm with WNBC in New York."

"Just lucky, I guess," I said, turning the other cheek and offering my hand. "Keith Hirshland with ESPN."

"Hi, Matt Lauer," he answered accepting my hand. "I worked at ESPN about ten years ago."

"Who do you need?" I offered without responding to what I perceived as his latest slight.

"Anybody," was his response.

"How about if I introduce you to Davis Love III," I said as I noticed DL III headed our way. I did just that and then headed in a different direction, not waiting for a thank you.

The next time I saw Matt Lauer, less than a year later, he was the news reader for *The Today Show*, and now I can see him every day if I want to.

While most guys on the PGA TOUR are nice, some are downright assholes, and one of them tried to kill me earlier that year.

In addition to seeking out the strange sights in each tournament town and recording all the shots Andy Young couldn't show live, one of my duties as an OCC replay producer was heading up the taping of golf-hole flyovers at various courses around the country. The flyover was a production element that Andy really liked because it gave the viewer a close-up look at the hole players were about to play and it interrupted the sometimes repetitive golf shot, golf shot, golf shot cadence that defined much of televised golf. In 1993 computers may have been sophisticated enough to generate stylized versions of golf holes, but they weren't even close to being cheap enough. They were so expensive that it was cheaper for us to hire a helicopter for half a day, have a cameraman hang out the side, and put the fly-by on videotape. Of course, the camera operator couldn't go up alone because someone had to push the button to start the videotape machine rolling and recording, and that someone just happened to be the new guy, me.

Luckily, once the hole description was captured, it could be used again and again for years, because most golf courses rarely redesigned their golf holes, especially ones that were used for PGA TOUR sanctioned events. The exceptions were when we arrived at a new tournament, one we hadn't televised in a few years, or that odd course that actually did remove a tree or add a bunker or a new teeing ground on one of the finishing holes. In that case, up I went. One such occasion was the 1993 United Airlines Hawaiian Open (now the Sony Open in Hawaii) at Waialae Golf Course near Diamond Head on Oahu. Plans were made to fly at first light Tuesday morning because the golf course looked beautiful at that time of day and, more importantly, there would be few, if any, golfers on the course that early. That was the case until we got to the par three 17th. A helicopter flying a few hundred feet above the ground over a golf course is loud and can cause a disturbance. The golf club had to get approval from both the Honolulu police and the homeowners association around the golf course because the "whoop, whoop, whoop" of a helicopter blade can be a rude awakening. To ensure we had a good recording of each hole, we'd fly over it at least twice, starting a few yards behind the tee and finishing by circling the green, starting at the 10th hole and finishing at number 18.

The 17th hole at Waialae is a beautiful par three, flanked by the Pacific Ocean on the left. The chopper pilot would fly out over the ocean and then swing around, just in time to reveal the tee box below, as he made his way on a straight line to the green a couple hundred yards away. As we swung out over the blue waters of the Pacific, I noticed a couple of players on the tee box waiting to hit their shots toward the green. One of them was a grouchy journeyman player named Bob Eastwood, who always seemed to have a bone to pick with ESPN because we never showed him on television. We weren't the only network that adopted this approach to Bob Eastwood's golf game, but we were the only network flying a helicopter right above his head first thing on a Tuesday morning. Bob Eastwood apparently felt the funny thing to do would be to try and hit the helicopter with his golf ball, and as we flew over he did just that. I couldn't believe my eyes as I closed them, hoping there was no way in hell he could hit a moving helicopter a hundred feet above his head with a five or six iron, and not quite sure what might happen if he did.

"What the fuck?" our pilot said as he saw the same thing I did. "Did that asshole just do what I think he did?"

"I believe so," I replied in a voice slightly higher than normal.

"We gotta go around again," my cameraman, Swanny, said, oblivious to the danger, because he was looking into a viewfinder instead of out the window at a knucklehead.

"He wouldn't be so moronic as to try that again," said the pilot, bringing the chopper around for a second pass.

"Couldn't be," I said/thought, but I was wrong. As we started for the green a second time, I saw Eastwood fire another golf ball in our direction. The fact that he was such a bad shot that he couldn't hit us did nothing to diminish the outrage I felt as we flew over the 18th hole and completed our mission. Once on the ground, I related the incident to a PGA TOUR rules official, who assured me action against Eastwood would be taken. I got back to the television compound and told the same story to Andy Young and asked him never to show that jerk on TV again, even if he was winning a tournament.

"Hadn't planned on it," was all Andy said.

OH, HOW THE YEARS GO BY

Bob Eastwood didn't win the Hawaiian Open that year. I'm not sure he even made the cut and, quite frankly, I couldn't have cared less, then or now. Historically the PGA TOUR golf season is a long one. Events start in January and continue, for some pros, all the way through the chance to compete on tour the following season at the annual qualifying tournament that ends the first Monday in December. In the early 1990s, four television networks shared in producing and broadcasting PGA TOUR events: CBS aired the most, followed by NBC, ABC, and then ESPN. Our crew was responsible for a handful of tournaments, mostly considered less important by many, like the Hawaiian Open, the New England Classic, the Southern Open, and the Hardees Golf Classic. Despite not being marquee events, those tournaments often featured marquee players and, on more than one occasion, those marquee players claimed the trophy on our air. It was always a thrill to be the network of record when Nick Price, Paul Azinger, Mark O'Meara, and Greg Norman won PGA TOUR events. Our ESPN team produced the TOUR Championship coverage that aired on ABC in 1992 when Paul Azinger won with a putter nicknamed "The Thing" because the head was only slightly bigger than the golf ball. They were all established players with big-league resumes and bulging bank accounts, but one of the most notable winners in my four years of work for ESPN's golf division came thanks to a kid with no professional experience.

PGA TOUR tournament fields are filled each week with professionals who qualify to play thanks to a lengthy, and sometimes complicated, list of eligibility requirements ranging from past championships to the position in which they finished on the previous year's money list to the number of "cuts" made in a player's career. In all, there are thirty-three ways a PGA TOUR player can qualify for the privilege of playing in a given event. If a player finishes between number one and 125 on the 2011 money list, he can play in any tournament he likes in 2012. If he wins an event in 2011, he is what they call exempt (or can play in any PGA TOUR event) for two full years, and if he happens to be fortunate enough to win one of the four major championships (the Masters, US Open, British Open, or PGA Championship), the ability to play anytime, anywhere is extended to five full years.

In addition to those players with various kinds of status, the PGA TOUR also gives people with nothing more than a great golf game and the desire to compete a chance to play through outlets, including Monday qualifying and sponsor's exemptions. Monday qualifying rounds are played almost every week on tour and offer a glimmer of hope to anybody who plops down the entry fee and wants to test his or her game against the best in the world. It's a one-day tournament, with hundreds of hopefuls playing for four starting positions. Most are pros who, for one reason or another, have lost their exempt status and tee it up every Monday, knowing they are one swing change, made putt, or good break away from getting back on tour full time. But some are dreamers, plain and simple, playing on a prayer. Dreams do come true, but it's rare. Arjun Atwal got into the Wyndham Championship in 2010 as a Monday qualifier and then went on to win the event. It was the first time in a quarter century that someone had accomplished that feat.

Another way to get into a PGA TOUR tournament is to obtain a sponsor's exemption. Corporations and companies spend millions of dollars each week to have their name attached to a professional golf tournament, and for that investment the company gets exposure, commercials, and a chance to have the CEO deliver a less-than-welcoming welcome message on the broadcast. Sponsors also get the opportunity to "invite" players of their own choosing to compete. Most times, this is another struggling former, or current, tour player who chooses this route instead of Monday qualifying for a second, third, or fourth chance, but sometimes it's a phenomenon. Tiger Woods was just old enough to get his California driver's license when he was offered, and accepted, an invitation to play in his first professional golf tournament, the 1992 Nissan Los Angeles Open. He shot 72 on Thursday and 75 on Friday, respectable for certain, but not good enough to make the cut and play the weekend.

Top-notch amateurs are always high on the list when sponsors consider to whom they'll extend an invite and, while it makes for decent public relations and generates some buzz, it rarely results in memorable results. It did in 1956 when officials running the Canadian Open asked twenty-three-year-old Canadian-born amateur Doug Sanders to enter. He played, captured lightning in a bottle, and won. That particular form of lightning didn't strike again for another thirty years, until the 1984 US Amateur Champion; Oklahoman Scott Verplank was invited to play in and then won the 1985 Western Open. Then it happened again, six years later, and I was lucky enough to help document it.

Before Tiger Woods dominated the American amateur golf scene, Phil Mickelson ruled the roost. Born in San Diego, California, in 1970, Mickelson took to the game early and, even though he was right-handed, he learned to swing the club left-handed by mirroring his father's right-handed swing.

He excelled at the game in high school and then became the face of American amateur golf while attending Arizona State University. Mickelson was just the second player to be named to the NCAA All America Team all four years in school, and won three straight NCAA individual golf championships, three Haskins Awards (signifying the country's top collegiate player), and the 1990 United States Amateur Championship. Our ESPN announcers talked about all of those accomplishments as he walked the fairways of the Tucson National Golf Resort and Spa and the TPC at Starr Pass (the tournament was contested on two courses between 1990 and 1996). He caused quite a stir by shooting a first round 65 and finding himself near the top of the leaderboard. A second round 71 wasn't as impressive, but he made the cut easily, and we had an interesting storyline heading into the weekend. Andy Young did what some producers do in that type of situation and sent us out early the next day to interview Phil, capture his swing on tape for expert analysis, and find out what we could find out about the young collegiate star. Mickelson wore the back of his collar turned up, carried an easy smile, and struck me as a polished, private guy, even then. He answered every question by saying all the right things,

"Are you surprised to be in contention?" I asked.

"I knew I had the game to compete, but these guys are the best players in the world," he answered.

"What are your expectations this weekend?" I continued.

"I just want to take it one shot at a time and try my best," he replied.

"Are you nervous?" I wanted to know.

"No," he offered, and I believed him.

We did find out that his caddie was Steve Loy, his golf coach at ASU; his sister also played golf; and he felt his short game (chipping and putting) was his strength. We recorded a couple of swings, thanked him, wished him well, and went back to edit what we had on tape. Phil then went out and shot 65 on Saturday and teed it up in the final round with a chance to win and be a part of history. His Sunday 71 seemed to show that he might have been more nervous than he claimed or, then again, it could have just been an early look into the window of what would become the wonderful world of Mickelson's golf game. He would hit a wayward shot off the tee and find himself in trouble in the Arizona desert or behind a cactus. But then he would wow the gallery and boggle our minds with a beautiful approach to the green. After 69 shots, he stood in the middle of the fairway on the tournament's 72nd hole, knowing he needed to make a birdie to beat tour veterans Bob Tway and Tom Purtzer, who had just finished. Mickelson and Loy (who would leave coaching and become Phil's agent when he turned pro) discussed the strategy, agreed on the shot, and then Mickelson selected a wedge, took one deep breath and two practice swings, then launched the ball toward the intended target. It landed on the green, took one hop and spun to a stop eight feet from the hole. Hatless, he smiled and waved, acknowledging the crowd all the way to the green. The birdie putt broke slightly from Phil's left to his right and was, as so many Mickelson putts would be in the future, pure. The ball rolled right into the middle of the hole; Phil took two steps to his left and pumped his fist. The crowd roared and so did the TV truck tape room, but Andy Young and Steve Beim were cool and collected as they delivered commands.

"Swanny, give me the crowd," ordered Beim.

"Recue the reax on red," said Young at the same time.

"Dawg, you have the family, stay with the family," continued the director.

"Cue up the line cut on one machine, the low angle slow mo on another, and the reaction again on a third," Young said to me.

"Putt's on white, low angle on blue, and fist pump on gold," I immediately replied.

"Record the hug somewhere!" they both said in unison.

"Got it on the line record and on red," I assured them both.

Golf is often described as a slow sport, even sleep inducing, and for good reason if you are watching it from the comfort of your living room couch. It is anything but that in a TV truck. The orchestration and cooperation to make a historic tournament finish air without a hitch is impressive, especially when you are in the middle of it, and incomparable when you are the one delivering the commands. Phil Mickelson celebrated a great achievement that day, but, because he was still an amateur, the first and second place money was split between Purtzer and Tway. Phil did receive a very cool, solid gold conquistador helmet, and he served notice that he would soon be a force in the world of golf. We celebrated a clean broadcast and the knowledge that we were lucky enough to get to do it again the next week.

Phil returned to Tucson and won another gold helmet four years later, and this time got to keep the winner's check, but by then, I was in charge of another television golf tournament production truck, thousands of miles away.

CALLING ON A NEW CAREER

Years before now, NBC golf announcer Gary Koch made his famous, to golf fans, "Better than most, better than most" call of Tiger Woods's birdie putt on the island green of the TPC Sawgrass's 17th hole. Years before that, he was better than a lot of guys on the golf course, and six times on the PGA TOUR, he was better than everybody. Born in Baton Rouge, Louisiana, Koch grew up loving golf and, after a successful high school career, he attended the University of Florida on a golf scholarship. He was a big part of a team that won the Southeastern Conference title and an NCAA Championship in 1973, and Koch would later join teammates Woody Blackburn, Phil Hancock, Andy Bean, and Andy North on the PGA TOUR. His first pro victory came in 1976 at the Tallahassee Open, and his best year on tour was 1984, when he won twice, including the prestigious Bay Hill Classic, a tournament hosted by Arnold Palmer and played on a course of his design. The last time Koch won was four years after that, in Southern Nevada, at the Panasonic Las Vegas Invitational, a tournament that aired on ESPN and was produced by Andy Young.

Golf announcers come and go. As I write this, the NBC team is calling the action at the Players Championship with Dan Hicks, Johnny Miller, Koch, Dottie Pepper, Mark Rolfing, and Peter Jacobsen, but it wasn't that long ago that Bob Murphy was part of that team, or Peter Oosterhuis was a constant, consistent presence during CBS telecasts.

Almost everyone on a network golf broadcast is a former or, thanks to the Champions Tour for guys over fifty, a current player. There are exceptions, most notably Peter Kostis on CBS (he's an instructor) or Jimmy Roberts on NBC (he's a reporter), but former players are the backbone of golf announcing. That's true in every sport, not just golf. Networks employ former athletes to serve as expert analysts for their sports coverage, but thanks to a multitude of games and events and expanded coverage on Golf Channel, regional sports networks, and the Internet, it seems a greater number of announcers are needed to cover baseball and golf than other sports. It was much more competitive in 1990. When I started working for Andy and Steve, the announce team, depending on the event, was anchored by Jim Kelly (the only nongolfer) as the host or play by play announcer, and then a list of former players including Bob Murphy, Jim Colbert, Jim Nelford, Andy North, John Schroeder, and others. Colbert had been a part of the team for years, but was closing in on his fiftieth birthday and was looking forward to rekindling his competitive juices on the Senior Tour. Murphy was two years younger, so his role in the booth seemed secure for several more years, but Andy was looking for someone to take Colbert's place as the team's top on-course commentator. Murphy, like Gary Koch, went to the University of Florida and knew Koch well. Because of that friendship, Bob Murphy knew the toll the game had taken on his fellow Gator, and was well aware that Koch was tired of the grind of professional golf. He also knew that Koch knew: as his game and the desire to play it deteriorated, his chances of winning again on Tour diminished. Murph (as everyone called Bob) spoke with Koch, and then went to Andy Young to tell him: he thought he had found the perfect replacement for Colbert. Andy respected Murph's opinion and, after a brief meeting with Koch, agreed to give Gary a shot at an upcoming event. Murph was right; Gary Koch made an impressive debut and Andy asked him to join the team.

Thanks to his impressive USGA Junior Amateur Championship and, more importantly, his six PGA TOUR wins, Koch had the resume to be instantly accepted by every player on Tour. His work ethic, intelligence, and desire to learn and get better every week won over his new colleagues in television. From the very first event, Koch worked hard, did his research, and brought his best effort to every broadcast. Covering golf as an on-course reporter is not as easy as it looks, or, perhaps more descriptively, as it sounds. You need to get out in front of the action to report on every circumstance that a player may face as he contemplates what to do with his next shot. Does he have a good lie? Are there trees or other hazards, like lakes or bunkers, between his ball and the hole? Which way will the putt for birdie, par, or bogey break? Those are some of the absolutes; but on-course reporters are also expected to comment on intangibles, like what is the player *thinking*? Or, *how many different approaches can he take* to playing a particular shot? Because the on-course announcer was once a player, the supposition is that he himself faced similar circumstances and can intelligently report on not only the absolutes, but especially the intangibles, and, in that regard, Koch was better than most.

The on-course reporter is also required to be in the proper position to be able to give an effective account of the shot and do it all while not distracting the professional who is trying to make a living or win a golf tournament. In the early days of golf on television, announcers spoke in hushed, reverential tones; many actually whispered, not because they had to, but because they wanted to—thinking it made them sound more "golfy"; but Ohlmeyer, and then his successor Young, would have none of that,

"Get into a position where you can use your normal conversational tone of voice," I heard Don, then Andy, say over and over again.

"If you have to whisper, you're in the wrong spot," both cautioned announcers on a number of occasions.

"If you whisper on my air, you can turn in your equipment," Don Ohlmeyer only had to say once.

That equipment was another issue, and sometimes a burden. The on-course announcer wore a headset, with muffs sometimes covering both ears, attached by a cord, plugged into a belt weighted down by batteries to power the gear. Also plugged into the belt was a microphone that the announcer held to his or her mouth when ready to speak. But the microphone wasn't the only thing an on-course announcer took with him to the fairways. Each announcer had notes on the players he would be assigned to cover, as well as a yardage book that had detailed descriptions of every hole on the course. Koch kept all of that together with a clipboard and then, ingeniously, held the clipboard in front of his mouth when he spoke to block the noise. He also instinctively knew to turn his body into the wind so his voice could not carry toward the players. The microphone featured a switch that, if pointed in one direction, put the announcer's voice and call of the shot on the air for everyone to hear. If the switch was flipped to the other direction, the announcer could speak exclusively to the production team in the truck, specifically the producer.

We had all travelled to the Glen Abbey Golf Course just outside of Toronto to televise the Canadian Open. The national championship of Canada had been contested since 1904 and won by some of golf's biggest names, including Armour, Hagen, Snead, Nelson, Palmer, Weiskopf, and Trevino. In subsequent years Greg Norman, Curtis Strange, and our own Bob Murphy all captured the tournament title, but, surprisingly, it was one of golf's few prominent national championships that had never been won by Jack Nicklaus. The tournament had a rich and interesting history, and Gary Koch was about to add to it. Koch's job was to follow and report on the action of the final group of the day, the leaders; and, as was his custom, he would position himself just ahead of the action to give himself a good look at the circumstances the players faced. He would then find the ideal spot from which to describe the action to our national and, in this case, worldwide audience. It was Sunday and the leaders were making their way to the 17th green, and Koch was in the moment and out ahead of the action. That is what Koch was doing when he flipped the switch on his announce pack and told the truck:

"Andy, I'm down."

"Audio, Gary's equipment isn't working," was how Andy responded, assuming that when Gary said he was "down," he meant his microphone.

The audio team heard it, I heard it, and Gary Koch heard it, and this is what we all heard next:

"No, not my gear, me. *I'm down!* I think I broke my ankle."

"Well, that sucks," Andy deadpanned. "Never mind, audio," he continued. "Office, can we get medical out to Gary Koch."

Gary had, indeed, broken his ankle by awkwardly stepping in a depression created by a sprinkler head near the green. He was taken to, and spent the night in, a Canadian hospital, spent the next couple of years honing his craft on Andy Young's announce team, and then was hired by Tommy Roy and NBC, where he has been a mainstay of their Emmy Award-winning golf coverage for nearly twenty years.

PAYING HOMAGE

A wise man (who you will actually meet later in this story) once said, "TV is like sausage; everybody likes it but nobody wants to see how it's made." Since I have already put the screws to that particular rule of thumb earlier in this tale, I might as well do it again. With that in mind, I hope you'll indulge me as I explain a little of the history and subsequent advancement of the way we are all able to watch golf on TV.

Frank Chirkinian is widely regarded as the "godfather" of television golf production, and rightfully so, but he wasn't a part of golf's first nationally televised tournament. That honor went to the folks at ABC, who brought the Tam O' Shanter World Championship into America's living rooms in 1953. Five years later, Chirkinian led his CBS Sports team's production of the PGA Championship at Llanerch Country Club near his home in Philadelphia, Pennsylvania, and the impact of his ideas was immediate. Until Chirkinian got in the truck, golf was a mostly silent sport on TV. The only sound you heard was that of an announcer watching on a monitor. That wouldn't work for Frank. He's quoted as saying, "Golf was like watching silent movies. It drove me crazy." So he fixed that. One of Chirkinian's early modifications put microphones on tee boxes and near greens so people at home could hear the natural sounds of the game. He followed that up with innovations like cameras mounted on cranes, in blimps, and on the shoulders of cameramen actually out in the fairways. He added "on-course announcers" who followed the action of particular players, up close and personal, and he developed communication devices that allowed him to speak with his announcers during a broadcast and, from what I'm told, he used that device liberally.

Chirkinian counts something else as the thing he "is most proud of." It was his idea in 1960 to list, on the screen, the player's score in relation to par instead of the total strokes struck during a tournament. All of a sudden, golf fans and viewers didn't have to be mathematicians to enjoy the game on TV. Instead of listing a player having taken 245 strokes, Chirkinian now showed that player at 17 under par. Immediately, fans of Arnold Palmer or Gary Player or Billy Casper or Don January knew exactly where their favorite player stood in the tournament. In addition to the roving announcers, Frank's team consisted of a host and an expert analyst (a former player on Tour) as well as announcers housed in treehouselike enclosures behind the greens at the four finishing holes. The host and his analyst partner occupied the "tower" behind the green at 18. The names included Summerall, Venturi, Wright, Melnyk, Nantz, McCord, Feherty, and more. They all followed Chirkinian's orders (and he barked them out like a military commander) or risked facing his legendary wrath. He was known affectionately, and not so affectionately, as "the Ayatollah," and he earned that nickname by ruling his broadcasts with an iron fist. He produced golf at CBS for thirty-nine years, won four national Emmy and two Peabody Awards, and was elected into the World Golf Hall of Fame by emergency vote on February 9, 2011. He died on March 4 of that year at the age of eighty-four. Gone now, but not forgotten. Never humble, he left the game with an amazing legacy and these words:

"I was probably the most inventive and brilliant person who ever worked in television. I have done so many things I can't remember half of them."

I met Frank Chirkinian on several occasions and he was always nice to me; I'm not sure he would have been as nice had I worked for him.

Even though Frank Chirkinian was making a major impact, golf was a minor sport on TV. Tournaments traditionally start on Thursday, but in the '60s and '70s, you couldn't see the action anywhere, other than the actual golf course on which the tournament was being played, until the weekend; and even then, only for ninety minutes at a time. My friend Karel Schliksbier helped announcer and former US Amateur Champion Steve Melnyk in his CBS tower behind the 15th green at tournament courses all over America. Karel remembers fondly that there were dozens of times when a program or sporting event (probably college basketball) that aired before golf coverage ran overtime on CBS, meaning the network got to its golf coverage later than expected. Because of that poor timing, the leaders or last few players on the course had already played and finished the hole at which Steve and Karel set up shop. The players were on to the 16th, and they were off to the bar. That changed with ESPN, the USA Network, and Tiger Woods.

OHLMEYER INNOVATES AS WELL

Don Ohlmeyer was born in 1945, grew up in Chicago, graduated from the University of Notre Dame with a degree in communications, and began his television career under the watchful eye of Roone Arledge at ABC in New York. Arledge helped start the network's sports division and provided the vision for ABC's first college football broadcast: a game between the Alabama Crimson Tide and the Georgia Bulldogs, in Birmingham, won by 'Bama 21–6. In addition to college football, Arledge also brought the weekly sports series *Wide World of Sports* to television and coined its famous catchphrase, "the thrill of victory and the agony of defeat." *Wide World of Sports* was the precursor of tape-delayed sports broadcasts utilizing the newest technology with the ability to expediently get the footage back to the New York studios for broadcast. Arledge hired Jim McKay to be the host and enlisted young creative minds like Chuck Howard and Don Ohlmeyer to work on the production side. Roone Arledge was named president of ABC Sports in 1968, and, less than two years later, flipped the switch on a national sports television treasure, *Monday Night Football*. His producer was the man I was hoping would sign my paychecks in 1989, Don Ohlmeyer. *Monday Night Football* wasn't Ohlmeyer's only accomplishment while employed by ABC. He also created the popular athlete/celebrity competition series *Superstars* and produced and directed three Olympic Games broadcasts for the network. Ohlmeyer was twenty-seven years old, in the truck, and in charge during the summer of 1972 in Munich, Germany, and had control of the broadcast when ski-mask-wearing Palestinian gunmen held hostage, then murdered, eleven Israeli athletes and coaches and one West German police officer, right before our eyes.

In those years, and for many years to come, Ohlmeyer was also the producer in charge of coverage for the Indianapolis 500 on ABC won by legends like Unser, Foyt, Rahal, and Mears. In 1977, he was wooed away from ABC by rival network NBC and there served as executive producer for the network's coverage of the Super Bowl and the World Series. He also created the sports anthology series *SportsWorld*, introduced innovative production techniques, was the driving force behind NBC's "Breakfast at Wimbledon," and even broadcast a network NFL game telecast without using announcers: a production experiment I would shamelessly copy thirty years later during a Nationwide Tour golf telecast. He was at NBC (the first time) for five years and left in 1982 to form Ohlmeyer Communications Company in West Hollywood, California. At OCC he produced several made-for-TV movies, series, and specials, winning an Emmy Award in 1983 for a movie called *Special Bulletin*. But OCC was built around sports.

Ohlmeyer signed contracts with the various broadcast and cable networks allowing OCC to produce and package the Indy Car Racing series called CART as well as several PGA TOUR and most Senior Tour (now Champions Tour) golf events. He also teamed with business partners at marketing, sponsorship, and athlete representation giant IMG to create golf's Skins Game: a Thanksgiving weekend, made-for TV, hole-by-hole competition that showcased the talents and the personalities of the game's greatest players. "Skins" is a weekend-golfer gambling game that OCC and IMG took global. The game is made up of eighteen individual, one-hole tournaments; each hole is awarded a monetary value, and the player who walks away from the hole with the best score wins the money that hole is worth. If two players tie, they all are considered to have tied, and the monetary value of the hole carries over to the next one. It's a blast to play with your friends for five bucks a pop, but it took on a whole new meaning when, in 1983, Jack Nicklaus, Arnold Palmer, Gary Player, and Tom Watson played eighteen holes against each other with nearly half a million dollars on the line. I realize that doesn't seem like a lot of money, given today's elevated purses, but in 1983 the very first The Skins Game offered more total prize money than every golf event, except for the United States Open Championship; and there were only four guys playing. By the way, Gary Player won the most money that weekend—$150,000, thanks to making a four-foot par putt on the second to last hole. The Skins Game became an instant sensation, and by the time its popularity waned three decades later, every single big-name player in golf hoped to be invited and wanted to be a part of it. And so did I; but I had to get in the OCC door first.

Don Ohlmeyer was more than an innovator in terms of programming: he looked for, and came up with, new cost-effective ways to produce the events he packaged. Like Frank Chirkinian, Ohlmeyer utilized roving cameras and announcers on the golf course, but he made changes, too. Instead of putting an announcer in a "treehouse" type tower, behind the final four or five greens, he trimmed the budget and streamlined the telecast by hiring one host and one analyst and put them in an announce position near the finishing hole. He hired Roger Twibell as the play-by-play host and an Australian with twenty-eight worldwide professional wins, named Bruce Devlin, as the analyst. He then supplemented that twosome with former players who followed specific groups to report their progress from the golf course during the telecast. The camera complement on all the networks was split between what we called "hard" cameras (big, heavy, studio style cameras with large lenses) built on scaffolding behind greens, and hand-held cameras (lighter, more mobile cameras with smaller lenses) that cameramen carried on their shoulders to get the shots. At CBS, Chirkinian built four hard cameras and placed them with a camera operator behind the greens at the 15 th, 16th, 17th, and 18th holes. He then, depending on the importance of the tournament, employed as many as eight hand-held cameras to cover the rest of the action. This meant that the play on earlier greens (anything before 15) had to be covered entirely by smaller cameras with shorter lenses. For the most part that was okay because, in the early days, CBS rarely allotted more than ninety minutes of broadcast time for the telecasts. ESPN and other cable networks, on the other hand, didn't have the luxury of extra programming and both needed and wanted as much golf as they could get, and two and a half or three hours was more the norm. The mobile production trucks that ESPN owned and used for golf carried as many as eight hard cameras; and you needed two of these tractor-trailer rigs to produce a golf tournament telecast. Ohlmeyer knew the number of cameras that rested in the bellies of these eighteen-wheel behemoths and he decided to use them. He also knew that for OCC to make any money, he had to keep the purse strings as tight as possible. A person costs more than a piece of hardware—after all, you have to put a person on an airplane, put him up in a hotel room, and feed him or her—so Ohlmeyer came up with the brilliant idea of using as many hard cameras as possible (most times ten), but only hiring six people to operate them. He then devised a "move" system that had those cameramen starting on one hole and then moving to another when a specific golfer or group of golfers went through. He had the coverage he needed but kept the budget manageable. He also decided that a calling card of a golf tournament produced by OCC would be a multitude of golf shots. In fact, one observer wrote, "Ohlmeyer's style is relentless. If something moves on the golf course, he shows it on TV." He believed golf as a television sport didn't have "inherent action" so he was going to create it by machine-gunning the audience with shots. OCC produced its first event in 1984, the J. C. Penney Team Championship in Largo, Florida. Five years later I would come knocking on the door.

"SKINS" FINDS A FUNNY BONE

Jack, Arnie, Gary, and Tom played the first two TV Skins Games. I already mentioned Player won the first in 1983 and then Nicklaus won the 1984 edition by sinking a dramatic ten-foot birdie putt on the 18th hole. That single shot put $240,000 in Jack's already-sizeable bank account, but it was his reaction that helped put the television show on the map. Normally a serious, stoic competitor, Nicklaus had won seventeen major championships, countless other tournaments, and millions of dollars. He is widely regarded to be the greatest golfer who ever lived, and he rarely cracked a smile. But as a ten-foot putt on the very last hole of a made-for-television event, on the Sunday after Thanksgiving, toppled into the cup, Nicklaus uncharacteristically heaved his putter twenty feet in the air and jumped; well, he kind of hopped into the air, then ducked, hoping not to be beaned by the very club that had earned him Skins Game gold. Jack Nicklaus threw his putter in the air! Unheard of.

The next year, Jack was back to defend his crown and Arnie and Tom were there again to challenge. But in 1985, Gary Player wasn't invited: his place was taken by the 1984 United States Open Champion, a gregarious, quick-talking practical joker named Frank Urban "Fuzzy" Zoeller. He had won the Masters (some say golf's most prestigious tournament) five years earlier, but it was his Open victory in June of 1984 that endeared Zoeller to golf fans all over the world as he battled an iconic Australian named Greg Norman. Norman joined the PGA TOUR that year and won the Kemper Open a week before teeing it up in the US Open at famed Winged Foot in Mamaroneck, New York. Norman shot rounds of 70, 68, and 69 during the first three rounds and teed off on Sunday in the penultimate pairing, just in front of Zoeller and fifty-four-hole leader Hale Irwin. Irwin started the day one shot ahead of Fuzzy, but erratic play early eliminated him from contention. So, that left Fuzzy watching Norman from the fairway of each hole and sneaking peaks at the fifteen-foot-high scoreboards scattered around the golf course to see where he stood. Near the end of the day, where he stood was tied with Norman in the middle of the fairway of the 72nd hole, watching the Aussie putt on the green ahead. He clearly saw Norman over the ball, shoulders moving to stroke the putt, and his arm rose in triumph as it trickled into the cup. Zoeller, thinking the putt was for a birdie that he would have to now match to force a play-off, grabbed the big white towel hanging from his golf bag and began to wave it in the air in mock surrender. Norman bowed, then backed away to sign his scorecard and wait for Fuzzy to finish. What Fuzzy didn't know then, but would find out soon enough, was that the putt Norman made was for par and a final round 69. A relieved, delighted, energized Zoeller made his putt for par, meaning the two would play eighteen more holes on Monday for the trophy. That Monday was warm and fuzzy as Zoeller shot 67 and won by eight shots. Norman returned the favor and surrendered for real, waving his own white towel when the round ended. Norman was toast and golf fans were hooked.

So Fuzzy Zoeller brought his personality and style to the Skins Game and gave it a shot in the arm. Ohlmeyer made sure the players wore microphones and Fuzzy joked, laughed, and kibitzed all around the golf course. He also won nine skins and took home $255,000; good enough for first place and an invite back in 1986. He returned and repeated in 1986, capturing four-teen of the eighteen skins and winning another $370,000; but even though the winner was the same, there were a couple of huge differences. For the first time, golfers and golf fans all over the world got a peek at the brand new PGA West Stadium Course designed by Pete Dye. The course featured railroad ties, yawning bunkers, and an infamous island green at the 17th hole—a hole he dubbed "Alcatraz." That year, 1986, was also the debut of the "Merry Mex," Lee Trevino. Fuzzy Zoeller was a showboat, but Lee Trevino commanded an entire fleet. He won six major championships, including the 1971 US Open, where he famously tossed a rubber snake at Jack Nicklaus before the start of the final round. At the age of forty-four, he remarkably won the 1984 PGA Championship, putting him back in the spotlight and in line for a Skins Game invite. He took advantage of it in 1986, finishing second to Fuzzy; but the interaction, especially with Zoeller, made Trevino an automatic invitee in Don Ohlmeyer's mind for three more years.

The 1987 Skins Game was a Trevino masterpiece. The competition was played over the course of two days, the first nine holes on Saturday and the final nine on Sunday. After day one Fuzzy Zoeller and Jack Nicklaus had each won four holes to tie for the lead. Trevino earned one skin and was a distant third. Then he grabbed Sunday by the throat. The 9th hole at the PGA West Stadium course is a slight dogleg right, around a big blue water hazard guarding the right side of the green. Ohlmeyer had decided he wanted the hole to be cut as close to that water hazard as possible without making the shot unfair. Zoeller, Nicklaus, and Palmer all played from the fairway and, with discretion as the better part of valor, played safe toward the middle of the green. Trevino hit last and saw an opening. He pulled a short iron and hit the shot he was famous for, a low-flying bullet that moved softly in the air from left to right. It landed on the green, bounced once, then again, and then hopped right into the hole for an eagle two. The crowd roared, Zoeller laughed out loud, and Trevino, ever the showman, gave his club a little toss in the air, then turned to the camera and said:

"I don't know what all the excitement is about. That's what I was aiming at."

Then, chuckling, he jogged up to the green.

That wasn't the only roar Trevino earned that day; the last and loudest came at Alcatraz. The tee at the picturesque par three sits a hundred or so feet above the clear blue water and the green below. The shot can be anything from a nine iron to a four iron, depending on the wind, but there was none that particular Sunday in November. Trevino reached into his golf bag, carried by longtime friend and caddie Herman Mitchell, and grabbed his six iron: he had the honor, so he hit first. Trevino never took long to play and there was no reason to now. He swung, launching the ball high into the air against the cloudless blue Southern California sky. "When I hit it, I knew it was close," the Merry Mex would say later, but close wasn't exactly what it turned out to be. The ball landed on the green and headed straight for the hole; and just like the shot on number 9, it didn't stop until it found the bottom of the cup for a hole in one, the first ever in a Skins Game. The crowd around the green went crazy and the dozen or so people in the production truck went crazier, but up on the tee out on the golf course there was stunned silence. Jack Nicklaus quipped, "He was speechless. I think that's the first time in my life I've heard him shut up," but the silence didn't last long. Trevino asked anyone within earshot if the ball had indeed gone in the hole and, when the answer was affirmative, he danced in the air and waved his sombrero-embroidered ball cap. Then he hugged and danced with Herman, all while Nicklaus, Palmer, and Zoeller waited, knowing they still had to play and one of them had to match Trevino's ace to save the skin. Of course they didn't, and Trevino reigned as champion. The shot was replayed later that day in a halftime update during an NFL telecast. The Skins Game had arrived completely. I know all this because I was fortunate enough to have access to the tapes and I watched the highlights of early Skins Games hundreds of times. Trevino's last Skins Game was 1989, my first was 1990; but I would get my fair share of the Merry Mex throughout the course of my career.

I GET "SKINNED"

Because a different mobile unit was assigned for the 1990 Skins Game, the production personnel setup was different from anything I had previously encountered. Previous events found me performing my duties in a separate truck, affectionately called the "B Unit," but for this, the biggest tournament production of an OCC career still in its infancy, I was stationed in the same truck as the main control room. The truck was configured in side-by-side fashion so the tape room (so called because that's where you could find both tape machines and tape machine operators) was on the left and the control room was on the right, the two separated by only inches and a sliding glass door.

In the control room the producer, in this case Don Ohlmeyer, sat in the left-hand seat closest to the tape room door. To his right was the director, Steve Beim, and on Steve's other side was the technical director, Dave Mazza. At every early Skins Game with which I was associated, Don ruled the roost. He was impressive in size and stature, to say the least, but what struck me most was the fact that he was held in such high regard, not only by network executives, but every single person on the crew, from the director all the way down to the utility who pulled camera cables or plugged in microphones. They loved Don and he loved them back. That's not to say he wasn't feared; he was. He demanded maximum effort and meticulous execution from everyone, and no one wanted to let him down or incur his wrath, including and, at the 1990 Skins Game, especially the new kid on the OCC block, me.

Don Ohlmeyer was a big man with a huge laugh that would at the same time, envelope and embrace you. He also had a big voice that seemed to get exponentially bigger when it was directed at you. TV producers and directors yelled back then, some still do, but in the '70s, '80s and early '90s, it seemed to be part of the job description. It was an era in sports television before lawsuits were filed over something as silly as hurt feelings or as sinister as sexual harassment. People were picked on and some producers took advantage of technicians and talent with thin skin. Some yelled simply to cover up their own inadequacies and mistakes, while others screamed because they had gained a reputation as a screamer and had to live up to that reputation every show. They yelled and screamed and swore all the time, every show. Ohlmeyer, on the other hand, only yelled when something happened that he felt adversely affected his ability to advance the story he was trying to tell during a broadcast. He could also cut the knees out from under you without ever raising his voice and that, in so many ways, was a much more intimidating and effective punishment. There are dozens of stories about that, but one I remember best was told to me by a friend on the crew and confirmed by others who frequently worked OCC shows. It was at an auto race, and one of the camera operators was having a particularly rough day. After being unable to adequately execute a command, in this case fill the screen with, and follow, a certain car around a turn and down the subsequent straightaway on several occasions. Don expressed his frustration the first few times and then finally he had had enough. He opened up the communication link between himself and *all* the cameramen and calmly said to the one who had offended him:

"Turn your camera around and point it at yourself." The operator, knowing he was in hot water, did as instructed and, while staring unsmilingly into the lens, he heard Ohlmeyer say through his headset, "I wanted to get a picture of this because it's the last time I'm ever going to see your face. Now do your best to find and lock off a beauty shot and take the rest of the day off."

He chose incomplete coverage over incompetence that day and every day.

There are many things about Don O. that I will never forget. At times he seemed larger than life, almost like one of the characters in his award-winning made-for-TV movies. He would sit in his producer's chair, acutely aware of every image in the more than fifty monitors that glowed in front of him, knowing innately the significance of each. He issued commands with, at various times, a cigarette, a can of Coke, or a hot dog, and sometimes all three, in his oversized hands. If he weren't so talented it would have tickled your funny bone. He was also extremely generous. Christmastime at OCC was a time of great anticipation because everyone knew that one day, usually the Friday before the holiday break, Don would don his custom-made Santa Claus suit and clamber down the office's spiral staircase, booming "Ho Ho Ho" and handing out always-more-than-you-figured-you'd-get bonus checks. He wasn't easy or particularly forthcoming with compliments, so when you got one, it meant something. The same way, it meant something when he let you know he was displeased with your performance, like he did with me Thanksgiving weekend 1990.

My job title during that show was associate producer and, in addition to writing and editing all of the teases and player feature packages, it was my responsibility to record golf shots, player reactions, and assorted interesting images during the telecast. I performed those last three particular duties physically standing in the tape room just a few feet, and a closed sliding glass door, away from Don O.

A golf show tape room is the busiest place in any production truck during any sporting event on the planet. It is today, and it was that day in 1990. It was a mosaic of spinning reels, flashing buttons, and fast-moving fingers. Nearly every image at which a camera points is recorded and available for the producer to decide its worthiness for broadcast. The tape machines were in constant motion, and we identified them by colors to separate and tell them apart. State-of-the-art mobile production technology in 1990 meant videotape was packaged in sixty- or ninety-minute reels mounted on half a dozen six-foot-tall machines. The tapes started, spun, stopped, and rewound to either play a certain golf shot or go back in record mode to capture the next one. Most of the action at Skins was shown live, so whatever happened was captured and beamed directly via satellite all over the globe. This time we were broadcasting the Thanksgiving event on a tape-delayed or prerecorded basis, so the competition took place in the morning but didn't appear on television until later in the day. But just because it aired later didn't mean you could ask Curtis Strange or Jack Nicklaus to repeat or replay a shot. It wasn't a movie unencumbered by immediacy; it was a live sporting event, and you had one chance and one chance only to capture each part of the passion play. Tape delay does give a producer some flexibility, and while he or she can't manipulate the action, he can massage time. It may take four players twenty minutes in real time to play a golf hole, but through the magic of videotape that can be accomplished in half the time by eliminating the unnecessary activity. If a player failed to execute a shot in a satisfactory manner, Don could choose to show that shot out of chronological order or even eliminate it altogether and simply start a segment with the next player's different, better-executed play.

So there I stood, over the shoulders of my friends Ed Kaufholz and Ed Beddingfield, working away, issuing commands to put "camera 4 into red and 7 green into blue" as we watched and recorded all of the golf shots played by four of the game's best players. I had four machines at my disposal (red, white, blue, and gold), each Ed operating two, as Don prepared to begin another segment of the show with an approach shot from Jack Nicklaus. He counted the crew and announcer team back from the intended commercial break, and the segment started with Nicklaus over the golf ball ready to play. I expertly ordered one Ed to record the Nicklaus approach shot in the red tape machine. Jack made contact and hit an indifferent shot that bounded off the back of the green. Ohlmeyer immediately decided he wasn't willing to begin that particular segment with that exact shot, so the red machine rolled on as Don said to all, "Forget that, Curtis is next, so we'll come back with that in five, four, three, two, and go, Vinnie." Vin Scully smoothly began again as Curtis pulled a club, addressed the ball, and swung.

What followed was another unsatisfactory result for Strange, and especially Ohlmeyer, who decided he was not going to start the segment with that shot either. Both shots were "killed" as far as the beginning of a segment, but they lived back to back right in front of me on good old red. Only Nick Faldo and Greg Norman remained as Ohlmeyer stopped Scully again and prepared to begin anew for the third time. Cameras moved into position as the always-deliberate Faldo prepared to play and Ohlmeyer barked out his next set of instructions,

"Okay, here we go again, Vinnie, with Faldo in seven, six, five, recue Nicklaus and recue Strange, two, one, and we're back." In case you didn't realize, what Don had said after five and before two was meant for me.

Immediately I deduced that I had screwed myself by not putting the two previous shots on different colored machines, and the reaction in the tape room confirmed my suspicions. Don was going to want to show Nicklaus and Strange via videotape after Faldo and Norman played, and I knew he wasn't going to be able to do what he wanted because I had misunderstood the original orders. It wasn't that Don didn't want those two shots at all, he just didn't want them at the moment they were struck, but he wanted them now. There was nothing for me to do but face the music so I keyed on to Steve Beim.

"Uh, Steve, we have a problem," I sputtered.

"What's up?" the director inquired.

"Don can't have Nicklaus *and* Strange because they're on the same machine," I admitted.

"Nice, but that actually sounds like *you* have a problem, not *we*. So *you* tell him," my friend said, covering his butt.

"Tell him what?" I heard the great Don Ohlmeyer say in the background.

"Don, it's Keith," I said after opening Ohlmeyer's channel. "Nicklaus and Strange are on the same machine," I managed to repeat without crying.

It wasn't what I heard next that is so solidly etched in my memory. It was what I saw as the sliding glass door started to slide open. The back of Don's chair appeared and then there was the man himself, who leaned back, looked me in the eye, and yelled, "What the *FUCK* is going on in tape?" as he rolled forward and slammed the door closed.

"Won't happen again, sir," I said, as we cued up the first of the two offending golf shots.

"You bet your ass it won't," I heard Don through Steve's channel. I also heard Steve chuckling. Don and I were both right; it never happened again.

IN THE "NICK" OF TIME

That Skins Game was memorable for me because of the personal baptism by fire, but golf fans probably remember it for the improbable playoff performance of Curtis Strange. As I mentioned earlier, Skins is set up as a hole-by-hole competition; but if two people tie for the low score on a hole, all four players tie and the money carries over to the next hole. That was also true on the first playoff hole if the competition wasn't decided in the regularly scheduled eighteen holes. If it went more than one playoff hole, then the worst score of the four would be eliminated. The 1990 Skins Game needed extra holes, and Norman, Faldo, Nicklaus, and Strange continued on. The 10th and 18th holes at the Stadium Course at PGA West are separated by a lake and run parallel to one another, and that was where the playoff would take place, starting at 10 and then on to 18 and back to 10 and on to 18, until one person played the hole better than the rest to take home the cash. The first time they played the hole, two tied, so all moved on to the next, where Nicklaus couldn't manage to keep up, so his day was done, and Norman, Faldo, and defending champion Curtis Strange went back to the 10th tee to play the third playoff hole. Norman found the fairway with his tee shot, as did Faldo, and then it was Curtis' turn. His shot was less than ideal and headed left, dangerously close to the water hazard that guarded the fairway. Norman's approach found the green, but ended up twenty-five feet from the hole;

Faldo did much better, sticking a pitching wedge to less than ten feet; and then it was Strange's turn. His ball was inside the lines that defined the water hazard, but not actually in the water, so it was playable; but to accomplish that, Curtis would have to stand in the lake to hit the ball. So off came the shoes, then the socks, which was followed by the rolling up of the pant legs; and the two-time US Open Champion dipped his lily-white feet into the murky water alongside the 10th fairway. To complicate matters, his ball had settled dangerously close to some rocks, so making clean, solid contact with his Titleist was problematic. He made a couple of rehearsal swings and then settled in to hit the shot, knowing that his ball could go anywhere or nowhere. Where it went was within five feet of the hole in one of the more amazing shots in both golf and Skins Game history. Curtis laughed; the people still in attendance cheered, and Norman gave Strange a tip of his then-famous wide-brimmed hat. Faldo wandered up to the green in a world of his own. On the green, Norman missed his putt and both Faldo and Strange made theirs, so the fourth playoff hole would be a twosome: Curtis Strange and Nick Faldo. I should mention that Curtis Strange had already won $150,000 and, effectively, the 1990 Skins Game title. Nicklaus left with seventy grand and Norman departed with $90,000, after failing to make birdie on the third playoff hole. Faldo was in possession of Skins worth $70,000 as they approached playoff hole number four, which was worth another $70,000 because of carryovers. Even though Faldo couldn't overtake Strange, there was money still on the table—money for which most people not named Nick Faldo would consider worth playing a hole or two or four of golf.

Englishman Nicholas Alexander Faldo wasn't well liked: not by his fellow professionals, most fans, and nearly every member of the media. But he was, at the time, the best pro golfer in the world. Nick was a taciturn perfectionist who preferred his profession to people. He had little regard or time for questions about his methods or those he considered unworthy to ask them. The golf world watched his every move during his preparation for, and participation in, a tournament, especially major championships, but as far as Nick Faldo was concerned, he operated within a very small space with room for only a handful of trusted companions, including his fastidious instructor, David Ledbetter, and his faithful caddie, Fanny Sunesson. Fellow professionals scanned the weekly tournament tee times, unhappy with the news that they were scheduled to play the first thirty-six holes of the event with Faldo, and many times it was even more unpleasant on the weekends. Playing the final thirty-six or eighteen holes with Nick was a double-sided coin; on one side, most weeks, it meant you were performing at high level—well positioned for a high finish or even a victory; but on the other side, it meant spending more than five hours a day with a fellow human being who would rarely say more than five words in your direction. It wasn't that Faldo was rude; he just didn't seem to acknowledge the existence of anyone other than himself when he was locked within the intensely personal struggle of constantly trying to hit the perfect golf shot. Perfection is rarely achieved in his chosen sport, but Faldo came close, particularly in what he considered the biggest tournaments: the Masters at Augusta National and his country's national championship. Between 1989 and 1992 he won six of those (three Masters green jackets and three Open Championship claret jugs).

I would later have the opportunity to be Nick's TV producer and, for at least several hours during a broadcast, his boss in 2006 when he joined our Golf Channel team. By that time he had mellowed, and I found a funny, intelligent, still somewhat conceited, very talented man who would develop into an excellent broadcaster. He had a droll sense of humor and was a deft storyteller, especially when the story was about Nick Faldo. I remember an intimate group of us having dinner one night during the Sony Open in Hawaii and Faldo was holding court, regaling us with the tale of his first face-to-face meeting with Her Majesty Queen Elizabeth II. He had been among a number of English dignitaries invited to Buckingham Palace and related, with pride and picture-perfect clarity, the account of the meeting.

"The doors opened and the whole room full of people turned to see the Queen Mum," he said, "but her entrance was preceded by her pups, a couple of cute but regal Corgies that were her constant companions." It was as if Faldo was back in that room when he continued.

"Her Majesty soon followed and was even more impressive than I'd imagined." Nick then admitted, "I was never nervous on the golf course, but when it came my turn to meet the queen, my knees began to quake just a tad," and he laughed to and, I imagine, at himself. We were rapt now and he knew it.

"She extended her hand; I took it and bowed and, when I rose, she asked who I was and exactly what I did to warrant an appearance in the royal palace." He looked us over and continued, "I'm your humble servant, Nick Faldo, Your Majesty, and I am a professional golfer." Nick then told us she allowed herself the smallest hint of a smile and looked him in the eyes and said, "Are you any good?"

Stunned, but just for a moment, Faldo told us he recovered and said, "Why, I'm the world's number one at the moment."

Releasing his hand, the Monarch, without missing a beat, said simply, "Excellent," before moving to the next in line.

Faldo spent a total of ninety-eight weeks at the top of the world golf rankings and was inducted into the World Golf Hall of Fame in 1997. He and Her Royal Highness had a chance to spend time together on at least two more occasions: once in 1998, when Faldo received the honor of Member of the Order of the British Empire, and then in 2010, when he earned the suffix "Sir" by being named Knight Bachelor, joining the likes of Elton John, Paul McCartney, Alec Guinness, Isaac Newton, and James Dyson (the guy who invented the vacuum cleaner with the ball). These days, I find Sir Nick Faldo to be delightful company, but at the Skins Game in 1990, he was actually rather boorish.

Strange and Faldo made their way to the tee box on the 18th hole for the second time in the playoff and the third time that day. It's an intimidating dogleg left with water all the way up the left side, the same lake from which Strange had, moments earlier, played his miracle recovery. Both players drove the ball in the fairway, Curtis slightly further from the hole than Nick, so he would play his second shot first. The approach from Strange was solid, if not spectacular, so it appeared unless Faldo hit a world-class second shot of his own, we were all destined for a fifth playoff hole. Competitors in the Skins Game were required to wear microphones, mostly so viewers at home could hear the lively banter between players throughout the day. Faldo was naturally reserved, and the fact that he was required, against his wishes, to wear the electronic device added even more to his reluctance to talk; but after Strange hit his lackluster shot at 18, Faldo was suddenly glib.

"How much is this hole worth?" the man who currently owned both the green jacket and the claret jug asked Executive Director Chuck Gerber, who walked the course with the players,

"Excuse me?" replied Gerber.

"What are we playing for right now?" the world's number one, now slightly more exasperated, asked again. "How much is this hole bloody worth?"

Seventy thousand dollars," Gerber answered with emphasis.

"Hardly seems worth it," quipped Faldo, who then, without a practice swing or a second thought, promptly stepped up and knocked his approach into the water hazard, giving the Skins win to Strange for the second straight year.

FROM THE MOUTHS
OF "BABES"

I attended a meeting in the upstairs conference room at OCC (although, for the life of me, I can't remember why I was invited) to discuss the upcoming Skins Game in 1992. Around the table sat the hierarchy of OCC; the brains, the brawn, the heart, and me. Ohlmeyer sat at the head of the table, flanked by the company's president, Howard Katz, and executive director, Chuck Gerber, who had a major say in the operation of the event. Also in the room was the show's director, my friend Steve Beim, who was always reverential, yet never afraid to speak his mind. Skins had been on television since 1983 and, as it approached its ten-year anniversary, remained extremely popular, claiming huge ratings, at least as far as TV golf was concerned. That year, the PGA TOUR and its members had the opportunity to play in forty-three tournaments, starting in Arizona the week of January 3 and ending across the country in Pensacola, Florida on October 30. When Ohlmeyer came up with the idea for Skins, he had, for the most part, the months of November and December all to himself. He picked Thanksgiving weekend, enlisted superagent Alistair Johnson from IMG to secure the Mount Rushmore of American golf, and he was off and running. By the time we held the meeting in OCC's upstairs conference room nine years later, the PGA TOUR had actually added one official event to its total schedule; but the winter months were littered with Skins Game

competition for golf viewers' attention. Greg Norman was playing his two-man team event, the Shark Shootout; Mark Rolfing
hosted his by-invitation-only Kapalua International; and the
Wendy's Three Tours Challenge and EMC Skills Challenge also
had dates. None of the money earned in these events counted
as official money on the PGA TOUR, but it certainly counted
in the participant's bank accounts; and players and agents were
lined up at production company and network doors, trying to
get their piece of the very lucrative pie. It had gotten to the
point that a sportswriter dubbed this part of golf's year "the silly
season," and even after nine incarnations, Don Ohlmeyer's Skins
Game still reigned supreme.

Curtis Strange won the United States Open Championship
back to back in 1988 and 1989. He was the first player in PGA
TOUR history to earn more than $1 million in a single season
(he accomplished that in 1988), and he made the Skins Game
invite list that very same year. If you ask most people in golf,
they'll tell you Curtis was never the most outgoing or likeable
guy on the PGA TOUR, but, at the end of that decade, he was
one of golf's biggest names; and those responsible for choosing the participants had begun to adopt the strategy of inviting current major champions, along with the Skins defending
champion, to join the fun. Arnold Palmer is credited with both
making golf popular and making it a television-worthy sport
in the late 1950s. The folks that followed him, around the fairways and at home in living rooms, called themselves "Arnie's
Army," and they loved their man. In 1992, he was still as popular as ever, but he had stopped being competitive, especially
on an unmerciful golf course like the Stadium Course at PGA
West. So, Arnie asked Ohlmeyer to make the 1987 Skins Game
his last. He would actually tee it up years later, in one more,
when he graciously agreed, at the last minute, to fill in for a
PGA TOUR-suspended John Daly, in 1993. In all, Palmer won

thirteen Skins and collected $245,000 in the Thanksgiving version of Ohlmeyer's creation. His record was much more impressive in the over-fifty-year-old version of the competition.

So, Strange played his first Skins Game the year after Arnold Palmer played his last. The US Open champion joined another first timer, Raymond Floyd, who had won the 1986 US Open and was widely regarded as the game's most intense competitor; Trevino, whose ace the year before made him the defending champ; and Nicklaus. Aside from the wisecracking Trevino, the 1988 edition offered few, if any, fireworks. Floyd walked away with the most skins (twelve) and a spot in the 1989 version; Trevino won five skins, and his personality was still enough to find him on the 1989 invite list, as well. Curtis Strange, on the other hand, was unfunny and unsuccessful—getting shut out in the skins wins department, making it unlikely that he would get an all-expenses-paid trip to the California desert the following year. Nicklaus won five skins; but he was Nicklaus and his invitation was, as it had been since 1983, automatic. Then Curtis did what no one had done in nearly fifty years: he won his second consecutive US Open, matching Ben Hogan, who was the last to defend the title back in 1951. The Skins Game wasn't around to celebrate Hogan's wins and offer him an invitation, but it was for Strange, and the invite went out. Surprising for those who worked on and witnessed the 1988 Skins Game, the 1989 edition offered the same four players. This time around, Curtis made sure he wouldn't have to repeat the feat of Willie Anderson and become only the second person in golf history to win three straight national championships to get invited back. He won the most skins in 1989 (twelve) thanks to a chip in on the 13th hole and a twenty-five-foot birdie on the last, making him, and of course Nicklaus, the only locks for the next go-around—the 1990 edition, which would be Jack's eighth and my first.

From 1983 through 1991 the Skins Game changed the venue on which it was played, the television network on which it was broadcast around the world, and the prize money for which its participants competed. Out of necessity, it changed those participants on several occasions. In all, twelve different players teed it up, but only one gentleman played in every single competition: Jack Nicklaus. Though Nicklaus had played in every single Skins Game and he had long been the brightest star in golf's sky, his record at Skins was less than stellar. He won once (1984), collected on average just three skins per year, and was shut out, collecting no skins, twice. Jack Nicklaus won seventy-three times on the PGA TOUR and led that league's money list eight times. He hadn't held a trophy on Tour since 1986, but he had celebrated his fifty-first birthday on January 21. The major players at OCC sat around the table and discussed who should be invited and who should not. Payne Stewart was the defending champion, so one slot was taken. The mercurial John Daly was still riding the wave of popularity among golf fans that he had first enjoyed the year before, when he came out of nowhere to win the PGA Championship at Crooked Stick in Indianapolis. He picked up seven Skins the year before and appeared to be the perfect player for this particular format. He hit it a mile, which was fun to behold, and he was inconsistent, which was even more fun to watch. But he was a train wreck. Ohlmeyer made it a priority to take excellent care of each competitor invited to his made-for-TV-money-grab. Players were wined and dined, shielded from the press, and given complete privacy. There are several amazing resorts in the Palm Springs California area, and many considered the La Quinta Resort to be the best of the best in the early 1990s. It wasn't often that a lower-level production staff person got lucky enough to stay where the top-of-the-line executives stayed, but there was an extra room at La Quinta in 1991 and, thanks to my friend Steve Beim, that room was given to me. I thought I had died and gone to heaven. John Daly was hell on wheels. I watched as he and his entourage checked in to the hotel, and the complaints were free-flowing as soon as he entered the lobby. The driver didn't recognize him at the airport, the car was cramped, it took too long to get to the resort, and by the time John arrived he was hungry, thirsty, and tired. It was a nonstop badmouthing barrage and apparently it didn't stop when he got to his room. I was told later that Daly immediately rejected the first two rooms offered by the resort and then trashed the third. John Daly may have been a great golfer, but he had committed a most egregious offense in Don Ohlmeyer's eyes—he was a petulant and unappreciative guest, so big bad John wouldn't be back. Curtis Strange had finally stopped winning (he took home the title in '89 and '90) and had clearly worn out his welcome, so, barring some miracle, Curtis had played his final Skins Game. That meant there were two open spots; but would there be another?

The subject finally came around to Nicklaus and, as far as Chuck Gerber was concerned, the conversation would be a short one. Of course Nicklaus would be invited; he was, after all, the greatest player who ever lived. First Katz, then Ohlmeyer himself, wondered if it wasn't at least worth a short conversation. Could Jack still compete? Were there younger, better choices available? The Skins Game, after all, was getting a little long in the tooth and Ohlmeyer wondered if it wasn't time to inject a little "sex appeal" into the mix. Both Greg Norman, the strapping Australian who had made his first Skins Game appearance in 1990, and Masters Champion Fred Couples, who had never before appeared at Skins, were available and chomping at the bit to compete. Tom Kite, who had won an emotional US Open at Pebble Beach on Father's Day, was also a worthy candidate. Ohlmeyer and Katz absolutely *loved* the idea of having two current major champions in the field, and Kite and Couples were penciled in to join Payne Stewart, but who would be the fourth—Nicklaus or Norman? Gerber continued to champion Nicklaus while it was clear Katz favored the younger, more competitive Norman; then Gerber tossed out what I'm sure he believed would be the clincher for the Golden Bear.

"Nicklaus is worth at least two ratings points."

As I mentioned before, The Skins Game was a ratings winner, especially for golf; in fact, five times in its first nine years, only one golf tournament could boast more viewers than Ohlmeyer's cash-for-some, fun-for-all golf party, and that was The Masters. The Skins Game could consistently claim viewership in the four to five million people range, at a time when most golf tournaments struggled to get half that many viewers, and here was Gerber standing firm on the fact that Nicklaus was responsible for as many as nearly half of them. I don't know if Ohlmeyer and Katz were skeptical, but I was and, for reasons known only to me, I blurted out, "How do you know?"

The silence, as some are fond of saying, was deafening. I considered Chuck Gerber a friend; we had played quite a bit of golf together and had lunch and dinner with one another on any number of occasions. I liked Chuck and I think he liked me, but when my question hit his ears, he turned in his chair and looked at me like he had never seen me before and had no interest in looking at me then. He didn't speak, but Howard Katz did and asked me, "What do you mean?"

I turned toward Katz slowly, certain that something thrown from Gerber's direction was about to render my response unintelligible, and looked the president of the company in the eye. When nothing knocked me out, I answered, "Mr. Gerber says Nicklaus is worth at least two ratings points, and my question is, how do you know?" I gulped, fully committed now, "You've never played a Skins Game without him."

I stopped, Ohlmeyer smiled, and Chuck Gerber dismissed me from the meeting. Greg Norman played The Skins Game for the second time in 1992, and Jack Nicklaus never played another one.

THE OCC FAMILY EXPANDS

Nineteen ninety-three was becoming an interesting year. Early on, rumors that Don was "getting out" started to spread around the office, and emotions ran the gamut between excited and worried. We had all heard the whispers: "Don's leaving," "Don's staying," "Don's selling," "Don's expanding," "Everything is changing," "Nothing is changing." But I knew something was actually happening when the great man himself called me into his office,

"Keith, you like water, don't you?" was the first and close to the only thing he said.

"Sure," I spit out, not quite understanding the question, but all the same hoping it was the right answer.

"I knew it," he continued. "That's why I'm giving you my Jet Ski." He looked at me and smiled and then went right back to the papers on his desk.

I smiled back. "Thanks," was all I could manage, and I left the office.

A couple of days later I came to work to find the registration and title to Don Ohlmeyer's two-person Sea Doo and trailer on my desk with instructions to retrieve it from the building's garage whenever I wanted. I allowed myself a moment to think I was being rewarded for a job well done and then, instantly, I had a more realistic thought. Don was trying to clean out his attic, or, in this case, his garage because he was moving on. No one knew for sure what would come next, who would still have a job, and for whom they would be working, but wherever I ended up and with whomever as a boss, I would go happily with a new toy. Of course my dream world soon crashed headlong into the real world. I had a wife, two infant children, and a house I could barely afford, so what in the world was I going to do with a damn Sea Doo?! Sell it, I thought, and sell it I did to one of the cameramen on the crew, Barry Hogenauer, who took it and put it to far greater use than I ever would have.

The rumors turned out to be true. Don was indeed selling his production company and, as it turned out, he was selling it to ESPN, but he wasn't selling us out. He made what is now reported to be more than $24 million on the transaction, but also got the guarantee that every employee of Ohlmeyer Communications Company would now be fulltime employees of ESPN, and we would enjoy all of the associated benefits, including stock options and vesting, at 100 percent levels, in retirement plans offered by our new employers, retroactive to the day we first started at OCC. So after all of these years, and despite the efforts—both positive and negative—of men like John Kosinski and Denis Sedory, I would now be receiving a paycheck from the "world-wide leader in sports." I later learned Ohlmeyer's connections to ESPN went further back. When the American Broadcasting Company (ABC) acquired ESPN in 1984, management needed help understanding the inner workings of the all-sports net-work, so they hired Don as a consultant. Ohlmeyer had recently left NBC sports and started the company for which Steve Beim, Andy Young, and I, among others, had worked. In addition to his consulting role, Don, with the financial backing of his busi-ness partner, Ross Johnson, went back to ABC and offered $60 million for a 20 percent piece of the ESPN pie. ESPN was any-thing but a moneymaker at the time, so the network agreed and gave Ohlmeyer the share he sought, along with a seat on the ESPN board of directors. In essence Don Ohlmeyer, in 1993, was part of the group that blessed the purchase of a production company and programming provider owned by Don Ohlmeyer.

We were employees of ESPN in name only, most of us anyway. Howard Katz had been Don's chief lieutenant and the chairman of OCC, and now he was moving to ESPN headquarters in Bristol, Connecticut, as an executive vice president because of the deal. To our new ESPN brethren, the rest of us were nameless, faceless, out-of-sight-out-of-mind men and women who worked on golf—a remote part of an ever-expanding sports universe that had little or no impact on the day-to-day lives of the folks at HQ. We provided dozens of hours of programming a week but rarely, if ever, dealt with the people who worked on programs that were making ESPN famous, most notably *SportsCenter.* Occasionally, producers of that flagship show would need special highlights from us, or one of our announcers to help preview or wrap up an event, but for the most part the relationship was that of distant cousins, which, by the way, was fine with us. But that didn't mean we didn't watch. We watched mainly because we were sports fans, but we also tuned in hoping to see the work we had done earlier in the day reappear on the network's number one studio show. Golf was never the most respected sport, especially on a program that concentrated on every sport, but occasionally we made the cut.

SportsCenter was, and remains, the program of record for news, human-interest stories, highlights, and scores from the world of sports. In the early 1990s, when we became part of the family, there were two main versions of the show: one at 6 p.m. Eastern Standard Time that mainly served to set up the action about to happen during the evening hours; and then another at 11 p.m. Eastern that included all the scores, highlights, and postgame interviews from the games and matches that had happened all across the country. The anchors (men and women who delivered the sports news of the day) for the 6 p.m. *SportsCenter* were Charley Steiner (who is now, with Vin Scully, the play-by-play announcer for the Los Angeles Dodgers), Robin Roberts (who now hosts *Good Morning America*) and Bob Ley (who was one of the first people hired, before the network even flipped the switch in 1979). At 11 p.m., ESPN paired Dan Patrick and Keith Olbermann. The trio at 6 p.m. was a professional group who delivered the information in a no-nonsense way; the twosome at 11 p.m. also delivered the sports news, but they were far more interesting and entertaining, and the late *SportsCenter* became appointment viewing for millions of fans, including me. Patrick and Olbermann were smart, clever, and funny, and even though we were now part of the same professional family, I hadn't even entertained the possibility of working with either one. It turned out I should have.

AGAIN A DAD

Hayley Virginia Hirshland was born February 20, 1991, on a Wednesday, at Cedars Sinai Hospital near Beverly Hills, California, with beautiful brown eyes and heart-shaped nostrils. Her younger brother, Jake Viertel, with a full head of hair and a big baby smile, followed a little more than two years later. Kathy and I were proud, partial parents. Partial, not only because we were both biased and prejudiced, but one of us wasn't always around. My dream job had me away from home more than twenty-five weeks a year, and many of those included holiday weekends during the summer, as well as Memorial Day and Thanksgiving. Our family grew as my responsibilities did the same, and eventually the two-bedroom apartment Les Kumagai had found for us years earlier had become too small. We loved the nearby neighborhood of Silver Lake and were lucky enough to find a small, cute, cottage-style house right across the street from the reservoir. Kathy and the kids stayed home when I travelled to tournaments across the country or halfway around the world, but they joined me when we could drive to events held in resort communities like Palm Springs, Ojai, or Napa. At least once a year Kathy, the kids, and I made trips to Hawaii so my mom and dad could get better acquainted with their newest grandchildren. My life was great as I worked and watched the best players in the game win tournaments that I had a hand in showing to the world. Kathy's life was clearly not as grand, as phone calls cataloging both specific and sweeping complaints continued to escalate. In an amazing display of what I can now look back on as arrogance, ignorance, and inattention, I was able to compartmentalize the protests, dismiss them as redundant and nonessential nagging, and forget them as soon as I hung up, or she hung up on me. There was one thing on which we agreed—life in Los Angeles with a home and two children was increasingly expensive, and surviving, let alone thriving, on one salary was more and more difficult. It was the end of the summer of 1993 and I knew something had to change. I either needed to make more money or it was time to leave Ohlmeyer and find something else to do.

Don had already sold his production company to ESPN and in fact was himself leaving to return to NBC as president of the network's West Coast Division. His right-hand man, Howard Katz, and lesser lieutenant, Chuck Gerber, were more and more in charge of day-to-day operations when I expressed my dilemma to Andy and Steve one night in Mexico when we were there to televise Senor Fred Funk winning the oft-interesting Mexican Open.

"I might have to quit," I blurted out as we walked to dinner.

"Is Kathy on your back again?" asked the always-sensitive Steve.

"Yeah, a little," I conceded, "but she has a point. I can't support my wife and kids on what I make right now. I've done the math and I need a big raise or I'm going to have to quit." I dipped my head and we continued walking.

"Howard and Chuck aren't going to let you quit," Andy added. "They wouldn't break up this team."

Steve nodded in agreement and then asked, "How much more do you need?"

"Twenty-five," I said. "Twenty minimum."

"Just talk to Chuck," was Andy's response.

"He'll take care of you," added Steve.

I hoped so.

Hope springs eternal, but cash is a hard and fast commodity and, unfortunately, my subsequent conversation with Chuck Gerber didn't go as well as Steve, Andy, or especially I would have liked,

"Can't do it," was the gist. "I don't have that kind of money to play with, and besides, ESPN would never agree to that much of a percentage increase year over year."

"I guess that's it then," I said, about to leave his office. "I guess I'm going to have to start to figure out what to do next."

"Sorry, pal"— Chuck tended to call people pal at inappropriate times. "Wish I could do more," he said, extending his hand.

"Me too," I said, taking it and shaking it.

THE END BECOMES A
BEGINNING

The 1993 golf season rolled along and, as it neared its end in October, it looked like Dave Stockton would lead the Senior Tour money list, thanks to six wins; and our own Bob Murphy would be the Tour's top rookie after doing the same thing Jim Colbert did, putting down the microphone and picking up the golf clubs again when he turned fifty. On the PGA TOUR, we had just watched Davis Love III win in Las Vegas, and now our broadcast team headed to Hawaii for the last event of our year, the Ping Kaanapali Classic on the Senior Tour. Kaanapali is a wonderful resort section on the island of Maui, said to be the spot where Hawaiian kings, such as Kamehameha I, came when the pressures of ruling the islands and its people became over-whelming. In the late 1700s and early 1800s, it must have been pure, pristine, and one of the prettiest places on earth, because in 2011, it's still one of the world's most beautiful spots, though no longer pure or pristine. Hotels, restaurants, and a shopping center dot the landscape, as does a golf course that in 1993, for one week, hosted the best over-fifty golfers in the world. ESPN put it on TV; I was a member of the production team, and my mom and dad were part of the volunteer corps.

Kathy, Hayley, and Jake joined me on that trip to the islands, and one night, after the kids had been put to bed, we sat around the dining room table in my parent's condo and discussed my future,

"What's the latest?" Dad asked, knowing my situation hadn't changed.

"Nothing new," was the expected reply. "Chuck still says there's nothing he can do about the number. He says his hands are tied."

"Do you believe him?" was my dad's next question.

"Not really," was my answer. "I just have a hard time believing that he can't fight for some more money," I shook my head.

"Maybe he doesn't want to," Dad said, looking away.

"What do you mean?" It was my turn to ask a question.

"I just mean, new bosses, new situation, maybe Chuck is covering his own ass and he hasn't even approached anyone else about your request." Now Dad was staring at me, and then he continued, "Does Howard know about your situation?"

"I assume so," I started to say, but saw Dad shake his head.

"Don't assume anything. Talk to Howard," he concluded.

Howard Katz scared me. Don Ohlmeyer was larger than life; a commanding, almost imperial presence that could certainly be intimidating, but he was fiercely loyal, protective of his people, and, once you got to know him, even friendly. He was a mensch and, more often than not, he wore his emotions on his sleeve. You knew when Don Ohlmeyer was angry with you, but you also knew when he wasn't. Howard, on the other hand, had a more exacting air; almost stern. I'm not sure I ever saw Howard laugh out loud and couldn't have told you, in the fall of 1993, if he liked me or hated me. Howard Katz never showed his cards. He was intimidating, and it came as no surprise that he didn't take my call when I phoned to ask for more money.

Steve Beim had a much more complex relationship with Howard. So did Andy Young; and I learned that, in an effort to be as prepared as possible if and when he did decide to have a conversation with me, Howard asked both Steve and Andy what it was I wanted. To their credit, both were true to their earlier word and told Howard that I was a valuable part of the golf team and would be difficult to replace, but having to replace me had come into play because of my financial circumstances. They also told him that I had gone to Chuck Gerber with a well-thought-out request for a raise, which had been rejected. I learned this because one day, as we were preparing for another show, Steve said to me, "Expect a call from Howard."

I don't want to give anyone the wrong impression about my dear friend Steve Beim. He was and is like a human Sour Patch Kid candy, a little rough and sour on the outside but sweet as can be if you could manage to get past the first impression. Some people never could. Steve could cut you with a word or a phrase, but he has a huge heart. He helped me so many times out of several situations that I'm sure I still have yet to repay him completely. I may never be able to adequately do that. For the most part the people who Steve doesn't like don't like him back, but the ones who have earned his trust and respect get the full measure of that back, too. He is one of my dearest friends and my daughter Hayley's godfather, but he could also be a pain in the ass.

I went to work every day waiting, hoping that call would come, but I'd leave each day disappointed when it didn't. Thankfully I could turn my attention to the upcoming Skins Game, figuring it would be my last, but hoping I was wrong. I had been involved in the game's most popular made-for-TV event since 1990 and loved every minute of the Skins and Senior Skins Game. The Thanksgiving edition featured PGA TOUR players, and the winner in 1991 and 1992 was one of golf's new breed of showmen, Payne Stewart, and he was one of the four again in 1993.

William Payne Stewart graduated from Southern Methodist University and hoped for a career in professional golf. His first attempt at the PGA TOUR qualifying tournament was unsuccessful, so he took his talents to Asia, where he competed for several years, winning twice. He finally qualified for the PGA TOUR in 1982 and won here in America that year. He won again in 1983, then for a third time in 1987, but 1989 was his breakout year. Golf, as a professional sport, is different from most because, unlike football, baseball, hockey, and basketball, it's an individual sport, not a team one. Golf, as a sport, also offers no multiyear or guaranteed contracts. An individual competes and if, during that competition, that person plays well enough on Thursday and Friday to make the cut and qualify for the weekend, then and only then does he or she earn a paycheck. The size of that paycheck depends on the score he or she shoots and how it stands in relation to what everyone else shoots. I mentioned earlier that winning tournaments does guarantee you spots in other tournaments, but it doesn't automatically earn you as much as a dollar in future prize money. You have to earn that, every round, every week.

One way a professional golfer *can* earn extra, guaranteed money is through endorsements. In 2009, Tiger Woods earned $10.5 million playing golf on the PGA TOUR, a healthy sum for sure, but he earned more than ten times that off the golf course, thanks to deals with businesses including Nike, PepsiCo, Gillette, AT&T, and General Motors. That was the eighth straight year Tiger Woods was the world's highest paid athlete. Payne Stewart was never in Tiger's stratosphere, but he did okay for himself, mostly through equipment and clothing deals. In fact, Stewart may have been more famous for what he wore on the golf course than what he shot. Stewart showed up at the course in the mid- to late eighties looking like every other PGA TOUR pro; but he emerged from the locker room clad in colors and clothing that would become his trademark and distinguish him from his fellow competitors. Stewart played PGA TOUR tournament golf in plus fours (knickers) and knee socks, and, thanks to an endorsement deal with the National Football League, he was dressed head to toe in the colors of various NFL teams. He'd save Sunday, if he made the cut, for the home or favorite team of the city in which the tournament was held, and that was why he was in the navy and orange of the windy city's beloved Bears when he captured the Wannamaker Trophy by winning the 1989 PGA Championship at Kemper Lakes Golf Course in suburban Chicago. Payne Stewart was no longer just a very good PGA TOUR professional; he was a star, and that star stayed high in the sky as he won two more tournaments in 1990, and then the United States Open—golf's toughest test—in 1991. Winning the Open, combined with his recognition factor and megawatt personality, got him into the Skins Game in November that year. Capturing more money and skins during that one weekend kept him coming back.

We had one more project in 1993, and it had nothing to do with golf, except for the fact that we could play at its location. It was a college football awards show that our group produced for ESPN from Walt Disney World in Orlando, Florida. Steve would direct and my job was to put together videotaped features on each of the nominees. For years college football handed out several "best of" awards to players who excelled at various positions throughout the year. There was a best quarterback award, named after legendary college quarterback Davey O'Brien; the running back award carried Texas Christian standout Doak Walker's name; and the linebacker award was named after Dick Butkus. But for years the only college football award that received national attention, and therefore television time, was the Heisman Memorial Trophy Award. This prize was awarded by the Downtown Athletic Club from 1937 until 2001, and is given by the Heisman Trust now. At first, it was simply called the DAC trophy, but in 1936 a Brown University and University of Pennsylvania football player named John Heisman died, and that year the award was renamed in his honor. It is annually given to the player sportswriters and fans determine to be the nation's best college football player. It's a big deal, even bigger a few years ago, and has been given to some of the greatest players in history, including Paul Hornung, Roger Staubach, O. J. Simpson, Tony Dorsett, and Barry Sanders. In 1986, the award's presentation began a near-decades-long run on network television, but the other awards were relegated to newspaper sports pages and mentions on *SportsCenter*, until ESPN decided to make a show of its own in 1990 and hand out all the awards, save for the Heisman, in one evening—live on national television. I didn't work on the show in '90, '91, or '92, but I did get the assignment in 1993. Players, coaches, fans, and families came to the Boardwalk at Walt Disney World to see who would win, and so did ESPN Executive Vice President Howard Katz. While he was there, he decided that was the time the two of us should discuss my future,

"Thanks for taking some time," I started, not quite knowing how to start.

"No problem," he said, certain, I'm sure, how it would end. "Tell me what's going on." And I did.

The conversation lasted about a half an hour. I tried to say all the right things and I'm certain I said some of the wrong ones. The gist of my side of the story was that I felt honored to work for him and Don and would happily do it forever, if I could afford to.

"What do you need?" he would ask.

I told him.

"And you gave that exact number to Chuck?"

I told him I did.

"And what did he tell you?" He sincerely seemed like he didn't know.

"He said ESPN would never go for that much of a percentage increase." I looked down at the ground, and then back up at Howard. "He said if it was still the old days it might be different, but it wasn't, and his hands were tied." I stopped for a second and Howard continued to look at me, almost through me, and I finished, "Then he said he was sorry."

I felt like crying. This was no power play or money grab; I *loved* my job and didn't ever want to leave, but the cost of living in Los Angeles for a family of four was beyond my current pay scale. Howard seemed to realize this and smiled. Then he said:

"Chuck's right, ESPN would *never* agree to a 40 or 50 percent increase year over year." My heart sank. My last hope was that Howard, in his new position in management at ESPN, could make something happen, and now it sounded like he couldn't. Then he continued:

"But he's wrong about not being able to do anything. Give me a few weeks to see what I can come up with," and then he stood and extended his hand. I stood as well and we shook hands.

"We don't want to lose you," was what he said as he let go of my hand and left the lobby.

So I waited, full of hope that a solution could be worked out, but at the same time fully preparing myself to quit my dream job and find another way to support my family. As the end of the year approached, I checked in with Howard's office at least once a week with no news, good or bad. I was, in the meantime, able to come to an agreement with Chuck Gerber on a deal that would bring me back, on a freelance basis, to work the tournaments that were played at the beginning of the golf season in 1994. It was a generous, per-week offer, but didn't include things like medical benefits and wouldn't, in the long run, be enough. The immediate plan was to take the family to Wisconsin for Christmas and visit Kathy's sisters, who were both now living in the Badger State. I called Howard Katz again and got the same "no news" answer, but he did give me hope by asking for the phone numbers of the places where I would be during the holiday. I still didn't possess a mobile phone, so I gave him the home numbers of both of Kathy's sisters and left it at that.

Christmas in Wisconsin is cold. It's pitiless, penetrating, take-your-breath-away cold; but beautiful. Kathy's oldest sister, Betsy, lived with her doctor husband and two beautiful children in an upscale neighborhood, just outside Madison, called Monona. They lived in a better-than-average-sized, more-comfortable-than-most house. The kitchen looked out into a wide-open dining room and living room, and that's where close to a dozen family members and friends were gathered, four days before my thirty-eighth birthday, when the phone rang.

"Joy, get the phone!" called Kathy's sister to her five-year-old daughter. The little girl, dressed in full-blown princess regalia, complete with tiara, appeared out of nowhere and picked up the phone.

"Rifkin residence," she said, in a tone and style well beyond her years, and then she listened. "Just one second," she answered.

"Uncle Keith!" she yelled, despite the fact that I was standing less than ten feet away. "It's for you," she continued, never looking my way but setting the phone on the counter and heading straight back to her imaginary kingdom. Chuckling, I picked up the phone.

"This is Keith," I said, not sure, but hoping I knew who was on the other end.

"Keith, it's Howard," was the response, and suddenly I didn't know whether to smile or vomit, as nervous as I could ever remember being.

"I have a proposition for you." I expected Howard Katz was about to make me an offer I wasn't sure I could refuse. "How would you feel about moving to Bristol, Connecticut?" Now *that* was unexpected.

"I'm not sure I follow," I said, pretty sure I didn't follow.

"ESPN2 has been on the air for a couple of months and they need help. They need producers, and if you're willing to relocate, one of those jobs is yours." He waited for me to respond, but I didn't know how, so he continued, "The money is close to what you want, but the cost of living in Bristol is far less than LA, so it's actually an impressive bump."

"Would I still do golf?" was all I could think to ask.

"Probably not," he answered quickly. "This is a full-time job, and quite frankly it's a hell of an opportunity." He was done selling it. The implication was clear...if I wanted to stay with this company, my immediate future was suddenly in Bristol, Connecticut, in an ESPN studio with complete strangers.

"When?" left my mouth, despite all of the words that stayed swirling around in my head.

"As soon as you can get there. Listen, I know it's quick, but that's how these things work sometimes. Talk to Kathy, enjoy your holiday, and let me know in the next few days." After I got over the initial shock that he remembered my wife's name, I realized my work was just beginning.

"Thanks, Howard, I really appreciate everything." I ended that conversation thinking a longer, more complicated one was about to take place.

HEADING BACK EAST

Surprisingly, or maybe not, Kathy was all for it. Despite the fact that her two sisters had moved from Connecticut to Wisconsin, she still had family and friends in the Nutmeg State. It was where she had grown up and she was eager to get back. She also *loved* the idea of me having a more sedentary job with more traditional hours, little or no travel, family dinners and holidays at home, and more time with the kids. That was what she pictured when I told her of the offer from Howard. A new job, completely out of my comfort zone, in a place and with people with whom I was utterly unfamiliar was what I thought about. But there was something about the challenge that intrigued me, and the opportunity to comfortably provide for my family was too important to ignore. On December 20, 1993, I called Howard back and told him yes. Nearly a decade after I had been hired, then not, as a director at ESPN, I would now be walking through those doors as a producer; but Kathy and I had a lot of work to do before that happened.

They wanted me to start ASAP, but there was a slight problem: I had agreed to produce the 1994 Senior Skins Game on the schedule to be played the end of January, and I was already well along in terms of putting together ideas for features and pieces that would air during the telecasts. The air days on ABC had been established—January 29 and 30—and hotel arrangements and tickets to Hawaii had already been purchased, so the nice folks at ESPN2 agreed to let me come to Bristol, work for a few weeks and then, almost immediately, take a week or so off to go to Hawaii for my final Skins Game telecast. While we were still in LA, it was my job to find footage, write pieces, and spend hours in a postproduction house editing the pictures. We were renting the three-bedroom dollhouse-like place across the street from the reservoir in the trendy Silver Lake neighborhood, so we gave notice there. The owners were sad to see us go, but not terribly so; the place was cute, well appointed, and we had kept it clean so they knew they would have no trouble at all finding another tenant quickly. Kathy enlisted the help of family and friends in Connecticut to find us a place on the other side of America, which they did, in the near-to-Bristol town of Farmington. We could move in February 1 and I had agreed, through Howard, to start on January 17. As part of the deal, ESPN had agreed to move our belongings across country and put us up in a Residence Inn near the studios until our newly found house was ready for occupancy. Things seemed to be falling into place, but I had an unsettling flashback to a decade-old conversation with someone else at ESPN and decided to pick up the phone and double check on the arrangements. My contact as "the guy in charge at ESPN2" was someone named Vince Doria, and I called ESPN HQ and asked to speak with him. Thankfully, no one said, "Mr. Doria no longer works here," and they put me through,

"Doria," was how he answered the phone.

"Mr. Doria, this is Keith Hirshland calling from LA," I started.

"Katz's guy," he interrupted. Oh boy.

"Yes, sir, I guess so," I replied.

"What can I do for you, Keith," he added, suddenly sounding much friendlier.

"Actually I was just calling to say hello and tell you how much I am looking forward to this opportunity." Was that too much sucking up, I wondered, as the words came out?

"Glad to hear it." I guess it wasn't laying it on too thick. "If you're half as good as Katz says you are then we're looking forward to having you. You can help us." No pressure there.

"I'll do my best," I said, trying to sound confident. What in the world had Howard told this guy?

"See you in a few weeks," he said, ending the call.

"See you, and thanks," I added, unsure of whether or not he heard. At least they were expecting me.

When I wasn't working on the Senior Skins features, we spent our last few weeks in Los Angeles saying good-bye to the friends we had made and packing up what we could before the movers came to put it all in a truck and drive it away. The arrangements were made through ESPN and the movers they hired told us to box up our personal items but leave the bigger stuff like the television set and furniture for them. They had also agreed to transport our two cars, so we were flying, and when it came time to go, we headed to the airport with two car seats and a couple of suitcases full of clothes. We left on Wednesday, January 12; the movers were set to come January 17, load the truck, and, after driving from the West to the East Coast, deliver everything we had accumulated in our lives together to our new home on February 1. A great plan; but you know what they say about the best-laid plans. On January 17, the very day the movers were set to pack up our house, put our stuff in a moving van, and hit the road, the shit hit the fan. At 4:31 a.m., a 6.7-magnitude earthquake ripped through the San Fernando Valley for as long as twenty seconds and shook LA out of its peaceful slumber.

SHAKEN, NOT STIRRED

Earthquakes have been both rearranging the concrete and a part of the consciousness of Southern California since 1769, when the first known tremor was felt by an expedition led by Gaspar de Portolo, near what is now Los Angeles. When I was a kid, my grandparents (Harry and Helen) lived in Rancho Palos Verdes overlooking the Pacific Ocean, and we went to visit every year. More times than I can count, my brothers and I would don our swim suits and hop over the fence to join the neighbor's kids in their backyard pool. We'd swim, splash, play water polo and water basketball, and at least once a trip, while in that pool, remark on the fact that it was the perfect place to be when the "Big One" hit and California slipped (as many "experts" predicted it would) into the ocean below. Obviously it hasn't yet, but some have never stopped thinking it might.

January 17, 1994, was my first day on the brand new job and one of my assignments was to shadow one of the producers of ESPN2's *SportsNight*, the brand new, supposedly hipper, cooler, younger brother of *SportsCenter* airing on ESPN. It was also scheduled to be a day filled with orientation, meeting people, and learning the ropes about my new place of employment. The day started early. I was supposed to meet my tour guide at 6 a.m., and I stopped at the local Dunkin' Donuts on my way in for a cup of coffee for me, and a couple of dozen donuts for the production team and talent (couldn't hurt, right?). I found my way to the prescribed meeting spot and was greeted by a young bespectacled man who, to me, looked more like a computer programmer than a TV sports producer,

"I'm Mark Gross," he said, extending his hand. "You must be the golf guy."

Oh, good, I already have a nickname, I thought as I took his hand and shook it.

"Keith Hirshland," I said, "it's really nice to meet you."

"You brought donuts, nice," he continued, looking at the boxes I was balancing in my other hand.

"Least I could do," I smiled as we went inside.

I quickly learned my new friend Mark went by "Grossie," grew up in Troy, New York, attended Ithaca College, and had always wanted to work at ESPN. He got his wish in 1988 and since his original hire date had been promoted up through the ranks, starting as a production assistant and getting to the point where he was now a producer on loan from *SportsCenter* to help get the company's brand new network off the ground. I followed him through the building he clearly knew well. The structure and its surrounding area were impressive, nothing like the sprawling campus that exists today, but impressive nonetheless, and we walked for a while before getting to the big room that would be my new home.

"I'm working on my show rundown right now and we have the first meeting at 10," Grossie said, reaching for a donut and heading for his workstation.

"First meeting?" I asked.

"Yeah, we have three a day: a production meeting, a show rundown meeting with the talent, and a final prep meeting a couple of hours before air," he said, talking and typing at the same time. "Olbermann *hates* them," he said, shaking his head, "but Vince and Norby think they're really important, and I agree." Vince I knew, or at least knew of; the Norby person was a mystery.

So I sat and watched Mark Gross meticulously prepare for the first of three meetings that would mold his and other's ideas into a national television show before the end of the day. He picked up the phone and gave instructions, handed out assignments, and banged away at his keyboard. I saw a handful of people come and go and figured they would soon be coming and going around me. At one point, he stole a glance at his watch, and I did the same,

"Nine forty-five," I said, more to myself than anyone, "fifteen minutes to meeting number one." But before I could attend my first ever meeting at ESPN, I heard something I never expected to hear at that moment.

"Keith Hirshland, please dial the operator," came over the speakers embedded in the ceiling. "Keith Hirshland, please dial the operator."

"Any phone?" I called out to Mark.

"Any one," he answered, "just dial zero."

I did.

The only person who knew I was there at that very moment was my wife, and I could imagine that the only reason she would be calling would be bad news.

"This is Keith," I said after dialing zero.

"Hold, please," came the disembodied voice. I held, and instinctively held my breath.

"Mr. Hirshland, this is Mark from Mayflower." It wasn't my wife, but I was certain it was still bad news.

The Northridge earthquake, as it would come to be called, actually had its epicenter in the Southern California town of Reseda, but, because that would take days to determine, the media attributed the quake to the larger, better-known community of Northridge. The monster quake directly resulted in the death of fifty-seven people and injured more than eighty-seven hundred others, and the damage extended as far as eighty-five miles away. It was eighty-five miles that included our house, still full of everything we had left behind, in Silver Lake.

Shaken by the news, I asked for, and received, the rest of my first day off and headed home to spend the rest of the day with Kathy, watching the kids playing, sleeping, eating, and basically being kids. They were almost three- and almost one-year-old children and couldn't have cared less whether they were in California or Connecticut. We were their parents, grown adults who at that very moment couldn't have been happier that we were somewhere other than Southern California. We watched with wonder the two of them alternately laughing and crying, the two of us alternately laughing and crying for entirely different reasons. We would never know what might have happened if we had still been in that house when the earth shook. What was left of our stuff arrived days later to our new address in Farmington, Connecticut. Personal possessions and things were cracked, broken, and shattered; but our lives were intact, and nothing else in the world mattered.

BUILDING SHOWS AND BUDDING NETWORKS

In 1993, plans for breaking ground on two groundbreaking television networks were being made. One had the muscle of a burgeoning cable sports powerhouse behind it and the other had the brains of an Alabama businessman. Steve Bornstein was president of ESPN at the time. His all-sports network had reached sixty million cable subscribers and was slowly and steadily seeping into the American consciousness. Dan Patrick and Keith Olbermann had made the 11 o'clock *SportsCenter* must-see TV, and the network had recently launched its own awards show, the ESPYS, which had seen former North Carolina State head basketball coach Jim Valvano, who was dying of cancer, give his now-famous inspirational, tear-inducing "Never Give Up" speech. ESPN aired a lot of live sporting events, but its president knew there was even more available; he just didn't have enough hours in the day to show it on one network. Bornstein was brilliant and apparently saw a world with multiple ESPN networks making all kinds of sports available to anyone who wanted to watch, and it would start with ESPN2. He would staff it and supply it with programming, but first he had to decide exactly what kind of sports television network it should be. For help, he brought in a man named John Lack, who had been one of the creative minds behind the creation of MTV. Many felt that network changed both music and television forever; and Bornstein was hoping Lack could do the same for his sports enterprise. With Lack on board, Bornstein escalated and elevated his plan for a second ESPN. ESPN2 launched on October 1, 1993, trying to attract mostly young, quite often distracted male viewers by offering a steady diet of action sports and hockey. It was determined that the tone of the new network, suddenly referred to as "the Deuce," would be no-holds-barred brash and irreverent. Insiders knew Bornstein also had ideas for, and plans to build, the ESPN brand through more networks, including one, already in the works, dedicated to twenty-four-hour sports news, and another focused solely on historic footage and games. He may or may not have already formulated the plans for a Hispanic network, a college-sports-themed network, and a network with the singular focus on golf, but that was all somewhere in the future; the present belonged to ESPN2, and time was of the essence.

Maybe Bornstein should have paid a little more attention to the network he thought could concentrate on the game of golf, because Joe Gibbs was busy beating him to it. Gibbs had taken his 1990 conversation with Arnold Palmer about an all-golf channel to heart and had then run with it, full speed ahead. He used a portion of the money he had made creating and growing his Alabama businesses and spent it on studies, focus groups, and research. He found that a cable television network dedicated to golf not only interested people, it excited them. Gibbs learned what he already knew: golf was more than a sport; it was a lifestyle. It had its own customs, character, fashions, and rituals, and, maybe most importantly, it had an extremely loyal and well-heeled following. Gibbs conducted more than half a dozen separate studies, including commissioning his own Gallup Poll, and they all helped him reach the same conclusion—a golf channel could work. Then, and only then, he reached out once again to Arnold Palmer. Armed with his positive research, Gibbs gathered potential investors for his Golf Channel in meetings and board-rooms all over America and, when he could, he brought along his ace in the hole, the great Arnold Palmer. Joe tells the story of how much Palmer meant to the enterprise when, early on in the process, the golfer addressed a group of advisors who were recommending caution.

"We had assembled a number of well-respected businessmen and professionals who were acting as advisors to me when this thing was getting off the ground," I heard that Joe Gibbs said, "but when Arnold was in the room the attitude changed."

"Gentlemen," Mr. Palmer is reported to have started, while looking around the room. "If I hadn't tried to hit the golf ball through the trees a few times, *none* of us would be sitting here now."

Advisors and investors alike may not have loved the go-for-broke, throw-caution-to-the-wind attitude of Palmer, but they had to respect it. With Palmer on board and research in hand, Gibbs got his initial backing and the go-ahead to create The Golf Channel.

Meanwhile, back in Bristol, plans for ESPN2 were humming right along as well. The decision had been made to create an anchor program; a nightly sportscast built on the model of *SportsCenter*, the runaway hit that was currently the defining program on ESPN. The immediate problem was in choosing the people to anchor it. One decision had been made—the female one—in the person of a West Palm Beach sportscaster named Suzy Kolber. The male half of the equation would prove to be much more difficult, literally and figuratively. Keith Olbermann had been around the radio and television block, working at various times for UPI and RKO on the radio side, and CNN and KCBS TV in Los Angeles in front of television cameras. He was brilliant and selfish, full of wit and, according to many coworkers, full of shit; and he was currently cohosting *SportsCenter* with Dan Patrick every night at 11 p.m., and people were watching. Because of that, some people clearly thought he would be the perfect person to help launch *SportsNight* on ESPN2; Keith never thought so. They did, however, convince him to take the job and, after several weeks of preparation and a handful of dress rehearsals, *SportsNight*, hosted by Keith Olbermann and Suzy Kolber, launched ESPN2 on the evening of October 1. The lights came on and a leather-jacket-clad Olbermann, without humor, stated the following words for the world to hear:

"Good evening, and welcome to the end of my career."

Joe Gibbs may have been feeling exactly the opposite at the time.

DEAD ON ARRIVAL

SportsNight was one of two signature shows on the fledgling network; the other was a thirty-minute talk show taped in LA and hosted by a consistently cocky, occasionally obnoxious, young Southern Californian named Jim Rome. While the Bristol show bumbled along under the weight of its unhappy star, the talk show had everybody talking. Rome could be impertinent, but he was almost always interesting, and the athletes who appeared across the table from him seemed to enjoy the forum—at least most of them did.

October turned into November and then became December, and the divide between Olbermann and everyone else working at ESPN2 and on *SportsNight* grew with his disdain for what he was doing. When I got there, in mid-January of 1994, the show was still trying to find a purpose, and Olbermann was trying harder than ever to find his way back to *SportsCenter*. My first few production meetings were remarkable, if only for the fact that I was struck by how little Olbermann participated or cared. Sometimes he didn't even show up. I never met John Lack, and I had been told that Vince Doria was in charge, but the guy who was my day-to-day if not hour-by-hour contact was Norby Williamson.

Norby, like Mark Gross and quite frankly about 99 percent of all the production people at ESPN, was an East Coast guy. He had gone to college at Southern Connecticut State and started at the all-sports network as a production assistant in 1985 (six years after the network launched), so he was almost a ten-year veteran when I came in on my first day. He and Gross were clearly friends, and again, like Mark, his career path was an upward one at ESPN. In fact, he rose slightly higher and slightly faster than Gross. Norby's title was coordinating producer, and that meant he oversaw the team of producers that put the show together every night. The best producers know that when you work on a live sporting event, there is only a certain amount of planning that can be done. For the most part you have to go with the flow and let the event take you along for the ride. The preparation for a studio show could be done hours and sometimes days, in advance and, as far as *SportsNight* was concerned, every idea had to be given the Norby Williamson seal of approval. That didn't bother me so much, but it bugged the hell out of Keith Olbermann. Williamson and Doria are still with the network; in fact, Norby may now be the third or fourth most powerful person at ESPN. He was then and, in my opinion, remains a confident, talented guy, blessed with great instincts and leadership qualities; but, at the time, at least one guy thought him overconfident, under qualified, and in over his head.

Olbermann might have been the smartest guy on television (I use the past tense because, as I write this, he is awaiting his next TV gig), and he was most certainly the smartest guy at ESPN; but the smartest guy in the room is rarely the most liked, and that was true with Keith. I attended several production meetings in mid-January as an observer, and I observed a number of young, gifted television people with can-do attitudes, working their tails off to try and make something new work. I also couldn't help but notice a contrary, sometimes petulant perfectionist with an "I'm better than you" attitude, sitting on the floor in the corner. It seemed unfortunate to me, but somewhere along the way someone had decided that every evening's

SportsNight program had to start with a *Saturday Night Live*-like skit. If you watch *Saturday Night Live*, you know how hard it is for card-carrying, check-cashing comedians to be funny once a week. Imagine putting that kind of pressure on a recently-out-of-college sports fan turned television associate producer or producer. Some of the ideas were clever, a few of them were even funny, but almost every one of them was greeted by an Olbermann shake of the head and the following phrase:

"I'm not doing that."

Then Keith would get up, take his copy of the rundown, highlighting the scripts and lead-ins for which he was responsible, and leave the room.

I remember mustering up the courage to seek out the oft-moody, always intimidating Olbermann and introduce myself. He still kept his desk on the other side of the building, the *SportsCenter* side, and I wandered in that direction to find him. Once located, I noticed him pounding away at his keyboard—typing words faster than anyone I had ever seen, with only the index finger of his right hand. I am a hunt-and-peck guy, never having taken a typing class, and I have to look at the keyboard when I type. When I find the letter for which I am searching I hit it with either the index finger of my right or my left hand. I wouldn't qualify for a *Mad Men* secretarial pool, but I do okay. While I might be described as a mechanic, Olbermann is a marvel. I stood, looking over his shoulder, mesmerized as his finger flew over the keyboard turning letters into words, words into sentences, and sentences into scripts, and then he stopped. The spell broken, my eyes wandered up to meet his. He had turned around and was now staring at me.

"Can I help you?" he inquired.

"I'm Keith Hirshland," I started to introduce myself.

"I'm happy for you," he interrupted, "but why should that mean anything to me?" Good question, but I had an answer.

"I'm a new producer on *SportsNight*"—at the sound of the show's name, he grunted, but I continued—"and I just want you to know that I will never ask you to do anything you're not comfortable doing," I finished.

"You're the golf guy," was his response. I nodded.

"Good luck," he said, turning back to his work and dismissing me.

That went well, I thought sarcastically, heading back to the other side of the building.

I didn't know it at the time, but Keith Olbermann was already negotiating his escape from ESPN2 and, in less than a month, word came down that the pardon from what Keith considered prison was granted and he would be returning to *SportsCenter*. It took another month for that to actually happen, but in the weeks that Olbermann and I actually worked together, I never broke my promise, and I can honestly say that we learned to coexist and, occasionally, even had some fun. At least that's the way I remember it.

LIFE ON THE DEUCE

There is something special about working on something new. Those of us busting our butts to steer what seemed, at times, like a rudderless ship, knew we garnered little respect from most of the building, but we didn't care. The group that produced *SportsNight* formed a bond and stood together, helping each other when help was needed, or requesting and minding our own business when that was what was required. Each had a different perspective, sense of humor, or idea of what worked or didn't, but we kept those opinions to ourselves unless we were asked to contribute. In those cases, ideas were exchanged freely and accepted or rejected with the proper perspective. We helped each other because we knew that was the only way this experiment was going to work. Stuart Scott replaced Keith Olbermann as the male anchor on *SportsNight*, and the tone and tenor of the show changed dramatically.

Stuart Scott is an African American graduate of the University of North Carolina at Chapel Hill, and if Olbermann was intentionally understated and shrewd, Stuart Scott was equally intentionally extroverted and bombastic. His was a hip-hop style of sportscasting and, because of the unconventional nature of the way he approached his job, people equally applauded and were appalled by him. He and Suzy couldn't have been more different, and that disparity created chemistry. They got along and developed a mutual respect for each other allowing show producers to concentrate on the program at hand. Part of that concentration each day was put toward trying to be clever. "The Deuce" was billed as ESPN's hipper, smarter, more irreverent little brother, and we were given free rein to present stories in a variety of ways.

SportsCenter would air an interview with Hall of Fame hockey player Wayne Gretzky and identify him as such. Over on ESPN2, *SportsNight* might air the same sound bite but, instead of identifying Gretzky as a member of the hockey hall of fame, we might put the words "third runner up in the Meryl Streep look-alike contest" under his name. While *SportsCenter* might show a full-screen graphic detailing Michael Jordan's basketball prowess by listing his points-per-game averages, *SportsNight* might instead compare his basketball numbers to his baseball statistics accumulated during his failed attempt to play another sport. We were encouraged to put a different spin on sports, and we were having fun, while good-heartedly making fun of some of the biggest names in sports. Then it all came to a crashing halt near the beginning of April.

James Samuel Everett III was born in Emporia, Kansas, in 1963, was a football standout at Eldorado High School in Albuquerque, New Mexico, and a college star his last two years at Purdue University. Everett, who remains the only Boilermaker quarterback to beat Michigan, Notre Dame, and Ohio State in the same year, led the NCAA in total offense his senior season and was drafted with the third pick in the first round of the 1986 NFL draft by the Houston Oilers, who then traded his rights to the Los Angeles Rams. He led the Rams to the playoffs that year and then again in 1988 and 1989, when the Rams made it all the way to the NFC Championship game, losing to the San Francisco 49ers 30–3. In that game, the quarterback was hounded, hassled, and harassed by the 49er defense, sending Everett to the ground on numerous occasions. He was so shell-shocked that, on one play, he went down not because of a sack, but just because he was anticipating being sacked, an action that led to criticism in and around the league. Everett was perceived by some as "soft" and never led a team to the playoffs again. At the end of the 1993 season, the Rams traded the beleaguered player to New Orleans, where he enjoyed a bit of a renaissance before his career ended in 1997. Before packing his bags and heading to Louisiana, he stopped by the talk show studios of Jim Rome for an appearance on ESPN2.

ROME FIDDLES AND
GETS BURNED

Rome fancied himself a controversial, argumentative fire-brand who delighted in a dispute and approved of any argument. Underneath the posturing pretense, he was nothing but a punk, and he proved it during a TV interview with an NFL quarter-back. Rome had been one of Everett's most vocal and demeaning critics, hammering the Pro Bowl quarterback at every available opportunity. It was Rome's unimaginative and uninspired idea to heap ridicule on Everett by calling him "Chris" in an effort to compare him to the female tennis star. Everett had heard it all before and had grown weary of the dialogue. Like most professional athletes, he knew he couldn't avoid the critics, but he preferred to discuss his accomplishments and speculate on the future that awaited him with his new team. That's what he thought he'd be doing when he agreed to do the ESPN2 inter-view. He also incorrectly thought he be sitting across the table from Roy Firestone, an accomplished interviewer who had had a talk show of his own on ESPN for years.

Instead, he was informed that the show was now hosted by Rome, and Everett knew it might get ugly. It didn't take long. Within seconds of starting the interview, Rome smugly threw the insult in his guest's face.

"Jim, good to have you on the show," Rome began.

"Good to be here, Jim, thank you," Everett answered, smiling.

"Check that, *Chris* Everett, good to have you on the show."
Rome was off camera but the joy in his voice at delivering the
slight was evident.

"You know what," countered a now-unsmiling Everett, "you
know you've been calling me that for about the last five years."

"Two years, actually, *Chris*," Rome interrupted his guest.

"Hey, you know what, let me say one thing," Everett said,
trying to regain some sense of control. "In that game, how many
sacks did I have, that we came back and won?" The camera cut
to a two shot to include the host of the show.

"How many sacks did you have?" Rome questioned, as the
director cut back to a single shot of the guest.

"Yeah, how many games, how many sacks?" Everett stopped
and looked at Rome while the director again changed shots to
show just the host.

"Yeah, but you see, this was back in 1989, and you may have
even been *Jim* Everett back there, but somewhere along the way,
Jim, you ceased being *Jim* and you became *Chris*." The director
cut back to the camera pointed at Everett, who was pointing his
left index finger at Rome.

"Well, let me tell you a little secret," Everett countered, as a
graphic appeared in that ESPN2 style, stating Jim Everett's name
and below it the words, *"don't call me chris, ok!"* Clever, don't
you think?

"You know, we're sitting here right now," Everett continued,
unaware of the wording on the graphic, "and if you guys want
to take a station break, you can." The quarterback shifted in his
chair and adopted a more threatening position, leaning toward
his interrogator, "But if you call me *Chris* Everett to my face one
more time—." Then Rome just *had* to interrupt.

"I already did it twice," Rome said, as the director again
switched to the camera pointing at the host, wearing a T-shirt,
sports coat, and a smug look on his face.

"You call it one more time: we better take a station break," Everett continued, as the viewer saw Rome's face and Everett's back.

"Well, it's a five-minute segment on a five-segment show," Rome said, "so we got a long way to go."

"We do," was Everett's two-word response.

"We got a long way to go," repeated Rome.

"We do," said Everett again as he started to lean back in his chair, clearly thinking he had diffused the situation.

"I'll get a couple segments out of you before," Rome continued.

"Well it's good to be here with you, though," said Everett as the camera showed Rome leaning back in his chair now.

"Well, it's good to see you too," the host chided.

"Because you've been talking like this behind my back for a long time," Everett pushed, thinking he now had the upper hand.

"But now I said it right here," said Rome, as the director cut back and forth between the cameras facing Rome and Everett. The viewer now saw the guest as he said, "Right, exactly."

"Well, we got no problems then," Rome said, off camera.

"You probably won't say it again," was what Everett said next.

"I bet I do," answered Rome.

"Okay," said Everett leaning back. The director cut to a camera that included a wide shot to show Everett, Rome, the table that separated them and the chairs in which they sat.

"*Chris*," said Rome, and Everett was no longer sitting. He rose, grabbed the table from underneath with both hands, tossed it out of the way, and lunged at the person who had spoken the offending words again. The host tried to stand, but the quarterback was on him, pushing him backwards and tossing him off the set. No punches were thrown, but Everett may have been about to when a stagehand entered the scene to pull the quarterback away from the fallen interviewer. Many thought at the time, and some still believe today, the whole thing was staged to create "buzz" around the fledgling network. Those that worked on the show, including a young Mark Shapiro, who would one day be in charge of all the programming for all the networks under the ESPN umbrella, swore it was not. Whether it was or wasn't doesn't matter now, and it didn't matter then. It happened on live TV, and everyone felt the consequences.

The very next day, the edict came down that the reins would be tightened, graphics would be more sedate, and ideas more sober. In short, ESPN2 would start to look more like ESPN; the age of irreverence was at an end. Jim Everett went on to have several more productive years in the NFL. Jim Rome was never sanctioned, suspended, or reprimanded in any way, and in fact, after a stint on a rival network, he had his own talk show on ESPN for a while before moving on. ESPN2 was never the same.

THE BEAT GOES ON

In addition to the *SportsNight* broadcasts, my day-to-day responsibilities also included producing something called "Sports Smash." These were "mini sportscasts," much like local news cut-ins during the morning shows *Today* and *Good Morning America*, with a blistering pace and, preferably, high-strung talent.

I was one of a handful of producers responsible for cobbling together *SportsNight* or the *Smash* on any given day, and it took all day to do either one. The days I spent doing *Sports Smash* were longer but, in many respects, easier. Each consisted of anywhere from three to five minutes and included scores, highlights, and graphics detailing the major sports stories of the day. The producer was responsible for the rundown (what story, score, or highlight went where) while the talent was mostly responsible for writing the scripts and coming up with an on-air personality with whom viewers could immediately identify. The men and women hired were unknowns from smaller markets, discovered, courted, and hired by ESPN's talent guru, Al Jaffe, and nurtured, coddled, and babysat by Doria, Williamson, and a merry band of producers. *Sports Smash* was where Stuart Scott, Bill Pidto, and Kenny Mayne were first seen on national television, and certain phrases—like "Boo Yah," "Peepin the madness," "We have a situation," and "I don't know what that pitch was, but *it tastes like chicken!*" were first uttered. Keith Olbermann never did a *Sports Smash*. Kenny Mayne did, but there was a question as to how many.

Mayne grew up in the Pacific Northwest and played football at the University of Nevada Las Vegas. Before graduating with a degree in broadcasting and becoming a TV personality, his claim to fame was that he backed up future NFL star Randall Cunningham for the Runnin' Rebels. He worked briefly as a reporter for a station in Las Vegas, and then worked for seven years at KSTW in Seattle as a reporter during the week and sports anchor on the weekend. He left KSTW in 1989 and started looking for work.

Five years later, he was still looking to continue his career in television and hoped a letter and a resume sent to ESPN Talent Coordinator Al Jaffe would do the trick. In classic Kenny Mayne style, the letter was simply a note with empty boxes asking ESPN if they would hire him. One option was "We'll hire you when there's an ESPN5"; another was simply "Yes." Something in the request must have piqued Jaffe's curiosity, because Mayne was brought to Bristol for an interview and then given a job. The job was anchoring various editions of *Sports Smash*, some produced by yours truly, including Kenny Mayne's very first appearance on the network.

Before hosting *SportsCenter with Dan Patrick*, *The Mayne Event* on *NFL Countdown*, an appearance on *Dancing with the Stars*, a cameo in the feature film *BASEketball*, and the release of a book on sports and pop culture, Kenneth Wheelock Mayne was staring into a camera with my voice in his ear, delivering scores and voicing over highlights on ESPN2, and he was *terrible*. He was clever and witty and funny and smart, but he was so nervous he could barely speak. He would sweat and stutter and forget to breathe and, thank goodness, most of the *Sports Smashes* he anchored on ESPN2 were taped because, when Kenny went live, a disaster almost always resulted. It would have been easy to make a beeline to Norby Williamson's office or beat a path to Vince Doria's door and say this guy was hopeless and had to go, but that wasn't my style. I also believed that his writing was creative and entertaining, and I wanted to put him in a position to succeed.

Kenny was as frustrated as others were exasperated. He wanted this, and I knew if he could get past his obvious stage fright, he would be good at it. He had personality, and he had some experience, and that's where I attempted to help him get better. I asked Kenny how he had managed to work in a major market for seven years but he couldn't sit in front of a camera for seven seconds without breaking out in a major sweat,

"That was just weekends in Seattle," was his response. "*This* is ESPN."

I told him I understood but, when he looks into that camera he shouldn't think about it being ESPN and millions of people; in fact, he shouldn't even think about it being weekends in Seattle and thousands of people. He should think about just *one* person on the other side of that lens, and think only of him or her. It was advice I had gotten from Ed Pearce way back when, in Reno, Nevada. It was good advice when it was given to me, and it was still good advice when I was giving it to Kenny. One day, Norby and Vince asked me if Kenny was worth keeping, and I said, "Definitely." He got better.

After the Rome/Everett debacle, we all settled in to a rhythm at the Deuce, and it was fun. I met and worked with some great production people, including Shawn Murphy, Matt Sandulli, Kevin Riley, Mike McQuade, Scott Ackerson, and Pete Esposito; many of them are still with the network. I was given the opportunity to connect with, and produce segments that featured, ex-professional athletes as well as award-winning authors and radio and television personalities, including John Feinstein, Tony Kornheiser, Nick Bakay, Tony Bruno, Al Morganti, Mark

Malone, and David Aldridge. I made friends and my work was well respected. We worked the front lines of sports reporting as the events of 1994 unfolded, delivering daily reports as Tonya Harding's figure-skating world unraveled, Andre Agassi became the first unseeded tennis player in history to win the US Open, and Major League Baseball forfeited on-the-field drama for off-the field-disaster as players went on strike, ending the sport midseason, forcing a cancellation of the World Series, and crippling America's pastime for years to come. I was still playing golf, for fun and recreation, and discovered Mark Gross, Norby Williamson, and Pete Esposito also shared a passion for the sport. On a late spring/early summer day, we had just completed an enjoyable round and retired to the snack bar to grab a bite to eat and a soda pop. It was June 17.

Once upon a time, Orenthal James Simpson was a true American sports hero. He won the coveted Heisman Trophy in 1968 by the widest margin in history, after scoring twenty-two touchdowns for the University of Southern California. He was drafted by the NFL's Buffalo Bills and struggled on bad teams for his first three years in the league. Then he rushed for more than twelve hundred yards in 1973 (the year I graduated from Reno High School) and then became the first player ever to run for more than two thousand yards in 1974. His career ended six years later and he was inducted into the Pro Football Hall of Fame in 1985, the first year he was eligible. His football prowess combined with an amiable nature led to a post-NFL string of successes. He was the spokesperson for a number of products and companies, including Hertz, and starred in a famous commercial that featured him running through an airport. He also could be seen on the silver screen in more than eight movies, the most memorable being the classic *Naked Gun* trilogy of comedies, co-starring alongside funnyman Leslie Nielsen. Once divorced, Simpson married again on February 2, 1985, this time saying "I do" to Nicole Brown. They had two children and then divorced in 1992. Two years later, she was murdered and, according to the Los Angeles Police Department, O. J. Simpson was the prime suspect.

We were playing golf when lawyers convinced the LAPD to allow Simpson to turn himself in. We had finished and were enjoying the last of our post round meal when the news hit that Simpson had not taken advantage of the deal and an "all-points bulletin" had been issued for the former football star. Norby turned to Grossie and said simply, "We better get into work. This is going to be a long night."

He was right. At 8 p.m. ET, with Simpson still nowhere to be found, his attorney and friend Robert Kardashian read a statement written by the missing sports star. An hour and forty-five minutes later, a police officer spotted the white Ford Bronco owned by O.J. heading north on Interstate 405. The officer pulled his cruiser alongside and saw not Simpson, but his friend Al Cowlings driving the automobile. Accounts would later say that Cowlings rolled down the window and yelled that Simpson was in the back of the car, holding a gun to his own head. The officer backed off and followed the northbound Bronco heading up the 405 at thirty-five miles per hour. More than twenty police cars joined the chase and an equal number of helicopters hovered above—some police choppers, others from news organizations, both local and national. CNN broke in first, bringing the live pictures of the "chase" to millions of Americans, including those working inside the walls of ESPN. NBC was covering game five of the NBA Finals—between the New York Knicks and the Houston Rockets—when someone in New York decided the Simpson story deserved attention, so the network split the screen into two boxes; the smaller one still carried the game, while the slightly larger one showed the white Ford Bronco trailed by as many as two dozen police, sheriff, and highway patrol cars. Sports fans glued to the game now knew what was going on in Southern California, and so did the decision makers at ESPN, Norby among them. What had promised to be a fairly routine night at the all-sports network became must-see news, late into the night, because a sports icon was at the center of the nation's biggest news story.

NEW OPPORTUNITIES ARISE

One story that didn't get a second of play *on* TV was what was going on behind the scenes in the world *of* sports TV. Joe Gibbs was launching his twenty-four-hour-a-day, seven-day–a-week, all-golf network; and he was busy assembling the team that would help him do it. At ESPN, word of the soon-to-be new television network had trickled down through whispers to the walkways, edit rooms, and studios of ESPN. People were getting phone calls, participating in interviews, and being asked to leave ESPN to join The Golf Channel. Word was The Golf Channel would begin broadcasting in January of 1995, and they needed people; some to put the shows together, some to promote the shows once they were complete, and some to put their faces in front of the camera to deliver them. As July turned to August, the whispers became a hum as more and more people from ESPN and other networks around the country were offered jobs. I knew people who got calls; but even though it seemed to me my golf experience warranted an inquiry, my phone didn't ring.

Joe Gibbs had cleared the first hurdle and acquired enough capital to start his fledgling network. Hurdle number two was staffing it. To accomplish that he turned to, and raided, one of the most respected cable networks in the history of television, HBO. Known for putting movies on television, HBO also had a sports pedigree. Some of the most compelling boxing matches in history made it into America's homes thanks to HBO, and the pay-to-view network also televised the grass court Grand Slam tennis event, Wimbledon. Ross Greenburg ran the sports division at HBO, and he did it with the help of Robert Greenway. Greenway was a TV veteran, having risen through the ranks at ABC as well as HBO. He had worked in all facets of production and, in 1994, was largely responsible for acquiring the rights to sporting events such as heavyweight title fights and Wimbledon for HBO. It wasn't uncommon for Bob Greenway to have a morning meeting in Las Vegas with headline-creating boxing promoters Don King or Bob Arum, and then hop on the HBO Gulfstream to head across the Atlantic Ocean, eventually landing in London to hammer out the latest proposal for early round coverage from the all lawn and tennis club. Maybe he tired of the travel; possibly he preferred the chance to spend more time with his wife, Janey, and children, Molly and Rory; or maybe Bob Greenway just cherished the chance for a new challenge. No matter the reason, he agreed to leave Ross Greenburg and HBO to join Joe Gibbs as head of programming, production, and operations for The Golf Channel.

Greenway joined the management group at Gibbs's brainchild, which included fellow Alabamans Chris Murvin, as the network's top lawyer, Del Wood, as its chief financial officer, and Matt Scalici, as the man behind the technology that would put the network on the air. He also enlisted the help of one of the sharpest minds at the PGA TOUR, Gary Stevenson, to be his chief operating officer. Stevenson was one of the tour's power brokers, working hand in hand with former Commissioner Deane Beman and the man who succeeded him, Tim Finchem. Many believed that Stevenson was on the short list in the line of succession if and when Finchem decided to leave; but instead of waiting, Stevenson decided to blaze his own trail. Gibbs handed a good deal of the network's reigns to Stevenson, who turned to Greenway to build a production team. Greenway started by bringing on board people with whom he worked at HBO; chief among them was Michael J. Whalen, who was given the title of executive producer.

Before the network ever saw the light of day, rights to televise tournaments had to be acquired and the fees for those rights negotiated; other programming had to be conceived, created, or placed under contract. Entire divisions had to be staffed; how the new network would look had to be decided, and studios and office space found or built, all on a budget determined by a finite number of dollars. The original business plan called for The Golf Channel to operate like HBO or Showtime, as a pay-per-view network. The idea was that people would subscribe to the network and pay $7 a month for the privilege of being able to watch it. Gibbs had enlisted a handful of the country's top cable operating systems, including Cox and Cablevision, as investors, taking their money, as well as their word, that each would clear channel space and offer up The Golf Channel to customers. It had worked with the movie channels and Gibbs had the research that showed it should work with The Golf Channel. People who played golf had money, and they were willing to give some of it up to watch their favorite sport on TV. Greenway and Murvin took care of the tournament rights acquisitions, the group as a whole started the process of creating divisions (Human Resources, Sales, Engineering, Programming and Promotion, News) and they all hired staff. Gibbs hired a young man he had met and liked in Alabama named Philip Hurst as The Golf Channel's first official employee, and they were off to the races.

FINALLY, THE PHONE RINGS

So, while the new all-golf network ramped up, I waited and wondered why I wasn't getting so much as an exploratory phone call. Colleagues and coworkers at ESPN and other networks were being courted, and some even got job offers. Originally, founder Joe Gibbs wanted The Golf Channel to be based in his home town of Birmingham, Alabama, but after careful consideration and the realization that hundreds of PGA TOUR members lived in or near Orlando, Florida, Gibbs decided the central Florida home of Mickey Mouse would also be the best spot for a twenty-four-hour TV channel devoted to golf. Being based in Orlando gave the network access to players, instructors, and golf facilities, while at the same time the city proved much more attractive to potential staffers.

As the summer solstice came and went and the days grew shorter in length, stories of the new network's ramp-up grew more plentiful. I had heard, through the grapevine and from friends that dozens of people had gotten jobs, both in front of the camera and behind the scenes, but Bob Greenway and Mike Whelan had still not hired either a producer or a director for their live, domestic tournament golf coverage. One of the issues was that there weren't that many people qualified to do the job and most, if not all of them, were not only currently employed and under contract with other networks but, more likely, supremely reluctant to leave posts producing the biggest events on the golf calendar to take a flyer on a start-up. Months later, I learned offers were proffered to nearly all of those broadcast network producers, and none accepted; but during the second week of August 1994, I had no idea. I just knew they weren't asking me. Then the phone rang.

My first conversation with Michael J. Whelan was short and sweet. He asked if I would be interested in being a part of television history, and I answered in the affirmative. Then we set a time and day to have a more extended conversation. That happened a few days later, and during that chat I learned of Whelan's broad vision for programming on the network, and tournament coverage in particular. He mentioned he had hired the bulk of a tournament golf announce team that included Jim Nelford, Kay Cockerill, Lori Garbacz, and Donna Caponi (people I had known or worked with, thanks to my years at OCC and ESPN) as well as people I didn't know, including an instructor named Gary Smith and a golf historian (Whelan's words, not mine) named Peter Kessler. He told me that the hiring of a play-by-play person was imminent, but the t's hadn't quite been crossed nor i's yet dotted on the contract. He said he had heard good things about me and then, right there on the phone, he made me an offer. I told him I was flattered (I was) but for the money he was offering, I wasn't interested (even though I was). We ended the call with him offering to "see what I can do" about making the offer more attractive.

My first call was to my dad and the second was to my friend Steve Beim. Both were excited for me about the prospects, and both stressed the importance of being up front with my current employers, meaning another face to face with Howard Katz. I called his assistant and set up an appointment,

"What's up?" Howard asked as I entered his office.

"I just got a call and a job offer from Mike Whelan at The Golf Channel," I answered, as he set his pen on his desk and leaned back in his chair. "They want me to produce their live tournament coverage."

"Interesting," he said. "Are you interested?"

I said I was and I mentioned their offer. I also told Howard I enjoyed what I was doing at ESPN2. He let me know that my superiors were impressed with my work so far and there had been discussions about giving me a slight bump in pay and moving me over to ESPN to produce the late night *SportsCenter*. He added that salary wasn't everything and working for a company like Cap Cities had long-reaching benefits.

"It's a start up," he added about The Golf Channel. "Chances of it making it are a long shot."

"I know," I replied, "but it is live golf again, and you know how much I loved doing that."

"I do," was his short response. "Thanks for letting me know and keep me posted on what happens next."

I got up and left the office. I knew he was right about everything: the money, the perks, the risks. But I *missed* working on live golf, and the opportunity to be lead producer was enticing. Regardless, Whelan was going to have to increase his offer, and less than a week later he did. Mike Whelan and I had a couple more conversations before the number became enticing enough for me to go back to Howard with an update. I told him about The Golf Channel's latest offer, which included a plane ride to Orlando to meet with the management team face to face. He encouraged me to go to the meeting and, again, asked only that he be kept in the loop. I called Whelan back and arrangements were finalized.

FIRST IMPRESSIONS

I had been to Orlando once in my life. I know we went to Walt Disney World but, for the life of me, I can't remember why we were in Central Florida. When I was a kid, Hirshland family vacation destinations, more often than not, involved places to which we could drive, unless we were travelling to Hawaii to visit family, or another exotic location. For most, we would all pile into the family's biggest vehicle (Mom and Dad in the front and Mark, David, and me fighting in the back) and drive to Los Angeles or Idaho or Yosemite or Zion National Park in Utah or British Columbia or anywhere else, stopping on the way to our final destination at various motels that had sprung up alongside the highway. We didn't care where we stayed as long as the place had a pool. We did visit New York City, Chicago, and many other places east of the Rockies, including Orlando, but my second visit was much more memorable than my first.

I arrived at the Orlando International Airport, headed for the tram that links the various gates with the main terminal, and was surprised to see a familiar face. Emmett Loughran, a technical director with whom I had worked on a number of ESPN golf events, had also just gotten off a plane. Emmett is a jolly, easygoing, talented TV guy who, at the time, lived in New York with his wife and two kids. There were very few reasons either one of us would be in Orlando without our families. Actually there was only one, The Golf Channel, and, as our eyes met, we both knew we were there for the same thing, if not the same job.

"Golf Channel interview?" Emmett asked, extending his hand in greeting.

"It seems they're looking for a producer," I replied, taking his hand and shaking it. "You?"

"With any luck, I'll be your director," he said laughing.

Standing there in the land of Mickey I thought, it is a small world after all.

We were each told to take a cab to The Golf Channel offices, so we decided to share one, and we headed to the appropriate address. Orlando is a blot on the map along Interstate 4, between the state's west coast and Tampa, and its east coast and the city of Daytona. It is home to a modest downtown, an NBA basketball team (the Magic), a few nice neighborhoods, Rollins College, the University of Central Florida, and the world's most visited theme parks: Walt Disney World, Sea World, and Universal Studios Florida. In the fall of 1994, it was also suddenly the home of the world's first niche sports television network, but when Emmett Loughran and I first visited, The Golf Channel didn't have much of a home. The cab driver had no idea what we were talking about when Emmett said our destination was The Golf Channel, but we did have a street address, so he took us there. We skirted the edges of Universal Studios on the east side of Orlando and turned down a side street, and then into a small parking lot that fronted what appeared to be a medical office building. It appeared that way because that's exactly what it was.

We climbed a flight of stairs, turned down a hallway, found the proper office number, and entered. The space had been divided into a small reception area and several offices. Seated behind a desk at the front was a young lady with a big smile.

"Welcome to The Golf Channel," she said, getting up and coming around the desk to say hello. "Which one of you is Keith and which one is Emmett?"

"Keith," I said, raising my hand.

"That would make me Emmett," my friend said, standing next to me.

"I'm Lori Dawson," was her reply. "You're meeting with Mike," she said, looking at me, "and you are meeting with Paul," she said, turning to Emmett.

I had no idea who Paul was, so I was happy to be meeting with Mike. Lori led us both down a short hallway, stopping at one door to hand Emmett off, and then she and I continued into another room where apparently I would meet with Mike.

"Is this The Golf Channel?" I asked, looking around. Lori Dawson smiled a smile that seemed to say everyone asks that.

"It is for now," she answered. "Mr. Gibbs has found a more permanent location, but for now he, Mr. Greenway, Mr. Whelan, and Mr. Farnsworth work out of here."

Mr. Farnsworth must be Paul, I thought.

"It doesn't look like much but it's really exciting," she said, somewhat conspiratorially. "Mike will be right with you." She turned on her heel and headed back to her desk. A minute or two later Michael J. Whelan blew into the room.

"I'm Mike," he said, shaking my hand and clearly not expecting a reply. "Let's get some lunch, we've got a lot to talk about."

"What in the world am I getting into?" I thought, as we breezed past Lori Dawson on the way out the door.

QUESTIONED ON THE COURSE

Lunch for Mike and me turned out to be a sandwich at a local golf course, and we made small talk over turkey and cheese on wheat and a Coke. I learned that Whelan, Greenway, and the golf historian/proposed on-course announcer, Peter Kessler, all came from HBO. Paul Farnsworth turned out to be Mike's right hand man, given the title of coordinating producer, and was primarily responsible for helping come up with programming ideas and hiring and managing the technical people charged with bringing those shows to life. That's why he was talking to Emmett. I would meet him later, assured Mike. He learned that I was a TV brat who really liked his job at ESPN but hungered to get back into live sports production, especially golf. I was excited, nervous, confident, and questioning. Mike made The Golf Channel sound like nirvana, but that was his job.

He was a smooth-talking, well-dressed, New-York-bundle-of-energy kind of a guy. Whelan was self-assured and, in many ways, impressive. He was also convinced that he was offering me the second best job in the world. It was the second best because, according to him, he had already laid claim to the best.

"Ready for the interview?" he asked.

"Sure," I said watching him get up and walk toward a golf cart loaded up with two sets of clubs.

"I do all my interviews on the golf course," he said, looking back over his shoulder at me. "Best place in the world to get a real sense of what someone is like."

"Goodness," I said, getting up and shedding both my sport coat and tie.

We teed off on number ten and I later learned Emmett and Paul Farnsworth were doing the same thing, but they started on the first hole. I played surprisingly well wearing slacks and a dress shirt, in rented shoes, and with a set of rental clubs, and apparently the interview went well, too, because after every other hole Mike offered me more money to join his band of merry men. While flattered, none of the offers reached the level of "leaving ESPN for" until we putted out at the ninth and last hole (I had a return flight to catch). Whelan patted me on the back and dropped what, at the time, felt like a bombshell by offering me more than twice my current salary. My response was a slight smile and a question.

"Is any of what you're offering guaranteed if the channel doesn't make it?"

"Nothing is guaranteed, and by the way, not making it is *not* an option," was his answer.

He drove me to the airport in a brand new Mustang convertible, and during the ride Mike talked and I listened to the production and programming foundation they were laying for the channel. Tournaments were at the top of the food chain, but the programming grid would include news, instruction, a weekly talk show he kept calling *Golf Talk Live*, and historical programming, gleaned from the library at the PGA TOUR. As we arrived at Orlando International, he shook my hand and made one more final "final" offer that came with a business card on which he had scribbled his home phone number and an ultimatum.

"I want you to join us, but I need a yes or no by midnight tonight."

"Understood," I answered, not really understanding, but already knowing what I wanted my answer to be. I wanted this opportunity. I knew the risks and understood the challenges, but Whelan's energy was contagious; and the chance to lead a remote production team on a history-making television channel was intoxicating. All that was left was to convince Kathy it was the right move to move again, and tell Howard that my way of thanking him for all the hoops he had jumped through to get me a job was to leave after nine months. That was all.

The trip from Orlando to Hartford flew by as I pondered my future and the future for my family. The money I was being offered was a huge positive, but the questions about the longevity of the channel were very, very real. Mike Whelan was a skilled salesperson and his vision was both exciting and seemed realistic, but I hadn't met any of the other decision makers at The Golf Channel, and the structure, stability, and future prospects for me at ESPN were hard to ignore. It was early evening in Connecticut when I jumped in my car and started for home. On the way I pulled out my ESPN-issued mobile phone and called my dad.

"Hey, Pop," our conversation began. "I've got a decision to make."

"I'm listening," is what I heard next.

I told him about my day and the escalating offers Whelan had made. We talked about the network's prospects, the effects another move would have on Kathy and the kids, and what leaving ESPN would mean, and then he asked the only question that mattered:

"What do you want to do?"

I pulled into the driveway, got out of the car, and walked into the house. Kathy had put the kids to bed, and I hugged her and told her we had to talk. For the next couple hours we discussed our future; she was happy in Connecticut, living close to family and the friends with whom she had grown up, but she understood that my work at ESPN wasn't 100 percent fulfilling and that I missed the energy live golf provided. The money was also enticing. We looked up the cost of living in Central Florida. The difference between Orlando and Farmington, Connecticut, made the salary even more impressive. We could buy a house, put some money in the bank, and enjoy the snowless winters in the Sunshine State. As we talked, the clock ticked and the "witching hour" of midnight quickly approached. Finally, I told her what I had told my dad—I wanted this. She kissed me and went to bed. In my mind, I wrestled a few more minutes with the pros and cons and then fished Mike Whelan's card out of my pocket and picked up the phone. It was 11:50 p.m.

"Hello," a sleepy voice answered the phone. Had I awakened him? Wasn't he the one who told me I had until midnight to decide my fate?

"Mike, it's Keith Hirshland," I started.

"Uh huh," was his contribution to keeping the conversation going. I took a deep breath and uttered the words that would change my life,

"I spoke with my wife and we've decided that it would be an honor to join The Golf Channel," I stopped.

"That's great news," he replied. "Call me on Monday and we'll work out the details," he said, hanging up the phone and most certainly rolling over and falling right back to sleep. At least one of us got some sleep that night. I had to tell Howard Katz on Monday morning that I was leaving.

So, as the clock struck midnight on September 23, 1994, there were a total of five people in the country whose number one occupation was to produce golf on network television: Lance Barrow, who had just taken over for Frank Chirkinian, at CBS; Tommy Roy, at NBC; Terry Jastrow, at ABC; Andy Young, at ESPN; and me.

HOWARD'S END

Much of the weekend was spent researching neighborhoods in Orlando and mentioning to our three-and-a-half-year-old daughter, Hayley, that she was about to be neighbors with Mickey Mouse. The Golf Channel wanted me there sooner rather than later, which meant one of us would have to make another trip to Orlando to find us a place to live. I wanted Kathy involved in this process, so we decided she would be the one to make that trip. We saw relatives, made hasty plans with friends for farewell get-togethers, and did some preliminary packing. I also spent time rehearsing just how I would tell Howard Katz. He had done me a great service by finding a place for me in Bristol, and part of me felt I was about to do him a great disservice by leaving. I resolved to meet the issue head on because, in the end, what mattered most was that this was too good an opportunity to pass up, and I hoped Howard would understand that.

Monday was a *Sports Smash* day for me, so I was at my desk, in my cubicle, bright and early. Everybody knew I was gone on Friday, but no one knew where I was except Howard, and, after fretting about relaying my decision all weekend, I wanted to get the deed done as soon as possible. I knew Howard was always at his desk by 8 a.m., so when the clock struck that number, I was out of my chair and headed toward his door. His assistant confirmed he was there and told me to go right in.

"How was your visit?" Howard said, without looking up from the paperwork that occupied him.

"Good," I said and that made him look up. I took a deep breath and told him what they had offered.

"We can't come anywhere near to matching that," he said.

"I know," was my response. "I didn't expect you to."

Howard Katz nodded, sat back in his chair, and looked me in the eye.

"Sounds like you've made a decision."

"I have," I said, but I didn't stop. "I want to thank you for everything, and while I know this is a risk, it feels like it's too good to pass up. I might be making a huge mistake, but I can live with that."

Howard smiled. "It is too good to pass up," he said, sounding fatherly. "You have to give it a shot."

Relief flooded over me as Howard continued, "Whatever happens, just know the door here is always open." He stood and offered his hand one more time, or should I say, one last time. I shook it, thanked him, and left his office thinking I had done everything right. I was honest with him the whole time, keeping him in the loop while considering all the options. I turned down several offers before finally accepting a very generous one, and, in the end, made the right decision for my family. I felt good about the entire process, but apparently I was the only one. I have no way of knowing whether that door was actually ever open, closed, or sealed shut, because Howard Katz hasn't spoken to me since.

A NEW NETWORK,
ANOTHER NEW START

The next couple of weeks were a crazy cacophony of circumstances, obligations, and tasks as we prepared for our life's next step. Kathy flew to Orlando on The Golf Channel's dime and, in one day, found us a place to live. A cute ranch house in the Conway area of Orlando, close to the airport and twenty minutes from The Golf Channel's new headquarters in a nondescript office park near Universal Studios, would be our home. Good-byes were said and promises to keep in touch made as we got ready for the move. Much of what we had was still in the boxes used for the last trip across the country, so putting our lives in a moving van wasn't quite as arduous as the last time.

I spent a number of hours on the phone with Mike Whelan mapping a direction for the channel's live tournament coverage. Executives Bob Greenway (senior vice president of programming, production, and operations) and Gary Stevenson (chief operating officer) were looking forward to meeting me, as was founder and president Joe Gibbs. It was all a bit overwhelming, and it could have been debilitating if there wasn't so much work to do. The channel was set to make its worldwide debut on January 17, 1995, slightly more than three months hence, and production and talent teams had to be assembled. Once in Orlando, I was going to have to hit the ground running.

Agreements in place with the Ladies Professional Golf Association meant our first live domestic telecast would be a tournament called the HealthSouth Inaugural, played on one of the courses at Walt Disney World in Orlando, taking place just two days after the network's launch. It was right in our back yard, but we were worlds away from being ready to put anything on television, let alone a professional golf tournament. Brilliant planning and negotiations by Gibbs, Greenway, and Stevenson with the various golf governing bodies meant The Golf Channel also had television and rights holder agreements with the European Tour, the PGA TOUR, and its feeder tour, sponsored in 1995 by the Ben Hogan Company, ensuring live golf would be the cornerstone on which the new network would be built. In all, the team I helped assemble would be responsible for twenty-eight live tournament telecasts, providing the network with more than a thousand hours of programming that first year. But when I walked through the doors on October 14, 1994, as the forty-eighth employee of Joe Gibbs's venture, the number of members of the live golf production team equaled two (including me), and the LPGA announce team Mike Whelan had cobbled together featured four television rookies. Only future Hall of Fame member Donna Caponi had any previous television broadcast experience. To say we had a long way to go in a short period of time was an understatement, but nobody complained; we didn't have that luxury.

The Golf Channel in 1994 was television's version of the wild, wild West, and Mike Whelan was the sheriff. In addition to bringing me on board, Whelan's other lieutenants included a brash, big-talking, TV veteran named Mark Friedman to assemble and run the news department; a creative yet hard-work-challenged son of a respected golf writer, named Marty Jenkins, to head up what would become the instructional department; and a wiry, anxious, bundle of energy named Jeff Hymes to produce a pregame show. Hymes, Jenkins, and Friedman technically reported to Paul Farnsworth, who reported to Whelan; but my observation was that people rarely reported to anybody, and, when they did, it was over drinks at Sam Snead's Tavern or Rachel's Steakhouse. Whelan may have run a loose ship but, in the beginning, his management style was exactly what the channel needed to spread its wings. He hired creative people who needed the freedom to create. That attitude helped get the network on the air, but it was an unstable foundation that would need constant attention lest it crashed to earth at the most inopportune time.

MY SHIP GETS AN ANCHOR

In the fall of 1994, I had two construction jobs: build both an announce team and a production team. The first task was already well under way, as Whelan had hired a generous portion of the group. We had people, some of them even professionals, to roam the fairways and inhabit the booth, but we were far from whole. The main missing ingredient was a play-by-play announcer, the guy or girl to serve as the anchor and traffic cop for the telecast. As with his efforts to try and find a producer, Mike had been down the well-traveled paths other networks had trod. He interviewed and was rejected by the folks who, at the time, had golf play-by-play jobs, and interviewed and rejected a dozen more who had, once upon a time, held golf play-by-play jobs. He hired a handsome, hard-luck Canadian pro-turned-broadcaster named Jim Nelford to be the main analyst for The Golf Channel's men's events, joining Donna Caponi, who had long been on board as the women's events analyst. Caponi, instructor Gary Smith, historian Peter Kessler, two-time US Women's Amateur Champion Kay Cockerill, and former LPGA Tour player Lori Garbacz would be on course at various tournaments; but, as October turned to November, we still didn't have a lead announcer. That changed when Whelan looked at another sport, on another network, and picked ESPN bowling announcer Denny Schreiner to be "our guy." Schreiner, a single-digit-handicap golfer, played in college at Akron during the midseventies and had served as the radio play-by-play announcer for the NBA's Cleveland Cavaliers for five seasons, in addition to his bowling duties at ESPN. In short, he was a professional announcer and just what the doctor ordered for a startup network devoted exclusively to golf. Plus, he *wanted* the job. With the announcer team intact, I could turn my attention to building a production team.

The only other person already on board was a quiet, thoughtful, Dartmouth graduate named Jeff Gershengorn, whom Whelan had plucked from the CBS Sports golf production team. "Gersh" would be my right-hand man, responsible for, among other things, the creation and implementation of our on-air graphics system. While Whelan came up with the "look," it was Jeff Gershengorn who decided what information was important to impart to the viewers, and in what way we would present that information. He had worked in the CBS system, while I had come from an ESPN golf world, created by Don Ohlmeyer and refined by Steve Beim and Andy Young. Gersh may have preferred to televise golf the way CBS did it, but he was smart enough to know we could only afford to do it the way it was done at ESPN—the way I knew how to do it.

The system depends on four pillars to be successful, all of equal importance. We had two of the four and now set out to find the other two. I concentrated on finding the guy that would serve the same role I served in Andy Young's world, the replay producer. I knew from experience, in the minute-by-minute world of television golf production, this is the hardest job. I decided to contact one of the people with whom I had worked in Bristol, Peter Esposito, and asked if he'd be interested in joining us on this adventure. Pete had been at ESPN for years and was widely recognized as one of the network's hardest-working production people. He was a Northeasterner who had grown up a Red Sox and Patriots fan in western Massachusetts and who had always wanted to work at ESPN. He had gotten his dream job, but had grown disillusioned due to the lack of advancement there. We had played a great deal of golf together, so I knew he had two things necessary for the job: a great work ethic and knowledge of the game. He accepted my offer and pillar three was on board.

We couldn't have gotten any of it done without Jeff Gershengorn and around the same time, Gersh was approaching a colleague at CBS to ferret out his interest in joining our group. Karel Schliksbier is a mountain of a man who played college football on the offensive line at the University of Wisconsin. At six foot five and close to 290 pounds, he was then the biggest man in the Big Ten conference. After leaving school, he bounced around a bit before landing a gig with CBS as an announcer assistant. In this role, he travelled the country with that network, providing companionship and much-needed information for Steve Melnyk, during their golf coverage, and Pat Summerall and John Madden during football season. According to Gersh, "the Big Man" was a gregarious, good-humored guy with a heart that fit his frame and a temperament that would fit in nicely with our group. I was in need of the fourth pillar, and what better person than a fun-loving former offensive lineman who tipped the scales at more than three hundred pounds to add support. On the phone, I explained to Karel that the job was primarily to provide support and information to me in regard to who the professional golfers were and what their order of play would be. He knew the job because he had watched his friend and colleague Chuck Will do it for Frank Chirkinian at CBS for years. The main difference, I explained to him, was that he would have to execute this more-difficult-than-it-sounds task with unpaid, unproven, and different tournament volunteers each week because, unlike the broadcast networks, our budget couldn't withstand the financial strain of travelling people to each event to carry microphones and report back hitting orders. I offered Karel the job over the phone and he accepted. Pillar four in place.

Now all we had to do was get the team together and find a place to practice.

PRACTICE MAKES PERFECT

The Golf Channel was going on the air in a matter of months and every single person was busy, inside and outside the building. Programming ideas were still taking shape, sets were being built, and budgets decided. Everybody had ideas, but only a select few (Gibbs, Stevenson, Greenway, Chief Financial Officer Del Wood, and top legal mind Chris Murvin, among them) knew how much money was in the purse. Production people want things, financial guys know things cost money, and word was sent out, then filtered down, that economics were just as important as production value. Chief Operating Officer Gary Stevenson, along with Bob Greenway, delivered the message to Mike Whelan, who passed it along to Paul Farnsworth and me.

I was lucky because my experience was limited to producing golf the "OCC way," the most economically prudent production system in golf. Even that wasn't cheap. Because of logistics, just to cover a tournament in the least complicated way, golf is by far the most expensive sport to produce, and we were starting from scratch. Some of the economics that swirl around the production of a golf tournament include the pre-event preparation. CBS, NBC, and ESPN had the luxury of having already set up and televised events at dozens of locations; we weren't so lucky. We had twenty-eight tournaments on the schedule for 1995 and we, as a group, had to go visit every single venue months before the first golf ball was struck. These adventures are called site surveys and, quite frankly, they are a pain in the ass.

Golf courses take up acreage and many feature lakes, trees, hills, valleys, rivers, and streams; and those are just the natural features. Many golf courses also are built around or near houses, resort hotels, power lines, and even airports; and one, two, or all of these things cause heartburn for a television crew. We had to go look at every hole, meet every tournament director, and find adequate housing (usually a Hampton Inn or Courtyard by Marriott) for a crew of close to a hundred hardworking people. While we were discussing where behind the green to put the camera tower, who might be the local copy machine and phone company contact, or how many cases of Coke the tournament might be willing to "donate" to our cause, Whelan, Farnsworth, and the rest of the boys in Orlando were busy building the other part of the channel. It was a team effort—our team and theirs—and rarely did the two meet.

My friend Emmett Loughran must have been equally impressive during his lunch/golf round trip to Orlando because he was chosen to sit by my side and direct all of The Golf Channel's live domestic tournament productions. He joined us on every trip around this great land, along with Vice President of Tournament Affairs Mark Oldham, Director of Remote Productions David Graham, and a handful of folks from the company that would supply all of our technical trucks and equipment, NEP. In some cities we had to convince tournaments that had never been on TV that we wouldn't come in like an invading horde and ruin their property; then we had to convince the ones who had once been on networks or cable channels that reached hundreds of thousands, if not millions of fans, that we wouldn't ruin their reputations. Many times that was a much tougher sale.

Between the middle of October and the end of December 1994, we managed to map out a plan and ease the minds at tournaments from Pensacola, Florida, to Tucson, Arizona, and we even were able to schedule and perform two dress rehearsal events as we prepared to do it for real. The first of these "practice" events happened in Orlando, during something called the Gary Player Tour. We rolled in the trucks, distributed the cable, built cameras on scaffolding towers, and pretended to make golf television. Emmett got used to me, I got a sense of what he was all about, the announcers tried to figure out when to talk and when to shut up, and we put it all on videotape to study it. A pro from Providence, Rhode Island, named Patrick Sheehan ended up winning the event, and our team ended up learning a lot, especially about ourselves.

The second and last time we had to "practice" televising an event was the first week in December, at what many players call golf's toughest tournament, the PGA TOUR Qualifying Tournament.

OUR FIRST Q SCHOOL TEST

Back in 1965, the PGA TOUR decided it needed a way to determine which players would be eligible to tee it up in their tournaments and compete for millions of dollars in prize money. That system became the PGA TOUR Qualifying Tournament, known almost instantly as Q-School. There are several ways to become a PGA TOUR pro, but, historically, Q-School has produced by far the most. Hundreds of household golf names, including Fuzzy Zoeller, Ben Crenshaw, Peter Jacobsen, and Paul Azinger, made their way to the PGA TOUR thanks to performing well enough at the qualifying tournament. Tiger Woods never had to go to Q-School; neither did Phil Mickelson. Michael Allen, a Champions Tour player who is also a major champion, has been fifteen times. Azinger, who recorded the best score and earned medalist honors at the 1984 event, once described it to me as "climbing up a cactus backwards, naked." Nobody wanted to be there, but everybody knew it was a necessary evil.

In 1994, the tournament was actually several tournaments that were competed in stages. Hopefuls teed it up against hundreds of fellow dreamers and, if their score was among the lowest, they advance to the next stage. It all culminated in the finals, held in alternate years on the West Coast or the East Coast. In 1994, the event was at a Central Florida resort called Grenelefe, and on the line were forty-five spots on the 1995 PGA TOUR.

In retrospect, I find it strange that, during what might be the most pressure-packed tournament in all of golf, with jobs for an entire year on the line, the PGA TOUR allowed our trucks, cameras, and technicians to invade this most genuine and, for many, life changing of events for a make-believe broadcast. To us, at the time, it made all the sense in the world, and our team treated it like the Masters.

The creative team at The Golf Channel, led by Steve Johnson, was still in the process of creating what would end up being the first of many "looks" that would grace the screen on behalf of our golf exclusive television network; but we wanted to "come on the air" with something that resembled a tease and an open, so I went to work. I racked my brain for songs about school and came up with "My Old School," by Steely Dan; "School's Out," by Alice Cooper; "Be True to Your School," by the Beach Boys; and "Hail, Hail Rock and Roll" ("Up in the morning and off to school"), by Chuck Berry, and tied them all together with video of participants and sound bites from PGA TOUR stars who had been through the process. What resulted was a forty-five-second-long piece that attempted to capture the essence of the event. We followed that with the first thirty seconds of a promotional video that the channel's sales and marketing department had put together to lure advertisers to spend money on The Golf Channel when it finally hit the air; hardly the stuff of Emmy Awards, but effective nonetheless. We had built the scaffolding towers, laid the cables, placed the microphones, equipped the volunteers, fed the crew, and assumed our various positions for a full dress rehearsal on Friday afternoon. No one would see this but us, but we knew it just might be the most important production in which any of us would ever be involved. Were we up to the challenge? Could we handle the scrutiny? Would we be ready to do it for real in less than forty-five days? We were about to find out. The plan was to "go on the air" at 1 p.m. ET and nerves were on high alert. Then something happened that ratcheted up the pressure one more notch. The door to the mobile unit opened and in walked Joseph E. Gibbs.

I had spent a total of three hours with Mr. Gibbs since the day I was hired. Maybe. It wasn't that we didn't like each other; it was just that we were both very busy. He was responsible for making history, and I had a small and remote part in helping him. Never before had a television network devoted exclusively to one sport been conceptualized, funded, staffed, programmed, and sold. Joseph E. Gibbs was a trailblazer and a visionary, but, more importantly, he was a genuinely nice man. Every single person that went to work for him, especially in the beginning, wanted his dream to become a reality. I was no exception. Joe had no real idea specifically what I or the close to one hundred people assembled that day did; he just knew our job was to put a golf tournament on his channel, and he had been told we were the right people to do just that. Before he walked in the truck, we were putting on a show for ourselves, but when he stood behind me, eyes fixed on the rows of television screens all lit up in front of him I felt the weight of knowing I was doing it for him. Our associate director, Chuck Whitfield, started the countdown,

"One minute to air," he boomed and, as I turned to acknowledge his trigger, he gave me a knowing smile.

"Okay, folks, here we go." I started pushing the appropriate buttons so everyone who needed to could hear my commands. "I'm proud to work with each and every one of you, and I know we are up to this challenge."

"Forty-five seconds," said Chuck.

"Just remember to have fun," I continued, and at that point I said six words that I am sure I had heard before, but for the life of me couldn't remember where or when:

"Cover me, boys, I'm going in."

I heard Joe Gibbs chuckle and I felt the weight of his hand as he rested it on my shoulder.

"Thirty seconds," counted Chuck. "Yatahay," he said, and later I would learn it was a Navajo saying that meant "it is good."

Emmett extended his hand for me to shake and I took it, as Chuck's count hit ten.

"Nine, eight, seven," Chuck said, as eyes scanned the screens. I asked Karel where my best golf was; Emmett readied the technicians, and then Chuck's count hit two.

"Roll yellow," barked Emmett, giving the final instruction to the tape machine operator that would start the piece that I had put together to begin this critical dress rehearsal. Yellow rolled.

All of a sudden, the largest screen in the monitor wall in front of us sprang to life with color as sound blared from the speakers mounted above our heads.

"Up in the morning and off to school," sang Chuck Berry, as golf images lit up the truck.

We were off and running. Several people talked and listened at the same time, a necessary skill in live sports production and, if there were any nerves, none showed. I alerted Denny Schreiner and Jim Nelford, seated and smartly dressed in our portable announce booth, that their role in this passion play was about to begin. The final screen image of the makeshift opening that I had edited together was the giant G that the creative types had designed, and Joe Gibbs had approved, as the network's logo. When it filled the screen, I took a chance and turned to steal a glance at the man who was responsible for this opportunity. What I saw raised goose bumps and made the hair on my neck stand up; Joe Gibbs had a satisfied smile on his face and a single tear rolled down his left cheek.

At that very moment, this was more than just a TV channel, or a business venture, or a pet project; this was that man's dream coming true, and we were all there to not only witness it, but actually help make it happen. I knew then and there that leaping into this adventure was the right decision.

Mr. Gibbs was long gone before we finished our two-and-a-half-hour rehearsal broadcast, but the man he had tabbed as the chief operating officer, Gary Stevenson, stayed until the bitter end. Before coming to The Golf Channel, Stevenson had been part of the executive management team at the NBA, as well as serving under Commissioner Deane Beman at the PGA TOUR. He had worked with and around athletes for dozens of years and knew bullshit when he came across it. Gary was a decision maker and, during the early days at The Golf Channel, there were hundreds of decisions that needed to be made every day. Another trait that defined Gary was the lack of a rearview mirror. He gave his blessing, or cast aspersion, on each program planned, aspect created, or dollar budgeted, with the best interest of moving Joe Gibbs's network forward. He displayed no self-doubt and, as far as I could tell, had no regrets. At the end of that very stressful, very successful afternoon, he invited the entire production and talent team to dinner to celebrate; so, after a meeting that started with a brief post mortem and ended with plans for the show we would practice producing the next day, we all joined our boss for a get together at Bob Evans Barbeque Restaurant (after all, this was Haines City, Florida!).

We were a relieved group of people. By all accounts, the rehearsal had gone beautifully and, despite small complaints here and a suggestion to change something there, the atmosphere was celebratory. Then the chief operating officer tapped the side of his mug with a spoon and commanded our attention.

"I don't know how much Keith told you, but Joe Gibbs was in the production truck this afternoon at the start of the show." That caused heads to turn and looks of both surprise and concern to creep across several faces, because I hadn't told anyone that Joe had seen at least the first half hour of the production. Gary paused briefly for effect, and then said with a smile:

"That was one proud man." He raised his glass and we followed suit. Then he looked around the table before his eyes fell on me.

"There is a tremendous amount of work left to do to get this channel on the air, but you need to know that, with everything on my plate, I am thankful that live tournament production is the *one* aspect of this operation that I don't have to lose one single wink of sleep over. Thank you for that."

There was probably a "hip, hip, hooray" tossed out, but I heard none of it. I was proud that we were worry free in Gary's mind, but knew it was my job to make sure it stayed that way.

SHOOTING STARS IN A
STARLESS SKY

As January 17, 1995, approached, the buildings The Golf Channel occupied in the nondescript office park located at 7580 Commerce Center Drive in Orlando began to fill up with bodies and equipment that would be needed to put the network on the air. Another Alabaman, Matt Scalici, was the driving force behind the technology, while a burly, fast-talking, big-thinking salesman named Gene Pizzolato would lead a group of mercenaries as they dealt with what may have been the toughest job of all...selling a concept. A television network dedicated twenty-four hours a day to news had launched (CNN, in June of 1980) as had a network that was all sports all the time (ESPN, in September of 1979) but this was the first time that fans of one single sport would be able to turn on the TV and watch their favorite subject twenty-four hours a day, seven days a week, 365 days a year. How much was that worth? How do you sell something no one had ever seen before? That was the challenge that confronted Pizzolato and his top lieutenants, Tom Knapp and David Manougian.

They started with the premise that Gibbs had figured out: golf was more than a sport; it was, in fact, a lifestyle. There was equipment, clothing, vacation resorts, books, magazines, and money. Research showed that golfers and golf fans were more economically well off than almost every other sport's fans. The majority of them were wealthy, most were white, and many were corporate decision makers who used golf as a tool in business. The sales team at The Golf Channel, armed with those facts, beat the corporate bushes with Joe Gibbs's idea and sold millions of dollars of advertising for programming that didn't exist. But that was only one piece of the economic plan; most important to the success of the network was the belief that, like movie channels HBO and Showtime, people would pay a monthly fee of close to $8 to their local cable companies for the privilege of watching news about, interviews with, instruction of, historical programming about, and tournaments featuring golf and golfers. Merely weeks away from the moment The Golf Channel would see the light of day, the number of people who had agreed that $8 a month was worth it was still south of one hundred thousand, nowhere near what Gibbs, Wood, Stevenson, and Greenway knew it would take to keep the channel afloat.

At the party celebrating The Golf Channel's tenth anniversary in 2005, Gibbs admitted to a small group of us that there were dozens of sleepless nights in those early days as he struggled, sometimes up until hours before the deadline, to pay the bills, keep the lights on, and meet the business's payroll demands. He smiled when he said that somehow, someway, deals were always struck and funds always made their way into the network's coffers so the dream could survive. Very few people ever knew how close we all were to having to find other work, and in those days and hours before the network launched, the energy in and around the building was inspiring. Joe Gibbs and Arnold Palmer literally flipped a switch (a great big artificial one with a golf ball on the handle), and Brian Hammons and Lynda Cardwell welcomed the world to one more brick along the road to the much-talked-about five-hundred-channel television universe.

My team was still inside the production trucks, stationed along the fairways of the golf course at Walt Disney World, putting the finishing touches on pieces that would be a part of our first live, domestic tournament production when a very small slice of the national television audience saw, and heard Brian Hammons bring The Golf Channel on the air. I didn't hear his exact words at the time, but I guarantee you they weren't, "Good evening, and welcome to the end of my career."

So The Golf Channel became a reality. People worked countless hours, secluded in the cocoons of their own worlds of news, instruction, sales, promotion, tournaments, or administration; all dedicated to a common goal...helping Joe Gibbs's dream become a success. Hammons and Cardwell were joined on the air by Jennifer Mills, Peter Kessler, Dwayne Ballen, and others on shows titled *Golf Channel Academy, Academy Live, Golf Central, Golf Talk Live, Golf Channel Classics*, and *Golf Channel Pre Game*. Each show had its own look, theme music, and ideas, for the most part conceived by the incredibly active mind of Michael J. Whelan. His fertile mind burned hot and so

did his temper. Stories of people being called on the carpet in Whelan's office started in Orlando and were embellished by the time they reached us out on the road. Friedman was inflexible in his management of the news team; Jenkins was too flexible in regard to the instruction unit; and Hymes lacked focus in his preparation for the Thursday through Sunday *Pre Game* shows. Whelan demanded perfection, but expected it from what amounted to a ragtag group of broadcast network castoffs and industry newbies, who came to the channel at both the beginnings and ends of careers. Everyone was making it up as they went along, and we all thought it was working, mostly because for nearly all of the hours the network was broadcasting, nobody was watching.

The history books will show that the first live tournament televised by The Golf Channel was the Dubai Desert Classic, a European Tour event that was played January 19–22 and won by American Fred Couples, but history is only partly right. The Dubai Desert Classic might have been the first tournament golf *seen* on The Golf Channel, but the network had absolutely nothing to do with its actual production. The tournament came to American TV screens via satellite and thanks to the efforts of a talented team of European production people. The only ownership The Golf Channel had of the event was that it aired on the network. The *real* first tournament telecast on The Golf Channel was under the capable control of the live tournament team I had built with Mike Whelan's, Paul Farnsworth's, and Bob Greenway's help, and it was being played on the Eagle Pines Golf Course at iconic Walt Disney World in Kissimmee, Florida. It featured the best women golfers in the world: the members of the Ladies Professional Golf Association, including superstars Beth Daniel, Betsy King, and Dottie Mochrie, as well as the still-competitive and Hall of Fame-bound Pat Bradley, and Patty Sheehan, along with two rising foreign stars in Sweden's Annika

Sorenstam and Australian Karrie Webb. The tour had existed for forty-five years and, in 1995, it featured thirty-three events and close to $20 million in prize money. The Golf Channel would televise ten of those events, more than CBS and NBC combined, and only a couple fewer than ESPN.

That first telecast was thrilling and each member of the team performed with aplomb. Denny Schreiner proved to be an agile and adept play-by-play man, directing traffic and bringing out the best in ever-likeable Donna Caponi in the booth, and Kay Cockerill, Lori Garbacz, and Peter Kessler on the ground. We didn't break any new ground in terms of the tournament telecast but, more importantly, we didn't break anything at all. The highlights included an expertly diagramed description of the mechanics of how to throw a club as Caponi took the viewer through the various slow motion plusses and minuses of Meg Mallon's form as she heaved her putter into the lake that bordered the 18th green. We also rejoiced in the victory by Pat Bradley, who walked away with the trophy at the HealthSouth Inaugural and into history as the very first tournament winner on the brand new Golf Channel. Years later, Pat would join our Nationwide Tour broadcasts via the telephone as she watched her nephew, Keegan, compete in that arena on our air. A year after earning his PGA TOUR playing privileges on the Nationwide Tour, Keegan won twice as a rookie on the PGA TOUR, first in Texas, and then in Atlanta as a major champion at the PGA Championship.

Two things did distinguish those early Golf Channel tournament telecasts, and the edicts came from both Joe Gibbs and Bob Greenway. First was the idea to include an extra half hour of programming daily, emanating from the tournament site, that would include the continuation of tournament play, as well as interviews and instruction from the practice tee. We called it *Scorecard Report* and we were the only network doing it. The other thing we did that no other network broadcasting golf would even consider was that we made a promise to our viewers to never leave golf on the golf course during a weekend telecast. Some of the most repeated words in golf broadcasting in those days were, "We are approaching the end of our broadcast window," but thanks to Gibbs and Greenway, there would be no end to the tournament broadcast window on The Golf Channel on either Saturday or Sunday. We didn't have *NBC Nightly News* or *Sixty Minutes* breathing down our necks; we were a twenty-four-hour-a-day network dedicated to golf, and if golf was being played on the weekend, we would stay on the air to show it. That meant excess hours of coverage on multiple occasions and, at times, we were on the air, broadcasting live, for six, seven, or eight hours during the day. Once, at a Nationwide Tour event in Salt Lake City, our Saturday broadcast window lasted nearly ten hours and ended with Carl Paulson holing a second shot from the fairway on the tournament's fifty-fourth hole...in the dark! It meant long hours, hungry stomachs, and strained bladders for an exceptional crew, but that was what we did, and it was the way it was as long as Joe Gibbs and Bob Greenway called the shots.

Two sources of programming were successful, and two others were necessities. Thursday through Sunday was the bastion of necessity with tournament coverage and news taking center stage, but Monday night was where you could find the unexpected success stories. Whelan and Greenway, though not really golf guys, were smart enough to know the mind-set of golfers and their desire for constant improvement, so it made complete sense to feature golf instruction on the television. The channel recruited and paid some of the game's top teachers to participate, and then handed the reins of the show over to Peter Kessler. If Whelan was Frankenstein in terms of the network's creation, then Kessler was his monster. Greenway and Whelan came to The Golf Channel from the unlimited resources/limited viewership world of HBO Sports, and when Bob and Mike came, they brought Kessler with them. At HBO Peter Kessler was heard and not seen, featured in that pay-per-view network's promotional spots as the voice of HBO boxing. He claimed to be a golf historian and he used his booming bass and bigger personality to become the face and voice of Gibbs's new channel. He was masterful at getting to the heart of the matter during the instructional shows he hosted, both live and pre-produced, but where Kessler really made an impact during the early days of The Golf Channel was during the hour-long interview program Whelan titled *Golf Talk Live*.

Kessler was Mike Wallace, Fred Rogers, and Alistair Cooke all rolled into one. He made both the guest and the viewer feel at ease and did just enough research to convince both that he was the smartest golf guy in the world. The show's guests during those first months included golf royalty and some of the biggest names in the sport. Palmer, Nicklaus, and Player joined Kessler on the set, and so did Sarazen, Snead, and Nelson. If you watched the show, you would also swear that Bobby Jones was a frequent visitor from the grave, because Kessler invoked his name or harkened back to his accomplishments during every broadcast. The people he interviewed ended each session by thanking him and showering him with praise, telling him he was the best interviewer they had ever encountered. Kessler not only thanked them for their kind words, but he started believing them. He was a studio star, and that was the mind-set he brought out on the road when he joined our group for live tournament coverage. The problem was the attitude to which we ascribed away from Orlando was that the stars were the ones who actually played the game for a living, not the ones who talked about the ones who played the game for a living. Peter Kessler may have been the big fish in the little studio pond, but as part of our live tournament team he was simply a fish out of water.

UP IN SMOKE

Our tournament group quickly became a family. We had to. The team was on the road together for more than half a year broadcasting LPGA, PGA TOUR, and Nike Tour (what would later become the Buy.Com Tour, then the Nationwide Tour, and now the Web.com Tour) events. The nucleus of the production team was always the same, and the announce team changed slightly, depending on the Tour, and in the beginning Denny Schriener, Donna Caponi, and Peter Kessler were a part of every telecast; but not for long. Kessler's fawning studio style didn't translate to the post round athlete interview, and the premise for which Kessler became part of the tournament team—because Mike Whelan felt having an "everyman" golfer talk to the "everyman" viewer would break new ground in golf broadcasts—never really took hold. Instead, it just broke down. It didn't take long for players, tour officials, and the most discerning viewers to see through the sham that was a single-digit handicap golfer describing and analyzing the play and thought process of professionals. Constant gaffes or misstatements in club or shot selection forced our other announcers (the ones who actually had professional golf careers) to consistently amend or correct Kessler's statements on the air. But misspeaking isn't what ended Peter Kessler's live golf announcing career in the end; misdeeds did.

I think I mentioned that we were on a tight budget and, in an effort to control costs, announcers were expected to share rental cars. Schreiner would swap keys with either Nelford or Caponi, depending on whether we were broadcasting a men's event or a women's. The on-course folks, Gary Smith and Kessler, also had one car between them, which became a constant source of frustration for the Englishman instructor turned excellent on-course commentator. On several occasions, Smith would pull me aside to complain that once he surrendered the car keys to Kessler during the week, he would never see them again. It wasn't fair and it wasn't right; it also wasn't in keeping with the family atmosphere I felt it was my job to foster. When I spoke with Kessler about it, he feigned surprise that it had become a problem and made promises to be more thoughtful in the future. Then the future would become the present and the same Smith complaints would arise anew. One day, Gary did get the car back, and, when he did, it came with an unexpected surprise,

"Keith, it's Gary," came the voice on the other end of the hotel room phone. The British accent told me it was Smith and not Stevenson.

"Hello, Smythe," I replied using the nickname he had acquired. "What's up?"

"I hate to bother you, but I have a problem with Peter and I didn't know where else to turn." I tried to recall whether Kessler had made another egregious call during the day's broadcast, but couldn't come up with anything. Then Gary continued, "When I got the car back tonight, there were two roaches in the ash tray of my car," he stopped.

That sounded like a rental car company problem, not a Peter Kessler problem, to me, and I asked, "Were they still alive?" Silence. Then laughter.

"Not bugs!" Smith burst out when the laughter had subsided. "Marijuana cigarettes." Boy, was I embarrassed.

Then Smith continued, "I can't have that in a rental car for which I am responsible," he said seriously. "If I get stopped by a policeman, it's my hide, not his." I couldn't argue with that.

"I'll take care of it," I assured him. "Did you keep the little buggers?" I said, trying to make a joke.

"The two roaches are in a plastic bag and I can hand them over to you in the morning," he said, and he did.

That Sunday was the final Sunday in the Peter Kessler-as-on-course- commentator experiment, but he would continue as the host of the channel's most successful studio shows for another handful of years. I'm sure he is still working somewhere in the world of golf broadcasting and remembered fondly by scores of viewers and, quite frankly, by me; but our tournament team became a better, tighter knit unit with his departure.

BLACK FRIDAY

Kessler's time with our tournament broadcast team wasn't the only thing that was short lived at the channel. The original programming grid called for a Thursday through Sunday studio show called *Golf Channel Pre Game* that was designed to get the viewer ready for the day's golf action. Dwayne Ballen, an African American veteran of local newscasts, was tabbed as the host, and it was determined that his analyst would be long-time tour player and one-time tournament winner Mark Lye. The intent of the show was admirable, its execution adequate; but the economics of both the program, in particular, and the channel, in general, meant *Golf Channel Pre Game* would have a short shelf life. Stevenson, Greenway, and Gibbs knew it, but they kept it to themselves for as long as they could.

The show had a staff of close to a dozen, and some of them (Ballen, Lye, and producer Jeff Hymes) were collecting hefty salaries. It was also, in its intended and ideal form, an expensive show to put on the air. The blueprint called for correspondents stationed across the country at the week's slate of tour events. These correspondents would report back each day, sometimes live, sometimes via videotape, on the circumstances surrounding each tournament. That meant reporters, equipment, crews, and satellite trucks had to be dispatched, fed, housed, and entertained in as many as three cities a week. That meant money; money Stevenson knew the channel could ill afford.

The first cost-cutting step came with an announcement that correspondents would be limited to the PGA TOUR event each week, with additional support from other tour events (Nike at the time or LPGA) if, and *only* if, a Golf Channel live tournament broadcast crew was on site. That way, the cost of previewing those events could be included in our much larger production budget. That's the way the show stayed on the air for the first part of 1995. Another way was to cross-pollinate crew's members, which meant that, on a weekly basis, our live tournament production crew would include one of the studio staffers. That person would, more often than not, become one of our graphics coordinators, responsible for making sure the names and numbers on the tournament-provided scoring system were accurate before we put them on the air in the form of a leaderboard.

We were in Richmond, Virginia, ready to broadcast a Nike Tour event, and a young man named Josh Berger, who, like Gersh, had come from the world of CBS golf, was our designated graphics coordinator. We fulfilled our duties in regard to supplying the pregame show with a three-minute live insert on Thursday, and then got to work with our own broadcast that day. As customary, when our three minutes were up, I thanked the person on the other end of the phone and ended the interaction with a hearty "see you tomorrow." The problem was, on this occasion there would be no tomorrow for *Golf Channel Pre Game*. Friday dawned hot and sunny in Richmond as I headed to the golf course the same way I always did—six hours before our scheduled air time with a coffee shop stop on the way. This was 1995 and Starbucks had yet to become a store-on-every-corner national phenomenon, so coffee for us, most often, meant a gas station or an occasional local vendor. Fortified, we parked in the clubhouse parking lot and headed to the trucks.

The morning before a tournament telecast is a bustling time as people are accounted for and fed, equipment is checked, and conditions are assessed. For me and the production team, mornings were then, and are now, spent compiling the various features, interviews, and highlights to be a part of that day's broadcast. In 1995, and for a dozen years after that, it all started with the writing and editing of a tease: the very first thing the viewer would see from our truck that day. The text was conceived and written the night before, usually on my trusty blue, graph, letter-size Topps note pad; but sometimes I had to improvise and teases were written on a cocktail napkin, an envelope, or even the skin on the palm of my hand. Inspiration sometimes comes at the most inopportune times. All of the components are laid down, back to back to back, on a piece of videotape, ready to be inserted at the appropriate time during the show. It's a steady stream of activity that is rarely interrupted by the telephone and again, then and now, never by the chief operating officer of the company. Well, almost never.

"Production truck," I answered, aggravated that particular day by the interruption.

"Bad day?" Gary Stevenson said on the other end.

"No, sorry, boss," I answered. "Didn't mean to be short. It's not a bad day at all."

"It's about to be," he said, and then he explained.

The phone call lasted about fifteen minutes, and during it he dropped the bombshell that *Golf Channel Pre Game* would not air that day, or any other day for the foreseeable future. The news had no short-term effect on us, except for Josh Berger, the one member of our group that was actually a member of that group. Gary laid out the process, saying it was Jeff Hymes who was making the majority of the calls in terms of who stayed and who would be leaving the network, and, as far as Gary knew, the way people were finding out was by coming in to work and logging in to their computer. Like the red light/green light system after you collect your luggage when you arrive in Mexico, the lucky ones got the green light and were able to log in; the rest were gone.

The first thing I did, after hanging up with Stevenson, was to shake my head and marvel at the impersonal way The Golf Channel was about to pare down the herd, then I set out to find the appropriate people to tell them that preparations for a live cut-in into *Golf Channel Pre Game* should be halted, now and forever. Then I looked for Josh Berger.

I found him in the second production truck (golf requires at least two) poring over statistics and creating graphics for that day's tournament coverage.

"Got a minute?" I asked, as he looked up.

We walked outside for privacy and then I asked one more, simple question,

"Have you tried to log in to the network this morning?"

"Not yet, why?" he asked, and I told him.

At that time, lower-level production people were not equipped with Golf Channel-provided laptop computers, so Josh had to call a colleague in Orlando and ask that person to log in to the computer system using his user name and password. I couldn't watch, but the technician with whom Josh worked during that particular tournament did, and she later related the events that took place.

On the first try, the log in attempt was unsuccessful. The same result followed the second attempt, and, at that point, Josh Berger, who had left the safety of a broadcast network giant to take a flyer on a startup, niche channel, put his head in his hands and moaned. The mood in the entire truck plummeted, because even though Josh wasn't a permanent part of our team, he was one of the good guys, and seeing him in turmoil was tough. He left the truck disheartened and walked into the portable trailer that served as our office that week.

"I can't believe it," he lamented, plopping down on a rental couch. "I don't know what I'm gonna tell my folks." His head went into his hands again.

Gersh and I, who happened to be in the office at the time, said nothing for a few minutes. What could we say? Then Gersh thought of something,

"Are you sure you tried to log in with the proper information?" he asked Josh, making him look up.

"What do you mean?" he asked Jeff.

"I know I personally have a couple of passwords because of safety concerns," continued Gersh, and at that young Josh Berger's face brightened.

"Oh, my God," he shouted, jumping up from the couch and looking for the nearest phone.

After reaching someone in Orlando, Berger hurriedly barked out different orders than he had relayed less than an hour before. Less than a minute passed as we held our collective breaths,

"Thank you!" he yelled into the phone. It seemed Josh Berger was still employed.

So was Mark Lye, who would become part of our tournament team the next time we televised an event.

LYE DOG

Mark Ryan Lye is a wonderful guy; I'm just not sure he realizes it. He had a better-than-average golf career, first as a three-time NCAA All-America team member at San Jose State, and then for pay after turning professional and joining the PGA TOUR in 1977. In an eighteen-year career, he played in 486 events, making the cut and playing the weekend 70 percent of the time. He finished in the top ten at a tournament forty-one times and won once, in 1983 at the Bank of Boston Classic. That's a better-than-average career in my mind. He was a member of Peter Jacobsen's all-golfer band, Jake Trout and the Flounders, which also included the late Payne Stewart, and he had a cameo role in Adam Sandler's *Happy Gilmore*. But Mark Lye tore a ligament in his right hand and was forced to retire from the PGA TOUR at the way-too-young-to-quit-golf age of forty-three. That's when he turned to television.

At the end of July in 1995, we were headed to the scene of Mark's only tour win, the Pleasant Valley Country Club in Sutton, Massachusetts, for what was then called the Ideon Classic, and Mark Lye was with us. We were a tight group during the time we were on the air, but we were just as much a family when the television broadcast day was over. Donna Caponi (or "Mama Caponi," as we lovingly called her) was frequently responsible for choosing an evening dinner spot, alerting and then gathering the group to enjoy a meal. There were always at least seven of us, and sometimes twice that many, not because we felt we had to work together *and* eat together, but because we wanted to. That week, Donna had learned about the area's most popular seafood place, the Sole Proprietor, so one night more than a dozen of us piled into a few of our rental cars and headed out. The restaurant had been in business for more than fifteen years and was the proud recipient of both local and national awards; but that night wasn't memorable because of the food; it was the company of fools that made it special.

The restaurant probably seated a hundred people, and that night it was packed. Donna had done what she does best, and, as people clearly frustrated due to the excessive wait grumbled, we waltzed past and headed to our table or, more precisely, a series of tables that had been joined together in the middle of the restaurant's main dining room. On the way to our seats, it was easy to spot the handful of PGA TOUR players who had also heard about, or had previously dined at, the Sole Proprietor. Paul Azinger was in a small booth; and Brad Faxon, Jeff Sluman, and the man who would end up holding the trophy on Sunday, Fred Funk, were all dining at separate tables. Donna and Mark said hello to their old friends while Denny inserted himself into the brief encounters and made his presence felt. The rest of us sat down. After the three of them rejoined the group, a couple of waiters appeared to take appetizer and drink orders. Karel was in charge of the app orders, while the rest of us asked for before dinner drinks, and then I had a brainstorm, so I touched the side of my water glass with a butter knife.

"Thank you, Donna, for once again taking care of your extended family," I started as the group turned their faces toward me.

"Yay, Donna," came out of multiple mouths.

"I also want to thank everyone for their hard work this week, and every week," I continued, "but now it's time to pay for your supper." I smiled as quizzical looks showed up on most everyone else.

"Here's the deal," I said. "We are going to go around the table and everyone is responsible for telling a joke." I looked around, trying to convey the fact that it was no joke. "You can pass, but *not* on the first go around, and after that if you pass, you risk the consequences." I saw a smile on almost every face, and the smiles stayed there as I finished. "Whoever tells the funniest joke gets free dinner."

"Who decides?" asked Karel, the biggest guy in the restaurant.

"You do," I said, acknowledging the biggest guy in the restaurant.

"I'll start," said Ted Byrnes, Donna's longtime companion and future husband.

In his distinctive New England accent, Ted told what he called "the penguin joke"— a tall tale about a john who is swindled out of his hard-earned money by a clever prostitute. She tells him her most popular "trick" is the penguin and, of course, he wants it. After eliciting the proper fare, the whore pulls the john's pants down around his ankles then grabs the cash and heads for the door. Imagine the just-pantsed john angrily chasing the whore and you know why the joke is called "the penguin." We were off to a good start.

We went around the room and the jokes varied, from Gersh's less-than-original effort—"A horse walks into a bar and the barkeep says, 'Why the long face?' "— to my also-bar-themed, only slightly funnier ditty about a drunk, a bartender, and some sweet-talking nuts that, of course, turn out to be "complimentary," to a Mark Lye classic:

"It's Halloween at the old folks home," he began, when the roulette wheel of humor landed on his seat, "and Gladys decided she'd come up with a costume that would, most certainly, get the attention of the single men still drawing breath in the building."

The joke's beginning had captured the attention of everyone at the table and Mark played to his rapt audience.

"She noticed Willard watching TV in the corner and approached," he continued with a twinkle in his eye. "With her eyes on Willard, she used both bony hands to lift up her skirt, revealing her God-given gifts in all their glory and screamed, "SUPer Pussy!'"

Half the table burst out laughing, thanks to the joke and the old woman imitation used by Mark. "Willard continued to stare at the TV even though Gladys's private parts were the only thing in sight. Undaunted, Gladys moved on to the next victim, a drooling Harry, who sat facing not the TV, but the wall. "SUPer Pussy!" cried Gladys/Mark, raising his arms to imitate Gladys lifting her skirt, and now the entire table was laughing and the nearby diners were suddenly interested.

"The only response from Harry was more drool," explained Mark, "so Gladys turned her sights on Nigel, who seemed busy puzzling over a crossword puzzle." We knew what was next but we couldn't wait.

"SUPer Pussy!" shouted Gladys/Mark with the full attention of not only our table, but the half a dozen that surrounded the one at which we sat.

"Nigel slowly put down his pencil and lifted his head to get a good look at the creature that had interrupted his crossword," Mark said, getting to the punch line. "As the monocle popped from Nigel's right eye, he gave one last look at Gladys's withered privates and then slowly looked up and into her eyes and said, 'I believe I'll have the soup.' "

The table, in fact a good part of the entire place, roared with laughter.

"I believe I'll have the soup," Mark repeated to himself chuckling. I believe we had a winner.

The jokes didn't stop there; in fact, it was an entire evening of having our funny bones tickled. Ted never ran out of sordid stories, and neither did Mark or Denny, whose efforts included assorted tales about farm animals, farmer's daughters, and travelling salesmen. It was impressive and has proved to be unforgettable. It was also one more illustration of how well we all got along during those early, uncertain days and how much we leaned on each other for support. Sadly, Denny, Donna, Ted, and a large percentage of those early trailblazers left, or were asked to leave, along the way, but Gersh is still part of the Golf Channel family, and so are Brian Hammons and Kay Cockerill; and surprisingly, considering some of the stories still to come in this book, so am I, for now.

A CHANGE OF PLANS

While we were having a laugh on a New England summer night, trying to keep The Golf Channel afloat was no laughing matter. The network was bleeding money and Joe Gibbs and his executive team knew that trimming staff or cutting shows outright was applying a Band-Aid when major surgery was required. They all knew what was wrong: the original business model was built on a shaky foundation, and the fundamental flaw was the belief that The Golf Channel could turn a profit as a pay-per-view network. Joe had some work to do, and he knew where he had to go to get it done: back to his friends at the cable companies that had agreed to carry The Golf Channel in the first place. The balance sheet was tipped far too heavily in favor of the accounts payable, which didn't favor the channel's long-term success. Advertising and sponsorship sales were making positive progress, but there just weren't enough people paying to watch us on TV. Gibbs was acutely aware of the issue and, at the same time, knew how to solve the problem. The Golf Channel had to join other successful networks that lived as part of television's basic cable service. Gibbs and the other members of the brain trust knew they had overestimated the golf viewing public's appetite for spending money on a niche sports network. The service had to be free for it to survive, so Joe Gibbs went back to work.

Cable television is one of the world's most competitive and interesting industries. In 1995, there were a handful of large cable companies (Time Warner, Comcast, Cablevision, and Cox among them) and several smaller ones. They carried similar programming, but each had channels the others didn't, and most made every effort to program their networks with channels and shows its paying customers wanted, unless, of course, it didn't work economically for them. You see, programming costs cable companies money, especially increasingly popular programming like ESPN. Cable operators paid the networks, sometimes pennies, sometimes more, and then turned around and passed the cost of that programming, plus a smallish profit for themselves, on to the consumer. The popularity of the channel also helped determine where on the dial it would land, and that's why you see ESPN consistently in the low twenties or thirties on your cable channel guide.

One other aspect of the cable business, in 1995, gave Joe Gibbs and his sales force heartburn, and that was the fact that cable operators, at the grass-roots or local level, weren't exactly beholden to the wishes, wants, or asks of the corporate fat cats. Picture the franchise system of a fast-food chain like McDonald's, where the menu at the corporate level features a Big Mac, a Quarter Pounder, and Chicken McNuggets, but as you change your view from thirty thousand feet to the streets of Anytown, USA, you find that the McDonald's in your town has the McNuggets and Big Macs but no Quarter Pounders, even though the folks at HQ in Chicago determined that the Quarter Pounder should be part of any well-rounded McDonald's menu. That's what faced Gibbs and his salespeople and meant that they couldn't get a sweeping decision at the corporate level. They had to, instead, appeal to every local cable operator in the country with the hope of persuading them to carry The Golf Channel on a basic tier. Getting the still-needed approval at the corporate level was easy, because a handful of the country's cable operators were among the initial investors in the channel, and they had a vested interest in its success. That would help with many, if not all, of the cable operators, so Joe needed another ace up his sleeve, and he had come up with one. While every other channel that appeared on cable TV demanded, and got, a negotiated sum of money for their efforts, Joe would ensure carriage of The Golf Channel by turning the tables and, instead of *getting paid*, paying the cable operators to carry his channel. That move cost him as much as ten cents a month, paid to dozens, if not hundreds, of cable operators; but it saved The Golf Channel. Suddenly, we went from having a viewing audience the size of Bismarck, North Dakota, to the potential of competing with the nation's most successful cable networks and being seen in major markets, including Chicago, Los Angeles, Miami, and New York.

It was one of two things that helped define the network and enabled it to go from heading down the road to oblivion to, amazingly, turning a profit in just three short years. The other thing that made The Golf Channel must-see TV had nothing to do with Joe Gibbs's business savvy, Gary Stevenson's drive, Bob Greenway's genius, or Mike Whelan's creativity. In 1996 a young man named Tiger Woods turned pro.

OUR FIRST TIGER TALE

Many people think that one day Tiger Woods will be golf's greatest player ever. Some think that day has already arrived. Regardless, I was around when the current or future king arrived on the professional scene. As I put pen to paper right now, the man has won more than one hundred professional golf tournaments; and I almost earned the distinction of being the producer in the TV truck when he won for the first time as a pro. The tournament was the 1996 Quad Cities Open (now the John Deere Classic) and Eldrick Tont "Tiger" Woods was a twenty-year-old PGA TOUR rookie. He turned pro with a "Hello World" announcement at the Greater Milwaukee Open, in August, with three consecutive US Amateur titles and more than $60 million worth of endorsements to his credit. He made the cut in Milwaukee and ended up tied for sixtieth, but his pro debut did feature a hole-in-one that resulted in a raucous celebration. He finished eleventh at a rain-shortened Canadian Open the following week and then came to the Quad Cities to play for the third time as a pro. He played on a sponsor's exemption from tournament director Kym Hougham, and it would be the first and only time he ever teed it up at that particular tournament. It was also The Golf Channel's live tournament production crew's first exposure to the young phenom.

People usually ask two questions when they learn I do work for The Golf Channel: "Can I get a job there?" and "Do you know

Tiger Woods?" The answer to the first question is almost always "you never know," but the answer to the second is always "no". I have met Mr. Woods on a number of occasions, sat with him face to face and interviewed him a few times, and watched him play up close and in person hundreds of times, but I wouldn't presume to say I know him. He would certainly say he has no idea who I am, but here is an attempt to refresh his memory.

Tiger was, for good reason, the talk of the golf world and, because this was our first chance to conduct our own intimate question-and-answer session, I was bound and determined to make sure everything went off without a hitch. In 1996, Tiger still did one-on-one interviews; it wasn't until a few years later that the only exposure the press and golf broadcast networks would get to Tiger was the weekly "gang bang" press conference in the media room. So, that week in 1996, we reached out to Woods's people and set up an interview for Tuesday afternoon. A professional golfer's week usually breaks down this way: arrive at a tournament site on Monday night or Tuesday morning; spend much of Tuesday at the golf course, hitting balls on the practice tee, chipping around the short game area, and putting on the putting green. Tuesday almost always includes playing the course (at least nine holes), especially when you aren't totally familiar with the layout, and most certainly when you are a rookie. Wednesday is pro-am day. This is the day the tournament makes its money charging corporations, businessmen, amateurs who wish they were pros, and ordinary blokes thousands of dollars to play alongside the tour pros. If you're a pro *not* playing in the pro-am (normally around sixty of the 152 pros get pro-am assignments), you make your way to the course for a few more hours of practice and "BS"-ing with friends, caddies, and fellow pros. Thursday morning, bright and early, the tournament starts. Everyone in the field plays the first two days, then the PGA TOUR makes what's called a cut—trimming the field down to the best seventy scores, and those players continue on to play the weekend. So, it was Tuesday, Tiger's practice day, and the day we were granted a few minutes of his time.

We were informed that Tiger would play a practice round in the morning, eat, and then practice. He would then meet us at a predetermined location (a remote area at the far end of the practice tee) at 4 p.m. and answer questions for fifteen minutes. We were free to ask him anything we wanted; after all, it was 1996, and he was twenty and still wet behind the ears. We gathered together our equipment (camera, lights, and microphones) and headed up to the designated area at 3:00, making sure we were ready to go when Tiger got there. He showed up at 3:59 p.m., smiling, enthusiastic, and polite. He spent close to half an hour with us that day; he answered every question openly and honestly, and then thanked us, and even signed a few autographs. In subsequent years, as the number of victories and the legend that was Tiger Woods continued to grow, I had the opportunity to be around him in an intimate setting on several more occasions and, each and every time, found him to be exactly the same way: polite, friendly, and always on time.

Tiger was also on time for his afternoon tee time on Thursday. Despite three consecutive US Amateur titles, saddlebags full of endorsement dollars, and fanfare rarely seen in the gentleman's game, Tiger did not receive preferential treatment when it came to tee times in 1996. As a rookie and a sponsor's exemption, Tiger was placed in the day's second-to-last group, teeing off at 1:54 p.m. Paired with Sean Murphy and John "Jumbo" Elliott, the threesome raced the setting sun to the finish. Oakwood Country Club, the host course, is not particularly long, but it featured tree-lined, sloping fairways and small, difficult-to-read greens. Tiger was treated to Thursday's largest gallery—estimated at more than twenty-five hundred, and he treated them to a one-under-par 69. That left him three shots off the lead of a trio of players after day one.

The PGA TOUR tries to level the playing field each week for every competitor. Players tee off in what are commonly referred to as "waves"; one in the morning and one in the afternoon. They also alternate between the 1st and the 10th holes to begin their rounds during the tournament's first two days. Tiger started on the 1st hole, in the afternoon, on Thursday, and that meant he would begin his second round on the 10th tee Friday morning. A smaller gallery turned out to watch Tiger blister Oakwood, shooting a six-under-par 64. The crowds would be back en masse on Saturday because, when play had been completed on Friday, the PGA TOUR made its weekly cut and seventy-three players were all looking up the leaderboard and chasing one guy: twenty-year-old Tiger Woods. Tiger stayed atop the field after fifty-four holes, thanks to a Saturday 67, and came to the golf course Sunday for a final-pairing tee time with Ed Fiori, a PGA TOUR veteran who picked up his first win when Tiger was three years old. Woods led Fiori by one shot and nobody gave the man, nicknamed "the Grip" because of the unconventional way he held the club, much of a chance against the long-hitting, future-so-bright-we-all-needed-shades, lionized Tiger. Nobody, that is, except Ed Fiori.

There was a tremendous amount of excitement around the golf course, The Golf Channel compound, and the Quad Cities. The area is called that because of the four municipalities straddling the Mississippi River along the Iowa-Illinois border: Bettendorf and Davenport in Iowa, and Moline and Rock Island in Illinois. The golf course that hosted the PGA TOUR event that year, and every year between 1975 and 2000, is in tiny Coal Valley, Illinois. According to US Census figures, it has never officially held more than four thousand people, but there were three times that many the only time Tiger Woods came to town.

Local area businesses in general, and nightclubs in particular, took advantage of Tiger's good play and the additional customers that flocked into town that weekend. Restaurants were full, bars packed, and dance clubs featured long lines for the first time in recent memory. A story about one of those lines made the rounds in our lunch line that week. According to several technicians on the crew, Tiger was spotted out on the town and attempting to enter one of the more popular haunts, but was stopped and asked to provide identification by the club's bouncer. Instead of showing his driver's license that would confirm he had not yet turned "of age" Tiger reportedly announced, "C'mon, man, I'm Tiger."

The doorman, not missing a beat, replied within earshot of our crew, "I don't care if you're the Lion King, if you're not twenty-one, you're not getting in."

Tiger left, followed moments later by a few of our guys who were also underage. This story has been told and retold (differently, at times, like in the February 28, 2011 issue of *Sports Illustrated*) and I can't confirm the validity of the Tiger tale, because I wasn't there, but I was one of the first to hear it that September week in 1996. It may be true, or it may be exactly what many people believe it to be, an urban legend. If it is, indeed, nothing but an urban legend, then its humble beginnings started underneath a rented Golf Channel crew tent.

Back to the story I know, for a fact, to be true: the final round of the 1996 Quad City Classic. We were scheduled to be on the air for three hours that Sunday. Our broadcast included play in the final round and then the *Scorecard Report*, featuring the introduction of the tournament sponsors and dignitaries, the presentation of the trophy, and the champion's interview. Everyone on the crew was hoping to be a part of history as the network of record for Tiger's first professional win. Admittedly, I experience a certain amount of nerves before *every* telecast, but I was particularly nervous and excited about this one. So too, apparently, was Tiger Woods. It normally takes two professional golfers between three and a half and four hours to play a round of tournament golf. We were on the air live for three, which meant then and still means now, the first five or six holes would have to be recorded on videotape and then made into a highlights package for the beginning of the broadcast. Shots or scores on holes that have no effect on the position of a player on the leaderboard are ignored, while birdies or bogeys that move one player up or down that leaderboard, are edited together in chronological order in an attempt to advance the story of the tournament. On Sunday, September 15, 1996, Tiger Woods advanced the story on the fourth hole. Tiger found the woods, thanks to a sweeping hook off the tee, and continued poor play on the hole led to a quadruple bogey eight and the loss of his fifty-seven-hole lead. His misery was compounded as we came on the air live with Woods and Fiori playing the relatively easy 7th hole. After reaching the green in regulation (two shots), Woods found the putting surface anything but easy. PGA TOUR pros hate to have to take three putts to put the ball in the hole after reaching a green. Through his amazing career, we've seen three putting might bother Tiger more than any other player. So you can only imagine his dismay that Sunday when, on number 7, he needed *four* putts to finish the hole. Tiger had made one quadruple bogey and one double bogey in his first seven holes and, for all intents and purposes, ended any chance he had to win for the first time. We weren't a part of history because Ed Fiori went on to claim his fourth, and last, PGA TOUR victory that day. Until Y. E. Yang came from behind to beat Tiger at the PGA Championship thirteen years later, it was the *only* time Tiger Woods lost a PGA TOUR event when leading after fifty-four holes; so, I guess we were a part of history after all.

A week later, our trucks, technicians, production, and announcer teams travelled to upstate New York and the En Joie Golf Club for the BC Open, named after the cartoon strip created by local Endicott resident Jonny Hart. We came and so did Tiger. The young man was the talk of the sport and part of our coverage, for the second straight tournament. Because of the hype that surrounded Woods, I was interviewed for, and quoted on, the front page of the *USA Today* sports section for the first and only time in my life. Weather was an issue all week, shortening the tournament from the normal seventy-two holes to just fifty-four in four days. It clearly didn't take long for Tiger to get over losing his grip on the lead the week before and losing the trophy to "the Grip," because he contended once again, shooting 68, 66, and 66 to finish tied for third.

ENJOY EN JOIE

That rain-soaked final round caused all kinds of problems for the players, galleries, and our production efforts. The crowds were massive—more people than the tournament had ever seen, or would ever see again, arrived by the thousands and crowded along the tree-lined fairways to try and get a glimpse of the kid who had become the talk of the town. En Joie is, by golf course standards, an intimate layout. Surrounded by houses, restaurants, and soccer fields, it's located on Main Street in the tiny town of Endicott and had hosted a PGA TOUR event since 1972. The golf course, at the time, could play as long as sixty-nine hundred yards, but it was much more comfortable at less; tees were close to greens, and fairways ran parallel to each other as one went one way and the next turned around and headed straight back the other way. All of this meant the mass of humanity following Tiger Woods moved as one when he was finished playing a shot on one hole, often interrupting the efforts of other players on other holes as they prepared and tried to play their shots. Amidst it all, our crew tried to remain inconspicuous as it did its job following the action.

In those days, budgets and Golf Channel money in the bank meant that the use of the newest RF (radio frequency) technology was not a part of our production plan. Instead, our camera operators were tied to good old-fashioned cable technology, which meant the first part of the week was spent lining the fairways with thousands and thousands of feet of coaxial cable that would serve as the vehicle to provide both the video and audio signal from the camera to the truck, which would then, through the use of other equipment, be transmitted from our mobile control room to a satellite millions of miles above the earth, down to the control room in Orlando, Florida, then back up to a satellite before finally ending up in your living room, bedroom, or man cave. I know it works, because, unlike most of you, I see the technology at work on occasion and, just like most of you, use it every day. I just don't know how it works—sorry.

Before almost every tournament starts, staff employed by the tour, the tournament, or both spend days lining each fairway with ropes and stakes to establish a boundary between the fans and the athletes. Players, caddies, and a handful of volunteers stroll up the fairways inside those ropes. Fans, en masse referred to as a gallery, stay on the outside of those ropes. To get the best angles for our viewing audience, a handful of network television camera operators, utilities, and microphone holders are also allowed inside the ropes, but the support staff needed to transport those people or fix the equipment if it breaks is not. Those people patrol the area outside the ropes, right along with the gallery, in golf carts, and spend most of their time trying to stay ahead of play and out of the way. Ideally, professional golfers hit tee shots that land in the fairway, and our cameramen stand stock still in prearranged spots, following the ball through lenses as it soars through the air, lands, bounces, and then rolls to a stop. Sometimes, even the best players in the sport miss their mark, and when that happens the ball ends up in a bunker, a water hazard, out of bounds, or in what is called the rough. Some rough is thick, some is sparse, and some grows wild and thick around trees, lakes, and bunkers, and it's rarely where a player wants his ball to end up. At En Joie Golf Course in 1996, while charging up the leaderboard on a rainy final day, it was exactly where Tiger Woods hit his tee shot on the 15th hole. The gallery scrambled to get a good look, and a member of our Golf Channel crew named Jonathan Schwartz drove his golf cart among them to do his job and provide support. We were in a commercial break and getting ready to return to our live broadcast when, over the headsets, we all heard the pained cry of Jim Huet, the camera operator on the tower behind the 15th green.

"Schwartzy just ran over Tiger's ball!" exclaimed Jimbo (if you haven't figured it out by now, *everybody* on the crew has a nickname).

"Say again?" asked an ever-calm Emmett Loughran.

"Schwartzy just ran his cart over Tiger's ball!" Jimbo claimed again.

"Are you fucking kidding me?" was what came out of my mouth.

"Office, we need a ruling at 15 fairway" were the much more productive words from Emmett, alerting our people to get in touch with the PGA TOUR rules officials on the radio.

Tiger's ball had nestled down in the thick wet grass, and Jonathan Schwartz had, indeed, in his haste to do a good job, not seen it and had accidentally run over it, putting it in an even more precarious position. People on the ground saw it happen; Jimbo Huet saw it happen and, thanks to the magic of videotape, everybody in the truck saw it, too. The television viewer was the last to get a glimpse, after I decided to show it, when we came back from commercial. Tiger arrived on the scene to assess his situation, heard from several members of the gallery what had happened, and then fixed his even-at-a-young age formidable stare on Schwartzy, who, to his credit, had stayed. Then Tiger smiled. He knew the rules, so he knew that because our technician had altered the position of his ball by running it over, he was entitled to what the Rules of Golf call "relief." A PGA TOUR official confirmed that, and Tiger got to pick up his golf ball and drop it in another spot, no closer to the hole. Then he pitched the ball on the green and made the putt for a birdie, inching one more shot closer to the tournament leader. He didn't end up winning, but the third-place finish was his best as a pro, and Schwartzy had a story to tell for the rest of his life.

ENJOYING THE END OF THE YEAR

Tiger Woods bettered that performance in the next tournament he played, beating Davis Love III on the first hole of a playoff in Las Vegas on October 6 and winning on tour exactly thirty-nine days after turning pro. It was his next tournament, but not ours. Tiger's victory was televised by ESPN, which meant my friend and mentor Andy Young would now forever be the TV producer of record for Tiger's first trophy hoist.

It was The Golf Channel's turn again to document Tiger, now a bona fide PGA TOUR winner, the following week when he teed it up in San Antonio, Texas. Because of the ever-increasing attention, he felt the need to warm up hundreds of yards away from the majority of his fellow competitors, and in virtual solitude, at the far end of the La Cantera Golf Club practice facility. A few of us had the pleasure of watching a then-still-friendly Tiger and his instructor, Butch Harmon, go through the paces of a post round cool-down session. For reasons known only to us, we had decided to bring half a dozen blue and white Golf Channel hats as a "gift" for the talented young player. After about thirty minutes, they took a break and spent the next several minutes shooting the breeze with us; then Tiger politely admitted he had "no need" for six Golf Channel hats, but took the time to scribble his name on each and every one before giving them all back. I still have mine tucked away, snug in a Ziploc baggie, in a box of memorabilia, somewhere in a closet. Woods made his sixth straight cut, but a Saturday 73 meant he wouldn't win for a second straight week; instead, he finished alone in third. The Golf Channel finally did get our own Tiger win the very next week, when he beat Payne Stewart down the stretch at the Walt Disney World/Oldsmobile Classic in Orlando, Florida, and stood, with trophy in hand, alongside Donna Caponi, who interviewed him, and Mickey and Minnie Mouse.

In 1996, Tiger Woods played eight tournaments after turning pro. He won twice and collected nearly $800,000 in official prize money, and, as we all know, that was just the beginning. I'm not the brightest bulb in the chandelier, but there are two things I know with relative certainty: The Golf Channel has had little to no impact on the success Tiger Woods has enjoyed since turning pro; but, conversely, Tiger Woods had a great deal to do with the success of The Golf Channel since it turned on the lights in 1995.

FAMILIAR FACES

During those first few years, The Golf Channel hired a couple of hundred people, some in high-paying, high-profile positions. While Hammons, Kessler, Cardwell, and Jennifer Mills saw a majority of the air time, other folks behind the scenes made sure they had something to talk about. Two of those people were young broadcast wannabes named Scott Van Pelt and Kelly Tilghman, and both were hired by Paul Farnsworth to work in the channel's videotape library.

The library functioned pretty much as you can imagine, but, instead of books, the shelves contained cases filled with music CDs and videotapes that featured highlights of past tournaments, interviews, and beauty shots of golf courses and resorts, some captured by the channel's cameramen weeks and even months before we actually went on the air. Friedman, Jenkins, and Hymes, or one of their producers, associate producers, or staff, in the process of putting programs together, would need the contents of what was on those videotapes to illustrate various stories that comprised each thirty- or sixty-minute program. All of the video was catalogued and could be recalled and found at the touch of a few keys on a computer keyboard when needed and in The Golf Channel's infancy those fingers often belonged to Van Pelt and Tilghman. Both wished for higher-profile jobs; both wanted to be *on* television and, along the way, both would get their wish.

Van Pelt was a natural. An instinctively funny, unquestionably intelligent, and completely engaging young man, he made friends easily and found his way in front of the camera by convincing, first, Paul Farnsworth, then Mike Whelan, and ultimately Gary Stevenson that he deserved it. He was right. There weren't a whole lot of people watching The Golf Channel in the beginning, and those that were didn't have a problem voicing both their approval and their complaints. The compliments were usually of a general nature, while the criticisms were almost always personal. Men and women were playing golf professionally somewhere in the country almost every weekend, thanks to both major and minor or mini tours. While Tiger Woods was teeing it up in Akron or Phoenix or Orlando and playing for millions of dollars, guys like Ryan Hietala, Harry Taylor, and hundreds of others were playing for comparatively pennies somewhere else, and they all had mothers, fathers, brothers, sisters, and fans who thought they deserved to be mentioned on a twenty-four-hour-a-day, seven-day-a-week network devoted to the game. Stevenson agreed and came up with the idea for a weekend show he called *Leaderboard Report*, thirty minutes of nothing but music and scores of tournaments played all over the country. All he needed was a host, and he found one in SVP. In a meeting before the first show aired, Gary told Scott simply:

"I want you to come on the air and say, 'Hi, I'm Scott Van Pelt, and this is the *Leaderboard Report*,' and thirty minutes later say, 'I'm Scott Van Pelt, and this has been the *Leaderboard Report*.' Anything more and I'll find somebody else to do this." Scott smiled and nodded and then said this on TV:

"Hello, I'm Scott Van Pelt, and my boss told me I was supposed to say only my name and welcome to the *Leaderboard Report* and then let you enjoy the music and the scores." But in a style that you can still see on ESPN, Van Pelt did much more than that. As third-round scores from the PGA TOUR event appeared on screen, Corey Pavin's name was there, and next to it was an uninspiring score of 76.

"Ooh, 76 for Corey Pavin," said Van Pelt over the music. "I guess you're sleeping in the garage tonight." And that was just the beginning as he continued to insert his personality throughout that first show and the many others that followed. At the end of his debut, Van Pelt actually did say what his "boss" had asked him to say, and afterward he was met by a happy Mike Whelan and a smiling Gary Stevenson. The Golf Channel had found a star.

Kelly Tilghman attended and played golf at Duke University, joining the team as one of Coach Dan Brooks's earliest recruits in 1988. A four-year college career included one tournament win and a tie for thirty-third in the 1991 NCAA Championship during her senior season. After that, Tilghman turned pro and Duke started winning national championships (1999, 2002, 2005-7).

She struggled as a pro, never qualifying for the LPGA and playing for four years in Australia, Europe, and Asia before giving up on one dream and beginning the chase for another. She interned at a West Palm Beach, Florida, television station before moving north in the Sunshine State and landing on Whelan's doorstep.

She combined hard work with a never-give-up attitude and parlayed that into an on-air opportunity after a couple of years in the library. Like Van Pelt, she started out filing reports for the various news programs, but, unlike Scott, Whelan wanted to try her out on tournament telecasts, so she became part of my LPGA announcer team, briefly. I have been around dozens of professional golfers turned broadcasters and know that most of them as golfers were perfectionists; the problem is, live golf television is an imperfect profession, and for many that can be unnerving. Like several, Kelly labored with the mechanics in the beginning, but thanks to help from a number of people, she got better. But apparently not better enough, because, unlike Kessler, it was Mike Whelan's idea to pull the plug this time: Kelly would make appearances on air for The Golf Channel, but those appearances would be as part of a studio broadcast team. We would work together again in the future, but a great deal happened between the first time we worked together and the next.

TROUBLE BUBBLES UP

While we were staying out of trouble in cities all around the country, spending weeks at a time showing the world (The Golf Channel had agreements with networks in Europe and Japan) American golf's best players, there was trouble brewing inside the walls at The Golf Channel. Gary Stevenson had complimented our group by saying he was glad he didn't have to worry about us, but the same couldn't be said for other departments or department heads. We didn't know all the details, but we had heard the rumors about several lawsuits filed against people in charge at the channel, mainly Mike Whelan. Marty Jenkins, whom Whelan had hired to be the producer responsible for instructional programming, fired the first salvo after Whelan fired him a year after we went on the air. Jenkins wasn't popular among his co-workers and carried the weight of a reputation that labeled him as lazy, unresponsive, and ineffective. Those charges led to his dismissal, but, instead of owning up to that reputation, he decided to sully someone else's by filing a "whistle-blower" lawsuit in state court alleging Whelan had sexually harassed several female employees, and both Whelan and Farnsworth had elicited free golf equipment from manufacturers and suppliers. Both Whelan and Farnsworth denied the charges, but Mike's troubles were just beginning.

A year later, a female studio director named Vicki Nantz hired an attorney and sued Whelan, Farnsworth, and the network in

US District Court for discrimination, alleging violations of Title VII of the Civil Rights Act and of the Equal Pay Act. According to Nantz, Whelan and Farnsworth were guilty of discriminating against her on the basis of gender because they denied her salary increases comparable to those of a male colleague performing the same duties. The lawsuit alleged that one of Nantz's coworkers was the recipient of raises not given to her, despite the fact that she was more experienced and had received more complimentary performance evaluations. Whelan and Farnsworth, through the channel's attorney's, denied those allegations, too, and offered Nantz an out-of-court settlement worth in excess of $135,000, but Nantz said no to any settlement that didn't include the dismissal of both Whelan and Farnsworth. True or not, in the end Michael J. Whelan couldn't survive those and other allegations that had sprung up during his brief but memorable tenure, and he resigned in July of 1998. His time at the channel will be remembered in different ways by different people; but one thing should never be forgotten—The Golf Channel would not have gotten on the air or been as successful without the countless hours Mike Whelan devoted to it. He left a lasting legacy, in more ways than one, but he didn't leave the channel in 1998 before we teamed up to make dozens of decisions.

MAKING MOVES

The TV business is a transient one; people come and go, owners buy and sell but, amazingly, the first decade of The Golf Channel was marked with, in hindsight, what seemed like an uncharacteristic amount of stability. Joe Gibbs, Matt Scalici, and Bob Greenway, among others, made it a great place to work, and, despite the behind-the-scenes tug of war with an ever-increasing payroll, those of us who worked the day-in, day-out jobs always had something to deposit in the bank. There was turnover, for sure. Whelan left because he had to; Gary Stevenson because he wanted to; and investors were alternately bought out and brought on board to help pay the bills. The Golf Channel was owned, in large or small part, by cable companies, including Comcast, a broadcast entity (FOX), and individuals (Palmer and Gibbs); but for more than a decade, nobody ever owned a bigger piece of the pie than Joe, and there was never any doubt that he called the shots at his own television network. It was that way until he sold the whole shebang to cable giant Comcast Corporation in 2009.

But, even these days, I hear people say, and know people who think, that Arnold Palmer "owned" The Golf Channel. I've never seen the books, so I don't know exactly what his financial investment was, but enough people in high places on the organizational chart have told me that investment was minimal, and so was the monetary gain the most charismatic golfer of all time received. While what he put in or took out wasn't anywhere near what people think, the impact he made on, and gravitas he gave to, the network was substantial. Gibbs, with Palmer in agreement, had already made the move from pay to basic cable, and things were looking up. The channel went from having subscribers numbering in the thousands to the tens of millions, but Golf Channel still had a long way to go. To get carriage on even more systems, enough to make a real difference, both Joe and Mr. Palmer knew they needed an event, a reason for people who hadn't yet given it a glance to watch the channel for the first time and, perhaps, decide it was worth watching again. The solution turned out to be easy.

For years, Palmer had hosted a one-day tournament for charity every August at his home course, the Laurel Valley Golf Club near Ligonier, Pennsylvania. The primary beneficiary was a local hospital, but every year the big winners were the golf fans of western Pennsylvania, who got the chance to watch their hero play golf with, and against, three of his friends. Those friends always included the best players of the day, year, or generation. In 1997, Mr. Palmer invited 1996 British Open Champion Tom Lehman and future PGA Championship winner Davis Love III to team up and take on him and Tiger Woods, who, since we had last seen him in person winning at Walt Disney World, had won four more times, including his first major championship, the Masters Tournament, by an astounding twelve strokes. Woods had gone from a prodigy to the winningest amateur golfer of all time to a professional phenomenon to a PGA TOUR winner to a major champion, carrying the weight of the expectations of millions who had him pegged as the heir to Jack Nicklaus and the future greatest player in the history of the game. Tiger Woods was not yet twenty-two years old.

It was the middle of summer back in Orlando and, inside the walls of The Golf Channel, my phone rang. I answered, and on the other end of the line was Mike Whelan with an invitation to join him in Bob Greenway's office. I didn't get summoned into the senior vice president's office often, but there had been times, and, as I gathered a notebook and a pen, I headed out the door feeling only curious, because I knew I had done nothing wrong. I made the quick trip to Bob's office and gave a sharp knock on the open door to announce my arrival before entering. I took two steps into the office and stopped dead in my tracks, because sitting at the round table in the corner of Bob Greenway's office were not only Bob and Mike, but Joseph E. Gibbs and Arnold Palmer.

Arnold Palmer had an office in the building. I had never been in it, but I knew it existed in the area affectionately called "the Green Carpet" by those of us who didn't have offices in that part of the building. In the early years, Palmer came by the channel once every few months, either to make an appearance on one of the network's studio broadcasts or to just check in with Joe Gibbs. When he was there, he also made it a point to walk the halls and say hello to people, not because he felt like he had to, but because he wanted to. Arnold Palmer had millions of fans all over the world, and we counted ourselves among them because of how he played the game and how he treated people. It was always the highlight of the month, and a topic of conversation for weeks, when he was in the building. I had the additional pleasure of interacting with him where he was much more com-fortable, on the golf course. He knew me by name, which I still count as one of the greatest honors I can imagine.

"Come on in, Keith," invited Bob. "You know Mr. Palmer." It was a statement, not a question.

"I do," I said, trying not to sound as intimidated as I felt. The great Arnold Palmer stood and offered his hand. I took it and was, once again, amazed at how big it was as I squeezed it and shook.

"Hello, young man," was all Palmer said, letting go of my hand and reclaiming his seat. I grabbed the back of the fifth chair around the table, set my pen and trusty blue pad of graph paper down, and sat.

"To what do I owe this honor?" was all I thought to say.

"I've got this little charity tournament," Palmer said, smiling, "and I was wondering if you'd like to help me put it on TV."

"Sounds like fun," I answered, "tell me more." And he did.

The meeting lasted about a half an hour, and the smile never left my face. Mr. Palmer and Mr. Gibbs left, but Bob, Mike, and I stayed and talked logistics. The event would be held at Laurel Valley on August 25, and we would maximize the exposure by broadcasting it, first live, and then again and again and again via tape delay, to maximize the viewing opportunities. In fact, as I write this today, September 10, 2011, it is Arnold Palmer's eighty-second birthday, and the Golf Channel is showing the *Arnold Palmer Golf Gala*, originally broadcast in 1997.

The channel could be seen, at that time, in approximately ten million homes. Conservative estimates predicted that cable systems would want the event badly enough to carry our signal, increasing the viewership by another twenty-five million to thirty million. If those people watched what we showed them and liked it, the theory was they would put enough pressure on their local cable operator to carry The Golf Channel permanently. If we disappointed them, they wouldn't pick up the phone and one incredible opportunity would be lost. No pressure. Greenway calmly explained all this to me, while Mike and I took notes. The meeting took place in early July. Woods had won the Masters, Lehman was about to defend his British Open crown, and Love III had yet to win the PGA Championship, but all three had agreed to join Mr. Palmer for fun, all in the name of charity. I had about six weeks to get ready.

THE GALA
APPROACHES

My Skins Game experience served me well as I prepared for the big event. When we weren't out on the road putting tournaments on TV, I was writing and editing features for the gala in the Golf Channel's Orlando home base. Director Emmett Loughran, Mike Whelan, and I took one trip to Latrobe to survey the golf course and decide on a coverage plan. We would use several small pickup trucks, with our cameras mounted on wooden platforms in the beds, to cover the action from behind the greens, while several truly mobile hand-held cameras, carried on the shoulders of capable operators, would patrol the fairways to capture the action from behind and alongside the players. We'd ask each one to wear a microphone to eavesdrop on conversations and have Donna Caponi and Mark Lye announce from the golf course while Denny Shreiner would serve as play-by-play announcer, all by himself, in an announce trailer.

While Emmett looked at the golf course to find the best camera angles, I walked the fairways with a note pad to determine how long it would take each golfer to get from one spot to the next, from the tee to the ball in the fairway, and then from the fairway to the green and from one green to the following teeing ground. This process helped me determine when I could take a commercial break, when I could show a feature, or when I should simply stay with the players as they walked from point A to point B. It all served to help Emmett get ready and help me get ready, while putting Michael J. Whelan's mind at ease. But we had one big problem. The Arnold Palmer Golf Gala was scheduled to be played in Latrobe, Pennsylvania, on Monday, August 25, and our tournament team was scheduled to be televising a Nike, now Web.com, Tour event in Odessa, Texas, that ended on Sunday, August 24. We had some logistics to figure out.

The Golf Channel had never televised two domestic events so close together, let alone in the same week. We broadcast as many as thirty tournaments in each of those first few years, many back to back, and sometimes all the way across the country, but they always had their own weeks. Now, The Golf Channel broadcasts between sixty and seventy tournaments on US soil and, thanks to an expanded production and talent pool, sometimes three, even four, events happen on the same week. But back in 1997, we were pretty thin. The fact that Emmett and I had to be in western Pennsylvania meant someone else had to produce and direct the Texas event and, after several days of deliberation, Bob, Mike, and I decided those responsibilities would fall on the shoulders of Karel Schliksbier and Peter Esposito. Donna Caponi didn't work with us on that tour, and neither did Mark Lye, but Denny Schreiner did; so we had to figure out how to get him, the big man, and Spo, as well as a few other essential production people, from the middle of nowhere, Texas, to the middle of nowhere, Pennsylvania, and, unfortunately for us, Delta didn't have that route on their schedule.

Luckily Karel, during his time at CBS, had become very good friends with not only the producer Lance Barrow, but the producer's brother, Mark; and Mark Barrow knew how to arrange private air travel. Before we all went our separate ways, a deal was struck and a private jet would meet our group at MAF, the Midland Odessa International Airport, Sunday evening and fly them all to Arnold Palmer Regional Airport in Latrobe. When Denny Schreiner heard he would be travelling from West Texas to Latrobe in style, he made it a point, all week, to let anyone who would listen know that "flying private is the *only* way to travel."

Emmett, Bob, Mike, and I were in the production truck in our compound at Laurel Valley Sunday evening, putting the finishing touches on graphics, features, and camera angles, when the phone rang. Phone lines at each tournament are temporary and were ordered by NEP days before the event, and very few people know the number, so, when the phone rings, it's either a computer-generated call or somebody looking for a specific someone. This particular call was not computer generated.

"Arnold Palmer Golf Gala production truck," I said, answering the ringing phone, expecting to hear the familiar delay before a computer started to ask me to buy or participate in something.

"General," came the non-computer-generated voice of the big man. Karel worked at CBS, under the watchful eye of Frank Chirkinian, and he knew the great TV golf producer was called "the Ayatollah." Early on in our professional relationship, he decided that I should have a nickname as well, and it was Karel who came up with "the General" for me, and it stuck. I was about to find out it wasn't the only thing that stuck.

"We have a problem," continued Karel. "We're all here at the airport, but there is no plane and it appears that there won't be one."

Oh, shit is what I thought, but what I said was, "Oh, shit," and suddenly I had company on the front bench of the truck.

"What's wrong?" asked Whelan.

"No plane," I replied.

"You're fucking kidding me," said Mike.

"Wish I was," and then the big man spoke again.

"It seems Mark Barrow couldn't come through, but we may have a line on another plane. We're working on it, but it's not going to be as cheap as the one Mark quoted us. Daisy says she'll put it on her credit card."

Daisy was Diana Phipps, our production assistant. She and Karel worked together at CBS and he convinced her to join our team when we started putting it together in 1995. She was hardworking, well educated, fun to be around, and very, very rich. Phipps money was "old" money going back to the days of US Steel, Carnegie, and Mellon. More recently, her family was better known for its horse racing interests: owning, training, racing, and breeding thoroughbreds. Daisy once told us her family "passed" on Secretariat when it came time to purchase the colt. Hey, even smart, successful, wealthy people make an occasional mistake. Daisy could have, and eventually did, join the Phipps family business; but before she did that, she was busy making a name for herself in golf television production and, at that particular moment, she was helping arrange a private jet and planning to put the cost of that emergency move (about $15,000) on her personal American Express card.

"They found another plane," I told the interested ears in the truck, "and Daisy is going to put it on her credit card."

"Give me the phone" were the next words I heard, and the first ones out of Bob Greenway's mouth.

We met our brethren at the airport long after midnight, knowing we all had to be back at the golf course at 6 a.m. The plane they got was paid for by Bob Greenway, smaller than the one Mark Barrow had promised, and it ultimately failed to deliver a luxurious ride, so Denny Schreiner's "only way to travel" became a several-hour, extremely cramped, bathroomless ordeal. But the rest of the team arrived, safe and sound, and the show would go on.

STAR GAZING

Thousands of adoring, interested, lucky fans showed up that day and got everything they had hoped for and more: so did we. The telecast went off without a hitch, the golf was exciting and fun, the features fit perfectly inside the broadcast, and the team of Arnold Palmer and Tiger Woods (it was his gala, so Arnie got to pick his partner) beat the team of Tom Lehman and Davis Love III. At one point during the competition, Woods and Palmer won a hole with a birdie putt from Tiger and, as they headed to the next tee, all four players stopped to sign autographs for fans, both young and old. According to the format I had painstakingly mapped out, it was an ideal spot for a commercial break, so that's what we did, and, when Woods, Palmer, Love, and Lehman reached the tee, the break still had another commercial in it.

The viewing audience at home was watching (I hope) a spot about the Latrobe Area Hospital (the event's charity) while, in the truck, we were looking at a $5 bill pierced by a lone white wooden golf tee, between the two tee markers. The camera zoomed out to show a quizzical look on Tiger Woods's face as he looked first at the ground and then at the big man.

"What's this?" asked Tiger.

"Take five," was Karel's answer, "we're still in commercial."

We heard and saw it all in the truck, and it was amusing, ice-breaking, and brilliant. Tiger's face broke out in a huge grin as he nodded at Karel, then picked up and pocketed the bill, just as Chuck Whitfield started his count alerting all of us that we were coming back from the break.

The Arnold Palmer Golf Gala aired live that day, and then reaired that night, and on many days and nights to follow. It featured four of golf's biggest stars, and it helped put Joe Gibbs's network on the map. When the show was over, we all let out a collective sigh of relief, and I know each and every one of us felt an enormous amount of pride and self-satisfaction, but it was a total team effort, and I made it a point to let each and every person know how honored I felt to work alongside them all. Then I headed up to the clubhouse to join the group that was having a celebratory cocktail.

Woods, Lehman, and Love were long gone, but there were still plenty of people in the room, most of them gathered around Arnold Palmer and Joe Gibbs, who were having a drink in front of a television screen showing *The Arnold Palmer Golf Gala* on The Golf Channel. Bob Greenway greeted me by patting me on the back and shaking my hand. When he did, he pulled me close and whispered in my ear, "You did good, Keith." Then he squeezed my hand a little harder and said, "Ah, hell, you did great!"

"Thanks, Bob," I said, as he let go. "It was fun," I added, and I meant it; then I turned to the TV to watch a little of the show I had only seen from the truck and saw Gibbs and Palmer looking right at me.

"Thank you," Joe Gibbs mouthed. Sitting next to him, Arnold Palmer smiled, winked, and gave me his patented thumbs up.

ON A LEG AND A PRAYER

Casey Martin had a dream, a ton of talent, and a bum leg. He came into the world in a Eugene, Oregon hospital on June 2, 1972, suffering from a birth defect in his right leg known as Klippel Trenaunay Weber Syndrome, a rare, congenital medical condition in which blood vessels and/or lymph vessels fail to form properly. At certain times, it caused blood to pool in his lower leg; at all times, it made walking painful. It slowed him down, but didn't stop him from attending and playing golf at Stanford, earning All PAC-10 honors three times, and winning a national championship, with Tiger Woods as a teammate, in 1994. A year earlier, he had won something called the Sahalee Players Championship, and in 1995 he decided it was the right time to turn pro. It seemed nothing was going to stop Casey Martin from playing professional golf, but the PGA TOUR certainly tried.

After turning pro, Casey did what thousands of aspiring PGA TOUR players did in 1997: he wrote a check for $3,000 and teed it up in the first stage of the PGA TOUR Qualifying Tournament. His scores there were good enough to advance to the tournament's second stage, where, again, he played well enough to earn a spot in the third and what was then the final stage of the process: ninety holes and five days of pressure-packed December golf, at the end of which Martin, depending on what he shot, could earn a spot on either the PGA TOUR or what was then the Nike Tour. But on his way to the Q-School finals, he found out his golf cart had hit a road block.

Earlier that year, the PGA TOUR had decided that, even though it allowed carts for the fifty-and-older players on the Senior Tour, golf carts could no longer be used during any PGA TOUR tournament, and that included Q-School. Martin had earned his way there on his own. He hit the shots, he made the putts, and now he was being told that despite that accomplishment, he would be denied the opportunity to compete at the highest level in the sport he loved. For the first time in the process, he needed help, and he got it in the form of the Americans with Disabilities Act.

In 1990, the United States Congress passed the ADA: a law prohibiting discrimination on the basis of disability and requiring accommodations be made. Martin's lawyers asked for a temporary injunction on this basis, allowing him to compete for his professional playing privileges during the first week of December 1997. The tour's lawyers set the stage for what would be its main legal argument for years by contending the PGA TOUR wasn't discriminating against Martin, it was simply holding the athletes who participated in its tournaments to a specific standard, maintaining that walking was an integral part of the game and riding in a cart would give one player an advantage. The judge sided with Martin, temporarily allowing him a cart and the opportunity to pursue his dream.

PGA TOUR veteran Scott Verplank, a diabetic with health issues of his own, walked and wound up the medalist at Q-School that year, but it was Martin who was the talk of our telecasts. He rode around the Grenelefe Resort golf courses, shooting 70, 69, 72, 74, and 70, finishing tied for forty-sixth and earning a card on what was then the Nike Tour. That tour's season started exactly one month later at the Grasslands Golf and Country Club in

Lakeland, Florida, and our TV trucks, equipment, crew, and announcers were there, as were Casey Martin, his golf clubs, and his golf cart.

The PGA TOUR had appealed the lower court's decision, but, while that appeal was making its way through the system, Martin was allowed to play and ride. In Lakeland, we watched as he opened with a six-under-par 66 on Thursday. He followed that up with a respectable 69 to make the cut and ensure making a paycheck in the first event of the year. Saturday, he surged to the lead with a splendid seven-under-par 65, and Casey Martin, who was attaining minor celebrity status because of his court battle with the PGA TOUR, would sleep on the very real possibility that he would be a winner on its second most important tour. During the production of the final round, we could tell Martin played with nerves on Sunday, but he did just enough, finishing with a par on the seventy-second hole to beat Steve Lamontagne by one shot. Our cameras captured his obvious pain and pleasure on the 18th hole, perfectly illustrating the fact that Casey Martin was both exhausted and exhilarated. Because of the PGA TOUR's rules, he was now able to play in any and every Nike Tour event for the next two years, and he wouldn't have to go back to anything other than the finals of Q-School for his chance at golf's biggest stage for five. But they were doing everything in their power to make sure he wouldn't be able to take advantage of the fruits of his labor. But he was now a champion and, court case or not, no one would ever be able to take that away.

He played the next week and missed the cut, and then the entire world of golf turned its attention to the arguments in federal court and the decision by US Magistrate Judge Thomas Coffin. The Nike Tour played on without Casey Martin, as the PGA TOUR argued in court that its competitions were places of public accommodation only outside the ropes, in the areas open to spectators, *not* inside the ropes, where the professionals conducted their business.

During the proceedings, The Golf Channel spent hundreds of thousands of dollars covering the case. The network hired satellite trucks and sent staff cameramen, producers, lead anchor Brian Hammons, and reporter Adam Barr to file reports on a daily basis. What was supposed to be an assignment lasting a couple of days turned into weeks, lasting until February 11, when Coffin gave his ruling, which came down on the side of Casey Martin, telling the PGA TOUR, in part, that "the operator of a public accommodation could not create private enclaves within the facility...thus relegating the ADA to hop-scotch areas." Despite testimony to the contrary from golf greats Arnold Palmer, Jack Nicklaus, and others, Casey Martin could play *and* ride, and our Golf Channel tournament coverage team would see him again on April 4 in Austin, Texas. We weren't alone.

Tournament organizers for the Nike Austin Open erected a large white tent near the parking lot to house the pretournament press conference featuring Martin. It was big enough for about one hundred people. They weren't even close. Close to two hundred reporters showed up with pens, pencils, notepads, and more than twenty television cameras. They crammed inside the tent and waited to see and hear from Casey. The PGA TOUR was playing one of its premiere events at Doral, in Miami, that same week, but the assembled press, which included first-time Nike Tour visitors ESPN, the *Los Angeles Times*, the *Wall Street Journal*, the *New York Times* and *Dateline NBC's* Stone Phillips, ignored Tiger Woods, Phil Mickelson, and the rest of the "big" tour to invade the hill country of Texas, outside Austin. Martin arrived (in a cart) wearing a hat with the familiar Nike swoosh (an Oregon boy, he had had Nike as a sponsor from the beginning) and sporting a few new sponsors as well, including The Hartford (insurance) on his bag, Spalding (golf balls), and Ping (golf clubs). He made a brief statement and then spent a little more than half an hour answering questions. At the end, he rose and limped toward the exit and then headed toward a portable toilet, as a cadre of close to twenty cameramen, armed with cameras, followed.

"You coming in here with me?" was all he had to say to finally get a moment's privacy.

Casey Martin made the cut that week, and fourteen more times that year. He also qualified to play in the United States Open at the Olympic Club in San Francisco and contended in our national championship for a brief time before falling back and ultimately finishing tied for twenty-third.

His pro career included one full year on the PGA TOUR, in 2000, and he was back on the Nike/Buy.com/Nationwide tours for a handful of years after that. His last year in professional golf was 2006, when, on an ever-deteriorating leg, he played in six tournaments and made one cut. Casey Martin won the Nike Lakeland Classic, and he never won again, except on May 29, 2001, when the United States Supreme Court, in a 7–2 decision, proclaimed, once and for all, that Casey Martin could, indeed, use a golf cart in professional competition. Justice John Paul Stevens wrote the more-than-five-page opinion, in which Justices O'Connor, Kennedy, Souter, Ginsburg, Breyer, and Chief Justice Rehnquist joined. Justice Antonin Scalia wrote the dissent and was joined in that minority opinion by Justice Clarence Thomas.

For far too short a time, Casey Martin got to live his dream inside the ropes, but now it seems he's still living it as the head men's golf coach at The University of Oregon. I was lucky enough to see him again and spend a few minutes with him outside the Eugene campus "Duck Store" in 2008. What I encountered was a very happy, relatively healthy young man who was keeping the fire that once burned so brightly in him alive in the hearts of his students.

FINDING FRIENDS IN FUNNY PLACES

There are few people in this world I know better or like more than Jerry Foltz. Foltzy was born in Las Vegas, Nevada, in 1962, grew up to be one of the state's best junior golfers, and competed with, and against, my younger brother, Mark. Jerry played golf at Oral Roberts University and the University of Arizona, won the Arizona Amateur in 1989, and turned pro the very next year. He played in one major championship during his pro career—the 1991 US Open, a championship at which he proudly says (with tongue firmly planted in cheek) he briefly sat atop the leaderboard. While true, the reason was simple: Jerry Foltz played in the very first grouping off the tee on Friday and had the best score when that grouping finished thirty-six holes. That meant until a better score was posted Jerry Foltz was the leader in the clubhouse at the United States Open. It was mostly downhill from there and he went on to miss the cut. He did win the 1994 South Carolina Classic on the Nike Tour, but, due to a back injury, by the time The Golf Channel flipped the switch in 1995, he was already exploring his options.

The door to our production mobile unit was always open, and, at the Pensacola Open, Jerry Foltz found and walked through it. He introduced himself to me, said he knew, liked, and played golf against my younger brother, Mark, and recalled that he was part of an Eddie Hogan Cup junior golf team from Nevada that I chaperoned once upon a time. I liked him immediately and would grow to like him more. I learned he knew more about that tour and its players than any PGA TOUR media person and certainly more than any of us at The Golf Channel. He offered to help me identify the various members of the tour we would be showing on television and assist our announcers by giving them information about what made those players tick. I told him we couldn't pay him anything, and he told me he didn't care. I accepted his offer immediately.

Over the course of the next few days, I recognized in Foltzy the qualities that I believed would make him a world-class broadcaster. It wasn't that he knew the game (he did), nor was it that he had played it at the highest level (he had). It wasn't even that he had a win on his resume (all overblown in the world of golf television announcers). It was that he was the most social person I had ever met. Jerry Foltz could and would talk to anyone about anything and you couldn't help but like him. I knew he would be

a welcome addition to the team and, eventually, I made sure that he was. He even started getting paid to do it. By 1999, Jerry was an ex-player and an integral part of our announce team as we toured the country covering golf.

I couldn't have been happier professionally, but I was growing ever unhappy at home. I loved my children with all my heart, but my "family" was the group of people with whom I worked and spent the lion's share of my time. We ate, drank, worked, and played together, and we had each other's backs... for the most part. The days were easy. All I had to do was bury myself in my work, but the nights in chain restaurants and $55-a-night hotel rooms could be endless. Thankfully, people like Chuck Whitfield, Denny Schreiner, and maybe especially Jerry Foltz knew it, cared, and took it upon them to make sure I didn't have time to let the loneliness and the dark get me down.

There are strip clubs, or at least one strip club, in nearly every city in America. Some are famous (Scores in New York City; the Spearmint Rhino in Vegas), most are not, and all are depressing. I mention this not to pass judgment on a billion-dollar industry, but to use it as the introduction to the only time I almost lost my job while working at Joe Gibbs's Golf Channel. Most of these operations were easy to find—just look for the purple neon lights and the packed parking lot—but some took a little more work to uncover. The one in Fort Smith, Arkansas, in 1999 was one of those.

The Cheyenne Gentlemen's Club wasn't even in Arkansas; in fact, you had to cross the Arkansas River into neighboring Oklahoma to get to it. It was a short trip, just a few miles, but knowing us at the time, we'd have gone even if it wasn't, and one night a group of us made the trek. This joint turned out to be like most of these joints: black lights, drinks that are priced too high, and girls whose self-esteem is way too low. Our group usually made a few friends, and this night was no exception.

Somewhere along the way, invitations to check out a golf tournament were extended, and, finally, we had had enough and headed home. Apparently, for a number of the folks on our crew, inviting strippers to a golf tournament was part of the inane banter that occurred between customer and professional. None had ever come to fruition until a couple of girls from the Cheyenne Gentlemen's Club, in a place called Arkoma, Oklahoma, decided it was the best offer they'd had in weeks—maybe ever.

My guess is, you can hide a couple of short-skirt, knee-high-boot wearing, overly made up, and clearly medicated girls at a PGA TOUR event attended by thousands of people; but this was the Fort Smith Classic, and "thousands" was more like tens of dozens, and our newfound friends were easy to spot. It didn't take long for our cameramen to find them and the players and tournament officials to notice. Jerry Foltz had traded his clubs in for a microphone, but, on many occasions, his former caddie and still best buddy, Patrick, joined him and us at events. Foltzy knew—hell, everybody knew—the girls had arrived and, thinking on his feet, dispatched Patrick to find them, serve as chaperone, and make sure they stayed out of trouble. Patrick may have been a great friend and a more-than-serviceable caddie, but he was a terrible chaperone, and it was clearer than ever that the girls had to go. I made an executive decision to bribe them and had Foltzy get word to Patrick that Golf Channel swag, in the form of coveted network shirts and hats, awaited them if they promised to come and get them and then leave. By the time word got to Patrick, and then the girls, we were on the air with our live broadcast. They came to the compound anyway, climbed the stairs, and walked right into the control room of the mobile production unit.

Thankfully, they accepted the bribe, took the hats and shirts, and, giggling, left the truck and, for all I know, the premises, for good. They didn't stay long, but they clearly made an impression. Some of us were mortified, most mildly amused, and a couple downright offended. One of the latter was Mark Lye, the one-time PGA TOUR winner who had replaced no-time PGA TOUR winner Jim Nelford as our main analyst. I didn't know it then, but I would certainly find out later, that Mark was so insulted by the presence of the invited, but unwanted, young women that he picked up the phone and called HQ in Orlando and voiced his displeasure to both Mike Whelan and Bob Greenway. When I arrived in my office the very next Monday, I was summoned.

I had been in Bob Greenway's office a hundred times, for dozens of reasons, but I can honestly say I had never seen him angry until the morning of August 23, 1999.

"We have a problem," Greenway said from behind his desk before I could even say hello. I looked at him, then at Whelan, honestly not aware of what was wrong.

"What's the problem?" I asked.

"Apparently, you are." It was Whelan this time. I stood still and then addressed Greenway, even though it was Whelan who had spoken last.

"Sorry, but I'm confused," I started. "What are you talking about?"

"What were you thinking?" Whelan spoke again, and this time I turned in his direction.

"What was I thinking about what?" I responded, still not sure what this was all about.

Mike Whelan formed a steeple with the index fingers of both hands, put them to his chin and spoke over them.

"Joe wants to fire you."

"Fire me for what?" I asked, first Mike, and then let the question linger in the air as I turned to Bob.

"How could you invite strippers into the truck?" said Bob, with a look of disappointment I can still see today.

"And give them Golf Channel shirts and hats!" added Whelan emphatically.

At that moment any real concern that may have been building inside evaporated. I wasn't worried anymore and I laughed out loud, then I said to both Mike and Bob, "Is that what this is all about?" I started in my defense. "Nothing happened," I told the truth, "and I have no idea how or why they were there," I lied, "but I gave them the shirts and hats because it was the only way I could think of to get rid of them," I told the truth again.

"You think this is funny?" Bob said, still upset. "It's not. Someone called (I found out later it was Mark Lye) and said strippers were in the truck, topless, and giving you lap dances during the show."

"Damn," I thought to myself, "sorry I missed that." Then I looked at them both and said, "Did either of you watch the show?" I waited for the reply. I didn't have to wait long.

"I did," said Whelan.

"I watched the tape," added Greenway, and then it was my turn again.

"Can you tell me exactly when it was during that broadcast that I was supposed to be getting a lap dance?" I paused, and looked right at Bob.

He couldn't; so I continued, "I'm good at what I do, Bob, but I'm not that good."

Now it was Greenway's turn to smile. "Tell us exactly what happened."

I did, to the best of my recollection.

Two months later our group was in Dothan, Alabama, to watch Casey Martin, Matt Gogel, Shaun Micheel, Mathew Goggin, and several others accept their PGA TOUR cards at the Nike Tour Championship. Because it was as close to The Golf Channel's founder and CEO, Joe Gibbs's, Birmingham home as we would get, he graced us with his presence and took our group to dinner. The meal was good and the banter free flowing and natural because, for a boss, Joe Gibbs was easy to be around. People peppered him with questions about the health of the network and the prospects for additional tournaments (more work for us) in the future, and Joe, like he always did, answered every one. Then he held up his hand and turned to me.

"Now it's my turn to ask a question," he started.

"Okay, shoot," I said, and Joe smiled, "Whose idea were the strippers?"

A moment (or was it a lifetime) of uncomfortable silence passed and, I swear, I was about to put the subject to rest with an admission when, at the end of the table, Jerry Foltz raised his hand. Joe Gibbs looked down the length of the table at Jerry and said, "So it was you?" and then he turned back to me and added, "Who is he?"

I said that his name was Jerry Foltz and he was one of the best announcers we had.

And that was that.

Period.

The end.

As we left the restaurant, I overheard Daisy Phipps talking to Jerry.

"I want you to be my best friend" was some of what I heard her say.

OUR CUPS RUNNETH OVER

The game of golf reveres its prizes. Players and avid fans know all about the history of, and the importance attached to, the claret jug (British Open trophy), the Wannamaker Trophy (the oversized award given to the winner of the PGA Championship), the green jacket (a sport coat the Masters champion gets to wear), and the United States Open trophy. Without question, golf respects and admires its trophies; but the game *loves* its cups.

The best are immersed in tradition. For example, the United States and Europe have been competing on a golf course every two years, with the exception of the World War II years, since 1927 to get a grip on the Ryder Cup. Highly competitive and supremely patriotic golfers from both sides of the pond had been playing "friendly" matches against one another since 1921, and in 1926 the get-together was held at the Wentworth Club in Surrey, England. In the gallery that day was a British seed merchant and avid golf fan named Samuel Ryder. Few people in the 1920s took up golf after their fiftieth birthday, but Ryder was one. He summarily worked his way to achieving a single-digit handicap; was accepted as a member of the Verulam Golf Club in St. Albans; and then, later, became that club's captain. Ryder decided these matches needed something for which to play, so he donated a golden keepsake, in the form of a trophy that bore his name, and an offer of five pounds sterling to each member of the winning team. So, in 1927, the first official Ryder Cup matches were held at the Worcester Golf Club in Worcester, Massachusetts. Today, the biennial competition is administered jointly by the PGA of America and the PGA European Tour and is one of television golf's most popular events.

Similarly, the United States Golf Association has cups named after historic figures and handed down over generations. The Walker Cup, like the Ryder Cup, is an every-other-year battle between golfers from the United States and other countries (in this case, Great Britain and Ireland); but, unlike the Ryder Cup, which features professionals, the Walker Cup match is reserved for amateurs. Its award is named after George Herbert Walker, grandfather to President George H. W. Bush and great-grandfather to his son, the forty-third president of the United States, George W. Bush. Walker was actually the first "president" in the family, having held that title at the USGA in 1920, when the Walker Cup was conceived. It was officially first played in 1922 at the National Golf Links of America on Long Island and, through the years since, has featured, as both players and captains, some of golf's most notable names, including Bobby Jones, Francis Ouimet, Michael Bonallack, Jack Nicklaus, Colin Montgomerie, and Tiger Woods.

Not to be outdone, the Curtis Cup, a women's amateur competition between the United States and Great Britain and Ireland, also administered by the USGA and the Royal and Ancient (R&A), was first played in 1932. Its trophy, a Paul Revere cup, was donated by sisters Harriot and Margaret Curtis, who, between them, won four US Women's Amateur Championships. Golf is quite proud of the Ryder Cup, the Walker Cup, and the Curtis Cup: three trophies with more than 250 years of history.

Because of, or, more sadly, maybe in spite of the honor bestowed on, and the history associated with, those cups, the powers that be in golf have given us a slew of other cups that owe no allegiance to the past nor bear any responsibility to upholding tradition. They seem to simply be sponsor-driven money grabs that serve no other purpose than to line the pockets of some of the world's wealthiest citizens. Competitions called the President's Cup and the Solheim Cup may survive scrutiny, but will anyone remember the FedEx Cup or the Charles Schwab Cup fifty, eighty, or one hundred years from now?

The cups we golf fans seem to appreciate most are awarded after one country or region's athletes square off against another's in a two- or three-day competition featuring a combination of head-to-head or two-person-team battles. Some are propped up, thanks to the weight of history, while others are, and have been, fly-by-night creations, hoping to make a buck, and maybe even provide entertainment. I have worked on both.

I know my cups. I've produced for television a Walker Cup match (Rickie Fowler and Peter Uihlein led the United States to victory in 2009); a Curtis Cup match (another US win); all four UBS Warburg Cups (an IMG-created, twelve-man-team competition between the United States and "the Rest of the World," captained, respectfully and respectively, by Arnold Palmer and Gary Player); the one and only Ganter Cup (this one pitted the PGA TOUR against the Nationwide Tour); the first several Tavistock Cup matches (Tiger Woods, Ernie Els, Retief Goosen, Annika Sorenstam, Ian Poulter, and other superstars, playing against each other for country club bragging rights); a couple of Charles Schwab Cup Championships (Champions Tour players, competing only for a big trophy and cash); and three Solheim Cup matches. All were challenging to produce, and each included memorable moments.

THE SOLHEIM STAGE
SHIFTS

The Solheim family makes PING golf clubs; they also made the Solheim Cup. Karsten Solheim was born in Norway, the son of a shoemaker who immigrated to the United States in 1913. The family settled in the Pacific Northwest, where young Karsten grew interested in, and then later studied, engineering, thanks to extension courses offered by the University of California. He eventually was hired, first as a salesman and then as an engineer, by General Electric. Colleagues introduced him to golf at the age of forty-two and he immediately found he not only liked the game, but he was good at it, except for one glaring weakness: he couldn't putt. Solheim decided the issue wasn't his stroke, it was the putter, and, being an engineer, he fixed the problem by designing and building himself a new one, in his garage. The concept of his new design was simple...move the shaft position from the heel of the blade to the center and apply specific scientific principles to the distribution of weight from the club head to the perimeter. With this new wand, the putts started to drop, and Karsten Solheim figured if it worked for him, it would work for everyone.

Solheim ended up in Phoenix and started making, and then trying to sell, his creation to what turned out to be a slew of not-so-accepting golf pros playing in tournaments and living in the desert. In 1967, he got the break he was hoping for when two-time US Open Champion Julius Boros used Solheim's signature club, the Ping Anser putter, to win that year's Phoenix Open. That success emboldened Solheim to quit GE altogether and begin the full-scale manufacturing of his perimeter-weighted Ping putters and irons. Today Ping clubs are played by millions of golfers and hundreds of touring professionals, and the company's products can be found in more than seventy countries.

I met Mr. Solheim once. It happened during my tenure at OCC, working on ESPN golf. We were in Arizona to broadcast a tournament and, while there, our crew asked for, and received, permission to bring our cameras and microphones inside the Ping factory. The Solheim family patriarch was gracious and interesting as he led us on a guided tour through his state-of-the-art plant. The employees clearly enjoyed their work and respected this bespectacled man, to whom they owed their livelihood. We saw how irons were molded, shafts inspected, and gold plating applied to putters (long before our visit, Solheim had started a tradition of sending each player who won a tournament using a Ping putter a gold-plated replica of the club, stamped with the name and date of the tournament, to commemorate the victory). At one point during the tour, we passed a set of double doors over which hung a sign stating simply, "Research and Development," and as we walked past, I posed a question to our host.

"What's happening in there?"

Karsten Solheim stopped and turned, looking first at the sign above the door, and then at me. He smiled a crooked smile.

"I could show you..." he paused, then added thoughtfully, "but then I'd have to kill you." Then he turned on his heel and continued walking.

I'd heard people use that phrase in jest on a number of occasions, but something in Solheim's eyes, combined with that crooked little smile, made me believe, at that particular moment, he actually meant it.

Karsten Solheim gave back to the game that gave so much to him by donating millions of dollars to build and maintain courses at both Arizona State and Oklahoma State universities. He was the driving force behind his company's sponsorship of LPGA Tour events in Oregon, Arizona, and Massachusetts, and in 1990 he created the Solheim Cup so the best players in America could go head to head with their counterparts in Europe. He kept Ping in the family, handing the reins of the company to his son, John, five years later, and then died in 2000 at the age of eighty-eight. His legacy lives on in the company he built from a single putter in a Redwood City, California, garage, to the golf club manufacturing behemoth of today, and a crystal cup handed out every two years that bears his name.

The first seven Solheim Cup matches were fairly lopsided affairs, won mostly by the United States team. The Europeans won twice, but never on US soil. Despite colorful competitors, like Laura Davies and Helen Alfredsson on one side, and future Hall of Fame members Juli Inkster, Pat Bradley, Beth Daniel, and Patty Sheehan on the other, the matches were not compelling enough to engage a huge percentage of the television viewing audience, and NBC's coverage was almost exclusively offered on a tape-delay basis, in weekend-only two- or three-hour blocks. By contrast, the network would be on the air for as many as ten hours a day offering coverage of the Ryder Cup matches or the United States Open Championship. Also, at the time, the Ryder Cup was played in odd years, and, not wanting to compete directly, the Solheim Cup officials decided to play their biennial team event in the even-numbered years. Then, in the fall of 2001, tragedy struck.

The attacks on America on September 11 changed lives, changed perceptions, and changed the world. Thousands of lives were lost, as was the way America conducted its business, and part of that business included professional sports. Following the lead of other leagues, golf restructured schedules and cancelled events, including the playing of the thirty-fourth Ryder Cup matches, originally scheduled for September 28, just over two weeks after the attacks on the World Trade Center and the Pentagon. The PGA of America and the PGA European Tour decided to postpone the match for a year, setting the Ryder Cup on its current even year rotation, the same rotation, at the time, as the Solheim Cup. As a reaction, the LPGA and its Solheim Cup partners made the choice to switch to an odd-year rotation, but, not wanting to immediately put the event on a three-year hiatus, the decision was made to play the Solheim Cup in consecutive years, on the old rotation in 2002, and then the new one in 2003.

While the changes in the schedule were happening, so were the behind-the-scenes machinations that would bring the Solheim Cup to The Golf Channel. Ping had been a charter sponsor of The Golf Channel, thanks to a relationship built by a tireless, creative salesperson named David Manougian. That same sales guy had climbed the corporate ladder and, in 2002, was the president of the network at which he'd worked since 1995. He knew what a signature event like the Solheim Cup would do for the perception of the seven-year-old channel, so he approached the Solheims and killed them with kindness and overwhelmed them with hours. The Golf Channel's promise was simple: for the first time in the history of the event, and regardless of where in the world the matches were played, a TV network would broadcast the competition from beginning to end...live. In addition, Manougian promised several hours of prime time rebroadcasts, bringing twice as much action into America's golf homes. A press release from March of 2003 promised twenty-seven hours of live golf from the Barseback Golf Club in Malmo, Sweden; and I'll give you one guess as to who would be responsible for that. I was, and I would be taking a very small, talented team halfway across the globe to help me accomplish it.

RIGHTS AND WRONGS

The Golf Channel's acquisition of Solheim Cup broadcast rights was just one of many changes in the way things were done in regard to TV golf after the millennium. During the first five years, the network had televised events from every major professional tour, but, at a press conference held on April 23, 2000, the world, and we, found out that was about to change. PGA TOUR commissioner Tim Finchem sat alongside, among others, NBC President and CEO Robert Wright and announced that, starting in 2001, the PGA Senior Tour (later rebranded as the Champions Tour) would be televised exclusively on NBC's sister network, CNBC. The announcement added the business channel would partner with another NBC-owned network, PAX, to bring all thirty-three events that the over-fifty pro golf tour played into America's homes. The reasoning behind the move was twofold, according to the commissioner: the demographics of both entities were a perfect match, and the PAX/CNBC combination offered consistent airtimes each and every week. The Tour announced that day that every Senior Tour event would air between 1 p.m. and 4 p.m. Fridays on PAX and from 6 p.m. to 8 p.m. Saturdays and Sundays on CNBC, and that meant two things to those of us who watched "old guys' golf": there would be no more events on either ESPN or The Golf Channel, and almost every single event would be broadcast on a tape-delay basis. I guess they thought it was a good idea at the time.

Besides Finchem, the driving force behind this move was then Senior Vice President of TV and Marketing for the Tour Donna Orender. She would later leave the Tour to become the commissioner of the WNBA, from 2005 through 2010, but before heading to hoops, she was hell bent on proving the PGA TOUR could manage and produce its own product on television, and she was going to start with the Senior Tour. For years, long before the creation of league-owned networks (NFL Network, MLB Network), leagues ran the competition and broadcast entities managed the television product. In CNBC, Orender found the perfect partner for her plan to have the Tour commandeer the broadcast end of the equation. Because CNBC had no history, infrastructure, or interest in staffing, managing, crewing, and broadcasting golf tournaments, that job would fall to the Tour's owned and operated TV arm, PGA TOUR Productions. Donna Orender thought they could do this, but she knew they needed help. PGA TOUR Productions had some television-savvy folks, but none that had much experience in live event production on the scale of an eighteen-hole golf tournament. There was also pressure from the players, who had just found out that they would no longer be featured on either ESPN or The Golf Channel, and many were concerned about how the CNBC shows would look. Orender knew she had to get an experienced producer in house to lead the effort, and, in an effort to accomplish that, she called me.

I had to admit, at the time, I was flattered; but I was also very, very happy at The Golf Channel. Like I had done a little more than five years prior, I went to my boss and told him about the phone call, and, like Howard Katz at ESPN, Bob Greenway encouraged me to drive up to PGA TOUR headquarters in Ponte Vedra Beach, Florida, and listen to the Tour's offer. I went, not once but twice, and met with Orender, her top lieutenant, Gil Kerr, and several PGA TOUR big shots, including Henry Hyde, Ed Moorhouse, and Tom Wade. I never got to Tim Finchem but, quite frankly, I knew I didn't need to; I didn't want the job. It seemed an exercise in futility and a project destined to fail. Orender explained to me that she had the bigger vision of establishing a foothold as the production arm for the Senior Tour and then graduating from there to producing PGA TOUR events, but I had a hard time looking past the obvious conflict of interest and the fact that the television networks currently producing golf events would have little interest in giving up the control they currently enjoyed. When I said thanks, but no thanks, Orender and the PGA TOUR turned to my team.

I was on the couch at home in Orlando when my phone rang and "the big man," Karel Schliksbier, was on the other end of the line.

"General, it's Karel," he started.

"Big Man, what's up?" I asked, even though I knew.

"I'm calling to talk about this CNBC job and to get your opinion," he said, confirming my supposition and starting a conversation that would last close to an hour.

Gil Kerr had called Karel and offered him the same job his boss, Donna Orender, had offered me, and the big man was not only flattered, but he had more to gain than I had. Karel was a valuable team member and had been producing a handful of events for me and The Golf Channel in the past few years, but, as he explained to me, this was his chance to be the leader—to "run the show." I knew and remembered the feeling, so I offered encouragement, but also warned him that I didn't think the premise was on such solid footing, and being the first person to do something was always a risk,

"I don't want to lose you," I said, as the conversation started to wind down, "but I understand the appeal of an opportunity like this." I paused for a second and then added earnestly, "If you take it, do what I did and surround yourself with good people." It was the best advice I could offer.

"I'll try," he started, sounding sad. "I'm gonna take it," he finished. I knew he would.

GIBBS REACTS

The way the whole rights thing works is simple: a league "owns" a product and it wants that product on television. If television executives think that the league's product will deliver ratings, in the form of viewers, and money, in the form of advertisers, it offers to pay the league for the "right" to broadcast its games. It gets a little more complicated when more than one network wants to broadcast a league's product; it also gets more lucrative for the league. The National Football League is a multibillion-dollar enterprise and a necessary piece to every American television network's programming puzzle. Other sports, while attractive, aren't the billion-dollar bombshell that the NFL is, and golf might be characterized as the wholesome, pretty-without-makeup girl next door in the grand scheme of broadcasting rights. But when it's the only sport you *can* put on the air because your network's name is The Golf Channel, it's a girl you can't afford to lose to another suitor; and that's exactly what happened to Joe Gibbs and The Golf Channel when Donna Orender and Tim Finchem strolled in with a prearranged marriage between the family's older, less-attractive daughter and CNBC.

So Gibbs went looking for another girlfriend, and he found one, purely by accident, while sitting on an airplane, flying across the country. Gibbs, Greenway, and Chris Murvin (The Golf Channel brain trust) were collectively livid over Finchem's

Senior Tour move and, although they knew they needed the PGA TOUR, they also knew diversity couldn't hurt. On this particular trip, Gibbs's seatmate serendipitously happened to be a high-ranking official in the Canadian Tour, golf's equivalent to the PGA TOUR north of the border. During a conversation, an idea was hatched and, on a cocktail napkin, a deal was struck. While this relationship was getting started, another one was becoming more permanent.

In March of 2000, the Comcast Corporation spent $98 million to buy an additional 14.6 percent of The Golf Channel, paying Joe Gibbs, Arnold Palmer, and other individual investors for the right to increase its stake in the network from 40.1 percent to a controlling 54.7 percent, with eyes on offering enough cash to the close to one hundred other minority investors by the time the Masters would be played in 2001, to gain another 7 percent. The network Gibbs had built from scratch, along with Chris Murvin and a handful of other friends, where, at several times during its five-year existence, he wondered if he had enough cash some weeks to pay his employees, was now valued at an astonishing $675 million. Gibbs started it, but by the spring of 2001, three entities owned it: Comcast with 60 percent, News Corp (Fox) with close to 31 percent, and Times Mirror with the rest. They owned the Golf Channel and, with it, among other things, the broadcast rights to the never-before-televised Canadian Tour.

Gibbs's move to secure the rights to Canadian Tour golf was brilliant. He, Murvin, and Greenway crafted a ten-year deal to televise a handful of events a year. The Golf Channel would pay the Canadian Tour for those rights but, before the t's were crossed and the i's dotted, a number of issues had to be ironed out: most importantly, a requirement that Canadian Tour golf events be played somewhere other than Canada. Before 2001 and The Golf Channel partnership, the Canadian Tour, in its thirty-year history, had never once played an event outside of

Canada, but with the new television agreement in place, there would be at least four each year, all broadcast live on The Golf Channel. Joe Gibbs was effectively thumbing his nose at Tim Finchem and the PGA TOUR, saying The Golf Channel can find events and succeed quite happily without your Senior Tour. He believed it, and he made it my job to make sure the television product was worth watching.

OH, CANADA

While the Senior Tour stumbled along on tape delay on an all-business network, The Golf Channel rolled out its coverage of the Canadian Tour from, of all places, Myrtle Beach, South Carolina. It was determined that the north-of-the-border golf tour would set up shop for a month at the brand new Barefoot Resort and host four events in four weeks. The resort included shopping, accommodations, and restaurants, but the main feature was the assortment of golf courses designed by some of the game's biggest names. Tom Fazio did one and it served as the host course for the first event of the series, creatively called the Myrtle Beach Open. From there, we moved to a Greg Norman design, on which the pros competed in the Barefoot Classic. Week three was the South Carolina Classic, played on the Love Course, eighteen holes designed by PGA TOUR standout Davis Love III; and the four-event, month-long South Carolina series ended with the CanAm Days Challenge, contested on the more-than-challenging Dye Course. The best players in the world ply their trade on the PGA TOUR, the next best play either the European Tour or the Web.com Tour, and the rest work their butts off and chase their dreams on places like the eGolf Tour, the Hooters Tour, or the Canadian Tour. Canada is proud of its pros and has had some excellent ones—Mike Weir, Dave Barr, and Ray Stewart, to name just a few—but most American golf fans were unfamiliar with the young, and old, men teeing it up in the Myrtle Beach Open on February 22, 2001. It was my job to give golf fans a reason to watch.

The first and, quite frankly, least creative idea we had was to put a microphone on certain players so the viewer could hear the "conversation" between the player and his caddie as he went about his business on the golf course. I say "least creative" because having professional golfers wear microphones during a competitive round was hardly a revolutionary idea. Don Ohlmeyer had all four players wearing mics during the Skins Game for years, and the PGA TOUR even agreed to try it in 1980 during the coverage of the Heritage Classic on Hilton Head Island in South Carolina. Tom Kite was the player who agreed to wear the microphone, but the grand broadcast experiment went "south" in South Carolina when, instead of talking golf and strategy while mic'd, Kite mercilessly criticized fellow professional John Schroeder for his slow play, for several minutes. The tour decided putting microphones on players was a bad idea and, to this day, has yet to agree to give live microphones on players another try; but we did it in Myrtle Beach, and it couldn't have turned out better.

Golfers are independent contractors and, because the game is a play-for-pay enterprise, no one can force a player to wear a microphone while he or she competes during a regular tour event. All you can do is ask, and we found the way you ask can make all the difference.

"Hi, I'm Keith Hirshland with The Golf Channel, and I was wondering if you'd wear this microphone while you play today?" gets a far different response than, "Hi, I'm Keith Hirshland with The Golf Channel, and I was hoping you'd agree to wear this microphone while you play today. If you do, I guarantee that every shot you hit will be on TV."

You see, golfers also make money through endorsements, and that means TV time is worth its weight in gold. But even with that enticement, there was no guarantee that players would agree to help us out, so we stacked the deck. One of the items in the small-print part of the Canadian Tour television contract indicated that The Golf Channel could control as many as four sponsor's exemptions in every televised event, so to ensure we would get someone to wear a microphone, or do anything else we asked, we would only offer one of those coveted exemptions to players who would agree to our terms. That would guarantee us a player wearing a microphone on Thursday, and another on Friday; but, again, because golf on the weekend is merit based, we had no control over which players would be among the leaders and in the last few groups on Saturday and Sunday. Thank goodness for a young Irish lad named Eamonn Brady, two enterprising members of our crew, and dumb luck.

Daisy Phipps (who you've met) and Elizabeth Wright (who you're meeting now) were the perfect pair to convince players to wear our microphone during Saturday's coverage. They were outgoing, smart, charming, and persuasive; a combination that,

I hoped, would mean a player saying no would prove impossible. They grabbed the gear—the power supply for the microphone is roughly the size of an iPhone—and, with high hopes and instructions from me to "get the thing on somebody!" headed for the practice facility to find a contender who would also to be our guinea pig.

Two players, Americans Marty Scheine and Aaron Barber, led at seven under par. They both said thanks but no thanks. Two of our sponsors picks, Steve Scott, who claimed a modicum of fame by nearly beating Tiger Woods in the 1996 US Amateur Championship, and my good friend and Golf Channel announcer Jerry Foltz, who followed up a disastrous first round 76 with a three-under-par 68, made the cut and would have happily worn the technology, but Daisy and Elizabeth felt they were too far off the lead to get enough airtime, so they were passed over. Three other American players, Dave Christensen, Brian Kontak, and D. A. Points, listened intently to the pitch and seriously considered the offer until deciding they had more to lose than gain by wearing the microphone and took a pass.

Derek Gillespie was, at the time, the best young Canadian golf prospect. He was a two-time Ontario Amateur champion and standout at the University of Arizona before turning pro. Gillespie would end 2001 as the Canadian Tour rookie of the year, but he started it by agreeing to try the microphone on the first Saturday of the season. Elizabeth and Daisy were thrilled as they hooked him up, then watched him walk over to the practice tee to start his warm up session. The two spent a few more minutes hanging out and shooting the breeze with Brett Bingham, Jason Bohn, and Joey Snyder III, players who had become friends over the years, and then turned to head back to their golf cart. When they did, they were met by an apologetic Gillespie, microphone equipment in hand, who said he tried, but it just didn't feel right. Back to square one.

For the Myrtle Beach Open, we had also extended an exemption to a young player named Jamie Neher. He hadn't nearly beaten Tiger; he wasn't a Golf Channel announcer; but the reasons for inviting him were just as compelling. Jamie Neher's father was a gentleman named Tim Neher, who just happened to be the vice chairman of Continental Cablevision, an early investor in The Golf Channel and a good friend of Joseph E. Gibbs. Daisy knew Tim's son, Jamie, and even though he had shot 74, 73 in the first two rounds, she also knew he was obligated to say yes to our request, because we were the only reason he was in the tournament field. With my earlier instructions still fresh in their minds, and time running out, they did what I asked them to do and "got" the microphone on somebody. That somebody was Jamie Neher. Jamie was great, actually thrilled, to help. He wasn't a name player, but he was a smart kid, and he knew he had made the cut by a single shot and, now, he was guaranteed TV time. He thanked Daisy and Elizabeth for the opportunity, and then thanked "us" by shooting Saturday's best round, an eight-under-par 63, and climbed nearly fifty places on the leaderboard. All of a sudden, getting somebody to wear the microphone on Sunday was going to be less of a problem. My bigger problem was getting our announce team to talk less on Sunday so the viewers could hear the player talk more.

Championship Sunday's final pairing was comprised of American Aaron Barber and Ireland's Eamonn Brady, both at seven under par. Barber would become part of a much more publicized piece of history two years later when he and Dean Wilson found themselves in the same group on Thursday and Friday as LPGA superstar Annika Sorenstam when she became the first female in more than half a century to tee it up in a PGA TOUR event at the Colonial Invitation Tournament in Fort Worth, Texas. But before Barber played in that historic threesome with Dean and Annika he had said no to Elizabeth and

Daisy on a Saturday in Myrtle Beach, so on Sunday they went right to Brady, who didn't hesitate in saying yes and grabbing the gear.

Grant Boone was my play-by-play announcer, and he is an excellent one. The nephew of legendary crooner Pat Boone, Grant was polished, professional, and, maddeningly, both articulate and loquacious. I have worked with many announcers in my time, and Grant is one of the best, and he is, without question, the smartest. You could always count on Grant Boone to turn a clever phrase or put a situation in the proper perspective. My challenge with Grant was convincing him to stop talking. I constantly asked him to talk 40 percent less because his 60 percent was better than everyone else's 100 percent, but, in the meeting before the final round of the Myrtle Beach Open, I worked hard to convince the entire team that we should let Eamonn Brady do most of the talking.

February 25, 2001, broke cold and gray, but Eamonn Brady was brilliant all day. He discussed strategy, reacted at different times with both humor and grace, and he gave our viewers an impressive glimpse inside the head of a professional golfer trying to win for the very first time in his career. With my constant badgering, the announce team did a credible job keeping the chatter to a minimum so we could get the maximum out of Brady. He methodically marched around the course and came to the 18th tee even par for the day and holding on to a three-shot lead over Barber, who had played over par for the first time all week. Brady's tee shot at the final hole headed toward a hazard to the right of the 18th fairway, but settled instead in the rough. He knew he had a fairly comfortable lead, but he couldn't afford a big mistake, and his sigh of relief was audible. At the same time, the excitement in the truck was palpable as we went to break.

When we came back from commercial, Brady was discussing his lie, in the ragged right rough, with his caddie, and, as Chuck started the countdown from ten, I gave one simple command to my announcers.

"Everybody, shut the fuck up," and they did.

Everybody in the truck, and every viewer at home, heard Brady and his caddie go back and forth about club selection and wind direction. The viewers didn't need to hear speculation from an announcer, because they got the information from the horse's mouth; Brady wasn't thinking about where he wanted to hit the shot, he was thinking out loud and telling all of us where he knew he "couldn't" hit the shot.

"Long is bad," Brady said to his looper. "I can make bogey from in front of the green, but long brings in the possibility of worse than that." The caddie said nothing, which said everything, and our cameras watched Brady steal a glance at his fellow competitor, Barber, whose ball was in the middle of the fairway.

"He knows he needs to make birdie," Brady continued, and now his caddie piped in.

"What he does means nothing if we make bogey or better. Play to the front part of the green," he finished, as he moved a step closer to his player. Brady nodded, grabbed a club, settled over the ball, and took a deep breath. Like he had done all day long, Eamonn Brady played a beautiful shot that landed just short of the green, then bounded onto the putting surface, about thirty feet from the hole location.

"Nice shot," his caddie said, after taking the iron back from Brady, who smiled, because he now knew the only way he could lose was if Aaron Barber holed his approach for an eagle two. He didn't.

By design, I had run all my commercials except for the one that would air between the final putt and the trophy presentation, in the hopes that this scenario would play out: a winner wearing a microphone, walking toward the green on the seventy-second hole, basking in the knowledge that the victory was his. Once again my instructions to the announce team were simple.

"Shhh, shhh, shhh, shhh," was what I said this time, and then I addressed our sound man, Billy Robinson.

"Billy Rob, pump up Brady's mic!" He did, and as Eamonn Brady crossed the bridge that left him about a hundred yards from the green, the soon-to-be-winner turned to his caddie and said, "This is the greatest feeling in the whole world."

I agreed.

GETTING THE "BUGGS" OUT

Jace Bugg was a good old Southern boy and a hell of a golfer. Cheerful and cherubic, Bugg had a ton of talent and a ton of friends. He was the 1997 Kentucky Golf Association Player of the Year and a member of the Canadian Tour two years later. He was on the practice tee at the Love Course in Myrtle Beach, South Carolina, on April 8, 2001, getting ready to play his final round in the South Carolina Challenge. Bugg had yet to do anything special in the event, shooting 72, 68, 71 to stand at five under par through three rounds and smack dab in the middle of the pack heading into Sunday. He was probably puzzled to see our crew heading his way as he went through the routine of warming up.

Jace was a nice guy, a good story, as well as a good player; and he was far from stupid. Daisy, Elizabeth, and technical manager, Eric Thomas, who had become a fan of our technology experiments, were desperate that particular morning, having asked and been turned down by every player with a tee time off number 1. To ensure everyone would finish during our television window, Canadian Tour officials had split the field on Sunday, meaning half would tee off 1 and finish on the back nine, where our cameras lived, while the other half would tee off number 10 and finish on the front nine, away from the glare of the cameras. The best scores were going off of hole number 1, the rest would tee off 10; and Jace Bugg was among the rest. He was also astute. Bugg knew others had worn the microphone, and he was well aware that technology translated into air time, so, when our group asked him if he'd wear it, he couldn't say yes fast enough. They had their man, but Emmett and I had a problem; Bugg and his grouping would be finishing on the front nine, and we didn't have cameras behind those greens. Emmett deftly reassigned the hand-held operators, sending two to follow Jace Bugg, who was a handful of shots off the pace, but proudly wearing our microphone.

Bugg started slowly that day and still trailed with nine holes to play when we came on the air, but then that all changed. He birdied his tenth hole, then four of the next five and, by the time he came to the last couple of holes, Jace Bugg was not only wearing our microphone, but cruising to a three-shot victory—his first as a pro. He would play the following season on the Nationwide Tour, and win there, too, capturing the Arkansas Classic, but 2002 was bittersweet, because, sadly, Jace Bugg was diagnosed with leukemia in November of that year. He fought the good fight for thirteen months before tragically passing away at St. Mary's Hospital and Medical Center in Evansville, Indiana. He was twenty-seven years old. There is now a Jace Bugg Award for Sportsmanship, handed out each year by the Kentucky State Golf Association, honoring a young man who had high standards, a wonderful outlook on life, and hundreds of people he called friends, who undoubtedly still think about him every day. I remember him fondly and always will.

MORE TOYS, LESS NOISE

Having tournament winners on two out of three champion-ship Sundays mic'd up validated the microphone experiment; but I had my sights set on other, actually innovative technology, and in 2001 I turned to instruments used every day to find it. Our group was on California's beautiful Monterey Peninsula in the fall of that year to televise the Buy.com Monterey Peninsula Classic: a week that started with me meeting Clint Eastwood for the first time and ended with Chad Campbell (who would later win on Tour, contend for major championships, and play for the United States in the Ryder Cup) winning. But it's what caught my eye in the middle that makes it part of this book.

Each week television networks park trucks full of equip-ment worth millions of dollars on grassy fields, gravel tracts and in golf course parking lots, fill them with people during the day and then leave them, silent and lonely, overnight. The Golf Channel pays for security—most times, off-duty police offi-cers—to stand guard over the trucks in the compound when no one else is there, and the Monterey Peninsula Classic was no exception. As we were leaving one day, the evening's security, an off-duty Monterey police officer, in his black and white, was arriving, and I noticed his radar gun on the dash, which trig-gered something in my brain.

Golfers, both professional and amateur, are obsessed with numbers. Not just birdies and bogeys, but distance, club speed, and ball velocity. At the turn of the decade, the only way to determine speed and velocity was a bulky contraption, mostly owned and operated by equipment manufacturers and reserved almost exclusively for the professionals who agreed to endorse their products. I had seen police radar guns hundreds of times, and even been nailed by one or two over the years, but when I saw this one, I didn't see a speeding ticket. I saw an opportunity to take everyday technology and apply it to our golf broadcasts. Radar guns were used by cops to track the speed of oncoming and receding traffic, but, more analogous to my needs, they were also used in major, minor, and, in some cases, little league baseball parks all over the land to measure the speed of someone's fastball. I wondered: if these devices could measure the speed of something coming toward them with enough accuracy to put fear in the hearts of major league hitters, or establish parameters for multi-million-dollar pitching contracts, could they measure the speed of a golf ball as it left the clubhead wielded by a professional golfer?

There was only one way to find out,

"Excuse me, officer?" I said, as I approached our security for the evening and he turned and looked my way. "I'm Keith Hirshland and I'm producing this event for The Golf Channel this week." He said nothing and betrayed nothing but contempt with a look, but I forged on, extending my hand. He took it and shook it. I continued, "I was thinking that your radar gun could measure the speed of a golf ball after it was hit, and I was wondering if we could borrow the gun for a few minutes and take it over to the practice tee to find out." I stopped my pitch and smiled again.

Again he didn't smile, but at least this time he offered a response.

"No."

"Okay, then, thanks," I said, and walked back to the car.

Being a baseball fan my entire life, I knew the machine that measured fastballs was called a JUGS gun. My next step was to contact that company and see if they would be more cooperative than the man in blue from the Monterey PD, and, to my delight, they were.

After I agreed to have Grant Boone mention the company at every opportunity during the broadcast, JUGS agreed to send me two guns, complete with batteries, carrying cases, and instructions ("point the JUGS device in the direction of the oncoming sphere and hold down the trigger until it clicks") for our use. They sent them to The Golf Channel and I took them to our next Canadian Tour event. The announce team (comprised mostly of former professional golfers) was skeptical when we dragged the guns out to the practice tee, but that skepticism soon turned to acceptance.

Getting a reading was tricky, because you had to hold the gun at the right angle to catch the ball the instant it left the club head. After experimenting with different variations, we found that if the operator held the gun about six inches off the ground, three to five yards directly behind the ball on the tee, we could get not just a reading, but an accurate one. PGA TOUR players Bubba Watson and Tiger Woods generate ball speeds in excess of 180 mph, but, according to statistics, the average ball speed generated on the PGA TOUR is 160 mph, and that was the number we used to measure the success or failure of our JUGS gun experiment. Squatting behind players on the practice tee, we aimed, held the trigger until it clicked, and watched as the club head smacked the ball and the readout indicated speeds from 152 to 177 mph. Soon we had attracted an audience of a couple dozen players and convinced even the most skeptical announcer that this thing could work. All we had to do next was put it on the air, during an event, live.

GUNS ABLAZIN'

So, we holstered our guns and headed out to the golf course to put our latest "technology" on TV. In my mind, and in theory, it always worked; in practice, not so much. There were a couple of issues when it came to getting results; first and foremost was the operator. Much of our help on the golf course came from a local volunteer base that, in many cases on our Canadian Tour coverage, was new to the game, and, in every case, new to television broadcasts of the game. When Karel left for what he perceived to be greener pastures, I promoted Daisy to the position of associate producer, in charge of the volunteer base that would serve as spotters, scorers, and now JUGS gun operators. It fell on her to train new people weekly, and sometimes daily, in the operation of the guns and then prepare them for a variety of situations, ranging from cramped muscles to crabby golfers and cameramen.

Emmett, our director, also had to rethink his technique, because we did not have the technology to independently show the JUGS gun results on the screen. Instead, the cameraman had to take his normal position behind the player, hold his "head to toe" shot through the swing, then quickly pan and tilt the camera to find the readout illuminated on the display of the gun. Simultaneously, the volunteer had to hold the trigger until it clicked, keep the gun placed directly behind the ball, pointed at the angle of launch, and then, immediately after contact, turn and tilt the back of the gun to meet the lens of the hand-held camera. It was a ballet and, when it worked, it was enlightening; when it didn't, it could be embarrassing.

Adding insult to injury, the gun had limitations. To get a reading, you had to pull the trigger no more than ten seconds before impact, and to show the reading to the world, the volunteer had that same amount of time to "meet" the cameraman. As you can imagine, there were occasions when the volunteer pulled the trigger too soon or too late and other occasions when the cameraman made his move to the gun at the same time the readout disappeared. If I had a dollar for every time the camera panned and tilted to show three horizontal lines, instead of numbers, I could buy you dinner at the restaurant of your choice, anywhere in the world. But honestly, it worked more often than it didn't, and the readings were surprisingly accurate. Our coverage even made a little news around the golf world when long-hitting Hank Kuehne, the 1998 US Amateur champion, won one of our Canadian Tour events in 2002 while consistently registering JUGS gun ball speed readings in excess of 185 mph. In my mind, it was an unqualified success. In at least one player's mind, it was a disaster.

That player was a journeyman PGA TOUR player named Bobby Wadkins. Bobby's big brother, Lanny, won the US Amateur in 1970, the PGA Championship in 1977, and twenty other PGA TOUR events along the way. Lanny competed on eight Ryder Cup teams and captained the American squad once during a more-than-twenty-year career. Lanny was always considered a great player; he was also known as a surly guy to everyone, save his closest friends; and maybe, in fact, even to them. Younger brother Bobby also had talent, albeit not as much as Lanny, finishing second six times on the PGA TOUR and winning four tournaments on the Champions Tour. He wasn't as good a player, but he could be just as big a jerk, and he proved it one day in front of our cameras on the Canadian Tour.

Our cameras and our JUGS gun operator parked themselves on a particular hole overlooking the beautiful Texas city of San Antonio. It was the perfect set-up for the gun: a wide open, downhill par five, at which every player pulled out a driver and attempted to hit it is as far as he could. The volunteer had been doing a great job, timing the start of the gun and turning the readout upward in perfect harmony with the cameraman's downward tilt. Group after group, we got great readings and, since the word was out, it wasn't unusual for the players, after hitting their tee shots, to approach our volunteer and our cameraman and ask at what speed their ball had launched. Everyone was having a good time and it made for good TV. Then Bobby Wadkins's group showed up. As Wadkins punctured the ground with his tee, the volunteer operating the JUGS gun squatted in place, catching Wadkins' eye.

"What's that?" he asked, pointing the head of the driver at the gun. Randy Koury, our hand-held-camera operator, kept his camera pointed at Wadkins and heard the volunteer answer, JUGS gun, sir!" he said.

It measures ball speed," added Randy

The player stared at Koury, slowly shook his head back and forth, grunted, and began to set up for his tee shot. This was all captured on camera and broadcast live to Golf Channel viewers all over the world, and so was what happened next. Wadkins addressed the ball and our volunteer started the process of getting a reading by pressing the JUGS gun trigger. As indicated earlier, when that happened the gun began to make a soft clicking noise, a noise that hadn't seem to bother any other player, but, for some reason, it bothered Bobby Wadkins, and he backed away from his ball and turned his glare once again on our JUGS gun operator.

"Turn it off," he growled.

"I'm supposed to get a reading from every player," our volunteer bravely replied, and, before our cameraman Randy could intervene, Wadkins took one more step toward the gun operator and let go with both barrels.

"If you don't turn it off right now," he said, again pointing the head of his driver at the gun, "I'm going to shove that thing all the way up your ass and we'll see what kind of reading you get then."

On the tee, our operator was mortified; in the truck, the crew was mesmerized; and Bobby Wadkins was clearly satisfied, as he hit his shot and walked off the tee box.

402

MY KINGDOM FOR A SEVEN-SECOND DELAY

The guns became a staple of not just our Canadian Tour coverage, but it overlapped into our coverage of other tours as well, and so did the microphones. Because of the success of the players who wore the microphones on the Canadian Tour (Aaron Barber, who refused to wear it week one, changed his mind the next week and won that event), it was an easy sell on the LPGA Tour. We were lucky enough to have Juli Inkster, Beth Daniel, Meg Mallon, Cristie Kerr, Laura Diaz, Janice Moodie, and many, many others wear our technology, but, despite that track record, we could never convince the PGA TOUR to let us put microphones on players and broadcast their conversations live during the telecast. Ten years later, they still refuse to do it. As successful as it was in the early 2000s, I wouldn't do it today, either, for the simple fact that having a player wear a microphone has become unnecessary. The sound that broadcast crews can gather these days through hand-held and parabolic microphones on the course is just as good, and nowhere near as invasive, as asking a player to clip on a microphone battery and run a cable up and under his shirt and around his body. But you still have to worry about the occasional slip of the tongue.

Live golf does not come with a seven-second delay, but there have been times that I wish it did. Jason Enloe certainly echoes that sentiment. Enloe retired from professional golf in 2011 a two-time winner on the Nationwide Tour to take a job as the assistant golf coach at his alma mater, Southern Methodist University. He turned pro in 1997 and found himself in the field during the Canadian Tour's Myrtle Beach Barefoot Championship the week of April 26, 2002. He was not only in the field, but he played well enough to lead the tournament as we came on the air on Friday afternoon. Earlier in the day, he had agreed to wear the microphone, and it was turned on and tuned up when Grant Boone brought us on the air.

"Welcome to The Golf Channel's coverage of the Myrtle Beach Barefoot Championship from the Dye Course at Barefoot Landing in Myrtle Beach, South Carolina. You're looking at tournament leader Jason Enloe." And with that, Grant stopped talking and Jason Enloe started after he took a mighty swing and hit a screaming low line drive.

"Run, you little cunt," was what he said, and then he added for good measure, "Oh fuck, I'm mic'd."

We had been on the air for less than twenty seconds and, for all intents and purposes, our show was over. Grant was speechless, the truck silent, and my heart must have skipped a beat because, all of a sudden, I had an idea for a different kind of technology.

HEARTS AFLUTTER

So Jason Enloe put his foot in his mouth (or he wished he had) and my heart was in my throat. By the way, to add injury to Enloe's insult, the scene replayed, in its entirety, bad words and all, later that night on The Golf Channel; but that's a subject for a completely different book on the inner workings of the network. I had hearts on my mind.

People constantly talk about the pressure of having to make a five-, ten-, or fifteen-foot putt to win a golf tournament and wonder how much that pressure affects players. We're told by former professionals, swing coaches, and sports psychologists that the reason pros practice for hours is to establish muscle memory that, in theory, takes over in times of duress. We also know, thanks to these same experts, that some players are better equipped than others to handle pressure because they are physically stronger (Tiger Woods), mentally tougher (Tiger Woods), or simply someone named Tiger Woods. But all that was just what they "thought." I wanted to know for a fact, so I turned once again to technology.

Several companies make devices that measure heart rate, and I wanted to convince one of them to construct a unit that would be nonintrusive enough to persuade a professional golfer to wear it when he or she played in a tournament. That company turned out to be Mortara Instruments, and a gentleman there named Mark Mentzer worked with his technicians to make my hope a reality. We ended up with a unit slightly bigger than the microphone transmitter that could be attached, through loops, to the player's belt. They also developed computer software that would allow us, through a portable laptop, to get heart rate readings from the player wearing the device, from a distance of up to fifty yards. The information would be displayed on the laptop and then audibly relayed, via a party line (PL) headset, to our graphics department in the mobile unit, and then inserted on air. That, it turned out, was the easy part.

The problem became evident the minute we opened the box from Mortara and read the instructions. The unit was the size they promised, and the software was installed without a hitch, but the issue was the leads that connected the device to the player—specifically the number of leads that needed to be attached to receive what the company called "optimum results." Initially, the number was eight, and I knew there was no way a player would agree to have that many extremely sticky patches, each with its own wire going from patch to transmitter, attached to his or her body and snaking from various points on and around the player's torso to the source. The diagram indicated the eight ideal spots on the body, which we immediately started eliminating because, after all, optimum results were needed in a life-and-death medical situation; results of any kind was what I was looking for in a Canadian Tour golf broadcast.

With the ever-willing Jerry Foltz as guinea pig, we started paring down the number of leads by half, hoping that four would work, and less than that if we could manage to get numbers, and, as it turned out, we could. With three "strategically placed" sticky leads on various spots on Foltzy's lower back, we could get his heart rate beating crystal clear on the portable laptop screen. Hooked up like a medical experiment, we took our patient/subject to the practice tee to prove to players that wearing it would cause no adverse effects. A lot of guys tried it, very few were convinced, but we only needed one to make it work. Luckily for me, we found one.

Jason Duehn Bohn was born in 1973, attended and played golf at the University of Alabama, and, while there, hoped to turn pro after graduation. As it turned out, he not only wouldn't wait...he couldn't. In 1992, Bohn was a sophomore, playing on the Crimson Tide golf team when he teed it up in a charity event being played in Tuscaloosa. As is often the case at charity golf tournaments, one of the par threes on the course was designated to offer a million-dollar prize for a hole in one, and this charity event was no exception. Bohn paid the entry fee, teed up his ball, took his swing, and then watched his ball sail skyward, land softly, and trundle into the hole for a 1—and $1 million! Suddenly Jason Bohn had a decision to make, because the United States Golf Association rules regarding amateur status simply stated that Bohn (or anyone) could either stay an amateur or accept the monetary award, but not both. Bohn immediately turned pro, gave up his Alabama scholarship, and became a million dollars richer. He would go on to win once on the Nationwide Tour and twice on the PGA TOUR but, ten years after his million-dollar golf shot, he was playing on the Canadian Tour, and on the practice tee when we approached with our heart rate device.

Jason Bohn was a good player and a good sport, and he was intrigued by the heart rate monitor. In the same vein as the JUGS gun, players, as it turned out, were curious to see what the machines said about them. Bohn was the first, but dozens of others would follow in his footsteps. We followed his footsteps on the air as he worked his way around the Circle C Ranch course. He was in good shape, as he played the first seven holes but wasn't close to catching the leaders, Hank Kuehne and Steve Runge, who were playing together in the last group. Before starting the round, we established a baseline, or resting heart rate, for Bohn by having him sit, breathe deeply, and relax for several minutes. That number was inserted on the screen, alongside a bar graph display showing beats per minute, developed by graphics designer and operator Tom Martin, exclusively for The Golf Channel. The bar would increase or decrease, by increments, as our technician following Bohn would call in numbers from the readout on his laptop. Based on the resting heart rate, we also established a maximum heart rate, and the bar graph would change from green (between resting and maximum) to red (above maximum) depending on the number called out by our guy on the ground.

Bohn birdied the 8th, and, while his heart rate bumped up a little, it wasn't a dramatic difference, but that was about to change. Bohn birdied the 9th, then the 10th, the 11th, and the 12th, for five in a row. He hit his approach close at 13 and we watched the bar graph inch up to the maximum line and glow from green to red, and he birdied again for six straight. The excitement of a player making six straight birdies was easily translated to the viewer as Grant Boone and our announce team set the scene and the expectations; but the addition of a real-time working heart rate monitor on the guy making all those birdies delivered a message that no former player, expert, psychologist, or even the best announcer in the world could deliver; there was pressure involved, and at least this professional was feeling it. Then the technology amazed us again.

Jason Bohn had made six birdies in a row and suddenly found himself in contention to win on the Canadian Tour. We watched and documented his rising heart rate as the birdies came at 10, 11, 12, and 13, but, as he settled over his ball in the middle of the 14th fairway, after another excellent drive, something interesting happened. I expected the heart rate to continue to rise, but the numbers called in by our technician, Mike Ruhlman, told a different story—a story any TV golf announce team wouldn't have told. Instead of Bohn's heart rate rising, an unexpected calm clearly came over the professional, and the heart rate number, instead of continuing to creep up, started going down! Bohn struck his approach, another good one, made his putt for his seventh straight birdie, and marched to the 15th tee, while his heart rate got closer and closer to the resting heart rate we had established, with his help, at the beginning of the day. It stayed there as he tied the Canadian Tour record with his eighth straight birdie, and then only moved up slightly as he putted for, and missed, his chance at holding the record alone on the 16th green. The technology was fascinating and, in my opinion, made for compelling television. Hank Kuenhe won the event, by a shot, over Runge and Bohn, but the heart rate monitor was the real winner that week, in my mind.

We continued to use the technology for another half-dozen years on the Canadian Tour, the LPGA Tour, and the Nationwide Tour and found, for the most part, that a professional golfer's heart rate rose the most not before he or she was about to hit a shot or a putt, but immediately *after* as they watched the ball in the air or rolling toward the hole. For the most part, the data told us the players are supremely confident over the shot or the ball, but the heart rate went up, and maybe the doubt crept in, when the ball was in the air, because the player never really knew where it would end up. By the way, the highest heart rate we ever recorded was in the 180s, as Robert Floyd (son of golf great Raymond) worked his ticker overtime, and the lowest barely broke 80, thanks to the calm demeanor of LPGA great Laura Davies, who proved her serene façade was no fluke.

Our Canadian Tour time lasted six years and it was time well spent. We watched young players blossom and become winners, including Jimmy Walker, Kuehne, Jeff Quinney, and Eric Compton. Compton's story is one of golf's most uplifting. He was born in November of 1979 with cardiomyopathy, a condition in which the heart muscle is inflamed and can't pump as hard, or as it should. He received his first transplant in 1992 when he was twelve, and a second sixteen years later, after attending and playing golf for the University of Georgia and playing for his country on the Walker Cup team in 2001, before turning pro. As a pro, he won twice on the Canadian Tour (once in Morocco and again, this time on our air, in California) and once on the Nationwide Tour. His Nationwide Tour win came in Mexico in 2011, and enabled him to finish high enough on the money list at the end of the year to earn playing privileges on the PGA TOUR for 2012.

The Golf Channel's programming department was looking for more live golf to put on TV, and they found it courtesy of the Canadian Tour. One idea being bandied about in 2001 was televising pro-am play on Wednesday, but, luckily, I was able to convince both the programming and the sales departments that less-compelling television may not exist. Did anyone really want to watch a professional golfer suffer through a five-hour golf round with a combination of rank amateurs and insufferable blowhards? They agreed not, but challenged us to come up with something better, and we did.

WEDNESDAY BECOMES A SHOW DAY

Rather than watching amateurs and pros struggle through their pro-am time together, we thought it might be fun to have a five-man, four-hole shootout on Wednesdays. Five players participating in that week's event would gather on the golf courses' 15th tee, where we would put microphones and/or heart rate monitors on them to eavesdrop on their conversations and contentment. The player posting the worst score on each hole would be eliminated, leaving two men standing on the 18th tee. It was a chance for them to have some fun, go for broke, and earn some money, since The Golf Channel put up $5,000 a week in prize money. Another wrinkle we added was to include, whenever possible, a celebrity, and at an event in Austin, Texas, we found one.

Like many musicians, Grammy-nominated Texas singer/ songwriter Pat Green wanted to be a professional golfer, but his true talents lay in music. Pat had been making country music since 1995. He was, and remains, famous in Texas and has enjoyed a modicum of success in the other forty-nine states. His 2003 Gold Record release, "Wave On Wave," featured a title track that reached number three on the charts and earned a Grammy nomination, but it hadn't come out yet when he walked into our TV production truck on a sparkling but chilly San Antonio Wednesday in March to take part in the shootout.

Pat is one of a great number of people who work at night and play golf during the day. He just happened to be very good at both. A single-digit handicap, Pat admitted he was a little nervous, but excited, about being a part of the party. Since we could make up the rules as we went along, we decided that the one amateur in the group (Pat) should receive an advantage, in the form of a couple of strokes, to even the playing field. He agreed, and so did the pros, and off we went. During the next couple of hours, Pat not only held his own, he made a natural birdie on the shootout's final hole to win the thing. We've been friends ever since, and, to this day, I make it a point to play at least a verse or two of one of his songs ("Carry On") in the production truck before every broadcast. In 2006, Pat Green released his seventh studio album, titled *Cannonball*, and on it was a song he'd written called "Feels Just Like It Should." I listened to it and thought it would be the perfect way to kick off our PGA TOUR coverage in 2007. The Golf Channel's CEO, David Manougian, agreed, so I asked Pat if we could use it; he said "sure," and so we did.

THE BIG MAN RETURNS

So, we were having fun, trying new things, and enjoying going to work every day while, sadly, my dear friend Karel Schliksbier was miserable. He had taken my advice when he had taken the PGA TOUR's job and surrounded himself with good people, or at least that's what he thought. As he was putting his team together, Karel reached out to a young man who had impressed him when they both worked at CBS—Brandt Packer. He was the son of then CBS Sports NCAA basketball analyst and noted blowhard Billy Packer, and, by all accounts, that was his entrée to the network's golf production team. Karel thought he was recruiting a hardworking team player who was going to help him build a PGA TOUR golf brand at CNBC. What he got instead was an ass-kissing, bullshitting, backstabbing, snake who poisoned the well at the new venture.

Packer was Karel's replay director, which made him responsible for recording the golf that was, for the most part, not the main thread in the producer's storyline. In nearly every production truck, the lines of communication are clearly drawn; the director and the replay director talk to the cameramen, while the producer is the main point of contact for the announcers. The director *can* talk to the talent, but rarely does; and the producer *can* talk to the cameramen, but displays an equal amount of restraint. I had spent more than fifteen years in golf production trucks and never once heard of a situation in which the replay director had a direct communication line to the talent *until* Brandt Packer installed one in his CNBC production mobile unit; and then he used it not to offer information or support the producer but, instead, to question or deride every decision Karel made during the telecast; and Packer didn't stop there. The malcontent sowed the seeds of discontent throughout the compound and up the ladder to Karel's boss, Gil Kerr, at the PGA TOUR in an effort to usurp the big man and take his place in the main production truck.

Nobody was happy with the road the Senior Tour barreled down during the mid-2000s. The players were well aware of, and hated, the fact that fewer people than ever were watching them, because nearly every weekend round was aired well after it was completed, thanks to tape delay on an all-business television network that no one turned to when it came to sports. The Tour was catching heat for making the move, and that heat ended up burning the big man. Brandt Packer was more than willing to distance himself from the guy that had given him the opportunity and kiss enough butt to convince Kerr that Karel was the problem and he, Brandt Packer, was the guy for the job.

Karel lost his job, and I was more than happy to welcome him back. Packer got the job for which he had so expertly maneuvered politically, and rewarded the Tour by producing unimaginative, uninspired, and uninteresting telecasts on CNBC until the day that we all ended up under the same roof.

HISTORIC HAPPENINGS

There were several meaningful moments in the life of the Golf Channel over the first several years of its existence, but the most significant may have occurred a week before the network's tenth birthday. Television broadcast rights are historically multiyear deals, but new deals are almost always negotiated well before the last day, month, or even year of the agreement. Those of us who worked at The Golf Channel knew the broadcast rights deal between the various TV networks and the PGA TOUR officially ended December 31, 2006; but we also knew that, at some point near the end of 2004, talks to renew had already begun. We were hoping the disastrous results of the PGA TOUR/CNBC arrangement meant that marriage would surely end in divorce, and we felt it was logical that the over-fifty tour would return to the channel's airwaves. No one would admit it in a large group of people, but we were also hopeful that a new TV rights deal would mean an opportunity to be a bigger player when it came to televising PGA TOUR events. Sometime near the end of 2004, an agreement was reached, and I sat on pins and needles as I listened in on a teleconference held on January 11, 2005. Much like the CNBC press conference years before, this one was attended by TV network executives, but it wasn't representatives of one cable network sitting alongside PGA TOUR Commissioner Tim Finchem; it was CBS's Sean McManus, NBC's Dick Ebersol, and Golf Channel's (somewhere along the way the network dropped

The from the name) David Manougian, who had been promoted from president to chief executive officer, making an announcement that was stunning and thrilling.

Finchem started with his broadcast partners and announced a new deal that would span six years, run through 2012, and see CBS increase the number of events it televised from sixteen to twenty tournaments, and NBC go from six to ten. CBS, with Lance Barrow in the chair, would broadcast the final event before the playoffs for the FedEx Cup, as well as the first event in the playoff series. NBC would then take over, televising the final events of the playoffs, including the TOUR Championship, as well as two of the four World Golf Championship events. They talked a little while longer about the number of hours and specific events, and each network head got the chance to say how happy he was with the agreement. Then it was time to turn to the cable rights, and for that he introduced Manougian, and together they dropped the bombshell.

CBS and NBC would divvy up the coverage of thirty PGA TOUR events, and that deal was good through 2012; in contrast, Tim Finchem told all who were listening that Golf Channel's deal to televise events was exclusive, and not for a six-year term, but for more than twice that length. I sat stunned as it soaked in. Golf Channel would be the exclusive (no other network) cable home of the PGA TOUR for fifteen years! In addition to every Thursday and Friday, our network would be the exclusive cable home of the Nationwide Tour, what was now called the Champions Tour, and the television home of the first three events on the PGA TOUR schedule (the Mercedes Championships, the Sony Open in Hawaii, and the Bob Hope Chrysler Classic), and the seven tournament fall series at the end of the year. It was a broadcast bonanza and an unprecedented deal. Reaction around the golf world was immediate, and mostly negative, as people wondered how and why the PGA TOUR would put all its cable eggs in one basket, let alone for fifteen years! Reaction in the building was jubilant. We had all worked hard, many of us for ten years, and now we were being rewarded in a major way. Personally, I couldn't wait for 2007 to roll around, and, as it turned out, we didn't.

A YEAR I'LL NEVER FORGET

Before we go there, I have to take you back to a most memorable year, 2003. Gary Stevenson was an integral part of Golf Channel's infancy and an equally important part of my professional life. He was at least partially responsible for hiring me to be the TV network's first and, in 1994, only producer for live tournament telecasts. Nine years later, he would turn out to be a considerable component in my personal life as well.

I was happily a father in an unhappy marriage. I loved my kids and my job. In 2003, Hayley was twelve, Jake ten, and the Golf Channel was eight. Our home was Orlando, Florida, but I lived for as many as thirty weeks that year out of suitcases, in hotel rooms, in cities all over the country, and I would be lying if I said I never thought about both cheating on and/or leaving my wife. The thirty weeks of work were a combination of PGA TOUR, LPGA Tour, Senior Tour, Canadian Tour, and what would, in 2003, become Nationwide Tour tournaments. The umbrella sponsorship change of the latter led to life-changing events, for which I will be forever grateful.

The PGA TOUR commissioner in 1990 was a pretty darned good golfer named Deane Beman. He won the US Amateur Championship twice before turning professional and joining the PGA TOUR as a player in 1967. Between 1969 and 1973, he won four tour events, including the 1972 Quad Cities Open (now the

John Deere Classic) by one shot over Tom Watson. In 1974, he became the second commissioner of the PGA TOUR and held the job for twenty years. During his tenure, he started the Players Championship, developed a national network of golf courses called Tournament Players Clubs, and was the driving force behind a third US tour that would give hundreds of professional golfers a place to play and hone their skills as they prepared to play on the PGA TOUR. In 1989, he helped find a sponsor in the Ben Hogan Company and, in 1990, launched the Ben Hogan Tour. In the beginning, the Hogan Tour featured thirty tournaments, playing for a typical total purse of $100,000 with $18,000 going to the winner. To put that in perspective Joe Ogilvie finished last at the 2012 United States Open Championship and won $16,512. Beman's idea was to create a place to play and get better, but not get comfortable. He didn't see the new tour as a place to make a living, but as a jumping-off point on the way to the PGA TOUR. Each year, the five players who earned the most money by virtue of their play during the season would "graduate" to the PGA TOUR the following season. After year one, the five players who were first to earn that privilege were Jeff Maggert, Jim McGovern, Dick Mast, Mike Springer, and Ed Humenik. Maggert led the way, earning $108,644. The Ben Hogan Company was a partner in the endeavor and the umbrella sponsor for three years, and then it was athletic apparel giant Nike's turn to take over the tour's umbrella sponsorship. The Nike Tour was the name when The Golf Channel started televising events, in 1995. The "swoosh" flew on that tour's flag for seven years and, under its sponsorship, the number of PGA TOUR cards granted at the end of the season grew from five to ten to fifteen, and among the players that received them were David Duval, David Toms, Curt Byrum, Jerry Kelly, Stuart Appleby, Chris DiMarco, and Stewart Cink. The money grew, too, and, by the turn of the century, the Nike Tour's top dog was taking home more than twice as much money as Jeff Maggert had in 1990, almost enough to make a living. But, at the end of 1999, Nike had had enough and the PGA TOUR went in search of another sponsor. What they found was an Internet shopping site called Buy.com, and what they got was an umbrella sponsor for three more years before realizing the investment wasn't worth it and sending the PGA TOUR sponsor shopping again.

The Golf Channel began televising these events in 1995, starting with the Pensacola Classic, won by Clarence Rose, and continued to do so for nine years, watching struggling journeymen, as well as future major champions, compete on a tour sponsored first by Hogan, then by Nike, and, eventually, by Buy.com; and never once did I see, meet, or have a casual conversation with anybody from any one of those companies, let alone have any substantive discussion about broadcast ideas or philosophy. In 2003, it was announced that the Nationwide Insurance Company, a Fortune 500 company based in Columbus, Ohio, would become the fourth umbrella sponsor of the tour Deane Beman had started in 1990. We had heard that this would be a huge companywide initiative for the insurance giant, and they had hired a sports marketing company out of Raleigh, North Carolina, to manage it, including the messaging delivered on Golf Channel. The sports marketing company just happened to be headed by former Golf Channel COO Gary Stevenson, and, in April of 2003, I heard my old boss was bringing his team to Orlando to talk turkey about Nationwide Tour television. As you might imagine, after nine years of being left alone in regard to these events, I had *no* interest in suddenly having company.

MESMERIZED

The Golf Channel's plan was simple: the bigwigs—Manougian, Greenway, VP of Production Tony Tortorici, and head of Sales Gene Pizzolato—would start the meeting in the executive conference room, a place Gary knew well from his time at the network. They would talk ad sales, air times, and hours and scheduling before calling me into the meeting to talk about production.

I had done my homework; I had a presentation ready, describing all of the great things we had done previously in our coverage and listing the amazing ideas we had planned for the future. I admit to having had a bit of a chip on my shoulder; after all, I had been proudly leading this unit since 1995, had few, if any, complaints, and wasn't about to let a sports marketing company, representing an insurance company, tell me how to "do" golf television. Even if that sports marketing company was headed by someone for whom I had the utmost respect, and the insurance company had committed millions of dollars over a five-year period to sponsor the tour. I was the expert. I was prepared, and I had an attitude, which I took with me down the hall after being summoned by my bosses. I was certain I was in control, right up until the moment I opened the door to the conference room and came face-to-face with the most beautiful woman I had ever seen. I thought Sarah Caitlin MacDougall was impressive; then I heard her speak and, at that point, I knew she was amazing. All the bluster, bombast, and bravado disappeared as I watched and listened to the OnSport (that's what Gary called his company) team state their case. The fact that Sarah was stunning was one thing, but, because she was sharp and smart, it was easy to see the merit in their presentation and, after a brief back and forth, during which both she and Gary complimented the Golf Channel on its coverage to this point, I was left with nothing to say but, "We'll work hard to make sure you get what you need." All I could think was, *"When can I see you again?"*

I learned later that Sarah felt a connection as well, but her focus was strictly on business. She had been told by Gary that salesmen, department heads, and network presidents didn't amount to a hill of beans. He let her know: if she wanted to get anything done in terms of delivering Nationwide's messaging, she had to convince the producer that it was a story worth telling. Silly me, I thought she liked me. It turned out, she did, and a relationship that started out all business soon included pleasure and became a courtship. I met her parents that Christmas and found them to be as impressive, intelligent, and loving as their daughter. It has been my pleasure to know them, and my honor to call them not only my family, but my friends.

BEDEVILED

Singular experiences affect us all at one point or another in our lives. Hearing a piece of music for the first time, reading and really understanding something someone else wrote, or ingesting or inhaling a foreign substance can positively or negatively alter one's vision of the world, forever. It's happened to me a few times, but one experience stands out.

I may have mentioned two things earlier in this memoir: I am an avid sports fan; and my dad went to Duke University. The first fact has more to do with this episode than the second. Being a fan, I had watched more than my fair share of sports on TV and, by 2004, I had even been lucky enough to witness, in person, some of America's best events, in many of the sports world's most iconic venues. I had been to, and kept tickets as souvenirs from, an Olympic Games, the US Open golf championship, Super Bowls, the Kentucky Derby, an NCAA Final Four, and both the Daytona and Indianapolis 500 automobile races. I had also watched those, and thousands of other sporting events, on television, including plenty of Duke Blue Devil basketball games from famed Cameron Indoor Stadium. Duke is, without question, the most polarizing college basketball program in the history of American sport; and I could even argue that it reaches beyond basketball to the realm of sports brands in general. Some might claim the same is true of baseball's Yankees or football's Cowboys, but, I guarantee you, there are sports fans ambivalent about both. Not Duke. The Blue Devils are either loved or hated. I was privy to the hate firsthand because of friends I had made while working at WTNH in the home state of the University of Connecticut. The UConn Huskies were back on the basketball map, thanks to Coach Jim Calhoun and an NIT tournament championship in 1988. Nearly a year after I had left the Nutmeg State, the Huskies were in the NCAA tournament and in a tight battle with Clemson, out of Duke's conference, the ACC. With a trip to the end-of-year tournament's "Sweet Sixteen" on the line, UConn trailed the Tigers by a point, but they had the ball and one second on the clock. In the time it took that second to tick down to zero, Scott Burrell threw a pass the entire length of the court and it was gathered in by senior Tate George, who wasted no time in launching a shot that sailed through the net, giving his team an incredible, and literally last second, win. My UConn-basketball-crazy buddies went nuts. What does this have to do with Duke, you ask? Two days later, Connecticut fell victim to the same kind of buzzer beater—this one at the hands of Duke and Christian Laettner. It was neither Laettner's only nor most famous buzzer-beating shot, but it capped a twenty-three-point performance that day and sent Duke, and not UConn, to the Final Four. That essentially ended Connecticut's chance to win a national championship that year, but began a decades-long distaste that both school's basketball fans still feel for each other. Duke eventually lost the title Connecticut fans were sure would have been theirs when UNLV blew the Blue Devils out of the gym 103–73 on April 2 in Denver, Colorado, but that provided little satisfaction. There was a fourteen-year-old girl living in the Mile High City at the time who probably had no idea there was a national championship game being played in her hometown. She didn't figure into that story; but she would certainly make an impact on mine.

It was the beginning of the rivalry between the two schools, but Connecticut's dislike of Duke wasn't uncommon. In fact, fans from nearly every school derided and decried the team and its fans, the "Cameron Crazies" —scores of students who camped out in front of their historic arena before games and then, painted in blue and white from head to toe, heckled, hounded, and unceremoniously gave the heave-ho to visiting teams on a nightly basis once they got inside. The basketball cathedral that is Cameron Indoor was dedicated in 1940; at the time, it cost $400,000 and was the largest gymnasium in the country south of the Palestra in Philadelphia. It was originally called Duke Indoor Stadium, but the name was changed in 1972 to honor former coach Eddie Cameron, who is said to have drawn up the plans for the building thirty-seven years earlier. Between then and 2004, Duke, thanks in large part to its renowned coach Mike Krzyzewski, had built a brand, sent dozens of players to the NBA, and won three national championships and almost every game at Cameron. On TV, the place looked like a madhouse; but like nearly everything else, TV didn't do it justice.

I met the one true love of my life in March of 2003 (that little girl in Denver had become a twenty-eight-year-old woman). Sarah MacDougall was, next to my dad, the most impressive person with whom I had ever been acquainted. She was also beautiful; but much more than her appearance, it was her substance that reached right through my skin and bones and managed to grab both my brain and my heart. We developed a working relationship, then a friendship, and, finally, a real relationship; and it was with Sarah, a Duke graduate (Class of 2001), that I discovered not just what true love was, but what Cameron Indoor Stadium was all about.

From the outside, the building looks like a cathedral, blending beautifully with the rest of the Gothic architecture that defines

the campus. In the era of domes, arenas, and outlandish excess, it remains oddly quaint. Duke's basketball program helps generate billions of dollars for the school and its entire spectrum of sports teams. While Duke's football team was once good, and may be good again, and various other sports have been competitive and even won national championships, Duke is a basketball school. It is also one of the world's most respected institutions of higher learning, boasting Nobel Prize winners and Rhodes Scholars, some of whom, I am certain, painted their faces blue and white and watched—standing the entire time in the student section—the Blue Devils win dozens of games. The school could have torn down the venerable old building, brick by brick, long ago and replaced it with a forty-thousand-seat, modern-day arena, complete with corporate suites and sexy scoreboards, then named it after their amazing coach. But Mike Krzyzewski is much more pragmatic than pompous. He put the student body front and center, the TV announcer team in the rafters, and created the greatest home court advantage in sports. It is a modern-day Roman Colosseum; the Blue Devils are the centurions and the visiting teams almost always end up being the vanquished. The night I went, they were playing something called the ACC Big Ten Challenge, and the opponents were, appropriately enough, the Spartans from Michigan State. The school from Lansing had an impressive program and a famous coach of their own, Tom Izzo, who had won the National Championship in 2000, and he led his talented team into Cameron Indoor at the beginning of the 2004 college basketball season. Michigan State also boasts a loyal and vocal fan base, and many of them were there that night.

We parked and walked toward the building, as Sarah pointed to the "Krzyzewskiville" sign and pointed out that it was the well-known spot where students would pitch tents and camp out for weeks before the yearly Atlantic Coast Conference battle of giants that was the Duke/North Carolina game. If you went to one, she explained, you hated the other. Duke fans abhorred their Chapel Hill neighbors so much that at least once, at some point during every game, regardless the opponent, the chant "Go to hell, Carolina, go to hell" is sure to be heard. The students didn't detest the Spartans nearly as much, but they unequivocally despised the Tar Heels, and their love for the Devils was unconditional. The outside of the building is dimly lit, with several side entrances manned by ticket takers. The fans, nearly all clad in something devilish, file peacefully into a small space leading to a flight of stairs that ascend to a main concourse that circles the arena. Sarah and I entered, climbed the stairs, and joined hundreds of fans filling the corridor and heading to their seats. I could hear the collective voice of the students already inside, chanting, and the Duke band playing as we walked past glass displays filled with balls, jerseys, and photos commemorating Duke's heroes, past and present. We turned left and suddenly the brightly lit "Coach K Court" presented itself for admiration. Immediately, something smacked me in the face; not literally, of course, and it took me a minute or so to figure out: it was history. I saw a sea of blue that, by virtue of TV, was familiar; but I felt something that was extraordinary and unique. I had once produced a story for *PM Magazine* on entertainer Wayne Newton, whose people placed placards on every table in the showroom, stating, "Mr. Newton expects a standing ovation"; there were no such placards needed at Cameron. I knew exactly what was expected of me.

I knew it would not be enough to merely observe what was about to happen in that building. This place, these fans, that moment expected me to be an active participant: I wanted to. I looked over at Sarah and she was beaming. For the next two hours, I was swept up in the emotion, the drama, and the passion of more than a college basketball game. The colors were bolder, the cheers louder, the sights and sounds more spectacular than I could have ever imagined. I felt every foul, sat on the edge of my seat, straining to catch a glimpse of Krzyzewski as he coached his team during every time out, swallowed whole every second of the "Our House, Our House" experience, and felt a certain sadness at the end when the student section advised everyone to "drive home safely" after another Duke victory. The Devils won, but I felt in a real sense everybody won for simply having been there. You don't often get the chance to become a different human being thanks to watching a sporting event, but it happened to me that night. I walked into the building one person, but knew as we walked out, smiling at each other and holding hands, that I was a different, better one. I would sit in those stands on several other occasions, including at center court on Senior Night for J. J. Reddick and Sheldon Williams against North Carolina in 2009, but no other night compared to that first night; not now—maybe not ever.

FAST FORWARD

Thanks to Sarah, my personal life was in a better place three years later as Golf Channel continued to prepare for what many felt would be our most important television broadcast, round one of the 2007 Mercedes Championships, from the Plantation Course at Kapalua on the Hawaiian island of Maui. Even though we had televised all four rounds of major championships and Solheim Cup matches in the past, all hands were on deck and all ideas were being considered for what was to come. We knew we were about to spend more money on a single event than we had ever spent in the history of the network, but we didn't have broadcast network money to throw at the telecast. We had to make a splash, but we had to spend smart.

Tony Tortorici was the vice president of production, so ultimately it was on him to make the decisions on the enhancements that would make the trip across the Pacific Ocean, along with our crew, trucks, and equipment. Tony was a nice guy with a big job. He knew his limitations and was smart enough to enlist both help and ideas from a long list of people. Most of the ideas were either too stupid (cameras mounted on caddies' caps) or too expensive ("smart" technology that immediately upon impact would display graphically, among other things, the loft, lie, and face angle of the club), but some made sense, and a couple seemed like winners. Eric Saperstein had worked at Golf Channel for several years and, in 2006, was one of the talented guys producing *Golf Central,* the network's thirty-minute studio show, primarily covering the PGA TOUR. Somewhere along the way, Eric had met a statistician, writer, and software designer named Mark Sweeney, who came to the table with two ideas. One was a mathematical formula, based on a PGA TOUR player's past performance, which would statistically predict the likelihood of a victory for every player in the field. Tony and others really liked this idea and decided to label it "The Win Zone." The other compelling idea was also based on math, but it was much more definable. Using GPS technology, Sweeney's team would map various greens on courses played by the PGA TOUR. Using that technology and adding equations that would take in variables, including growing grass and blowing wind, the Golf Channel's viewers could see a line on the green that would show which way the putt would curve or bend if struck at what the computer considered a "perfect" speed (the ball coming to rest approximately twelve inches past the hole). In addition, the computer would graphically generate the exact point on the green at which the player would have to aim his ball to get the ball rolling on the proper course to the cup. That is why we decided to give this piece of technology the on-air branding of "AimPoint."

While Tony, Eric, Jeff Gershengorn, others, and I were working on the substance of the upcoming telecasts, David Manougian, Don McGuire, and Bob Greenway had turned their focus to the style. The network had a couple of very capable play-by-play announcers in Rich Lerner and Brian Hammons. It also had an excellent one named Brian Anderson, but instead of going with one of those proven, professional play-by-play people, Manougian and the others decided to take a flyer. At some point in 2006, I was informed that bringing us on the air for what was without question the channel's most important PGA TOUR telecast would be someone who had never done that job before: reporter and golf news reader Kelly Tilghman.

I remember sitting in Tony T's office and hearing Manougian coming down the hall. Our president never snuck up on anybody. He was a bundle of energy, always thinking, seemingly constantly in motion. He was a classic multitasker, able to split his attention and share his feelings on, and between, several topics in a matter of minutes. I liked him, but I had reservations about his latest decision the moment he stuck his head in Tony's office to give him and, because I was sitting there, me, the news.

Tony was the polar opposite of David Manougian: the tortoise to Manougian's hare. David thought big thoughts, made big plans, and swung for the fences every chance he could. Tony was a singles hitter, your classic utility player who, given a task, would concentrate all his efforts on that one job until it was done. Dave Manougian was a head-in-the-clouds guy, while Tony, more often than not had his head in his hands. He heard the news about Kelly, knew it didn't affect him directly, and turned his attention back to AimPoint and the Win Zone. My attention was equally split, half on innovation and half on a sudden sense of impending doom. Days later, it was Don McGuire who put it in perspective.

McGuire had been around the television block. He was, and still is, one of the most respected executives in the industry, and in 2006 he was effectively in charge of production at the Golf Channel for the second time. Don started his career my freshman year in college, worked for Don Ohlmeyer at NBC, producing studio shows for the network's college basketball coverage in 1978 and '79, and then features for its Olympics coverage from Moscow in 1980. He helped start Raycom Sports in the early '80s, and then, later in the decade, turned TBS into a sports television player as the network's executive producer at two Olympic Games, a Pan American Games, and a World Cup. McGuire was the guy responsible for hiring, among others, Don Sutton, Hubie Brown, Ernie Johnson, Jr., Doug Collins, and

Charles Barkley. He also made the sausage comment about TV production. He knew what he was talking about, and when he spoke to me, I listened.

From the other side of his desk, he explained: Manougian's logic was simple—Tilghman was different and she and the network would make history by having the first female play-by-play announcer in television golf. He also dropped the bombshell that the Golf Channel was in serious talks with six-time major champion Nick Faldo to partner with her in the booth. This was quite a coup, because Faldo was known to be in discussions with CBS to be the analyst for their golf coverage (they, in fact, hired Faldo in October).

"I know you have reservations about Kelly, but David thinks this is the right move," he paused, and considered his next words, "and so do I."

THE KELLY EXPERIMENT
BEGINS

Just because we were embarking on a new chapter in regard to our PGA TOUR coverage didn't mean we could abandon our focus on the thirty or so events we were charged to broadcast that year. While I was out on the road working, Tony was overseeing the transformation of Kelly Tilghman from studio show host to live golf play-by-play person. The move had still not been made public, but inside the building people knew something was up. Audio booths were booked and marked off-limits as Kelly practiced being a play-by-play announcer by watching tournament coverage and pretending to be the one giving the call. Tony also brought in Brandel Chamblee and Mark Rolfing to sit next to her and serve as her pretend analyst in many of these exercises. Tony firmly believed this was the way to prepare her for her new role.

During the dog days of summer, I received word that Kelly's practice sessions would move from the secluded comfort of a back-room audio booth to a live dress rehearsal, on site. She would join us at the Jeld-Wen Tradition at the Reserve Vineyards and Golf Club in Aloha, Oregon, the last week in August to hone her skills in a real-life, real-time coverage setting. The Tradition was one of the Champions Tour's biggest events, considered a major, and it required everyone's full attention. The tournament was played at a course outside of Manougian's home town of

Portland, Oregon, and it came as no surprise to anyone that he would be in attendance, along with Tortorici and McGuire.

In addition to our normal production plan, we established a "Kelly Rehearsal Plan" that would give her at least ninety minutes a day in the play-by-play chair, with a large "on-air" monitor in front of her, a producer and director in her ear, and our everyday Champions Tour analyst, Frank Nobilo, by her side. Our cameras and microphones would be set up, and enough of our crew would be in place by Wednesday afternoon, so that would be our first chance to give this a go. I was uptight, which created a trickle down that made everyone else uncomfortable. My guess was Don McGuire knew that as he stood over my shoulder on Wednesday, August 23.

It didn't go well, and it wasn't Kelly's fault.

I mentioned earlier in this book that Wednesday is pro-am day in golf, the day that tournaments get to pay the bills and, if they're lucky, make a little profit. On the PGA TOUR, major championships are exempt from having to play Pro-Ams because event organizers want to give the participants as much time as possible to prepare, but some LPGA and Champions Tour majors are perceived differently, so pro-ams get the green light. The Jeld-Wen Tradition was one of those. The allure of a pro-am is the opportunity for average golfers to spend a handful of hours practicing their favorite hobby alongside professionals whom they watch on TV nearly every other week of the year. The problem with pro-ams, if you're trying to rehearse a real golf television broadcast, is that there are five people playing in every group; only one of them is a pro, and that pro could not care less how well, or poorly, he hits a tee shot, a wedge, or a putt. My only option was to have Emmett point his camera at the first player I saw and then tell Kelly, in her ear, to ignore the fact that it was John Smith, general sales manager at Any City Cadillac, and pretend it was Tom Watson hitting his second shot at the 15th hole. Then John Smith/Tom Watson would take a mighty swing and gash the ground and advance his golf ball all of twenty yards. Ever the pro, Frank Nobilo did his best to take it seriously, but, in fact, it turned out to be impossible to do the exercise justice and, after about twenty minutes, McGuire tapped me on the shoulder and told me to pull the plug,

"We'll try it for real tomorrow," he said leaving the truck.

And we did.

A REAL PRO REHEARSAL

When I awoke Thursday morning, it was with the realization that I had two jobs that day: preparing the team for the afternoon broadcast of a Champions Tour major championship; and getting Kelly Tilghman ready for what many hoped would be hundreds of afternoons in a brand new career. The first part was easy. As I have said before, at the Golf Channel, with a few notable exceptions, I was blessed to work with a creative, hard-working, professional group of men and women who knew their roles and did their jobs as well as, or better than, anyone in the business. Laying out the production plan for that day's show took only a matter of minutes, and then I turned my attention to Kelly.

During the show meeting, I had noticed Kelly, nose buried in her laptop, working in a corner of the makeshift office. After getting her attention and asking her to join the discussion that would now involve her, I discovered that the morning had found her busy compiling and committing to memory statistics and media guide fodder related to some of the players we would feature in our rehearsal, which was now just an hour or so away. While I believe in the power of research, I also know that a huge part of being good at play-by-play is the ability to watch, and then react to, what it is you are watching.

"Great," I started, "now take everything you read and memorized and file it in the back of your brain to use only when necessary." Frank Nobilo smiled, because I had given him the same one-line speech many months before as he got ready for his first broadcast on our air. I waited half a beat and then added:

"That stuff is, at worst, background babble, and, at best, situational. It's nice to know what Jay Haas's sand save percentage is, or how many fairways Loren Roberts hits, but that can't be your narrative. Every situation is different, and what is happening at that moment, on this golf course, is what should drive your thought process." Then, I said the words I had said to every play-by-play person with whom I had ever worked:

"You are the traffic cop, *not* the expert. It's your job to get the conversation going, not be the last word on the subject." Sitting together, Don McGuire, Rich Lerner, Frank Nobilo, and others nodded affirmatively.

I went through the basics of the game plan; highlighted the groups on which our cameras would focus; and gave the meeting over to McGuire, who thanked the group for the professional way the other members of the announce team were handling this new initiative. I knew there were unhappy people because of the play-by-play turn of events, but I made a mental note to stress that it was in everyone's best interest to help Kelly succeed. The meeting broke up and everyone headed to our separate stations to pull together as a team.

Immediately, this dress rehearsal was 180 degrees different from the previous day. The biggest change was that we actually had golf, played by professionals, to show; and, from the beginning, Kelly was more focused, more proficient, and just plain better. We would do a segment or two, each lasting anywhere from four to eight minutes, and then stop. When we stopped I asked, over the headsets, if anyone had any questions or concerns. When none became apparent, we soldiered on.

In addition to calling golf, I would ask Kelly to lead me to interviews or features, and she handled those duties with aplomb. Throughout the course of my career, I found one of the hardest things to do, as an announcer, is to speak and maintain a coherent and intelligent train of thought, while someone else is speaking *to* you, in your ear. I had been careful not to do too much of that with Kelly, but, as the test proceeded, I did a little more. The rest of the rehearsal didn't go quite as well as the beginning but Don felt we had made significant progress.

I had structured the schedule so that our Friday would look exactly like our Thursday. A morning meeting, followed by an hour or so rehearsal with Kelly, followed by lunch, and then another half hour to forty-five minutes of rehearsal with Kelly and the on-course announcers. Then we would have to reset the announce team and get ready for a real show. Everything Friday looked like Thursday, except Kelly showed up late.

"Meeting started at 10," I said, looking at up Kelly as she came through the door.

"Sorry, I was in my room doing a little extra research," she offered.

"Okay," I said, turning my attention back to the group as a whole, "take a look at the groups that will be in our rehearsal window and let's be in position in twenty minutes." The meeting was over.

The second dress rehearsal went much like the firs,t but I felt Kelly was falling into the trap of relaying the information she had gleaned from her research instead of watching the action and reacting to it. One of the monitors in the production truck is focused on the announcer desk, and I could see Frank Nobilo getting a little frustrated as well, because he didn't have time to analyze the live action. I found myself agreeing and vowed to mention it to Kelly before we started rehearsing again after lunch.

"Getting more comfortable?" I asked Kelly, when I found her in Friday's lunch line.

"Yep," she said, "I got it."

"Okay, cool. There are a couple of things I want you to work on as we move forward," I said, reaching for the salad tongs.

"No, I'm good," she said, stopping me, "I told Dave I got it. It's not as hard as I thought it would be, so I'm heading back to Orlando."

"Really," I said, only a little surprised. "Okay, then I guess we're set."

I found out later that when she went back to Orlando, she continued to work, as clandestinely as possible, in sound-proof booths, with Chamblee, Rolfing, and even Nick Faldo in an effort to perfect her style. Manougian's choice of Kelly Tilghman as the number one play-by-play announcer would make waves the following year, and, in 2008, headlines.

ONE STEP FORWARD, TWO STEPS BACK

We tested AimPoint in October at the Houstonian during the Nationwide Tour Championship and then again at the PGA TOUR Qualifying Tournament at the Stadium Course at PGA West. It was terrific, telling, and new to golf. Other networks had visuals that could, through various techniques, show the contours and elevation changes on the greens, but Golf Channel was the *only* place where you could see the line of the putt *while* the professional was actually playing the shot, and know immediately if the ball had *any* chance of going in the hole. The most beautiful thing about it was that it was *never* wrong. Sweeney and his team and the technology experts at a small Texas company called Vistas Unlimited had hit a home run. We couldn't wait to show off the technology for real on the incredibly sloping greens at the Plantation Course at Kapalua.

While I was sure AimPoint would make a splash, Eric Saperstein, Tony Tortorici, and others in the building were equally, if not more, gung-ho about Sweeney's other brainchild, which the Golf Channel called the Win Zone. The folks at the network loved the Win Zone so much that they made it the main technological initiative in our coverage and a main promotional element, right behind the announcer team pairing of Kelly Tilghman and Nick Faldo. The Win Zone was going to revolutionize the way networks told the story of PGA TOUR events and the way the viewer at home watched them. According to the Golf Channel, it was a statistics-based bonanza that could almost always guarantee the winner of a PGA TOUR tournament. Sweeney and Saperstein had gone back a half dozen years and, applying Mark's mathematical formula, could prove, without a doubt, they could have predicted the winner or, at least, the person who had the best chance to win every tournament. What is it they say about hindsight? Oh yeah. It's 20/20.

The Win Zone was such a big deal and was going to be such a huge part of our coverage going forward that the network, with Saperstein as its producer, gave the green light to the production of a program designed to explain the wonderful analytical tool to the viewers. The show aired over and over again, as the countdown ticked toward our first PGA TOUR telecast on January 4, 2007. During the show, our announcers explained, or tried to explain, the system, touting its historically heavy credentials, and announced that The Win Zone would favor the following players: Stuart Appleby, David Toms, Vijay Singh, Geoff Ogilvy, and Jim Furyk.

Those of us who weren't completely sold on the predictive powers of the computer program confidently pointed to the fact that picking those five guys out of the thirty-four in the field was as far from genius as you could get; in fact, it was a no-brainer. After all, a first-time player had *never* won this tournament at the Plantation course (except, of course, when David Duval won it the first time it was played there, in 1999) and there were thirteen of them in the field in 2007. Add to that the previous year's PGA TOUR winners that *did* qualify, including Stephen Ames, Rod Pampling, John Rollins, Kirk Triplett, and Corey Pavin. Nothing against any of those, especially Pavin, who is one of golf's toughest competitors, but, before his surprising victory in Milwaukee the year before, the "gritty little Bruin" hadn't won a tournament in more than ten years. Stuart

Appleby was the computer's favorite (tough choice there, since Appleby was returning to Kapalua having won the tournament in 2004, 2005, and 2006) and Vijay was number two on the hit list, and the reason for that was equally easy to see. Singh had won fourteen times between 2004 and 2006, including the 2005 Sony Open in Hawaii, and, at the age of forty-three, was still one of the longest hitters in golf, a trait that serves everyone well at Kapalua.

But the fact that the very first tournament of the year was a winners-only, limited-field (thirty-four players) event meant we would not be using the Win Zone during our coverage. Instead, we would save it for the following week at the first full-field event of the year, the Sony Open in Hawaii. By the way, Vijay ended up winning, which served to bolster the Win Zone's reputation as we prepared to use it the next week on O'ahu. In the meantime, in my opinion, we had something better up our sleeves; and it wasn't Kelly and Nick.

FOLLOW THE PRETTY BLUE LINE

The Win Zone, and Kelly and Nick, were getting most of the attention, but AimPoint was the thing that actually turned heads. The technology reminded people of the first-and-ten line in football and, in many ways, it was the same technology. But, the first-and-ten line didn't have to deal with all the variables that AimPoint needed to overcome in terms of slope, speed, grain, and wind on a rock in the middle of the Pacific Ocean. The first-and-ten line gave the viewer an idea of where the offense would have to move the football to get a new set of downs, but, in reality, it didn't have to be exact; the officials had the chains for that. Our claim was that AimPoint was the exact line the putt would have to follow to go in the hole; sure, there were variables, and we explained them, but the bottom line was, if the putt followed the line, at the exact speed gauged by the computer, the ball could not miss; and guess what—it didn't!

At the beginning of the week, Nick was skeptical, which wasn't good, because he was the lead analyst, and if he didn't "buy in" to the technology, we were sunk. So we took him out to the 18th green and told him to pick a spot from which to putt. He did, and set the ball on the green. Next, we asked him to "read" the putt (a term golfers use to look at the slope of the green, the length and grain of the grass, and other variables that go into making a decision on how and where to hit the ball), and then strike the golf ball. He missed the hole. He tried again and missed again. Then, electronically, we showed him the spot on the green that AimPoint had figured out a player of Faldo's caliber would have to hit his ball to make the putt. Faldo couldn't believe it, because it was several inches away from the line his own eyes had told him the ball would have to follow. He shook his head, smiled, and then settled over the ball. Nick Faldo had made many more important putts in his life, at least more important to him, but when this one went in, and the next one, and the next one, the AimPoint technology had a convert and we had an on-air advocate. AimPoint was amazing and the viewers, the players, and the people that write about golf agreed:

TheSandTrap.com, January 9, 2007
"…it was addicting to watch."

Detroit Free Press, January 11, 2007
"I can already say with absolute certainty that AimPoint will revolutionize golf telecasts."

LA Daily News, January 18, 2007
"Unique and exclusive graphics such as the AimPoint, a football-like '1st-and-10' blue line on the green to show the break of a putt as the golfer is actually striking the ball, is one sure thing the networks will soon want to steal."

NBCSports.com, January 18, 2007
"Mutual of Omaha AimPoint, computer-generated laser technology that traces the ideal line of a putt before a golfer strikes it, was a neat high-tech addition to the telecast, and in the future should be used more often."

TheSportsCritic.com, January 21, 2007
"…the AimPoint feature is quite a treat."

GolfBusinessWire.com, February 10, 2007
"This might be the best new graphic for any sport in a long time. The graphic charts the ball's projected and ideal path to the hole. An arrow shows where a player should aim, while a dotted line from the ball to the hole allows viewers to track the ball's path. Putting is what wins tournaments, so this is a great new toy."

Golf Week, February 10, 2007
"Golf Channel also rolled out a new toy, AimPoint, which is golf's version of football's first-down line, giving viewers some much-needed perspective of the two-dimensional putting greens."

The greens at the Seth Raynor-designed Waialai Country Club, near Waikiki Beach on O'ahu, are small and flat; in other words, not the greatest ones to illustrate the AimPoint technology. So we broke down that technology and broke out the Win Zone for the first and, thanks to Paul Goydos, the last time, at the 2007 Sony Open in Hawaii. Heading into that event, Goydos had been a professional golfer for almost twenty years, and he had won two tournaments (one on the Ben Hogan Tour in 1992, and one on the PGA TOUR in 1996), so the Win Zone gave him less than a 1 percent chance to win during the second week in January of 2007. Defying the odds, Goydos played well enough on Thursday and Friday to not only make the cut, but tie for the lead at eleven under par; but, even after that stellar play, he wasn't on our radar and remained off the chart in terms of the computer's likely, or even possible, winners.

We were, instead, thrilled about, and enthralled with, the story of a young Hawaiian named Tadd Fujikawa, who birdied the thirty-sixth hole and, at the ripe "old" age of sixteen years and four days, became the second youngest player ever to make the cut and play the weekend in a PGA TOUR tournament. As the Hawaiian sun was setting on Friday, Tadd walked up the final fairway to thunderous applause. Our cameras showed the crowd, gathered and standing to welcome him, and then cut to a shot through the window of our announce booth, showing Kelly and Nick on their feet as well, applauding the young man's accomplishment.

Goydos stayed in contention Saturday, but fell out of the lead, giving more fuel to the Win Zone's fire that he not only wouldn't, but couldn't win (I *know* you know where this is going). He started Sunday trailing, among others, Charles Howell III and Luke Donald, and, because he was behind on the leaderboard, he was ahead of them on the golf course when our telecast was coming to an end. Paul Goydos birdied the 15th and 16th holes during the last round, but the computer still spit out its lackluster opinion of Goydos and we graphically announced his chances of winning were less than 10 percent. In fact, when his eagle chip hit the flagstick on the final green, guaranteeing his second PGA TOUR victory, the computer was still more than 90 percent positive he wouldn't win the golf tournament. Luckily, as it turned out, I had stopped using the graphic and had ordered the announcers to stop talking about the Win Zone after Goydos played the 16th hole. That initiative bit the dust, but the technology behind AimPoint won our crew and the Golf Channel their first and, to this date, *only* Emmy Award. Despite mixed reviews, Kelly stayed in the announce booth and would make national news of her own in 2008. But there was still controversy yet to come in 2007.

CAPTAINS
COURAGEOUS

On January 26, 2012, one of American women's golf's best and brightest stars was named United States Solheim Cup captain for the matches that would be held in 2013. Meg Mallon played more than twenty years on the LPGA Tour, won eighteen times, including four major championships, and represented her country on eight Solheim Cup teams. She was Beth Daniel's assistant captain in 2009 when the US team beat Europe 16–12 at Rich Harvest Farms near Chicago, and that body of work made her a logical choice to head the American effort in 2013—a logical choice, but not the only choice. The succession of US captains had read like LPGA royalty: Whitworth, Carner, Rankin, Bradley, Sheehan, Lopez, King, Daniel, and Jones had all led American players during the biennial matches, and the entire golf world figured the favorites to grab the baton would be Mallon or Hall of Fame member Juli Inkster. The problem with choosing Inkster was clear; she was still competitive, finishing in the top ten four times in 2011 while showing no signs of slowing down. She was a playing part of nine Solheim Cup teams and would be the first to admit she had every intention of playing in her tenth. In addition to Mallon and Inkster, there was a third possibility, who, for many, was the personification of the American Solheim Cup effort, Dottie Pepper. Her seventeen victories (two majors) and a 13-5-2 record in six Solheim Cups was only part of the story.

Dottie Pepper may have been the most intense, aggressive, and hard-as-bright-red-painted-nails player the LPGA had ever seen. Dottie was the emotional leader of every Solheim Cup team on which she played; in fact, she was so disliked by her European opponents that, on more than one occasion, they rallied around each other by railing against Pepper. Dottie would have been the ideal choice as Solheim Cup captain for the US team, but events that unfolded in September of 2007 had most people thinking Pepper, though ultimately and completely deserving, would *never* become captain. Events that, if truth be told (and it's about to be), would more than likely never have occurred if not for me and my big mouth.

DOTTIE GETS BIT BY A "FREAKIN' DOG"

Our Golf Channel production team had headed to Sweden for the second time in five years for our third Solheim Cup together, but, to my dismay, thanks to the budget, two members who had joined us for the event played in Malmo the last time, Jeff Gershengorn and Elizabeth Wright, did not make the travel squad. Our group consisted of me (producer and director), Peter Esposito (associate director), Mel Hundley (replay producer), and Scott Kazakewich (graphics coordinator); and we were joined by several crew members hired by our partners at European Tour Productions to serve as camera operators, technical directors, and audio technicians. We had all done this before and knew we were in for long days, short nights, and plenty of action, both on the golf course and in our compound.

Brian Hammons was there to serve as the host and play-by-play announcer, paired with Dottie Pepper as the analyst and joined by Kay Cockerill and Val Skinner following matches on the course. This was a small, yet professional, group that knew broadcasting the Solheim Cup matches on Golf Channel meant twelve- to fourteen-hour workdays that started, and ended, in the dark. They knew they had to bring good attitudes and foul-weather gear, because the middle of September in Halmstad, Sweden, could be windy, cold, wet, and raw; and it was. The winds turned out to be so strong that, like the big bad wolf, it huffed and puffed and blew our announcer tent down on Friday, forcing our folks to scramble and retrofit a makeshift announce booth in a trailer in our compound so Brian and Dottie wouldn't catch pneumonia. And that's where they were when the proverbial shit hit the fan.

The last and, for that matter, only time the American team had won the cup on foreign soil was 1996, at the St. Pierre Golf and Country Club in Chepstow, Wales. This time around, the best player on either team was still the great Annika Sorenstam, but, overall, the Americans were considered stronger, came into the weekend the favorites to retain the Solheim Cup, and held a slim 4½ to 3½ point lead after the first day. Eight points were up for grabs on both Friday and Saturday, after a combination of foursomes (what most golfers call alternate shot, because four players each hit "some" of the shots), and four ball (best ball, in layman's terms, in which all four golfers hit all the shots and count the best score) matches, while Sunday was saved for twelve head-to-head singles matches. There were 28 points in total and, because the United States held the cup due to its win in Indianapolis two years before, they needed only to earn 14 points, or a tie, in Halmstad to retain the prized possession. Saturday was damp and chilly, and gloves, wool hats, and foul-weather gear were required for the morning foursomes matches. Despite the inclement weather, the American team grabbed early leads in three of the four matches, hoping to grab a commanding advantage halfway through the competition.

Pat Hurst and Angela Stanford did their part, jumping out to a 4-up lead on Iben Tinning and Bettina Hauert and closing out the match on the 16th hole, putting up 1 point for Team USA, but the other three matches didn't follow that script. Juli Inkster and Paula Creamer were teamed against European Solheim Cup stalwarts Suzann Petterson and Sophie Gustafson, and, like Hurst and Stanford, had an early lead; but, unlike their countrywomen, Creamer and Inkster couldn't hold on, giving up holes late to lose their advantage. In another match, the same scenario was unfolding as Americans Sherri Steinhauer and Laura Diaz were locked in a battle with the European team of Gwladys Nocera and Maria Hjorth. Steinhauer and Diaz led late, but missteps, in the form of missed short putts, gave the Europeans life. We documented it all and were bringing it to American viewers live as Steinhauer looked over a four-foot par putt on the 18th hole that would give Team USA the match and another full point. Steinhauer had already missed a putt of similar length two holes earlier that would have put this particular contest-within-a-contest out of reach; then she missed this one, opening the door for Hjorth to make her similar-length putt and give Europe a tie and a coveted ½ point, from a match that, just a half hour ago, was surely a loss. Before Hjorth putted, our coverage shifted to the Inkster/Creamer match on the 18th tee, another match that had seen the USA give away holes late and, with it, chances to close out their opponents. Back we went to the green as Hjorth first lined up, and then stood over, her putt to win the hole and halve the match. In it went, completing the comeback and gaining the ½ point by beating Steinhauer and Diaz and, as the pro-European crowd around the green at 18 went wild, I pushed the button that allowed me to talk to the announce team and, out loud, I exclaimed:

"Choking fucking dogs!"

Then I released the button and called for a leaderboard and a commercial. The leaderboard appeared on the screen and I began to count Brian Hammons on the air and Peter Esposito off it, to commercial. When I got to two, I heard Espo give Orlando the command to roll the commercial break, which I expected them to do when I got to zero. A full eight seconds later, Dottie repeated an edited version of the three words I had in frustration uttered in her headset:

"Choking freakin' dogs."

Unfortunately for all of us, and especially Dottie Pepper, her words were the ones heard round the world.

Should Dottie have said it? Probably not, even though the words rang true, because both American teams had missed very makeable short putts that would have, at multiple times, closed out matches; but, knowing Dottie, my guess is she never would have said those words if I hadn't just seconds prior. Whether she should or shouldn't have ultimately gets lost in the fact that nobody but Brian and the audio technician in the booth should have heard those three damning words. Orlando was *supposed* to be in break; *should* have been eight seconds into a Cadillac commercial; but, because someone in Orlando, more than 7,700 miles away from Dottie Pepper, was asleep at the switch, her reputation, and ultimately, her standing in the women's golf community, and the Solheim Cup specifically, was in mortal peril.

Words like those spoken by Dottie are uttered *all* the time. You'd be surprised (or maybe you wouldn't) by what is said by announcers, producers, and directors during commercial breaks, but those remarks stay where Dottie's should have: in private. This wasn't a slip of the tongue, or Dottie blurting out some knee-jerk reaction, knowing full well cameras were rolling and people were listening and watching. This was Dottie, having been there and done that, remembering making and missing similar important putts, agreeing, when she had been told we were not on air, with a producer who had done none of those things. More than agreeing with me, Dottie was guilty of nothing more than holding up her end of the trust equation that is so important in our business. I told her we were clear and she trusted me. Then someone in Orlando let us both down.

We continued our coverage, but the reaction was immediate and brutal. There were calls to the Golf Channel to remove Dottie from the broadcast immediately and, because of the Internet and word of mouth, it wasn't long before the American team and its captain, Betsy King, heard about what Dottie had said and found it unacceptable. Feelings were hurt and egos bruised, but Dottie knew of none of it, because we were still on the air. The highest-ranking Golf Channel person on site in Sweden was programming executive Wayne Becker, whose company-issued Blackberry was blowing up, and he was in full crisis mode when he entered our production trailer.

"We've got to get Dottie to issue an apology!" he shouted, pointing at me with one hand and pocketing his mobile device with the other.

"Excuse me?" I said, without turning from the dozen or so television sets in front of me.

"Dottie has to apologize!" Wayne repeated, and, again without looking at him, I responded:

"First of all, lower your voice," I said, as I continued to call out commands and push buttons on the switcher, "and, secondly, what the hell are you talking about?"

"Apparently Dottie insulted the US team during our coverage, and she has to issue an on-air apology," Becker answered, in a lowered voice.

"Let me get into a commercial," was my reply.

During the break, Becker laid out the complaint and that was when I first learned that Dottie's private comment had, instead, been very, very public; but Dottie still had no idea. I felt sick to my stomach, but knew Becker was right, Dottie needed to apologize; but, first, she had to be told what had happened, and that was my job.

Dottie not only apologized immediately, but she has "owned" the remark since the minute she said it. She showed tremendous integrity, took the heat, repaired the relationships she felt were worth repairing, and moved on, never once mentioning or blaming me. Meg Mallon told Golfchannel.com's Randall Mell the day she was named 2013 USA Solheim Cup captain that she thought Dottie should get the consideration she deserves.

"I do believe Dottie Pepper should be captain someday... Dottie was the face of the US Solheim Cup team in the '90s. She deserves to be captain."

A day later, Pepper choked back tears on TV as she reacted.

"I made terms with what happened five years ago and, you know, you take the penalty or whatever you term it to be. You come to terms with that as well, and you move on." Then, all of a sudden, she paused to compose herself and measure what she would say next.

"I still don't know what to think of all of it, 'cuz I'm kinda blown away."

She became one of the best and most respected broadcasters in the business and will, one day, be a great team captain. I'm proud she was then, and is still today, my friend.

YEAR THIRTEEN ENDS

We ended our broadcast year in 2007 the same way we ended the previous twelve broadcast years, at the PGA TOUR Qualifying Tournament. This one was held at the Orange County National golf complex outside Orlando, Florida, and twelve-year PGA TOUR veteran Frank Lickliter II walked away the medalist, so my year saw a member of the World Golf Hall of Fame (Vijay Singh) start it and a three-time winner nicknamed "the Blade" end it. In between, I watched on monitors mounted in NEP trucks as talented players, including Charlie Hoffman, Justin Leonard, Chad Campbell, Hale Irwin, Joe Ogilvie, Mike Weir, George McNeil, Jay Haas, and Nick Flanagan celebrated on the Golf Channel's air. Grant Boone, Brian Hammons, Rich Lerner, Kelly Tilghman, and others called the action, to mixed reviews.

Comcast was in full control of the Golf Channel by this time, and the company had installed one of its own, a man named Page Thompson, as president, operating under Manougian. David's influence was waning, Don McGuire's was nonexistent because he had once again left the company, and those of us with Golf Channel history who remained could feel the breeze from the winds of change. We just weren't sure what that change would mean for any of us. Page was a smart guy, but he was learning on the job about golf and broadcast television. Before taking the reins at Golf Channel, he was responsible for building the company's video-on-demand service from conception to an industry-leading platform that offered more than nine thousand programs each month. With Don gone, and Manougian around less and less, we prepared for our second season at the home of the PGA TOUR's opening event, the Mercedes Championship, at Kapalua, on Maui.

Travelling to Maui, especially to televise golf's best players, was always memorable, but this time the trip would be unforgettable for all the wrong reasons.

I WISH I HAD BEEN HANGING ON HER EVERY WORD

The feeling on Maui the second time around was far different from the first. Page was running the day-to-day operation of the Golf Channel, and Tony Tortorici was his main production lieutenant. The year before, I had fought for a production team change and championed the addition of both Steve Beim and Andy Young. The change was a blow to my friend, colleague, and director for years, Emmett Loughran, but I felt Steve was the best in the business, and Andy's counsel would make every broadcast better. Tony agreed that this was the best course of action, and the three of us reunited to broadcast the Golf Channel's first three PGA TOUR events in 2007, and we did so again to start off the year in 2008. Thirty-one players teed it up on Thursday, and the broadcast started on time, with Stephen Ames hitting the first shot, and ended with Nick Watney grabbing the lead after shooting a five-under-par 68. That score was one better than the 69 shot by eventual winner, Daniel Chopra, and it meant those two players would comprise the final pairing for Friday's second round. Unlike 2007, there was no post-first-round party at the Ritz-Carlton/Kapalua; no champagne toasts to celebrate the dawn of a new Golf Channel era. It was business as usual and everyone went about his or her business like he or she had been there before. But there was a big hole in my heart in January of 2008.

My father had passed away in May of the previous year. I missed him every day, and the hurt was more intense the moment I set foot back on Maui, but my pain was nothing compared to how my mom must have felt. We could only remember my Dad, but Sarah and I had convinced my mom that she should join us for the tournament in 2008, so she returned to the island on which they had shared so many happy moments. But this time she was a much sadder and more introspective person. She was doing her best to enjoy the experience, and we were having a nice dinner at a Napili restaurant that Thursday night after round one. Page Thompson and his family happened to be at the same restaurant, and he stopped by our table on his way out. After I introduced him to my mom, he congratulated me on the day's telecast.

"Good job today," he said, patting my shoulder, "and thanks for entertaining my son." Page had brought his family into the truck during the telecast and, during a commercial break, I had let the boy wear my headset and speak, over the party line, with the cameramen.

"Thanks, and no problem," I answered. "He's welcome any time. Just let me know when he's ready to produce a segment or two." Page laughed and, as he left, let me know he was headed back to Orlando and wouldn't be around for the remainder of the weekend. As it turned out, he probably wishes he had stayed.

Friday started out as another day in paradise. Kapalua is roughly five-and-a-half square miles on Maui's northwest coast. Once upon a time, it featured amazing beaches and miles and miles of pineapple fields. Most of the pineapples are gone, replaced by homes, condominiums, and golf courses, but the beaches remain, and they are still spectacular. Maui is both the second youngest and second largest Hawaiian Island and has diverse landscapes, thanks to a pair of volcanoes. Millions of years ago, the Hawaiian island chain was formed by lava that poured out of thousands of volcanic vents. Two of the volcanoes were close enough to each other that lava flows overlapped, creating not two, but one island, the island of Maui. The older volcano eroded to form the West Maui Mountains, while the larger, younger volcano to the east, Haleakala, rises more than five miles from the ocean floor and serves as the island's signature sight.

If you've been on Maui, you know south Maui is the sunny side of the island and that's where you'll find the resort communities of Wailea and Makena. The northwest side, while still warm and beautiful, is windier and wetter, and that's where you'll find Kapalua. There is a Ritz-Carlton there, and that's where most of the Golf Channel's executive and announce team stayed during tournament week. The crew, on the other hand, had to "suffer" the indignity of staying at the Sheraton on Kaanapali Beach. It took about twenty minutes (thanks to a stop at Starbucks) to get from there to the Plantation Course, and it was along this route that associate producer Elizabeth Wright and I discussed just about everything, besides work, on the way to the compound. We had driven similar drives, from different hotels to other golf courses, in a variety of cities, since she had agreed to become part of the production team in 2001, but it was safe to say, what was about to unfold would be unlike any other day.

Most PGA TOUR events are structured so the competitors play in the same threesomes on Thursday and Friday, with one of the rounds played in the morning and the other in the afternoon. Tournaments are set up this way in an effort to level the playing field, with the hope of ensuring all of the contestants play the first thirty-six holes of the tournament under like conditions. With a full field (anywhere from 144 to 156 players) on most courses, the PGA TOUR officials plan on an average round taking five-and-a-half hours, from the first tee shot to the final putt. When the field is trimmed, thanks to the cut on the weekend, players then tee off in pairs, with the leaders playing last; and, because of that and the fact that the better players that week qualified for the final two rounds, officials usually plan on each round of golf taking three-and-a-half hours to play.

The first event of the year is a limited field event (winners only from the year before) and, because of that, the tournament is played all four days under the formula devised for weekends only during the rest of the season—twosomes, re-paired each day by score. Our broadcast window was scheduled for four hours, which meant the first few pairings of the day would be finished and the last couple not yet teed off when we came on the air. The hope is always that the final pairing finishes in just enough time to allow for a quick interview with the leader before the play-by-play man or, in our case, woman, says good-bye. For reasons that are too numerous to list, Kelly and Nick had a few more minutes than that to fill on Friday, January 4.

The beginning and the end are the two busiest times during a television golf broadcast, and that Friday was no exception. At the beginning of that telecast, Orlando was talking to the associate director, Scott Barke; the replay director (Pete Esposito) was talking to the cameramen and videotape operators; the director (Steve Beim) was talking to the cameramen, the technical director, and the graphics operators; I was talking to the announcers, the replay director, the features producer, and the graphics coordinators; and everyone was talking to me. You learn to filter out what you determine to be the most important messages, and that means different things to different producers, but one voice is universally respected at the very beginning and the very end of every show: the associate director, because, when that count gets to zero in the beginning, you're on the air; and zero at the end, you better be finished. Getting on the air that day was no problem, and neither was getting off, or so I thought at the time.

Play finished early on Friday and we had interviewed every player we wanted to interview so Steve, Andy, and I knew there was going to be a little time to "fill" at the end of the telecast. When that happens, a producer has options that include running tournament or daily highlights featuring players who have just completed their round, or putting the play-by-play person and analyst in front of the camera and letting them BS until the clock hits the top, or bottom, of the hour. Vice President of Production Tony Tortorici was still in the truck, and his preference was for the latter option, so I hit the all call and warned Kelly and Nick that we were coming "on camera."

"Turn on the lights in the booth," barked Beim, into his headset.

"Okay, guys, I need you to fill for about ninety seconds and we're coming on camera to do it," I gave the command to Kelly and Nick.

"What do you want us to talk about?" Kelly asked.

Tiger Woods was far and away golf's best player. In the three prior years, he had won twenty-one times on tour, five major championships, and more than $31 million. He was the game's dominant force and the subject of conversation at every event, whether he was entered to play or not. In fact, some people who watched most of the programming on the Golf Channel during that time complained because they thought Golf Channel treated Tiger Woods like he was professional golf's *only* player. Most of the events we televised were ones that Tiger skipped but featured some of the game's best stories and young talent. The Nationwide Tour tournaments were further evidence of that; and several players near the top of the leaderboard after Friday's second round of the season-opening Mercedes Championships (Brandt Snedeker, Nick Watney, and Aaron Baddeley) were young players with whom I was familiar, and I knew they had game, so I answered Kelly's question this way:

"Why don't you ask Nick which guys in the current crop of young players might challenge Tiger?"

Kelly and Tiger were friends and had a great relationship, so I knew any chance to talk about Tiger would be okay with her, so I turned my attention to the normal course of business that happened to get us off the air. The first broadcast of the year was an "all hands on deck" situation, which meant, in addition to Kelly, who performed the duties of play-by-play, we had Rich Lerner, who was there to serve as the "host." That meant the last forty-five seconds to a minute of the broadcast were Rich's responsibility as he wrapped up the day and urged viewers to stay tuned to what was coming up next and then join us again Saturday. Rich was brilliant at doing just that, and I knew I only needed to give Rich time cues and he would adhere to them precisely. After looking at the ticking clock, and double checking with Scott, I asked Rich how much time he needed; whether or not what he was about to say needed video support; or if that last few seconds would be him, looking into the camera to promote *Golf Central*, coming up next, and our coverage, at the same time tomorrow. He answered, through a tiny speaker in front of me that was turned up loud enough for Steve to hear, and then I heard Scott:

"Two minutes off air," was his command to me.

"Wrap it up and send it down to Rich," was my command to Kelly.

"Stand by, Rich," I said to Lerner. Rich did, Kelly did, and we got off the air on time.

I had no idea that, while I was adding and subtracting seconds, and asking questions of, and issuing commands to Rich, Kelly had asked Nick about the young guys challenging Tiger and Nick, in part, had offered this strategy: "…to take Tiger on, well, yeah, maybe they should just gang up for a while until…"

Then, for reasons to this day that are known only to Kelly, she interrupted the six-time major champion and analyst by chuckling and then dropping this bomb:

"Lynch him in a back alley."

REALIZATION AND REACTION

There was still work to be done on site as our crew provided content for the various studio shows back in Orlando. Clearly, I wasn't alone in the truck when Kelly made her racially tinged, insensitive remark. In addition to the crew members, there were a couple of people representing the PGA TOUR's broadcasting arm; two graphics people; event Coordinating Producer Andy Young; and Golf Channel VP of Production Tony Tortorici— perhaps as many as twelve people, all within fifty feet of each other, who apparently hadn't heard Kelly's comment either. There were also people along with Kelly and Nick who could, but must not have, been paying close enough attention either. Because no one heard it, we couldn't, and didn't, get a jump on a reaction to the comment, so we finished our work, congratulated each other on another good show and headed back to our hotel rooms. I got a good night's sleep, not realizing, at the time, it would be my last one of those for a while.

In January 2008, the social networking website Twitter was only nine months old and years away from being an avenue for instant discussion, but the Internet was, obviously, alive and well. One of the features on the network's website, Golfchannel.com, was a discussion board, where viewers of the channel could log on and display their views in regard to what they liked (very little) and didn't like (a lot) about what we were putting on the air. For the most part, the discussion board was confined to a handful of complainers who spent more time criticizing each other than us, but there was a specific section devoted to tournament coverage and, to satisfy some sort of perverted itch, that's where I went, occasionally, when my computer was on. Eight o'clock in the morning on Saturday, January 5, was one of those occasions.

I expected to find someone who called himself "Papi" complaining about the fact that we didn't show enough shots hit by Vijay during the coverage, or another discussion board "member" who called himself "TheGeorgePBurdell" telling me, in writing, that Nick and Rich talked too much. But I didn't expect to find a thread titled simply, "Kelly Messes Up." *Oh, boy,* I thought, as I clicked on the title, wondering what I might find, and I didn't have to wonder long. Right there, in front of me, were more than a hundred responses, going back and forth, about what Kelly could have possibly been thinking when, at the end of the telecast, she suggested the other professional golfers "lynch" the world's best player and the sport's only black athlete "in a back alley."

"What the hell?" I remember saying, perhaps louder than I should have.

"What's up?" asked Elizabeth, who rode in to work with me and was just then settling into her work station a few feet away.

"I think we might have a problem," I said to her, and myself. "Where are yesterday's show tapes?"

As a matter of course, we recorded two copies of every broadcast on site. At the end of the week, one goes back to the videotape library at the Golf Channel in Orlando, while the other one is sent, via Federal Express, to the PGA TOUR. I found Friday's tape, put it in the machine, and fast forwarded it to the end of the show, hoping to find what everyone was talking about. Right there, in living color, were Nick and Kelly, facing the camera and then each other, addressing the topic of who could challenge Tiger, and how. I watched as Nick, almost apologetically, made the point that there wasn't one single player in the world of golf at the moment who was equipped to catch up to, let alone take down, Tiger; and then, he suggested a better tactic might be for the younger players to do it collectively and "gang up" on Woods. He was finished, but Kelly decided that was the appropriate time to chuckle and stick her foot in her mouth.

"Lynch him in a back alley." Stop. Rewind. Play.

"Lynch him in a back alley." Stop. Rewind. Play.

"Lynch him in a back alley." Stop. Rewind. Stop.

"Oh, fuck." It was me, live and in person, not Kelly on tape, who spoke. "I have to find Tony."

It was 8:30 a.m. Hawaii-Aleutian Standard Time.

Tony didn't answer the phone in his hotel room or his Blackberry the first five times I called. I knew we had a problem, but I also knew I had work to do to prepare for Saturday's broadcast, and Tony would show up in the compound sooner or later. I can't say for sure exactly when he arrived, but I finally found him, around 10 a.m. (3 p.m. in Orlando), and told him there was something he needed to see, so he followed me into the tape room of the truck.

"Give us a few minutes," I said to the technicians who were there, and waited until the only people left in the mobile unit were me and my boss; then, I inserted the tape into the machine and played it. Tony watched, for the first time, what I had committed to memory and, much to my surprise, didn't react.

"Well?" I asked.

"What am I looking at?" He answered my question with one of his own.

I rewound the tape and hit play again. This time, he heard the offensive comment and I doubt I'll ever forget his reaction.

He let out a long breath, put the palm of his hand to his forehead, rubbed it, and said softly:

"I guess that was an unfortunate choice of words."

My comeback was immediate as I told him, in my opinion, it was far more serious than that; the use of the word "lynch" was offensive enough, but to connect it with Tiger Woods was more than simply unfortunate.

"Let me hear it again," was all he said next.

After playing the offending several seconds two more times, I told him I thought we needed to get out in front of this and call Orlando before the end of the business day. Tony thought for a moment, then said, "I don't think we need to go that far. I think we should just do nothing and hope nobody heard what she said and it just blows over." I couldn't believe it.

"Somebody has *already* heard it," I replied. "It's all over the Internet discussion boards."

"I'm not going to do anything right now," he reiterated. He turned and left the truck, and me holding the bag.

NEXT STEPS

I tried to go back to work, but Tony's reaction, or lack thereof, ate at me, and it wasn't long before I found it to be unacceptable. I couldn't talk to my dad; he was gone. But there was someone I felt I could speak with, so I picked up my phone, left the truck to find someplace private, and called Dave Manougian. The Golf Channel's CEO was much more than just my ultimate boss; he was my friend, and we had been together at the network from the beginning. I trusted him and knew I could depend on an intelligent, thoughtful reaction to the dilemma which I now faced. He picked up the phone on the second ring and said hello. I returned the greeting and got right to the point, relating the story, the issue, the fallout, and Tony's reaction.

"Tell me again exactly what she said," he commanded when I had finished, and I did.

"Wow," he reacted, then asked me a question: "What do *you* think should be done?"

I had already asked that question of myself and had given it a good deal of thought, so I answered quickly.

"I think, at the very least, she should offer an on-air apology at the top of today's show and, at most, we should tape an on-air apology and send her home." But that wasn't all I had to say. "I also think we should tell senior management—Page, Chris, or Gene—so that they aren't blindsided by this." Then I asked him what he would do.

468

"Right this second, I don't know what I *would* do, but I sure as hell know what I *wouldn't* do. I *wouldn't* stick my head in the sand and hope it went away." Then he advised me to speak with Tony again and try to impress upon him the need to be proactive in handling this story. I thanked him, ended the call, and went to find the VP of production.

Tony was in the office trailer reading the paper when I approached.

"Can I talk to you outside?" I asked. He answered by putting the paper down and following me out the door and down the steps. I told him I wasn't comfortable with doing nothing, and if he wasn't willing to discipline Kelly that day, the least we should do was to alert his bosses about the situation. I even offered to make the call or write the e-mail to Page, Chris, and Gene.

He nodded his head, then said, "Okay, go ahead and write an e-mail, but just send it to Page and copy me." So at 11:30 a.m. HST, I sat down and wrote, then sent, an e-mail message to the president of the Golf Channel, Page Thompson, describing what had happened, quoting Kelly and Nick verbatim, and offering my opinion on what we should do about it, repeating what I had told both Tony and Dave. A couple of e-mails went back and forth, but in the end the decision was made to wait and see what might unfold.

As far as the Golf Channel was concerned, that was the end of it. On Saturday we would go on the air as if nothing had happened, and that's what we did. I had made my argument, and lost. After the broadcast, during which no mention of the incident was made, I opened my e-mail and learned that while we were on the air ignoring the issue, it had been far from ignored in the halls of the Golf Channel in Orlando and Comcast headquarters in Philadelphia. I was copied on a message that said Kelly had chosen some "particularly unfortunate words" and she would call Tiger personally to apologize. The hope, according to the e-mail message, was that the incident would not "take on a life of its own." As we would all find out, in the coming days, it was far too late to worry about whether or not it had done exactly that, but first we had to get through Sunday.

ON THE SEVENTH DAY
NO ONE RESTED

Sunday might have been the weirdest day I had ever experienced in my television life. In a career that has lasted more than a quarter of a century, I found many people in this business more concerned with what people thought than what made them tick. Several famous folks have used this proverb to make a point: "Great minds discuss ideas, average minds discuss events, and small minds discuss people." For the purposes of the industry in which I have spent most of my professional life, I amended it to read, "Some people like talking to people, others like talking about people."

On Sunday, everyone was talking *about* Kelly, but I knew I had to talk *to* her, and I spent the majority of my morning thinking about what I would say. So far the Golf Channel had decided to handle it by not handling it; but in my heart I still believed it was in everyone's best interest to get in front of it. I thought she should offer an on-air apology, and I was bound and determined to offer her the opportunity to do just that. I couldn't tell her until after noon, because she didn't show up before that. When she did arrive, it was in the middle of our production meeting and she was visibly upset. Someone had already spoken to her, and after the meeting it was my turn.

"You got a minute?" I asked, and she answered by nodding her head, so I pressed on. "Let's go outside."

It was almost the same spot at which I had convinced Tony a day earlier that we had to move this up the food chain, and now I knew I had to try to convince Kelly to admit, on the air, in front of hundreds of thousands of people, that she had made a mistake and was sorry for it.

"How are you holding up?" I started.

"I'm hanging in there," she answered. "I'm just hoping this goes away quickly." I didn't see how that could possibly happen without her taking full responsibility, so I made my pitch.

"I don't know which direction this is supposed to go, but I really think you should offer an on-camera apology at the beginning of the show. Get it out of the way and try to move on." She looked like I had slapped her.

"I didn't do anything wrong," was a response I never expected to hear. "They want me to apologize, but I'm not doing it on camera. The decision has been made to have me address it over a shot of one of the younger players at some point early in the show." She stopped and looked at me. There was clearly nothing more for me to say.

That was, indeed, the decision. I later learned from Tony that Kelly had called, among others, Tiger, and everyone she spoke to told her it was no big deal, that people knew she hadn't meant it racially or maliciously, and the quicker she moved on, the quicker it would go away. Early in the broadcast, twenty-six-year old Nick Watney, who had won on the PGA TOUR for the first time the year before, was surveying a long birdie putt on the Plantation Course's second hole, and I thought it was as good a time as any for Kelly to issue her statement.

"Okay, kids," I said into all of the announcers headsets. "Before Watney putts, let's lay out for Kelly," and I proceeded to count backwards from seven. When I hit zero, Kelly offered up the words she surely had practiced for hours. The statement lasted no more than fifteen seconds, and I don't remember the word "sorry" being in it. When she was done, I looked at Tony, who had been sitting next to me since the beginning of the show, and asked if he was good with what Kelly had just said. He nodded affirmatively, and I turned my attention to the rest of the telecast. It seemed just about everyone else in the world turned their attention to Kelly and the Golf Channel.

ON TO OAHU

If Kelly thought the issue would fade away, she couldn't have been more wrong. In fact, the Golf Channel's delayed response, and Kelly's offering, only added fuel to what was becoming a national fire. Normally, Tuesday is a slow day in a PGA TOUR media room, but when I entered the space on Tuesday, January 9, it was standing-room only; and the reason was, social rights activist and political pundit the Reverend Al Sharpton was on the warpath. Sharpton had just helped get radio talk show host Don Imus fired from CBS after Imus called the Rutgers women's basketball team "a bunch of nappy-headed hos," and now the right reverend was turning his guns on Tilghman.

Before he got his own show on America's most liberal television network, Al Sharpton had been on just about everyone else's TV shows for years. Alfred Charles Sharpton, Jr., was born in 1954 and fifteen years later teamed up for the first time with Jesse Jackson when Jackson appointed a fifteen-year-old Sharpton as youth director for something called Operation Breadbasket. The organization was established to focus on new and better jobs for the African American community.

Sharpton founded the National Action Network in 1991, became a Baptist minister in 1994, ran for president of the United States in 2004, and for nearly half a century has been a very public face speaking out against anything perceived to be even remotely racist in nature. A comment on national television linking America's most racially motivated hate crime and the world's most recognizable African American athlete qualified as something that would arouse Sharpton's interest.

"Lynching is not murder in general. It is not assault in general," Sharpton told a CNN audience about Kelly's comment as we watched on television in the media room at Waialai Country Club on Oahu. "It is a specific racial term that this woman should be held accountable for." But mere accountability wasn't what Sharpton was after. "What she said is racist, and whether she runs around at night making racist statements is immaterial."

While Sharpton was railing against Kelly in an attempt to make headlines, the people who literally did make the headlines were making Page Thompson's Golf Channel phone ring off the hook. *USA Today*, the *New York Times*, the *Washington Post*, and all of golf's trade magazines were among the dozens of news organizations that wanted an explanation and a statement from Thompson about what disciplinary action might still come. Page apologized publicly on behalf of the Golf Channel, and Kelly issued another statement. But very quickly the Golf Channel came to the realization that words were not going to be enough, and the very next morning they took action, suspending Kelly Tilghman and relieving her of her play-by-play duties for two weeks.

That news of the suspension made news of its own, as reports of Kelly's punishment aired on CNN, Headline News, *The Today Show*, and several more outlets. The insensitive remark also changed the way the Golf Channel conducted its business. The network announced soon after that it was, among other initiatives, renewing and increasing its commitment to the First Tee Program and was in the process of producing a documentary titled *Uneven Fairways* that would chronicle the rich history of African Americans in golf. It also prompted respected TV critic and *New York Times* reporter Richard Sandoval to write the following in a January 11 column, titled "When An Apology Is Not Enough":

> "Tilghman now belongs to a group of experienced broadcasters who have paid for their missteps about race, religion or gender, including Don Imus, Michael Irvin, Jimmy (The Greek) Snyder, Steve Lyons, Rush Limbaugh, and Ben Wright."

He then continued:

> "But the six males above said nothing to evoke the brutal racial violence that produced nearly five thousand lynchings between 1882 and 1968, according to records kept by the Tuskegee Institute, the *Chicago Tribune*, and the NAACP."

After a few paragraphs outlining the offenses of the aforementioned other broadcasters, Sandoval once again trained his laser-like criticism on Kelly.

> Faldo's remark prompted Tilghman to glibly raise the verbal ante to a level that would make anyone shudder and wonder, what would make her say that? Or, what else is in her oratorical toolbox? Sadly, her remark made her and Faldo giggle. Page Thompson, the president of the Golf Channel, said Thursday, by telephone: "Quite frankly, I don't know what she was thinking. I found the comment to be offensive. No one here thinks that Kelly meant the remark to hurt Tiger Woods, or anyone else, but the words were hurtful and that's why she was suspended."

Despite her apology to Woods on Saturday, Tilghman said nothing during the network's four-and-a-half hours on the air. She finally apologized on-air Sunday.

So far, in his *New York Times* column, Sandomir had concentrated on Tilghman and Thompson, but in the very next paragraph he brought me into it:

That raises some disturbing questions. One: if she knew enough to apologize to Woods the next day, why not the public? And two: if no one at the Golf Channel ordered her on Saturday to apologize (could the lynch reference not have been heard by anyone in the production truck?), why didn't she approach her producer?

Page Thompson said he did not yet know the answers.

"That's something we have to fix," he said, adding that if he had heard her say "lynch" on Friday, "I would have definitely told her to apologize immediately."

"TOM"FOOLERY

Helping through the firestorm was my wonderful wife, Sarah. In front of family and friends, we were married on a beautiful Aspen, Colorado, day, in August of 2007. Her practical view and wise, thoughtful recommendations helped me through what turned out to be a volatile and complex professional situation.

In April, the "Comcastization" of the Golf Channel was complete when the company announced that Comcast Sports Network executive Tom Stathakes would be coming on board as senior vice president of Programming, Production and Operations, putting the entire network (international sales, programming, production, and new media) under the management of Comcast execs. What was it again that Brian Roberts said in front of nearly three hundred Golf Channel employees a few years before? Oh, yeah, "we love what you're doing and don't plan on changing a thing."

Nobody knew what to expect from a Stathakes regime, but nearly everyone who thought his or her job might be affected went to work on the new guy in charge in an effort to make sure that if there were any changes made, those changes would at best benefit and at worst not harm him or her. The new boss had been in charge for a couple of months, but he and I had yet to meet when June and one of my favorite events rolled around, the PGA Professional National Championship, conducted in 2008 at Reynolds Plantation in Georgia.

There are three distinct organizations that are most associated with the game of golf in the United States: the United States Golf Association, the PGA of America, and the PGA TOUR. The latter is the group that represents professional touring players, their tournaments, and their business affairs. It really has little or nothing to do with the bigger picture of being a caretaker of the sport. That falls to the other two. People often confuse the PGA TOUR and the PGA of America, and sometimes it's easy to see why. They were, after all, once one and the same and still share the same three big block letters in their titles. All over the country you hear people refer to the PGA TOUR as simply the PGA, thinking they are synonymous, when nothing could be further from the truth. The PGA of America represents more than twenty-seven thousand men and women who are golf professionals, as opposed to professional golfers. They are the instructors, head professionals, and administrators at thousands of clubs, practice facilities, and businesses around America that work dawn to dusk in order to help, in their words, "grow the game."

The USGA is different from both. It was founded more than half a century before the other two with the primary purpose, at the time, to conduct national golf championships, and as of 2013 that list included thirteen events. Since those humble beginnings in 1894, the USGA has evolved. Its main objective is to "preserve and promote" the game, and to do that the United States Golf Association takes on the responsibility for establishing and overseeing the rules of golf for both amateurs and professionals. From offices in Far Hills, New Jersey, it also tests equipment to make sure every club, ball, shoe, and piece of equipment conforms to the rules and specs the USGA has put in place. The organization also oversees the system almost every amateur uses to establish a handicap, leveling the playing field between amateur and amateur as well as amateur and golf course. Folks don't normally confuse the USGA with either the PGA of America or the PGA TOUR, but even some avid golfers think the PGA TOUR is responsible for the rules of the game. Then, to add the cherry on top, all three organizations run golf tournaments; the PGA TOUR has the most, but none of the four most important. The USGA (the United States Open) and the PGA of America (the PGA Championship) each control one of golf's majors, which remains a constant source of envy for the PGA TOUR people in Ponte Vedra Beach, Florida.

Another event that the PGA of America stages is the PPNC, and it identifies the best of the best of the teaching professionals mentioned above. In 1997 the PGA of America and the Golf Channel decided the time had come that this particular event belonged on national television, so we loaded up the trucks and headed to famed Pinehurst, North Carolina, and a brand new course at the golfing mecca, Number 8, to put the twenty-seventh incarnation of the event on TV. Whether or not it's great TV is debatable, but I think it's a great event because, for the players who compete, it's the only chance to appear on national television, to the delight of friends, family, and club members who gather around TVs at homes and in grill rooms at courses across the land. The event moves around the country every year, and in 2008 I found myself in Georgia getting ready to produce the broadcast and meet my new boss.

MEET THE NEW BOSS, NOT THE SAME AS THE OLD BOSS

Like most events in professional golf, the PPNC conducted a pro-am, but, unlike most, this gathering was intimate, involving no more than a dozen groups featuring sponsors and special invitees. The Golf Channel, under Gibbs and Greenway, had been a big supporter of not only the PGA of America in general, but this tournament specifically, and several of the company's top executives were invited and gladly accepted the opportunity to play.

Most of the men and women who were initially responsible for running the Golf Channel played the game, and those that didn't spent a good deal of time learning how. They all believed it was important, and some of the Comcast folks who took over the reins, Page Thompson among them, did, too, but it was crystal clear that Tom Stathakes did not.

As I maneuvered my golf cart around the Reynolds Plantation Great Waters course, in an effort to introduce myself to Stathakes, I saw and stopped to chat with the other members of the Golf Channel executive team that were playing in the pro-am. I saw Chris Murvin (a very good, single-handicap player), Tony Tortorici (another good player, though not as good as Chris), and Page Thompson (a better-than-average player who wanted to get better). Everyone with whom I engaged was having a ball and happy to see me, and then I saw Tom Stathakes, who was neither.

Following the cart path, I wound my way past a green and slowed through a strand of trees that, on the other side, would reveal the next hole's teeing ground. Athletes are gifted physically, but they are also able to impressively summon their powers of concentration to perform specific tasks. I always marvel at the ability of basketball players to sink a game-winning free throw or a baseball player to blast an epic home run, all while thousands of people, just a few feet away, are screaming their silly heads off. But a golfer as gifted as Tiger Woods or Jack Nicklaus can't shake home a one-foot putt unless the only sound is silence for miles. That's why I slowed my golf cart to a crawl as I approached the tee box. As it turned out, I could have been driving Dale Earnhardt's number 88 Chevrolet at top speed and it wouldn't have made any difference. I eased to a stop and, through the trees, saw a middle-aged, silver-haired man, with shirt untucked, take a mighty hack at his teed up golf ball and… miss. After slamming his club on the ground, he made another attempt, this time making contact, and sent his golf ball skittering off the tee to the left into another stand of trees about forty yards on the left. I stayed, transfixed, and continued to watch as Tom Stathakes, driver still in hand, stomped, unsmiling, to his ball, quickly took his stance, and swung away again, propelling the ball about fifty yards, all the way across the fairway into the trees on the other side of the hole.

"Shit." And that was the first word I heard my new boss say. It wouldn't be the last. I put my foot on the gas and headed his way.

"Tom?" I asked, getting out of the cart and extending my hand. "Keith Hirshland, it's nice to finally meet you."

"Hi," he semi-grunted. "This game sucks." He grabbed my hand and shook it. "I don't play very much," he continued. "Don't like it."

"It's a frustrating game," I said, smiling as we walked to where his third stroke had come to rest on some pine straw in the middle of the trees. He looked at the ball, then through the trees at the green some three hundred yards away, then he leaned over, picked up his ball, and put it in his pocket.

"I'm done!" he yelled at the members of his foursome and then he looked at me. "We'll talk later," he said as he turned and headed toward the cart carrying his bag filled with rental clubs. I turned the other way and went back to my own cart and got back to work.

HAVING TO SAY GOODBYE AGAIN

My mom loved my dad, wholly, completely, unfailingly. At work, at play, in life, and in love, they were inseparable for more than half a century, and when my dad died in May of 2007, with him went the spark that lit the flame of my mother's life. She didn't know how to live without him, despite the best efforts of those of us left on the planet who loved her. After Dad died, she went back to Reno but found it too painful, thought about returning to Maui but rejected it as too lonely, and eventually found some sort of peace and sense of belonging with her younger sister Susie and her husband, my uncle, Lyle, at their home in Oregon.

Looking back I would tell you my mom was generally a happy person, but upon closer inspection I would have to admit that her happiness was fragile, always dependent on something or someone else. She was fiercely loyal and always put the well-being of her husband and three sons above her own. She worried constantly that we were all okay and felt responsible when we said or she felt we weren't. That worry consumed her, weighed her down, and ultimately made it impossible for her to have her own life. Had my mom passed away first, my dad would have been devastated, but he would have found the inner strength to forge ahead; but that didn't happen. Cancer took my father and my mother couldn't take it; her heart busted up into so many little pieces that no amount of love from those of us who were left could find a big enough piece left to fill it with even the smallest amount of joy. She didn't want to live without my dad, and as it turned out she couldn't.

With him by her side, she started a business, built an empire, raised a family, and led an enviable life, but when he left her behind, she wanted nothing more than to catch up to him again. I danced with Mom at my wedding in August 2007 and felt the lightness of a person who was suddenly only half whole. Living in the Pacific Northwest, the happiness continued to drain out of her, one drop at a time, until the sadness and the cancer that were inside her consumed her and she was rushed to a Portland hospital during the summer of 2008. My older brother, David, visited first, I followed, and my younger brother, Mark, saw her last. When she had seen each of us and we in turn had one by one held her hand, told her that we would be okay, and she was free to leave us behind, she died of a broken heart on July 5, 2008, and was reunited with my dad. I think of one, the other, or both of them every single day.

OUT OF TOUCH

Summer and early fall were always the busiest weeks and the ones spent most away from home or corporate headquarters. There were tournaments being played every week on just about every tour, and when one Sunday ended, it meant either a quick trip home to unpack, do laundry, repack, and get on another airplane or staying another night in one city before heading the next day to wherever the following tournament was being played. While we were on the road doing our thing, Stathakes was in Orlando doing his.

When I wasn't on the road, I was home with Sarah in North Carolina, not in Orlando, where decisions that would shape the Golf Channel for years were being made. Most of the people who started and subsequently built the channel were gone, and those that remained, like Jeff Gershengorn and Tony Tortorici, were busy trying to maneuver through the machinations of the new regime. Out on the road, we got bits and pieces of news and information, but little explanation, which led to anxiety, uncertainty, and a string of suppositions and rumors. The consensus was that some people would lose their jobs or be reassigned within the growing Comcast family of networks, while others would get the opportunity to be more powerful and influential going forward. I felt confident that my situation fell into the latter category, not the former. Silly me.

Our tournament production team was in Utah for a Nationwide Tour tournament and I was headed to the gym when my phone rang and I looked at the screen, which indicated Eric Saperstein was calling. Eric was basically running the newsroom and overseeing many of the studio shows for the network, so he and I spoke quite frequently.

"Hey, Sap," I said after pushing the green accept button on my Golf Channel-issued BlackBerry.

"Hi, Keith," Eric answered not sounding like Eric.

"What's new?" I asked.

"I just got fired," he said flatly.

"What the fuck?!" was all I could think to say.

Eric Saperstein had been at the Golf Channel for more than a decade. He was a smart, dedicated, hardworking employee who sometimes rubbed people the wrong way, but he always, in my mind, put the good of the network ahead of himself. He was innovative and creative, and now he was out of a job,

"Stathakes called me into his office," he started, "and said he is bringing in his own people from Philadelphia and I just didn't fit into his plans."

"Jesus, Sap," I started but he stopped my train of thought, and me dead in my tracks, with what came out of his mouth next.

"And he doesn't think very much of you either."

People who know me best know I battle with insecurity at times, and this was suddenly one of those times. I had suddenly lost the desire to work out and had an overwhelming urge to call my wife.

SOUND ADVICE

I did that a lot (call Sarah) during the days and months that came later, and on that day, as she did on every day, she gave me thoughtful, measured, unemotional words of wisdom, because I was a scatterbrained, paranoid, overly sensitive mess when I called.

"Hello, this is Sarah," she answered, the way she always did.

"Hi, Doll, how's your day?" I asked, trying to sound calm.

"Fine, what's up?" She got right to the point so I did as well.

"I just got off the phone with Eric Saperstein at Golf Channel," I started. "He got fired today." I waited for her reaction.

"You're kidding!" she said, surprised. "Why?"

"According to Eric, Stathakes told him he was making changes and bringing in his own people," I paused for a second, "and then Eric told me Tom doesn't hold me in high regard either."

"Why would he say that?" she asked, and I let that one hang in the thousands of miles of air between us. "I mean, he doesn't even know you." I nodded and still said nothing. "Maybe it's a case of misery loves company."

"Maybe," I said.

"He just got fired and he wants someone else to feel pain, too." If that was the case it was working, I thought. "I've got to run to a meeting but we'll talk more later," she said. "Don't worry about it right now." She added those last six words knowing in her heart that's all I would do.

We spoke again later that day and she told me I should do my best to get out in front of the conversation by calling Tom Stathakes myself and setting up an appointment to meet, which I did the very next day. He was nice enough on the phone, and we set a date for me to travel to Orlando and get together as soon as my schedule allowed. Immediately after hanging up, I started to develop my strategy, and by the time I got off the plane a few weeks later in Orlando, I had a plan. I put pen to paper—my vision of all the ways Stathakes could take the channel forward in terms of tournament coverage—and was excited about making the case that I was the one to help him do it. That excitement lasted until the minute I entered the space that Stathakes had decided to occupy at the Golf Channel, Arnold Palmer's old office.

"C'mon in, man," he said, quickly shaking my hand, "have a seat." He let go and walked around his desk and sat. I did what I was told and, as I was reaching into my backpack to retrieve my carefully thought out, written notes, I heard him say, "I just want you to know that none of this is personal."

Immediately I retracted my hand from my backpack, realizing I wouldn't need my notes. He then spent the next thirty minutes explaining that he was hired to "shake things up" and outlining his vision for a new Golf Channel that had very little to do with me. I was devastated but did my best not to show it, and when he had finished stripping me of my responsibilities and my pride, I knew I had much more to say to my wife than to him.

"Okay, well, thanks for the time," I managed to get out as I reached for my bag and began to stand. Stathakes pushed himself away from his desk and came out of his chair with his hand extended and a smile on his face. We met near the middle of the room and shook hands again.

"I want to thank you for not busting my balls on this," he said as he led me to the door.

In this new Golf Channel world led by Tom Stathakes, Brandt Packer would produce the bulk of the events on the network going forward, including all of the ones perceived to be important. A woman who I had made the first female producer in golf television, Beth Hutter, would lead the LPGA team, and I would handle the Nationwide Tour and a handful of other events. I went into the meeting hoping to have a say in the big picture of how events were brought to life on the network, and left knowing my influence would instead be on a very small segment of the product. It was disheartening but, after a few days of retrospection and some very encouraging words of wisdom from Sarah, I realized the only way to approach this was to make the tournaments for which I was responsible the best they could possibly be, and that's exactly what I did.

CLEANING HOUSE

In addition to altering my workload and responsibilities, Stathakes changed my employment status. As of January 2009, I was no longer a full-time salaried employee of the Golf Channel, meaning, for the first time in almost two decades, I was back in the freelance world, this time producing as many as twenty golf tournaments for the network as an independent contractor. I found myself working fewer events for less money and taking a further financial hit because an employer was no longer taking care of medical and other benefits. I also found myself further removed from the tournament production decision-making process when Stathakes and the Golf Channel hired former ABC golf producer Jack Graham to ultimately take Tony Tortorici's place in Orlando. Tortorici was still with the network, but only until his contract ran out at the end of 2009.

Graham had been a fixture at ABC Sports for a quarter of a century, working for producer Terry Jastrow as that network pretty much owned golf on television in the '60s, '70s, and '80s, broadcasting three of the sport's four major championships (CBS televised the Masters). But then things changed. In 1991, ABC Sports head Denis Swanson fired longtime and much-beloved analyst Dave Marr, and that same year ABC lost the rights to broadcast the PGA Championship and the Ryder Cup (CBS got the championship and NBC got the matches). Later that year Swanson made another controversial decision, signing veteran broadcaster but rookie golf guy Brent Musberger to host ABC's events. In 1992 Musberger served as the play-by-play announcer for his first US Open, this one at Pebble Beach, and a year later he hosted his last, because in 1994, after twenty-nine years, the USGA followed the PGA of America's lead and dumped ABC as its broadcast home.

ABC had spiraled from being the broadcast home of the game's biggest events to, in 1996, hanging its golf hat on a handful of tournaments, including the Diner's Club Matches, the Wendy's Three Tours Challenge, and the J. C. Penney Classic. ABC did still have the British Open but, at the time, that coverage was essentially no more than a shared proposition with the BBC, who handled the majority of the telecast. ABC Sports' steady slide coincided with the rise of the ESPN brand and, in 1996, the transformation was taking more solid shape. Swanson was forced to resign as the division's president, and ESPN honcho Steve Bornstein took over. One of the first moves the new boss made was to put Steve Anderson in charge of golf, and Anderson decided that Jastrow, who lived in LA and had his hand in projects other than ABC's, was no longer the right guy for the job. Jack Graham took the reins.

One of Graham's first moves was to help find an analyst who, like Johnny Miller at NBC, would have people talking golf around Monday's water cooler. He convinced Anderson that two-time US Open Champion, renowned curmudgeon, and longtime friend Curtis Strange was that guy. A handful of years later ABC/ESPN was virtually out of the golf business, Strange found himself getting ready to play on the Champions Tour, and Jack Graham was working freelance when Tom Stathakes was on the other end of a ringing phone.

CAN I GET A PROOFREADER, PLEASE

The year 2009 was a tumultuous time at the Golf Channel. The only thing that seemed certain was the uncertainty felt by people who showed up for work on a daily basis. The new regime, installed by Comcast, preached a more communicative workplace but then made decisions behind closed doors. Much of the communication then came in the form of demotions or outright firings, especially of people who had been longtime Golf Channel employees. I saw friends and colleagues lose face and lose jobs. Many of them were people that had worked at the channel since launch but garnered no respect as the times, culture, and values changed. One thing the network had always done in the past was honor its long-term employees. Those of us who had put in five years of continuous service received a beautiful Tiffany gold alarm clock. After ten years the gift was an engraved Tag Heuer wristwatch. A number of employees had received these trinkets, but very few had been around long enough to reach the next milestone, fifteen years. It was so special that one of the first to get there, Sue Heard, was given her own parking space as a token of the company's appreciation, and those of us who had been around that long, but came after Sue, wondered what our special gift would be. But the Comcast takeover made individual awards next to impossible. There were just too many employees, so Golf Channel adopted the Comcast system of rewarding longevity, and employees were allowed to choose an appropriate gift from a catalog. My fifteen-year anniversary had come and gone but, despite a couple of requests, I had yet to get a copy of the catalog. In hindsight, this seems so inconsequential and petty, but at the time I was hurt and offended. I took all of this change personally and acted emotionally rather than professionally, hanging on to the misguided notion that, despite all of the changes going on in Orlando, there was still a protective bubble around me. A pragmatist knows everyone is replaceable, but no one has ever characterized me as pragmatic and, despite seeing some very obvious signs, I decided to continue to treat my professional world like it was still 1999 and not a decade later.

Don McGuire had once characterized my approach to things as a "ready, fire, aim" strategy, and never was that more evident than at the end of 2009. Summoning all my stupidity, I didn't get ready or aim, I just fired, sending an e-mail to Golf Channel President Page Thompson asking about the status of my fifteenth anniversary reward. While I had his attention, I figured it was as good a time as any to relate feelings I harbored about the channel losing its soul and appearing to disrespect the very people who helped make it something Comcast valued enough to buy. I wrote the e-mail, but didn't run the idea by my brilliant wife or ask her to read it. I thought it was okay because Page and I were friends. I hit send. I was wrong, and I found out just how wrong when my phone rang a few days later.

"Hello, this is Keith," I answered, and over a speaker phone I heard the following:

"Keith, this is Linda Wingate calling." Linda was head of Human Resources at Golf Channel. "I have Tom Stathakes with me." Uh oh, I thought. This can't be good.

"Hi, Tom. Hi, Linda," I swallowed hard, "What can I do for you?"

"Well, we're calling," it was Stathakes this time, "to tell you we're tearing up your contract. We can't have you working for this network." I was dumbfounded and defensive.

"What? Wait. Why?" The three words popped out of my mouth as my mind was reeling, looking for a lifeline, and Linda answered.

"You sent an e-mail to the president of this company that was disrespectful and critical, and that's a breach of your independent contractor agreement." My mind continued to race; what had I written? When was I disrespectful?

"Wait a second, please," I pleaded. "I wrote the e-mail but at *no* time did I mean any disrespect. I wrote to Page as a friend and as someone who loves the Golf Channel." I meant that.

"That's not the way he or we read it," Stathakes again. "We're gonna have to let you go."

"Don't do this." More pleading on my part. "I have been a loyal employee for more than fifteen years and I would love another chance to prove that loyalty." That was met with silence. "Can I come to Orlando and state my case in person?" I didn't stop or wait for a response this time and just kept going,

"I am asking you for one more chance." I didn't know what else to say. I didn't want to lose my job. I felt like throwing up.

"We'll think about it," Linda this time, "and call you back."

"Thank you," I said, and we all hung up.

Thankfully, after a few agonizing hours, Stathakes did call back and told me to be in Orlando two days later, giving me the second chance for which I had begged. Now I had to face my wife.

"You have to go down there with your hat in your hands and your tail between your legs and beg them in person for your job," Sarah said matter-of-factly, after I 'fessed up to my misstep.

"What in the world were you thinking?" and she left it at that.

So down to Orlando I went, with hat in hand and my tail firmly placed between my legs. I faced Stathakes in his office— Linda Wingate was not in attendance—and stated my case. I admitted I had misread the situation and overstepped my bounds, but reiterated that I was loyal, hardworking, and a "network first" kind of guy. I talked some and listened a lot and took my medicine, which was a ripping up of the three-year deal I had signed and replacing it with a one-year contract and a threat of immediate unemployment if Stathakes so much as heard a rumor about insubordination.

As I was leaving, relieved, Stathakes mentioned that I should stick my head in across the hall and say hello to Page. After what had transpired, I found it odd that the president of the company would want anything to do with me, but I did as he suggested. Page greeted me warmly, asked about Sarah and my family, and wished me happy holidays, and then asked if I had gotten the catalog for my fifteen-year anniversary gift yet. I said I hadn't but I wasn't worried about it, and then he promised to take care of it.

A week or so later the catalog showed up in the mailbox with dozens of items from which to choose. Quite frankly I have no recollection what I picked, if it ever came, and, if it did, where it is now, but I do remember a conversation I had with my friend Jerry Foltz from Hawaii as he was preparing for 2010's first PGA TOUR event.

"What happened with you and Stathakes?" he asked after we had exchanged pleasantries.

"What are you talking about?" I asked, knowing what he was talking about.

"Did you send an e-mail to Page?" was the next question.

"I did," was my answer.

"Why didn't you tell me this story?" he asked a third question.

"Nothing to tell, and it wasn't about you," I answered honestly, and then I asked him how he came to know the facts of the story. Foltzy casually mentioned that Stathakes had told him the tale over a beer at the bar.

"What did Stathakes tell you?" I wondered aloud.

"He asked if I had heard what he did to 'my guy.' " I listened but didn't react, and when I didn't say anything, Foltzy continued, "I said I had no idea what he was talking about and he was shocked that you hadn't told me."

"Uh huh," I said, suddenly very happy that Sarah was the only person to whom I had confided.

"He said he fired you but then gave you your job back," Jerry went on. "He also told me he was never really going to fire you but he had to put you in your place."

"I guess he did," I responded.

"Then he said he had to let you know that this wasn't Keith Hirshland's Golf Channel anymore." Jerry stopped.

One of us never thought it was.

During those days and in many of the weeks and months that followed, I finally came to the stark realization that what it wasn't was Joe Gibbs's Golf Channel anymore. I often wondered whether Joe would have made the same decision to sell had he known what the network would grow to become. I thought about my father, too, who decades before had seen Channel 2 in Reno change in much the same way. Both men built their business with passion as the foundation and strong belief and an unshakeable integrity as the building blocks. Because their intentions were pure, they hired and then inspired a loyal, enthusiastic team that collectively and individually busted its butt every day to be the mortar that held it together. They provided people a livelihood but, more than that, they gave people a purpose and showed, by example, that giving their best built a shared success. That kind of give and take creates a moral pact and forges a lasting bond. At least it felt that way. Then deals were done and they were gone and we were left to make sense of what was left.

Despite lucrative results, and the obvious lifestyle upgrades both entrepreneurs were afforded after selling off what they had built from scratch, I debated internally if the two of them, separately or together, would say the cost of the loss of a certain culture at their companies was too high a price to pay. Would either make the same deal they made then, today?

I know my father wouldn't have.

BETTER THAN MOST

Surprisingly the next two years turned out to be among my most enjoyable. The Nationwide Tour and the group with whom I was privileged to work was a joy. While Stathakes and the rest of the honchos in Orlando fussed and fretted and fawned over the PGA TOUR, we were on our own, having fun and producing some pretty entertaining television. The second round of every tournament became "fun Friday," as we created features, focused on the players, and brought back to television a concept I had come up with years ago on the LPGA Tour, bringing players into the mobile unit to perform production jobs during the telecast.

Players had been serving as guest on-course commentators for years, but this was different. Instead of giving them a microphone and asking them to talk about the course, the competitors, or certain shots, we put a headset on them and plopped them behind camera or in front of a videotape machine or in the director's chair to actually shoot the shots, record the shots, or call the shots. It was a blast and it was a hit. The players loved it, the crew loved it, and from the reaction we got in print and in person, the golf world loved it. At the first television event of 2010 in Northern California, I sought out one of the Nationwide Tour rookies who I hoped would be interested in operating one of our videotape machines during Friday's broadcast. His name was Keegan Bradley, the nephew of World Golf Hall of Fame member Pat Bradley, and a willing guinea pig in the plan.

Friday's broadcast arrived and so did Bradley, keeping his word despite shooting a 78 on the way to missing the cut. We gave him a headset and about sixty seconds worth of training and put him to work. Keegan Bradley spent the next twenty minutes recording, rewinding, and replaying golf shots and operating the controls of our recording device to show a player's swing in slow motion intentionally forward and unintentionally in reverse, much to the delight of the crew, our announcers, our audience, and the television critics like *GolfWeek*'s Martin Kaufmann, who wrote about it in his weekly column. Bradley would go on to finish fourteenth on the year-end money list and earn his PGA TOUR playing privileges for 2011, where he won his first tournament (the HP Byron Nelson Championship), his first major (the PGA Championship) ,and the PGA TOUR Rookie of the Year award.

In addition to having the players involved, I continued to do my best to have the announcers working on the shows less involved. I have consistently preached to all who get paid to talk on TV to do more listening instead of talking; just ask Grant Boone, Brian Anderson, Kraig Kann, Jerry Foltz, and others. Sometimes my message was received, other times ignored. Then, for one day of one week, I decided to take complete control of the situation.

SWEET SILENCE

Don Ohlmeyer shared my views that announcers tended to talk too much long before he started signing my paychecks. In 1980 the man who produced the first *Monday Night Football* game, headed three Olympic Games broadcasts, won sixteen Emmy Awards, and would end up in the Broadcasting Hall of Fame made one decision about silencing announcers for one football game that had everybody talking. It was December 20 and NBC was scheduled to air an NFL game that featured two teams long since eliminated from any postseason possibilities, the New York Jets and the Miami Dolphins.

"Here we had this dog of a game," Ohlmeyer is quoted saying, "and part of my thinking was, what could we possibly do to get fans to watch this?" His answer was simple: try to make it worth listening to. The production team was excited to give it a try, but the announcers, led by the great Dick Enberg, weren't so sure.

"My first reaction was of incredible nerves, nervousness," Enberg remembered in an interview with ESPN. "We all gathered together hoping Ohlmeyer was dead wrong. I mean, he was flirting with the rest of our lives. What if this crazy idea really worked?" Well, it wasn't perfect, but by many measures it did indeed work. The Jets ultimately won the game 24–17, but that score wasn't the one in which Ohlmeyer was interested. He looked at fan reaction, and by the tally registered by the

NBC switchboard, there were 1,349 phone calls—831 positive and 518 negative.

"It certainly did a much better number for us," Ohlmeyer would say, talking about the TV rating, "than that dog deserved." While Ohlmeyer was sending a not-so-subtle message to announcers, he wasn't taking the first step toward what Enberg feared was the elimination of that part of the process altogether. He was just looking for a way to get more eyeballs interested in a game that, on its own, generated very little interest.

I knew all about that experiment and Don Ohlmeyer's feeling that, in general announcers talked too much during sports broadcasts, and it was the latter that motivated me more than the former in pushing for trying something that had never been tried in golf television. The idea I proposed for Saturday's broadcast of the Alberston's Boise Open, thirty years after Ohlmeyer's football experiment, was not "announcerless," it was more "announcer lite." Jerry Foltz, Curt Byrum, Phil Parkin, Kay Cockerill, and Stephanie Sparks would each have a role; it just would not be the traditional roles undertaken by announcers on golf telecasts. The idea was similar to Ohlmeyer's three-decades-old initiative, and so was one announcer's reaction.

"If it works, it could be to golf announcers what reality TV is to actors," said Stephanie Sparks in an interview two days before the broadcast. But, just like Ohlmeyer, my idea wasn't to pave the way for a future that didn't include announcers; it was just to try something new on a telecast of a tour that lent itself to creativity if someone was willing to take a chance, and I was. I mapped out the plan: Foltz and Byrum would plant themselves on a couch outside the confines of a restrictive booth and become observers as well as participants in the broadcast. They would introduce the show at the beginning, explain the concept, and then, at various times, react to the play on the course before sending the viewer back to the golf. We would also incorporate social media, with Foltz and Byrum responding and reacting to Twitter and Facebook posts as well as interviewing by phone Matt Kuchar, Stewart Cink, and Zach Johnson, current PGA TOUR stars who once competed on the Nationwide Tour. Cockerill and Sparks would be stationed at two back-nine tee boxes to conduct interviews with players (Hillcrest Country Club in Boise was perfect for this because players always waited on the difficult par three 13th and the drive-able par four 15th), and Parkin would patrol the putting green and practice tee, looking for players to interview either before or after their rounds. The bulk of the telecast would just be the sights of the players hitting golf shots and the sounds of the players and their caddies discussing the shots before they played and reacting to them after. We bulked up the resources on the ground by adding "shotgun" microphones on the course and asking one player to wear a microphone during the round. Hunter Haas agreed to be the mic guinea pig and ended up shooting one of the day's best rounds, a 67. He also just happened to go on to win the tournament. I presented my plan to Jack Graham, who wasn't 100 percent sold on it, and Tom Stathakes, who was, so the plan, to my delight, became a reality.

Did it work? I thought so, and so did about 60 percent of the viewing audience, as well as a number of people who look at golf TV critically. Was it my, or anyone's, vision of golf TV's future? Hardly. It was simply one way to look at one of close to a thousand rounds of golf broadcast by the Golf Channel in 2010, and it was fun.

MERGING COMPANIES AND CULTURES

While we were traveling around the country minding our own business during 2010, the business world was keeping a close eye on the pending merger between Comcast and NBCUniversal. The original deal for one (Comcast) to acquire the other (NBCUniversal) was valued at close to $30 billion and was struck in December of 2009. Since then it had been stuck on Capitol Hill, with proponents and opponents arguing the merits and faults of the corporate marriage. Despite the rhetoric, most experts felt it was just a matter of time before the FCC approved the merger, and as 2010 came to a close most felt the deal was imminent (the FCC and the Department of Justice did put the stamp of approval on the merger on January 18, 2011). The talk around our water cooler centered on which entity would lead the decision-making process at the Golf Channel.

Comcast was the buyer, so many opined that the one writing the checks would determine the philosophical bent of the channel. Others argued that it was NBC that had all the production experience and Comcast would be foolish not to take advantage of that. In September industry publications reported that Page Thompson would be stepping down as president and leaving the channel by the end of the year, and added that NBC Sports and Olympic Chairman Dick Ebersol was seen taking a tour of the Golf Channel. Speculation ran rampant, but as far as we knew nobody was certain, or, if they did know, they weren't talking. The fuzzy picture seemed to clear a little when we were all called to Orlando in the days following Arnold Palmer's PGA TOUR event at Bay Hill for a special production seminar and corporate come-together.

A group of about a hundred of us (producers, directors, and announcers) gathered at a nearby hotel for a couple of days to review the previous year and look ahead to the next. It usually included pep talks from company muckety-mucks and feel-good videos about the state of the channel's efforts across the board, including ratings, news, production, and sales. It was also the time to discuss plans for new features, graphics, and personnel for the year ahead. We assembled in a conference room complete with a podium, stage, and big screen for show and tell. As I looked around the room I saw colleagues, friends, and Golf Channel leaders, including Tom Stathakes. I did *not* see Page Thompson, who had indeed left the channel by then, having been promoted up the Comcast corporate ladder. That didn't surprise me, but the folks at the front of the room did. Waiting to impart their wisdom to us all were Dick Ebersol, Tommy Roy, Johnny Miller, Gary Koch, and Roger Maltbie—all from NBC Sports.

Dick Ebersol was legendary in our world, but I had never had the honor or the pleasure of making his acquaintance. He got his start in the business in 1967 after dropping out of Yale to join Roone Arledge and the folks at ABC Sports to become the network's first-ever Olympics researcher. Seven years later he jumped ship and joined NBC as the director of weekend late-night programming, and in 1975, along with another NBC staffer named Lorne Michaels, came up with the idea for and developed *Saturday Night Live*. He was named vice president of late-night programming at age twenty-eight (the network's youngest ever VP), the president of NBC Sports in 1989, and chairman, NBC Sports and Olympics, nine years after that. As the network's sports president, Ebersol either acquired or renewed the rights to broadcast the National Football League, the National Basketball Association, Major League Baseball, and Notre Dame football. During his tenure in the 1995–96 sporting event season, NBC broadcast the World Series, the Super Bowl, the NBA Finals, and the Summer Olympics. It marked the only time in television history that all four of those major sporting events were telecast by the same US network. At the end of the year *Sporting News* magazine named Dick Ebersol "the Most Powerful Person in Sports," and now he was one of several people preparing to address our group. First, as the only Golf Channel person with power in the room, Tom Stathakes stood before us and started the seminar with some housekeeping tidbits. Stathakes started by telling the assembled masses that *Morning Drive*, the channel's daily golf-talk radio show on TV, was an important initiative heading into 2011, and he added that in his opinion the Comcast/NBCUniversal merger came at exactly the right time.

"Recently I spent some time with Tommy Roy (NBC's golf producer) and he taught me everything I need to know about golf in three hours," he chuckled, and then he introduced the channel's new president, NBC's Mike McCarley.

COMINGS AND GOINGS

It was no secret that Stathakes wanted to be, and thought Comcast honcho Jeff Shell would make him, Page's successor, but in February of 2011 word came down that the job would be McCarley's and not Stathakes's. McCarley was Ebersol's protege and in fact had gotten his start at the network as the Olympics division's communications director. It was Mike McCarley who was credited with coming up with NBC's "big event strategy." Promotions up the ladder within the organization started in 2003 and continued throughout his NBC career, thanks to "wins" that included the network's incredibly successful "Sunday Night is Football Night" campaign and the industry's first-ever Emmy Award for sports promotion. One story goes that in 2006 McCarley was out the door and on to business school to work toward his MBA when Ebersol reportedly said, "Stay here and get your MBA from me," and then promoted the rising star to senior vice president, strategic marketing, promotion, and communications. McCarley stayed, and less than five years later Ebersol handed the thirty-four-year-old the keys to the Golf Channel kingdom, a kingdom that would now be branded "Golf Channel on NBC." Suddenly there was very little confusion about which network would be calling the shots, at least the golf shots.

Mike McCarley was the first of the "new" Golf Channel/ NBC group to speak. He didn't regurgitate the old line about "not changing a thing" but instead told us that "passion and authenticity were hallmarks of both networks" and the goal was to work toward "consistency in coverage between both." Then he told us we should all "check our egos at the door and absorb what Tommy Roy says, because you'll walk out of here a better broadcaster." Roy, NBC's golf producer since 1993, spoke next, explaining his philosophy that would now become Golf Channel's, and he was followed by PGA TOUR great, World Golf Hall of Fame member, and NBC lead analyst Johnny Miller. Finally, after about an hour, we got to hear from the man behind the curtain, Dick Ebersol.

"I remember having dinner with a reporter a dozen or so years ago," Ebersol recalled, "and he asked me if I had any regrets. I thought for a second and then answered honestly that professionally my one regret was that I didn't buy the Golf Channel in the mid-'90s when I had the chance." He laughed, we laughed, and then he added, "A generation later, you guys did it. It's a terrific brand, an amazing story, and you all should be very, very proud." I don't know about anyone else in the room, but I was.

Ebersol then spent some time telling his story, discussing his philosophy, and revealing what motivated him.

"Curiosity has always dominated me," he told the group, but I felt like he was talking to and about me. "Passion is extremely important, but curiosity is critical." Then he continued making a point that was ingrained in me years before by Don Ohlmeyer, Steve Beim, and Andy Young.

"You are producing a live event," Ebersol said. "You can't *produce* a live event. You can only hang on and try to manage it. Do not hesitate to drop anything you had planned for that day. Be prepared, but then be prepared to give everything up because the event takes you in a different direction." It was easy to see why Dick Ebersol had risen to the top of his profession, and I was one of many in the room prepared to make the most of what the future held under his leadership. Then, as soon as we thought we could get comfortable, we all had to adjust.

On May 19, after failing to agree to the terms of a new contract, Dick Ebersol resigned as NBC Sports Group chairman less than four months after the takeover of NBC by Comcast. He had run the network's sports division for more than two decades, and in the blink of an eye he was gone.

Around the same time my daughter Hayley was finishing her sophomore year at Beloit College, a small liberal arts school in Beloit, Wisconsin. She was double majoring in international studies and Japanese and is not only fluent but proficient in both that language and Mandarin Chinese. Thanks to her dad, she was also fluent in Golf Channel and knew the network had a division that concentrated on an international partnership with networks in Asia that televised golf. I had worked closely with that department's head, Debra Conrad, and called one day to inquire about the possibility of an internship. Debra remembered Hayley as a child interested in learning Japanese and revealed to me that she was, in fact, looking for a summer intern. She ended the conversation by saying she would be very interested in speaking with my middle child about the position.

If you're thinking I got my daughter a job at Golf Channel, you would be wrong. I made the initial call inquiring about the position and, armed with that information, told Hayley about the opportunity. It was up to her to contact Debra and convince her she was qualified for the job. She did, and, starting in the summer of 2011, another Hirshland was roaming the halls of the Golf Channel in Orlando. Debra asked her back for another summer in 2012, and at the end of that internship offered Hayley a full-time job when she graduated from school in December. Hayley accepted. She now has her own cubicle, a most impressive double-sided business card (one side English, the other Japanese), and gets to work alongside some of the same people with whom I had the pleasure to work for so many years. I couldn't be more proud.

2011 COMES TO A CLOSE

The Nationwide Tour boasts by far the most exciting and dramatic season-ending race in all of golf. The PGA TOUR finished up with what was in 2011 labeled the Fall Series, where near millionaires play against other near millionaires in an effort to stay inside the top 125 on the money list to keep their playing privileges and play for millions of dollars again the next year. There is some drama, because occasionally a player drops out while another one moves in, but that drama is tempered by the knowledge that if you finish between number 126 and number 150 on that same money list, you will have a place to play during the following season. It may not be as often or in places that the player would prefer, but he still has a chance to earn millions. Life on the Nationwide Tour is very different.

Nationwide Tour players tee it up all season long with one goal: finish in the top twenty-five on that tour's year-end money list. If that goal is accomplished you get a promotion to the PGA TOUR the following year. J. J. Killeen led that list in 2011, earning $414,273, while Billy Hurley III hit enough good shots and made enough putts to grab the twenty-fifth spot on the list and the last automatic PGA TOUR card, earning $181,191. By contrast, there were eighty-nine millionaires on the PGA TOUR that same year, led by Luke Donald with $6,683,214. The player finishing in the 125th spot and earning the final exempt spot on the 2012 PGA TOUR was former Nationwide Tour player D. J. Trahan with $668,166 in earnings. You can make a living playing on the Nationwide Tour, but life is a whole lot better in the big leagues.

Our team was in Ponte Vedra Beach, Florida, following the Nationwide Tour as its season ground down to the final two weeks. The home of the PGA TOUR is a busy, boring, ninety-minute drive from Golf Channel headquarters in Orlando. Tom Stathakes had been in charge of production for the network for forty-one months, and he had never attended a Nationwide Tour event or set foot in a Golf Channel Nationwide Tour TV compound, but early in the week we got word that that was all about to change. The boss would make the drive over on Thursday, watch the broadcast from the truck that afternoon, take the team out to dinner, and then do it all again on Friday. We couldn't wait...in a good way. To a person, our group saw this as an opportunity to show Stathakes what the Nationwide Tour team could do, but sadly we never got the chance.

About an hour before air, my phone buzzed in the truck. I looked down to see that it was the senior vice president of production on the other end of the line, and, thinking he was looking for directions to the compound where our trucks were parked, I answered. As it turned out, he was not looking for the trucks; in fact, he had not yet left Orlando, but he wanted me to know he was coming. He was sorry he would miss the broadcast, but he would see us all at dinner and would watch the show from the mobile unit on Friday. Okay, we could wait; I could wait.

Earlier that month Stathakes' right-hand man, Jack Graham, had started discussions with me about the 2012 production season. According to Jack, my event schedule would start with the PGA TOUR stop in Puerto Rico in March and then pick up again at the first Nationwide Tour event the last week in June, nothing before and nothing in between. That was troubling to me, and

I had mentioned it on several occasions to Jack. He was apologetic on the phone, telling me there was nothing else he could offer me despite the fact that the network had dozens of broadcasts in that time period. I later heard he told other people that he didn't know why I was upset because, after all, my wife had a great job and I didn't even have to work. I decided it was time to voice my concerns to his and, ultimately, my boss. I was hoping to do just that between the broadcast and dinner on Thursday, so the delay just meant my conversation would have to wait until Friday morning.

I was a bourbon fan at the time, thanks in part to my friend Frank Nobilo, who introduced me to the Kentucky libation with a Maker's Mark Manhattan on the rocks and in part because of a trip Sarah and I took to Blackberry Farm, a wonderful getaway in the Smokey Mountains outside Knoxville, Tennessee. Among the dozens of bourbons the Blackberry Farm bar stocked was a powerful, sinus-clearing, unfiltered George T. Stagg, which was nearly impossible to find anywhere else. Nearly, but not impossible, because the liquor store near the TPC Sawgrass Marriott just happened to have a bottle, which I bought and brought to the hotel bar after our team dinner with Stathakes. Jerry Foltz, Kay Cockerill, and a few others were gathered around the boss when I entered and asked the bartender for a couple of glasses. I poured a couple of fingers of the caramel-colored liquor into each and handed one to Tom.

"What's this?" he asked as I handed him the glass.

"It's bourbon," I replied, "George T. Stagg unfiltered. Pretty rare, but I found a bottle. Thanks for coming to visit," I continued, "it means a lot to everybody," and I raised my glass in salute.

We touched glasses and drank, me clearly enjoying it more than him. I knew we were going to talk the next day, but I took the opportunity to start the conversation at that moment.

"You and I got off to a rocky start," I said, still feeling the burn of the bourbon in my throat, "but I think we've managed to earn an appreciation for one another."

"We did and we have," he agreed, setting his glass down.

"You know I'm the best you got," I finished my comment and my bourbon.

"I'm realizing that," he said, not bothering to take another sip. "We'll talk more tomorrow."

The next day was like many in Florida in October, crisp and beautiful. We were on the air early, so I had arrived shortly after 6:30 a.m. Stathakes came a few hours later and we found a quiet place to talk.

"I can't stay," was how he started the conversation. "Something's come up at home and I have to get back to Orlando."

"When do you have to leave?" I asked, guessing that it was soon.

"Right after we talk," was the answer meaning his record of never seeing a Nationwide Tour telecast from the truck perspective would remain intact. "Tell me what's on your mind."

I took a deep breath and measured my words, "This is a terrific group, a great team, and it's been my honor and pleasure to lead them."

"You've done a great job," he interjected.

"Thanks," I said, "but I wasn't fishing for a compliment. I got my schedule from Jack and, quite frankly, I was surprised and disappointed. I have one show between March and June and nothing the first two-and-a-half months of the year." I didn't wait for a reply. "I know I'm good at what I do; in fact, I think I'm better than anybody else you have in the truck, and I want to be a bigger contributor."

Stathakes smiled and nodded, and then I continued, "I am tired of being marginalized. I love my job and I love this channel and I have a lot more to offer."

"Why is your schedule so light?" was his question.

I didn't have to offer up an answer.

"You have done everything we've asked of you and then some. I know this has been hard on you, and I want you to know how much I appreciate everything you've done." I liked the sound of this, I thought, as he continued, "I'm on your side here, and I plan to talk to Jack as soon as I can, and I promise we'll get this fixed."

He stood and offered his hand. I shook it, thanked him, and watched him walk to his car, not knowing if I believed him or trusted him, but when push came to shove, I knew I didn't have a choice. I wouldn't know until later that while I may have gotten something off my chest, our conversation didn't really matter much. As events unfolded over the next several months, it became clear that when Tom Stathakes "promised" to fix my situation, he was already out the Golf Channel door.

514

FULL CIRCLE

I started this as an effort to honor my father and explain some of the things that were happening in the world that shaped him growing up, and one of those things was the Japanese attack on Pearl Harbor on December 7, 1941. It looks like this particular collection of memories is about to end as I look back on that same day of the year, more than 145,000 words and exactly seventy years later. I didn't plan it that way; it just seems to have happened.

On Monday, December 7, 2011, Brian Hammons signed off the air and we faded to black on the PGA TOUR Qualifying Tournament played at PGA West in La Quinta, California. A young man who had honed his skills, in equal parts, by playing at the University of Georgia and then the Nationwide Tour, Brendan Todd, was the medalist. In all, twenty-nine players received their PGA TOUR playing privileges for 2012: some you've no doubt heard of, including Jeff Maggert, Colt Knost, and Bob Estes. Others will one day be famous, because Harris English, Sang Moon Bae, John Huh, and Brian Harmon have what they call, in the golf business, "plenty of game." It was my eighteenth Q-School seen from the inside of a Golf Channel production truck.

The very next day, I got on an airplane and flew to Orlando to attend another mandatory, annual, year-end meeting that, this particular time, was kicked off by a get-together hosted by Golf

Channel President Mike McCarley. Tom Stathakes was there, and from what we all had heard, he was still trying to stake his claim to overturn McCarley and eventually run the channel himself. That effort finally ended for good when Stathakes was "reassigned" by Comcast less than a month later.

Dick Ebersol was not among the seventy-five or so people at the December party, but several colleagues with whom I had worked, and grown to respect and like, mixed and mingled with perfect strangers. As I surveyed the room, going from familiar to unfamiliar face, my eyes fell upon two men for whom I had as much respect as any in the world: Joe Gibbs and Arnold Palmer. After getting over the initial shock of seeing those two welcoming faces in a mostly unwelcoming setting, I made my way across the courtyard to say hello. I hadn't seen Joe since he had sold his creation to Comcast, and, seeing him now, I couldn't help but notice that he looked great. All smiles, steady on his feet, and proud, he welcomed my approach and greeted me with, first, a firm handshake and then a hug. I was struck by how happy he looked, and that made me happy. We spoke for several minutes, catching up, asking after each other's families and, finally, promising to keep in touch, before seeing Arnold and Kit Palmer, standing just a few feet away. I wanted to pay my respects to them, so I said a last goodbye to Joe and, as I did, he leaned in a little closer to me and said, "Thank you again for everything."

A little stunned, I made sure my response was heartfelt and brief.

"It was always my pleasure," I said, and then squeezed his hand a little harder and added, "I wish you'd never left."

I turned to say hello to the Palmers. I don't know if I'll ever see Joe Gibbs again, but I'm glad I saw him that night.

Later that evening, Mike McCarley asked for, and got, everyone's attention in order to make a toast to both Joe and

Mr. Palmer, and, as I watched those two listen to the man most recently charged with taking their baby and leading it into adulthood, I couldn't help but feel, in my heart, a little sad, because at that moment I wasn't sure if I would ever produce another event as a contract employee of the Golf Channel. I had been a part of history, and the weight of that hit me and brought a tear to my eye. Many people were a part of the network's success, and most had been under- or unappreciated in the dozens of months since Comcast seized control. McCarley, standing next to Joe and Mr. Palmer, congratulated the group on a fantastic year and, through his words indicated that the winds of change may indeed be blowing again.

"Twenty eleven was another record-setting year for Golf Channel, and I am so happy to have Joe and Arnold here to hear me say that." McCarley turned to look at them and then back to the assembled group. "We cannot celebrate the present and look forward to the future without recognizing what has been accomplished in the past." He raised his glass and we raised ours. "To Joe Gibbs and Arnold Palmer and everyone else who put it all on the line to get this started."

I realized there was reason for optimism, and I hoped my association with the Golf Channel was far from over.

SO MANY THANK YOUS

I have worked with, been around, and met thousands of people, and every single one of them helped make my life what it is today. Hundreds of those people are in this book, and hundreds more are not. They all have their own stories to tell and, in many cases, those stories are better and more interestingly told by them, so I'll leave them to that. As for my story, it would have never been put in readable form were it not for my extraordinary wife and partner in life, Sarah. We were sorting through a box of memories left behind by my mom and dad when she remarked about the remarkable life my parents had led and mentioned it was a shame that my folks never "wrote any of it down in a diary" to leave behind to their kids, and their kids, and their kids. That's when she suggested that I not make the same mistake. Honey, you didn't want to read this while it was being written, but I so hope you enjoyed it now that you have.

Jared, Hayley, and Jake, ultimately this is for you.

The first and only person, besides me, who did read this from stem to stern was my amazing mother-in-law, Susan Green. To say I respect her opinion is an understatement, and I can never thank her enough for the guidance she offered during this process. She didn't hesitate to tell me when a turn of a phrase, or a chapter, was good; but, more importantly, she was quick to effectively criticize and skillfully eliminate the many sentences, segments, and parts that were awful. This book is about me, but Susan, it's so much better because of you. Thanks.

There were many stories I could have told but didn't, and maybe some of the ones I did tell I shouldn't have, but the bottom line is I am glad I wrote them all down and hopeful you all enjoyed reading about a life in television as much as I enjoyed writing about it. I made countless acquaintances, many turned into friends, and some became loved ones. The first group has no idea what the other two know for certain—I am a terrible correspondent—but I hope they don't hold that against me because it has nothing to do with how much I value their friendship and love.

Everything in this is what I remember to be true. Others may have different memories, but these are mine, and I stand by them with conviction. If you were a part of any of these stories and remember them differently, then write your own damn book. As for me, the best part of my story is that it isn't over, and I look forward to what's next.

CPSIA information can be obtained
at www.ICGtesting.com
Printed in the USA
BVHW031924180821
614720BV00011B/117